Epistemology and Inference

The University of Minnesota Press
gratefully acknowledges assistance provided
by the McKnight Foundation
for publication of this book.

Epistemology and Inference

Henry E. Kyburg, Jr.

University of Minnesota Press *Minneapolis*

Library of Congress Cataloging in Publication Data

Kyburg, Henry Ely, 1928-
    Epistemology and inference.

    Includes index.
    1. Knowledge, Theory of — Addresses, essays,
lectures.   2. Probabilities — Addresses, essays,
lectures.   3. Inference (Logic) — Addresses, essays,
lectures.   I. Title.
BD161.K9   121   82-4836
ISBN 0-8166-1149-1   AACR2
ISBN 0-8166-1150-5 (pbk.)

To my teacher, Ernest Nagel

Preface

The essays collected here were written over a period of nearly twenty years. Only three of them have not been previously published, but those that have appeared elsewhere have appeared in a widely scattered collection of journals and edited volumes. Since they concern a single theme—rational belief and scientific inference—it seemed that it might serve a useful purpose if they were collected in a single place.

Putting such a collection together, I discovered, is easier intended than accomplished. All of the essays required minor corrections here and there; quite a number of them contained serious mistakes that needed to be dealt with; and some expressed views that I no longer hold, or hopes that are as yet unfulfilled. Clearly it would be inappropriate (as well as a monumental task) to rewrite the essays so completely that I could now agree with everything that is said in them. Inappropriate, and also pointless, since I expect that my views will continue to change. At the same time, it is surely desirable to correct obvious mistakes. The problem is that the three categories of correction mentioned above are not neatly distinguishable. Something that I see as calling for a minor correction at one time seems to be a serious mistake calling for extensive rewriting at another, and to be quite hopelessly wrong-headed at yet another time.

The net result has been that I have done some rewriting of all of the essays, but I have also attempted to let them retain their temporal identity. In the case of the three essays that have not appeared before, I have felt relatively unconstrained in making changes, but even they will be recognizable to those who heard them as originally delivered.

The papers that follow are divided into five groups. Part I addresses some very general philosophical (and practical) questions, which seem to call for the results of abstract philosophical analysis. The first paper, "Prophecies and Pretensions," was written for a general audience, in 1977, and used the controversy surrounding the Club of Rome report as a springboard to show that even large, practical, and pressing problems require us to look more closely and more abstractly at such matters as scientific inference, prediction, laws, and theories. The second essay, "Two World Views," attempts to sketch two quite different ways of approaching the world—through contemplation and through action. The first tends to lead to scientific realism, a logical or epistemological view of probability, or sometimes a frequency view of probability, and a rationalistic view of scientific method. The second tends to lead to instrumentalism to subjectivistic views of probability, and to a decision-theoretic view of scientific method. The intended evenhandedness of my characterization was marred (perhaps "destroyed") by my all-too-obvious partisanship. The third essay, "Tyche and Athena," attempted to show that the contemplative approach, as based on the notion of epistemological probability, could do justice to both chance and wisdom in guiding action as well as in seeking truth.

The papers in Part II are primarily critical and comparative. Together they help to locate epistemological probability in the space of possible interpretations of probability. The first paper, "Probability and Decision," contains the original version of the tale of Prince Hogarth, and attempts to show that the question of interpreting probability is not merely a matter of abstract philosophical interest, but is of direct and immediate concern in making decisions in the real world. "Bets and Beliefs," presents a critical consideration relevant to both subjectivistic and logical interpretations of probability: that as ordinarily construed these theories entail the rationality of very strong beliefs about long-run frequencies in the absence of any evidence whatever concerning those frequencies. The following piece is a frank (indeed, polemical) attack on the subjective view of probability, and in particular on the cogency of the Dutch Book argument. In this connection one might also wish to consult Patrician Ballie, "Confirmation and the Dutch Book Argument," (*British Journal for the Philosophy of Science*, 24, 1973, pp. 393-397), and Charles Chihara and Ralph Kennedy, "The Dutch Book Argument: Its Logical Flaws, Its Subjective Sources," (*Philosophical Studies* 36, 1979, pp. 19-33). "Chance" is my attempt to deal with propensity views of probability. It has been claimed—for example by Isaac Levi, in "Direct Inference," (*Journal of Philosophy* 74, 1977, pp. 5-29)—that even if some such view of probability as mine is to be accepted, it nevertheless requires an underlying theory of chance on which to base probabilities. I conclude that while there may be special theoretical contexts in which we might want to base our probabilities on chances, these are rare and special, and that in ordinary cases the arguments calling for chance statements as premises in direct inference are not weighty. The final paper of this group traces the connections and comparisons between my notion of probability (misleadingly called "logical") and Fisher's notion of fiducial probability. The paper was delivered by invitation at a meeting of the International Statistical Institute at Fisher's instigation.

Papers in Part III are those in which I have attempted to present my own view of probability in relatively brief compass. If it is presumptuous to think they might be of historical interest, yet a characterization or a turn of phrase which does not appear in the more extensive treatments may ring a bell with some readers. The first paper has not appeared in print, and represents my efforts to produce a college outline of epistemological probability for friends and students. "Probability and Randomness" is the oldest paper in the book. It was written before *Probability and the Logic of Rational Belief,* and despite its mistakes and obscurities represents the first statement of epistemological probability. It also contains the first statement of the lottery paradox, although the first to appear in print was that in the book just mentioned. "Probability and Informative Inference" was written for statisticans, and intended to show the bearing of my interpretation of probability on the foundations of statistics. It contains a detailed discussion of an example, which, in the original version, contained a serious mistake. I have corrected the mistake, but the result is that the example is not so poignant as it could be. "Epistemological Probability" is the paper in which my view was finally christened "epistemological;" it represents my last attempt to give a fairly informal presentation of some complicated and technical matters.

The canonical technical formulation of these ideas is *The Logical Foundations of Statistical Inference* (Reidel, 1974). As is clear from that work, the program confidently described in the early papers was not so easy to carry through. And recent discussion has shown that there are still technical difficulties. (See Isaac Levi, "Confirmational Conditionalization," *Journal of Philosophy* 75, 1978, pp. 730-737, as well as "Direct Inference," cited above, and particularly the critical essays in Radu Bogdan [ed.], *Profile of Kyburg and Levi,* Reidel, 1981.)

In Parts IV and V I return in full circle to the beginning and treat some general philosophical questions by means of the machinery provided by epistemological probability. The fourth group of essays concerns epistemology. "Epistemology and Induction" is a hitherto unpublished paper written for a symposium with Isaac Levi and Stephen Spielman. Since it depended heavily on references to a detailed example provided by Levi, and since it contained serious mistakes concerning his views on conditionalization, it has been extensively rewritten, both in order to be self-contained, and in order to avoid spreading lies about my good friend. "Conjunctivitis" traces the connections among various forms of deductive closure, consistency, and conjunction in bodies of knowledge, and embodies my views concerning the lessons to be learned from the lottery paradox. "Probability, Rationality, and a Rule of Detachment" provides a statistical version of the lottery paradox. It is one thing to say that the lottery is so special and artificial that we need not take it seriously; it is another thing entirely to say that we need not take seriously the fact that inconsistent sets of statements may be inferred from the same body of data by means of standard statistical procedures. The final essay of this section—it might also have been placed in the last group—argues in favor of a global approach to epistemology and induction rather than the local approach that Levi has made popular. I claim that the only way we can really solve the problems of local induction is by providing a framework that in principle can be extended arbitrarily far in the direction of a global approach.

Part V contains three essays. The first two, "How to Make Up a Theory," and "An Interpolation Theorem for Inductive Relations," are very short. They were written as philosophical jokes, but jokes with a point. "How to Make Up a Theory" shows how Craig's technique can be used to replace a theory with given observational consequences, employing a certain set of theoretical terms and axioms concerning them, by another theory having an arbitrary theoretical structure, but having exactly the same observational consequences. The next paper argues that in any of four natural ways of interpreting "inductive systematization" it is demonstrable that the introduction of theories (with or without "theoretical" terms) does not lead to inductive systematization. The final paper, "All Generalizations Are Analytic," was also conceived as a provocative philosophical joke, but I have now come to regard it as embodying a view of scientific inference that should be explored more thoroughly and seriously. The word "analytic" should be replaced by *"a priori"* throughout the paper, and of course much more needs to be said about the grounds for choosing between two languages embodying what I would now call different *"a priori* commitments." Book-length treatments of measurement and of theoretical and linguistic change are in the future. This final essay, I hope, gives a foretaste of their flavor.

Henry E. Kyburg, Jr.
University of Rochester

Acknowledgments

The author wishes to thank the publishers and editors of the various volumes in which some of these essays first appeared for permission to reprint them here. Individual acknowledgments appear as footnotes in the corresponding essays.

Special thanks are due to Ms. Lynn McCoy and particularly to Ms. Anna Harrison who far exceeded the call of secretarial duty. Incorporating the mysterious and arbitrary changes demanded by the author, always under the pressure of time, keeping track of often unnumbered pages, remembering who had the scissors last and to keep the top on the glue, might well have driven lesser mortals to a nervous breakdown. Lynn and Anna not only survived, but remained cheery and good-humored.

A number of the essays that have previously appeared in print represent research supported by various grants from the National Science Foundation, to which gratitude is hereby expressed. Those essays that appear here for the first time were rewritten this year (1980-81) in the course of research undertaken as a Guggenheim Fellow. Although the main fruits of that research will appear elsewhere, the author is pleased to take this as his first opportunity to express his appreciation for the generosity of the Guggenheim Foundation.

Contents

Preface   vii

Acknowledgments   xi

Part I. General
1. Prophecies and Pretensions   3
2. Two World Views   18
3. Tyche and Athena   28

Part II. Critical Probability Papers
4. Probability and Decision   49
5. Bets and Beliefs   63
6. Subjective Probability:
   Criticisms, Reflections, and Problems   79
7. Chance   99
8. Logical and Fiducial Probability   132

Part III. Constructive Probability Papers
9. The Nature of Epistemological Probability   153
10. Probability and Randomness   158
11. Probability and Informative Inference   180
12. Epistemological Probability   204

Part IV. Epistemology
13. Epistemology and Induction   221
14. Conjunctivitis   232
15. Probability,
    Rationality, and a Rule of Detachment   255
16. Local and Global Induction   264

Part V. Theory and Generalization
17. How to Make Up a Theory   287
18. An Interpolation Theorem for Inductive Relations   291
19. All Acceptable Generalizations Are Analytic   296

Index   315

Part I. General

1

Prophecies and Pretensions

There have always been prophets, and generally they have prophesied doom. The prophets of the Old Testament foretold, over and over, and in relished detail, the punishments the Lord had in store for stiff-necked and sinful Israel. No doubt there was no lack of cranks and crackpots foretelling the collapse of the Roman Empire. In recent decades we have been threatened with the exhaustion of resources, the explosion of population, the outbreak of global nuclear war, the disaster of widespread starvation, the depletion of our fuel and energy supplies, and an ignominious and final collapse of our collective moral fiber. Many of these prophecies are alleged to have scientific warrant, and therefore epistemic justification. It would be reasonable to suppose that philosophers who claim some understanding of scientific inference and of the principles of epistemology, might have something useful to say about such claims.

A striking contribution to the literature of Doom is *The Limits to Growth*,[1] the outcome of the Club of Rome Project on the Predicament of Mankind. As in all doomsday literature, there is in *The Limits to Growth* a mixture of moral outrage and factual forecasting. Although Isaiah was long on outrage and short on facts, the authors of *The Limits to Growth* attempted to soft-pedal their moral concerns and hew as best they could to the line of hard facts.

The Club of Rome is an international group of industrialists, scientists, educators, economists, and statesmen who are, like many of us, concerned about the course of world events. It was founded in 1968, and in 1970 launched a project to examine the complex of problems—poverty, pollution, urban decay, inflation—that beset the world. A team at MIT under the leadership of Dennis Meadows, undertook this project, employing the methodology developed by Jay Forrester and known as System Dynamics. The result is a computer model of the world—that is, a computer program reflecting on the world scale not only various trends in industrial expansion, population growth, and so on, but also the various ways in which these factors interact. (For example, if the population is larger, there is a greater demand for industrial output; if there is a high per capita income, birthrates tend to fall.) Once we have the model at hand, and are

3

convinced that it reflects the tendencies of the world, we can use it to see what general effect various courses of action will have on those tendencies. The model is not a categorical forecasting device, but only a conditional one: it says that if such and such historical tendencies remain unchanged, then such and such will happen; if some tendencies remain unchanged, and some are altered by social action, then such and such another thing will happen.

The outcome of this computer modeling exercise at MIT was both gloomy and somewhat surprising. The team looked at five factors involved in economic growth on the planet: *population, agricultural production, natural resources, industrial production,* and *pollution.* According to the basic model there is a sharp decline in food per capita, industrial output per capita, services per capita, followed by a rapid decline in population owing to a rapidly rising death rate that occurs sometime during the twenty-first century. Double the assumed supply of natural resources, and the same thing happens: growth is stopped in the twenty-first century by rising pollution. Assume that the world has unlimited resources and imposes severe pollution controls: the result is that sometime during the twenty-first century the population begins to fall owing to a high death rate, indirectly owing to a shortage of food, and to the diversion of capital into agricultural production. Make the same assumptions, and in addition assume that land yield is doubled in 1975: population and the standard of living plummet during the twenty-first century. Many people have said, for many years, that the problem is that of population pressure. Run the computer model with unlimited resources, pollution controls, and perfect birth control; the result is that the food crisis of the previous model is postponed for only a decade. Finally, assume that resources are fully exploited and 75 percent of those used are recycled, that pollution generation is reduced to one-quarter of its 1970 value; that land yields are doubled in 1975; and that effective methods of birth control are made available to the world population. I quote from Meadows: "The result is a temporary achievement of a constant population with a world average income per capita that reaches nearly the present US level. Finally, though, industrial growth is halted, and the death rate rises as resources are depleted, pollution accumulates, and food production declines" (p. 147). Food, food, food. It all boils down, as it always has, to getting enough to eat.

Are there no stable worlds available? Yes: but to achieve them, we would have to defuse the two exponential bombs of population growth and capital accumulation simultaneously, as well as to implement the policies already mentioned. We would have to restrict the number of births to the number of deaths, thus instantly obtaining a fixed population size; and (surprisingly) we would have to restrict the rate of capital investment to the rate of depreciation to avoid industrial growth.

We would seem to be in a dreadful fix. But where there is a Cassandra, there is a Pollyanna. A group of scholars at the University of Sussex has provided an extensive critique of the methodology and results of the MIT group. Their results have been published in a group of essays called *Models of Doom*.[2] Although they agree with the Meadows group that the world has problems which should be addressed, they argue that the specific projections of the Meadows models are essentially worthless as predictions. They argue that the data base is dreadfully weak and cannot support the extrapolations involved. They argue that the technique of aggregation (of using world averages for GNP, capital accumulation, food supply, etc.) renders the model so unrealistic as to be perniciously misleading. They argue that the major limitation of the MIT group is that "they have chosen to be unconcerned with politics, unconcerned with social structure, unconcerned with human needs and wants" (p. 212).

There are a number of issues involved here, and quite a few of them fall within the purview of philosophy. To take the last one first: the MIT group quite explicitly restricts their concern to the physical limits to growth. They are concerned with the constraints that the physical world imposes on potential solutions to the problems that the world now faces. They attempt to characterize some of the physically possible alternatives that would alleviate those problems. They simply do not concern themselves with the social and political problems of implementing those alternatives; they do not explore the additional constraints imposed by social and political realities. Perhaps they should have; perhaps the social and political constraints should be explored before the physical constraints. In any event, we certainly need to be concerned, ultimately, with both sets of constraints. More than this, however, when we consider the viability of certain social and political alternatives, we find ourselves embroiled in two sorts of concerns: one is feasibility; the other is justice or fairness, the question of moral acceptability. In the literature of this problem, including that of the Sussex group, there has been relatively little contribution from philosophers who have a certain amount of expertise in evaluating moral arguments and moral claims; what ethical argument there is, is of a rather elementary level. But we shall put this issue aside and concentrate on epistemological and inferential issues.

Consider how the MIT and Sussex groups construe the world model. The Sussex group construes it as a mechanism for making predictions, on the analogy of a system of celestial mechanics being used as a mechanism for predicting an eclipse. If the eclipse doesn't come off, your system of celestial mechanics is wrong—according to a traditional notion of science. But the analogy is a poor one, as a little reflection will show, and the traditional notion of scientific testing is oversimplified.

Suppose we have a heavy steel ball rolling down a plane. We know when it was released, the angle of the plane, the coefficient of friction; we predict the time of arrival of the ball at the bottom of the plane. A trivial problem in high-school physics. But note: we cannot predict the time of arrival perfectly. We know the time at which the ball starts—but only within certain limits of accuracy; we know the angle, the coefficient of friction—but only within certain limits of accuracy. In fact we only know the value of the gravitational constant g to a certain number of decimal places. So all we can conclude is that the ball will arrive at *approximately* such and such a time. This does not vitiate our projection. To decline to make the projection on the ground that our knowledge was imperfect would be stupid—we can do very well indeed (and indeed be very accurate) with the information we have.

Again, there are certain *constraints* assumed in our problem. We assume that no one snatches the ball away before it gets to the bottom of the plane; we assume that no one bumps into the apparatus accidentally, we assume that there are no earthquakes or atomic wars. We not only *make* these assumptions, however. We make them on good grounds. We have *reason* to make them. They are justified assumptions. If we are interested in the time of arrival of our steel ball, but know that the experiment is to be performed in a room full of practical jokers, some one of whom is almost bound to stop the ball from rolling, we can make no sensible projection.

There are three lessons to be learned from this trivial example. (1) Predictions are inherently both uncertain and approximate. (2) Predictions depend on the best information we have about the world. (3) Predictions are warranted if and only if certain assumptions may *reasonably* be made.

Let us look at a more complicated example. I am a farmer—I have a farm in upstate New York—and in making plans for the next year I have to make a projection of my farming income. Now in this instance we have all the old uncertainties, but in addition we have an entirely new set of problems. These new problems are introduced by the fact that the farm income is strongly influenced by what I *decide* to do.

What I must do is suppose that there is a certain definite range of alternatives open to me. Those are the ones I am willing to consider. I can plant so many acres of corn and so many acres of wheat; or I can put all those acres into oats; or I can let some of them lie fallow. My forecast, my projection, is now a function of my decision among these alternatives. Even *given* a decision, however, the projection of my income is fraught with perils and uncertainties. There are the same uncertainties of measurement that we encountered in the inclined plane example. There are the new uncertainties introduced by the fact that, our knowledge of genetics being what it is, the yield of a plant is only a probabilistic function of its growing conditions. These new uncertainties are not great, since the number of plants involved is so large: the probability is enormous that the yield of a field of plants under certain conditions of growth will be very close to the typical (average) yield of plants of that kind grown under those conditions. So far we are dealing with what we might call laboratory uncertainties—that is, uncertainties of measurement or of sample selection that can be made very small by taking suitable precautions.

Now we come to a different kind of uncertainty. Given growing conditions, we can predict yield relatively well. Some growing conditions (soil acidity, major nutrients) are under our control; but others are not. I can't simply decide when to plant—it depends on the wetness of the ground, which in turn depends on the weather. I can't decide how much rain will be available for my crops. I can't decide what the temperatures will be. I can, on the basis of past experience of the weather, make some pretty good probabilistic projections. But these are in a different class from the earlier ones. The yield of a corn plant may vary by a factor of two under given conditions; but in an acre there are thirty thousand corn plants and under those conditions—owing to the law of large numbers— we can make a prediction of the yield per acre that is accurate within less than one percent. When it comes to the weather, however, we can get no help from the law of large numbers. My corn will respond to the weather we get next year—not to the average weather over a hundred years. I must simply take my chances. It is quite true that I can project a most probable range of production, given a decision; but I must also take account of the fact that even that approximate production will vary widely according to the particular weather conditions I happen to run into next summer. The law of large numbers offers me no protection here.

There is yet another source of uncertainty: the value of my crop next year depends on social, political, and economic conditions over which I have essentially no control, and which (as we have discovered in recent years) are at least as unpredictable as the weather. These conditions, in fact, are unpredictable or uncertain in a very deep sense.

So far it has been relatively easy to distinguish between the constraints we justifiably and rationally assume to be satisfied when we pose a problem of projection, and the laws and statistical generalizations we employ in making the projection. We assume nobody will snatch the ball off the inclined plane; we assume that the gravitational constant will not suddenly change its value; we assume that a volcano will not suddenly emerge in the North 40 of the farm; we assume that the biochemistry of corn will not undergo a radical change; we assume that an extremely large comet will not enter the solar system and pull the earth out of its orbit, thus profoundly changing its weather, and so on. All of these assumptions are uncertain, but we have no grounds on which to reject any of them. This is the same old uncertainty we have to live with every minute of every day. It is in principle no different from the uncertainty of measurement: you can measure an inclined plane and even in principle come up with nothing better than a result that is in error by a small amount. There is no more certainty in physics, at this level, than there is in roulette, where, *practically speaking,* the house is certain to win.

All this is to say that the assumptions we have made so far are practical certainties: under ordinary circumstances, we have every reason to accept them and no reason to reject them. I can't assume that there will be just so much rainfall next season, but I can assume—as practically certain—that there will be no major change in weather patterns, and thus that past years provide good grounds for assuming a certain probability distribution of rainfall.

Now in the case of the social, political and economic factors that affect the value of my crops, this is just what I cannot do. The assumptions I make, which I have to treat as practical certainties, are much looser, much more subject to modification in the light of new evidence, than the assumptions I make about what is (falsely, I think) characterized as the "natural world." (As though politics and economics were unnatural!) Nevertheless, I can assume, justifiably, for lack of anything better to go on, that the predictions of economists and market analysts will not be very far off—and this suffices to allow me to make a relatively informed probabilistic and approximate projection of my income for next year, although it does not allow me to arrive at a relatively precise probability distribution for that income.

Projections, economic and otherwise, for the whole world over a long range future, are of course even more complicated than the projection of a farmer's income for the next growing season. They also introduce new factors, both of knowledge and of uncertainty. The latter obviously; the former because certain social decisions may (by the law of large numbers) turn out to be relatively predictable while individual decisions are not. Thus Sir Charles Galton Darwin, in his book *The Next Million Years*,[3] writes that, while predictions over a hundred years are extremely difficult, if not impossible, to make, predictions over the span of a million years become much easier because the trivial local fluctuations—the rise and fall of empires, the evanescent appearance of religions, and the like—average out in the long run. According to Sir Charles, the one constraint that controls human numbers is starvation—his whole forecast of the next million years is based on the principle that populations expand to the limits of the available food supply—a principle for which, as far as the long run is concerned, there is plenty of biological evidence. On the other hand most of us deliberately control the number of offspring we generate. Although other species control their populations in response to the weather, in response to the density of their populations, we are the first species to be able to control our population in response to projections extending far into the future. Thus it *may* be that expansion to the limits of food supply is not characteristic of future human populations.

However this may be, the projections with which we are concerned are more limited in scope and should therefore be somewhat more detailed. Our model, in this sense, is not the kinetic theory of gases, which Sir Charles employed, but the model of the ball on the inclined plane or the model of the farmer's projection of his income. In principle, despite the added complications, the dearth of data and the fact that individual and social decisions enter into the calculations more explicitly, the methodology of projection is the same in the social sciences as it is in the physical sciences.

The mechanism of prediction, even in a physical theory, is conditional: *If* the initial conditions are thus and so; *if* such and such events (which may well be within our control) do not intervene; *then* the outcome (probably and approximately and within the limits of error) will be so and so. These conditional predictions can be very useful, even when we know in advance that the conditions will not be satisfied. To take the most classical example, one of Newton's laws states that a body not acted upon by external forces will continue in its state of rest or straight-line motion indefinitely. Further laws in the same system of physics state that there is no body that is not acted on by external forces. But this does not render the original law uninteresting or useless: it is precisely the original law that we might call on to explain how a coasting truck demolished a parked Volkswagen. We would say that the Volkswagen was called upon to provide those external forces that would alter the tendency for the truck to continue in its state of rectilinear motion indefinitely.

The MIT group construes their model as giving a broad picture of the interaction of certain dynamic tendencies. Thus they don't construe it as a mechanism for categorical prediction at all, but rather as giving a picture of the way certain forces in the world tend to operate, and have operated historically. For social and political reasons, it seems quite apparent that none of the forecasts of the model could ever come to pass. Long before the population of the world begins to fall in the way predicted by the original model, social and political unrest would be so violent as to knock the parameters of the model wildly askew. Thus the actual predictive power of the model is quite irrelevant to the question of whether it gives us insight into operation of the powerful forces set loose in the world of mankind.

How much insight does it give us to the dynamics of growth? That's a question, and a rather deep question, in the philosophy of science as well as in social science. How well it measures up, depends on what sort of insights it is reasonable to ask any model to give us. My own feeling is that their world model is more helpful than any other; but the competition here is not very severe. The MIT model certainly gives us more insight than that of Herman Kahn and Anthony Weiner, in *The Year 2,000*,[4] who simply use statistical time series to plot trends and extrapolate "likely developments" to produce what appears to be a categorical characterization of the world in the year 2000. Such a prediction either comes off or it doesn't. In either case, we gain little insight into the mechanism of the forces that produce that future, and thus little guidance in *how* to tinker with the carburetor or adjust the timing of the world engine if such be possible and desirable.

Despite the obvious shortcomings of the MIT model, it does at least purport to reveal something about the mechanism of this engine—something quite independent of the way the operators run it. Consider, in this context, the question of aggregation. As the Sussex group points out, the technique of aggregation renders the model very defective as a mechanism for prediction. One cannot be satisfied with aggregated food when one's larder is empty; per capita GNP can have no effect on one's progenitive propensities if one never sees more than a tiny fraction of that GNP; if I live in the clean air and among the fresh streams of rural upstate New York (as I do), pollution in Minamata Bay in Japan will be of only the most indirect concern to me. But as a mechanism for indicating trends, for revealing the interaction of forces, aggregation may do no harm at all. Indeed aggregation may well lead to errors on the side of conservatism: if things are going to go to pot when the *average* amount of pollution is such and such, on the assumption that it is evenly distributed, then things will surely go to pot sooner in regions that have a disproportionate share of pollution. So far as the model is taken as an indicator of trends we should like to avoid, and aggregation tends to minimize the intensity of those trends, it is difficult to see how aggregation can mislead us into thinking trends are less severe than they are.

Finally, let us look at the weakness of the data base. The question of how much data will support how much extrapolation is a classical philosophical problem—the problem of induction. It is also one of the problems of statistical inference. This is an area that is rich in controversy, that is undergoing very active development both by statisticians and by philosophers, and in which there are no canonical and universally accepted principles that we can bring to bear on a problem of the sort the Club of Rome report deals with. Nevertheless, one can say a few things. The data suggest a certain set of related problems. It *could* be said that the data are actually misleading and do not at all support the model used by the MIT group. Except in matters of small detail, even the Sussex group does not make this claim. Alternatively, one could maintain that data are simply insufficient to support the conclusions of the MIT group. This is reiterated in almost every contribution of the Sussex group. But although this does support the contention that the model is not very reliable, it does not at all support the claim that we need not take it seriously. When faced with a practical decision, you have to use the data you have: getting more data, waiting for better information before you do anything may simply not be one of the options open to you. You have to plant when the ground is ready. You can't wait until after the race is over to decide which horse to back. Delay, in a case like the one under discussion, may simply truncate the alternatives available. (So, of course, may premature or ill-advised actions.) In making a decision, one takes into account not only what the data suggest, but also the reliability of the data and the costs of various courses of action under various circumstances. Such an argument, though not made explicit, may underlie some of the objections of the Sussex group to the Club of Rome report. To evaluate it, we would have to have some indication of the costs of action or inaction under various circumstances. It is difficult to estimate these costs even roughly without making use of essentially the same sort of roughly quantitative model that the Club of Rome has provided us with.

In any event, in the context of decision and action, the mere claim that the data base is weak is itself insufficient. As the British philosopher David Hume pointed out long ago, the data base is *always* too weak to support categorical predictions of perfect reliability. Despite centuries of investigation, and untold amounts of data, we may in fact be wrong about the law governing the behavior of a ball on an inclined plane. We may in fact be wrong about the law of falling bodies. But the man, plummeting past the tenth floor of a twenty-story building from whose roof he has just leaped, who depends on the falsity of that law to save him from destruction, is surely even more irrational than the classical optimist of the old joke who argues inductively: Well, everything is all right so far.

I do not mean to suggest that those who have expressed doubts about the value of the Club of Rome report are as irrational as the man in the joke. But I do mean to suggest that the arguments that have been offered by the doubters so far—in particular those found in the Sussex report—are simply not good enough. The weakness of the data base, the obvious inadequacy of the world model as a mechanism for categorical predictions, the fact that the model takes account neither of political feasibility nor moral acceptability—none of these things keep the model from being informative, none of them suggest we need not take the model seriously, none of them provide an excuse for not getting on with the next step, which is that of trying to discover what alternatives are open to us, what courses of action can in fact be implemented, and by whom, and what ethical, political, and social constraints it is possible to impose on those alternatives without eliminating them all.

Let us therefore focus briefly and tentatively on the problems of food and social policy. In all of the projections of the Club of Rome, and in Sir Charles Darwin's general million-year forecast, the constraints on the food supply play a fundamental role. This would already seem to pose an ironic social dilemma: On the one hand, in some parts of the world, it is too unrewarding to produce food. On the other hand, there are parts of the world in which large numbers of people starve: people who would pay with year-long hard labor for enough food to keep themselves alive.

Where are the famous forces of the free market? There is no real anomaly: labor in India does an Illinois farmer no more good than wheat in an Illinois elevator does starving Indians. And yet the constraints that keep the labor and the wheat from getting together are not merely the constraints of time and distance—they are not merely physical constraints. They are largely social constraints. This does not make them "unnatural" or "perverse;" but it does mean that in some respects and to some degree, they can be changed. This is one thing we might think about, though it is a very complicated and difficult thing to think about: How might social policy be changed to benefit both the farmer and the starving Indian?

There is another thing we might think about. It is only in response to economic motivation that the farmer can be led to produce the food needed by a starving world. It often costs the farmer more money to produce a bushel of wheat than he can sell the wheat for. Under these circumstances he cannot successfully be *exhorted* to produce more wheat. He will grow some wheat, because he has always grown wheat, because it fits into his crop rotation, because next year the price may be better. He will grow some wheat because it is beautiful to look at and he is motivated partly by aesthetic considerations. But there are obvious economic limits to the amount of wheat he will produce, and these limits will not be changed by exhortation.

There is a third thing to think about, which brings us back full circle to the Club of Rome. There are limits to the production of food imposed by the geography of the globe. We are obviously nowhere near those limits—and of course the more valuable food is, the more those limits can be expanded. At the same time, they are finite, and the *potential* for human reproduction (as Sir Charles pointed out) is bounded only by starvation. Furthermore, there are factors at work that are reducing those limits: we are paving good farmland at the rate of so and so many thousands of acres a year; we are losing so and so many thousands of acres a year to erosion and housing. Thus our conjecture that there might be better ways of distributing food and labor in no way supports the long-run validity of the often-heard claim that our food problems would be solved if only we could solve a few distribution problems. (Such claims tend to naively ignore the fact that distribution itself has an economic cost.)

There may be any number of things we can do right now to implement a social policy that would benefit both the Illinois farmer and the hungry Indian; but we have every reason to believe that in the long run this would not reduce, but increase, the number of Indian children like those whose pictures you glance at in the *New Yorker* before you turn the page and take another sip of your Chivas Regal. This is clearly implied by what we know, or have good reason to believe, about world food production, industrial production, population growth, the relation between population growth and standard of living, capital accumulation, and so on. That projection is dependent on the assumption that social and political constraints remain constant. This assumption is like the Newtonian assumption that a body is subject to no external forces. There is no such body. And there is no such world as that in which social and political constraints remain constant.

This leads to a final and fourth thing to think about. A long-run solution to the world food problem requires balancing birth and death rates. It is inevitable, obviously, that in the long run birth and death rates will be balanced—that is a simple matter of arithmetic. The one sure thing is that zero population growth will be achieved. What is at issue is just when the balance will occur, and at what economic level for whom, and how long it will last. In most of the Club of Rome models the balance is only temporary and is rapidly followed by an increase of death rates over birth rates. How we respond to this, whether by advocating general decreases in birth rates or general increases in death rates or selective increases and decreases in the rates in different populations—is a matter of social policy writ large and philosophical. Social policy, as embodied in our laws and institutions, can no doubt go a long way toward alleviating the immediate distribution problems, at least in principle. (Whether such social policies are politically feasible is another matter.) But this is a matter of local social policy in which nobody (nobody we *know*, that is) will get hurt. In contemplating the larger social issues, the questions of social philosophy, we must face up to the fact that untold numbers of people are going to get hurt. To deny this fact is to close one's eyes to the most simple and straightforward applications of intelligence to the world. It is to take an irrationally selective attitude toward empirical evidence: when it doesn't hurt, when it concerns the time it takes a ball to roll down an inclined plane, we regard it as persuasive and indeed irrefutable. When it concerns something we don't like to think about—for example the relations between food supply, industrial production, capital investment, and population—we regard it as fraught with uncertainty, inaccuracy, irrelevance, and perversity.

I suggest that in either case, evidence is evidence and we should attend to it. I suggest that the results of programming world models in computers are relevant to our decisions, even though they are not—and were never intended to be—categorical forecasts of the future. I suggest that we have more than adequate grounds for thinking about food production, investment and population.

Let us turn, finally, to some of the popular general methodologies of salvation. Consider, for example, zero population growth. Its proponents say that the population of the world is pushing against the limits of the world's resources, that it cannot continue to grow without leading to more and more misery and starvation, and so on—all perfectly true. It is implied that zero population growth, if it could be achieved, would make a difference. (It is acknowledged that it can't be achieved—at least not soon—but that is not in itself reason for rejecting it as a goal.) But this is clearly shown to be in error by the MIT model: when the model is run with a population maintained at the 1975 level, catastrophe from other sources strikes only a few years later than when population is allowed to expand exponentially. To be sure, no one ever said that zero population growth would cure all the world's ills. And although zero population growth is inevitable in the long run, there are more and less painful ways of achieving it, and it is surely a worthwhile exercise to think about these alternatives. But the rates at which population growth is slowed have by themselves very little bearing on the projections of the Meadows model.

Or consider energy, which we have all been doing recently. Barry Commoner recently wrote an excellent series of articles in the *New Yorker* on energy and the need for its more efficient use and conservation. In the Meadows model energy appears as a natural resource, and in the model run in which death from depletion of resources is avoided, we encounter catastrophic food problems. Commoner points out that it takes more energy to produce a bushel of corn now, despite (or because of) our new varities, fertilizers, pesticides, and the constant pressure on the farmer to produce more corn for less money, than it did ten years ago. Implicitly he suggests that more energy-efficient ways of growing corn should be used.

For example, if we look at thermodynamic efficiency, it might well be that we could grow corn with more thermodynamic efficiency by utilizing solar energy to grow hay and oats, feeding the hay and oats to horses, who will provide both nitrogen-rich fertilizer and horsepower to pull our plows and till our fields. The image is rather attractive.

But there are certain costs. There is another datum I encountered in a recent issue of a farm journal. There it was pointed out that despite the fact that more land can be tilled with horses than can be tilled with tractors (horses don't tip over on side hills) we already have a level of agricultural production that does not leave room for horses. That is, it would require so much land to grow the feed to power the horses that would replace tractors, that we could not produce as much food for human consumption as we do now. Thus if we accept certain constraints—for example, that our contribution to the world's food supply should not decrease—we have already gone beyond the point at which we can use energy as efficiently as we might. We have reached a point, not of diminishing returns, but of diminishing thermodynamic efficiency. What the Meadows model shows is that this is what happens in general.

Let us consider one more recipe for our troubled world: sharing the wealth. It has often been claimed in the past that poverty and suffering in the world are not the result of a dearth of goods, but rather a result of their misdistribution. In particular this has been claimed to be the case with regard to food. But a 1977 article in *Crops and Soils* points out that if it were possible to provide a fair and even distribution of the calories produced in the world, instantaneously, the immediate result would be that everyone in the world would be suffering from malnutrition.

This is not to say that the distribution of the world's goods and foods is not something we should think about. As in the matter of population control and energy conservation, the distribution of the world's benefits will have a bearing on the future course of the world. It represents one of the variables, like population and energy use, over which, in some degree, we have some control.

I say that "we"—you and I—have some control over some of these factors. In what sense is this true? It seems obvious that, at least in a personal way, we have some control over them. We can decide to have no more than two children. We are free to decide that because we have available a wide variety of contraceptive devices and techniques; we have the economic wherewithal to employ them and we are not dependent for our welfare in old age on having a large number of children to support us. We can conserve energy: we can turn out lights, we can indulge in energy conserving sports (sailing rather than water-skiing); more generally, we can decide to spend a smaller fraction of our income on energy and a larger fraction on services. (Note that we had better not *save* a larger fraction: that goes into capital growth which is energy consumptive.) We are free to do this because the fraction of income we spend for what we middle-class Americans quaintly think of as "necessities" is relatively small. As for the redistribution of the world's goods, we can subscribe to various charities: we can send food to Biafra, farming equipment to India, medicine to Pakistan. We can voluntarily give up a certain fraction of our economic share of the world and pass it on to the poor in other parts of the world. Again: we are free to do this because our standard of living is so high that it will not be compromised by the redistribution of a small fraction. But we would not be likely to agree to change places with the Indian peasant. If one of our children needed such expensive surgical treatment that it would use up our entire spare income, we would put our own child first. Even orthodonture, in our segment of society, would generally be regarded as one of the "necessities" that would have to precede unilateral efforts to redistribute the world's goods. And thus you can see how far that proposal goes.

How effective are these proposals? If, as seems evident, the population of the world tends to expand to take up the room available to it, your contribution to the population problem will be precisely balanced by the survival of more individuals elsewhere, unless your self-control serves to modify that tendency toward expansion. But there is not the slightest reason to think that your behavior in this regard has any impact on global tendencies, or even that the behavior of a large number of middle-class Americans will have any impact on global tendencies for population to expand.

How about the conservation of energy? How about the redistribution of goods? The answers we obtain from the models are the same: as long as the problem is a dynamic tendency, rather than a static or local difficulty, such maneuvers are irrelevant. The one thing that does seem to emerge from the models — even when they are regarded with the degree of skepticism they no doubt deserve — is that the sacrifices made with such high moral purpose by the members of the liberal intellectual establishment are, so far as the state of the world over the mid-length run of the next hundred years is concerned, completely pointless. Of course in a local sense they are not pointless: to send a CARE package to Biafra may give a family one more meal before they starve, which is hardly pointless to them, and of course it also gives a boost to the self-esteem of the sender. But we are supposed to be looking a hundred years ahead here, and in that perspective, it couldn't matter less.

What can we do about the state of the world, then? Surely there is something better than this absolute negativism? Is there no methodology of salvation?

Yes, there is a methodology of salvation. It is precisely the methodology of the doomsayers. That is, it is the method of making the most careful and responsible projections we can make with the data we have at hand, based on various assumptions concerning the choices that will be made by various parts of the world's population. Thus Meadows ran his machine model on various assumptions regarding population control, resource conservation, agricultural productivity, technological development, pollution controls, and so on. One set of assumptions in *Limits to Growth* produced a world in equilibrium (pp. 169-170). It is worth repeating them here: set birth rate equal to death rate in 1975, worldwide; set industrial capital investment rate equal to depreciation rate as of

1990, and reduce resource consumption to one-quarter of the 1970 level. Economic preferences of society (worldwide) are shifted (as of 1975) toward services and away from material goods. Pollution generation per unit of production is reduced to one-quarter of the 1970 level. And so on. Remember that these are worldwide changes and that they are instituted in 1975. The model indicates that if these changes are delayed until 2000, it is too late: stability is no longer attainable. And now what would we have attained, had we been able to perform these miracles in 1975? More than twice as much food per person as the average value today, higher industrial output per capita and triple the services per capita. Splendid? The model assumes relatively perfect distribution, and Meadows points out that this corresponds to an income of about half the present U.S. average. He doesn't mention food, but that average, too, would be well below current U.S. standards. Furthermore, it is obvious that to have achieved stability in 1975, totalitarian powers undreamed of by the world's most megalomaniacal dictators would have had to have been employed.

This seems to be about the best that Meadows group can come up with, and it doesn't sound much like salvation to me, any more than it does to you. But what we're after is not a prescription, but a method. The method of computer simulation, fraught though it may be with inadequacies, does indeed give us a way of projecting the net result of various trends and interactions into the future, subject to whatever constraints and assumptions we wish to impose. We are perfectly free to program a scenario according to which a new uninhabited land mass, oil rich and equal in area to the combined land masses of Asia, Europe and the Americas, is discovered in the South Pacific in 1977. But there isn't much point in making assumptions like that. On the other hand, it seems to me that it might be well worthwhile trying out assumptions (such as skewed distributions of goods or food) that fly in the face of liberal-intellectual predilections. Perhaps one should try higher death rates, rather than lower birth rates. As long as we are operating on a computer, and not on the real world, it seems to me that the only limitation we are subject to is that of imagination. And I think people have been inhibited in what they will allow themselves to experiment with for fear of being thought monsters by the liberal intellectual establishment.

So what I suggest as the most worthwhile methodology for salvation, if any, is the methodology of careful, responsible projections, using the best data that can be gathered, combined with as rich a variety of social modifications of the imputs as anyone can come up with. Don't abandon the hard data and don't abandon the search for better and better techniques of probabilistic projections; but at the same time don't be afraid to shift any of the boundaries that are or might be under human control, and don't be afraid to shift them in any direction—regardless of what your academic neighbors may think.

NOTES

1. Donella Meadows, Dennis Meadows, Jorgen Randers, and William Behrens III, *The Limits to Growth*, New American Library, New York, 1972.

2. H. S. D. Cole (ed.), *Models of Doom*, University of Sussex, Sussex, 1973.

3. Sir Charles Darwin, *The Next Million Years*, Doubleday and Co., Garden City, New York, 1953.

4. Herman Kahn and Anthony Weiner, *The Year 2000*, Macmillan, New York, 1967.

2

Two World Views

1. There is a classical distinction, which has now and then been raised into a metaphysical principle, between two human attitudes toward the world. The distinction is that between the contemplative and the active. Often these poles are personified: Socrates, the seeker after truth; Alexander, the man of action. In more contemporary terms, the contrast is between Thought and Action. It is of course true that we all partake of both these principles, the contemplative and the active. Nevertheless, there are times and places when they can be encountered in fairly pure form. The mathematician in his study devising the proof of a theorem comes close to the contemplative pole, and the director of a sales campaign managing her staff seems to come close to the active pole.

Both of these attitudes or viewpoints are to be found in science. The theoretician is concerned with how things hang together, with explanation on a variety of levels. The experimentalist is concerned with devising experimental setups, and with how things are going to turn out. In the philosophy of science this contrast of viewpoint seems to be reflected in the dispute between realists and instrumentalists.

In a similar way, we may discern both points of view in the application of statistics. Statistics, as used in science—in agriculture or psychology or the theory of errors—is concerned with getting at the truth, or as close to the truth as possible. Its concerns are epistemic. Statistics as used in quality control or decision theory is concerned with improving the success of our actions in the world. It is concerned with action and decisions.

Although both thought and action are involved in every aspect of human life (the quality control engineer must design his procedure; the mathematician must sharpen his pencil), there is a serious tension between them. The tension is not always recognized. In statistics, it is sometimes claimed, we have a field that abounds in healthy controversy and argument, but not one in which the goals of some practitioners are in conflict with the goals of others. In the sciences, there

Reprinted, with modifications and additions, from *Nous,* no. 4 (1970), pp. 337-348, by permission of the publisher.

is little conflict, because the goals of experimentalists as well as of theorists are ultimately epistemic. But in the philosophy of science, again, we find implicit conflict between those who take the concern of science to be to develop a vision of the world, and those who take the concern of science to be the correct descriptions of the outcomes of experiments.

In the following three sections we shall attempt to establish and characterize the tension between the two world views concerned with action and thought in statistics. In the next section we shall draw a parallel with the issue of instrumentalism and realism in science and provide a single schematic framework in which both can be characterized. In the final section I shall attempt to characterize a connection, in this framework, between the two points of view.

2. We will be better able to see what the situation is in the foundations of statistics, with respect to thought and action, if we approach the matter with the help of a thumbnail history. In statistics the distinction that concerns us is that between decision and informative inference. In the early days of the development of statistical tests the background was agricultural experimentation. People wanted to know whether treatment A was any better than treatment B; the difference between the two treatments might not be very large; intuition alone might well be wrong. So careful statistical treatments of the data were developed. This is clearly a matter of informative inference. One may wish to withhold the name 'inference' for it surely isn't the sort of inference one encounters in mathematics. The premises may be true and the conclusion false, for one thing. For another, a warranted inference from a certain set of premises to a conclusion may cease to be warranted when the set of premises is enlarged. Inference or no, the kinds of actions to which statistical procedures led at this time were essentially epistemological actions, such as accepting (perhaps only for further testing) the hypothesis that compound Z increases the yield of strawberries. Such an action may be described in an involuted way, as rejecting the null hypothesis that compound Z has no beneficial effect on the yield of strawberries. However the outcome is worded, it does involve adopting a certain epistemological stance toward the hypothesis about compound Z. Our body of knowledge has changed as the result of our experiment and its statistical analysis.

The next stage in the development of statistics took place against a very different background. It took place at the time of the burgeoning of a serious interest in quality control in manufacture and a serious appreciation of its economic importance. It is natural that the same techniques, and what is more important for our purposes, the same terminology, was employed in testing lots of of manufactured items as was employed in testing plots of agricultural items. One still spoke of selecting a null hypothesis H_0 for testing; of the result of the testing procedure being the rejection or non-rejection of the null hypothesis. Mathematical progress continued, of course. The theory of uniformly most powerful tests was developed, and the concept of efficiency. The general properties of statistical decision functions were explored, and the theory of sequential tests was established. The name of the game is now decision theory, and more outcomes are available than the rejection or non-rejection of H_0: one can continue testing, for example. But the general terminology remains the same.

Although the terminology remains the same, the ideas are very different. Whereas in the classical rustic framework in which this terminology developed, the rejection of H_0 was an epistemic act, taking place in the realm of knowledge and belief, that is, in the world of contemplation, in the new framework "rejecting the null hypothesis" has become an indirect way of saying, "O.K., boys, go ahead and act as you would if you knew that the null hypothesis were true." The act that is referred to here is not an epistemic act at all—it is not an act of adopting a certain attitude of belief or knowledge or doubt toward the hypothesis in question. It is an act in the proper sense, an act in the realm of action. It is sending a lot of items back to the manufacturer, or putting a drug on the market, or redesigning a school curriculum, or . . . It would be more accurate and less misleading to refer to the outcome of a testing procedure, in this context, as an act (a non-epistemic act) of executing behavior B. The fact that B seems appropriate to us when H_0 is false is a fact which in one sense is external to the testing procedure. Of course in another sense we can perhaps make a connection in some cases: it may be possible to argue that act B maximizes an expectation of some sort when H_0 is false, and this may be regarded as an ingredient in the statistical analysis. In any event, the outcome of the statistical test is the performance of a certain act, rather than the adoption of an epistemic attitude toward a hypothesis.

Note that the split between the active and contemplative roles played by statistical methodology appears quite independently of any underlying interpretation of probability. The interpretations of probability adopted by most statisticians—to the extent that they selfconsciously adopted any interpretation at all—were generally empirical interpretations of one sort or another. Some statisticians, following von Mises, adopted an explicit limiting frequency interpretation; some, like Cramér, adopted a theoretical-counterpart-of-empirical-frequencies-in-finite-classes interpretation; some adopted the attitude that probability theory and statistics were mathematical disciplines, and as such not concerned with interpretations, and therefore that the question of interpretation could and should be left to the peasants out in the country who were applying the mathematics; some still clung to the primordial equally likely cases interpretation. Whatever the interpretation of probability, however, statistics came to play both a contemplative role, as in the testing of hypotheses in agriculture or psychology, and an active role, as in quality control and executive decision theory.

Personal probability now enters the confusing scene from stage left. Personal probability is from the very outset designed as a theory of action; but it is expressed in epistemic, or more properly credential, terms. Personalistic probability is alleged to be concerned with degrees of belief; degress of belief in turn are measured by tendencies or dispositions to act in certain ways. It might be felt here—and is no doubt felt by many personalistic theorists—that what we have here is a great new unification of the contemplative and active world views. I think this feeling is mistaken, and that what we really have in personalistic statistics is rather an activistic methodology in very nearly a pure form. Furthermore, I think many of the objections to personalistic probability, including some of my own, have missed the point precisely because they have been directed toward the role of statistics in the world of contemplation rather than in the world of action. Finally, I think that some personalistic theorists fail to see—perhaps because of their tendency to talk about belief—that their theory is a theory of action and not a theory of thought, and that if their theory is to be taken as sufficient for scientific methodology, they are committed to a radical and startling view of human scientific activity. These points must now be substantiated.

3. The development of personal probability is tied up with the development of a theory of utility, and both are based on the concept of preference. Preference is expressed in choices between actions; but the outcome is interpreted as a set of constraints on belief. Thus if I prefer to stake a possible gain on the occurrence of A rather than on the occurrence of B, this is interpreted as indicating that my degree of belief in A is greater than my degree of belief in B. For the personalist, probability is degree of belief. The usual axioms of the probability calculus follow from a few relatively plausible assumptions about preference. If someone's degrees of belief fail to conform to the probability calculus, then his preferences fail to satisfy these assumptions, and insofar as these assumptions merely express conditions of rationality of preferences, he is irrational.

A typical instance of the kind of argument that might be used to support an axiom of the probability calculus is the following argument for the principle that if my degree of belief in A is p, then my degree of belief in not-A must be (or ought to be) $1 - p$. The behavioral measure of a degree of belief is the willingness of the person whose degree of belief it is to act on it. A typical sort of act—though it is not at all necessary that it be taken as in any sense fundamental or basic—is the act of making a bet. Subject to some relatively innocuous assumptions about disinterested betting, a behavioral measure of a degree of belief in A is given by the least odds at which the person will bet on A: if the odds at which I am indifferent to taking either side of a bet on A are $s : t$, then my degree of belief in A, my subjective or personal probability for A, is $s/(s + t)$. Similarly, if the odds at which I am indifferent to taking either side of a bet on not-A are $u : v$, then my degree of belief in not-A is $u/(u + v)$. Now, the argument goes, $u/(u + v)$ and $s/(s + t)$ must add up to 1, for if they do not, the person will be forced to lose no matter what happens, either by betting on both A and not-A, or by betting against both A and not-A according to whether the sum is greater than 1 or less than 1.

We leave aside the question of why someone who is willing to bet at odds of

$s:t$ on A and at odds of $u:v$ on not-A should feel committed to accept both bets at once when they entail, *independently of any probabilistic considerations at all*, that he loses in every case. One's degrees of belief need not obey the probability calculus in order that one should decline to have a book made against him.

The arguments concerning preferences between actions directly impose constraints on actions: given a few natural assumptions about preferences, it follows that you should not simultaneously make bets at odds of three to one on A and at odds of three to one on not-A. The next step, and it is a different step, is that you should not *commit* yourself to making both of these bets simultaneously; i.e., you should not offer odds of three to one on A and at the same time of three to one on not-A. Of course you could make this offer, and then as soon as one bet is accepted, withdraw the other; but under these circumstances we would not say that you had *committed* yourself to both types of bet. As step three, we say that you should (subject to these natural axioms concerning preference) not have a *disposition* to offer bets at these two sets of odds, where by a disposition we mean something relatively permanent, i.e., such that if during a small interval of time, I have both the disposition to offer odds of three to one on A and of three to one on not-A, and if I find customers for both of these bets, I will in point of fact make both bets.

As the fourth and last step, we identify these dispositions with degrees of belief. We say that one should not have a degree of belief equal to ¼ in A and at the same time a degree of belief equal to ¼ in not-A. This step is clearly gratuitous. We can get the same sound bookmaking advice from the personalistic analysis without taking dispositions to bet at certain odds to be necessary and sufficient conditions for having certain degrees of belief. To take this step is possible; it amounts to adopting a certain behavioristic view of belief; but it is surely a mistake to regard this bit of behaviorism as an integral component of the personalistic interpretation of probability.

If we now excise this questionable talk of beliefs from personalistic statistics, replacing it where necessary with talk of dispositions to act of the relatively stable sort already alluded to, we have a species of statistics which is beautifully adopted to industrial and executive applications. Misleading talk about rejecting the null hypothesis H_0 becomes replaced by such lucid talk as: Send lot number 278 on to the shipping room. In classical terminology, we talk of the relative importance of two kinds of errors: the error of rejecting H_0 when it is true, and the error of failing to reject it when it is false. The relative importance of these two kinds of errors, on the personalistic analysis, is reflected in the prior probabilities of H_0 and its complement, combined with the relevant values. Eschewing talk of belief, what this amounts to is that before performing a test or experiment, we have a certain disposition to act A_H (misleadingly described at acting on H), that after the experiment we have a new disposition to act $A_H{}^*$, and that the classical talk of the relative importance of the two kinds of errors can be interpreted plausibly as reflecting something about our initial disposition.

Personalistic statistics is thus a normative theory of dispositions to certain sorts of actions. As such it very properly replaces the classical theory, and especially the terminology of the classical theory, which was developed with an eye to epistemological applications, rather than applications in the world of action, in the context of decision making.

4. We can characterize the field of application of personal statistics as being concerned with the world of action. We can also be both more formal and more specific. Suppose that we have a formal language of science, in which appear observation terms, theoretical terms, reports, generalizations, and so on. We can distinguish two kinds of statements in this language: statements that may be taken as actionable, or as proper subjects for bets, or as the direct basis of an action, and statements that cannot be so taken. Instances are easier to come by than a formal characterization: 'the next swan I see will be white', 'the next swan I see will be black', 'of the next 1000 swans investigated not more than 5% will be black', are statements that can form a proper direct basis for action, or that it is appropriate to bet on. 'All swans are white', 'less than 5% of swans are black', 'The weight of full grown swans is normally distributed with mean 25 and standard deviation 4.3' are statements on whose truth it does not seem plausible to bet. We cannot definitively verify or refute them in the sense that we can definitively verify or refute the statement 'less than 5% of the next thousand swans will be black'. 'Definitive' is a relative term, of course; in the case of a thousand swans we can easily enough lose count, and we take the possibility of error seriously. In the case of 'the next swan will be found to weigh less than 25 pounds' we take the possibility of error even more seriously. Yet in either case we allow that for all practical purposes verification or falsification is definitive. The notion of what is definitive being relative to a context, there is some fuzziness here, which I think should be taken seriously; but for the moment let us simply let it go. In a given situation, at any rate, there is a certain set of statements we will be able to decide are true or false, once and for all, in a specifiable finite period of time, and these are the only statements that are of relevance for our actions for that period of time. Not only are these the statements that can be bet on, and the bets settled; they are also the statements on which the outcomes of our actions hinge: indeed we may take them to include statements *of* the outcomes of our actions.

Some personalists feel that it is appropriate that the personalistic probability function be defined over the algebra of all statements of our scientific language, thus having in its domain such statements as 'all swans are white' as well as such statements as 'the next swan will be white'. Other personalists, taking the betting background more seriously, have doubts about including in the domain of the probability function statements whose truth or falsity cannot be settled in a predictable finite length of time. Of course if the truth or falsity of a statement cannot be settled in a finite length of time, it is not the sort of statement we have to worry about in itself, so if we want to include it within the domain of the probability function we must want to do so because it simplifies things in some way, or helps us in our calculations, or some such thing.

5. Let us explore this possibility. Let us call the statements whose truth or falsity can be determined in a finite predictable amount of time *D*-statements. ("*D*" for "determinable.") The set of *D*- statements is a Boolean algebra, since if *S* belongs to that set of statements, then *S* can be verified or falsified for all practical purposes in what we are regarding as a finite period of time; but to verify or falsify *S* is just to falsify or verify the denial of *S*. Further, if *S* and *T* belong to the set of *D*-statements, then so do their disjunction and conjunction. This is a little doubtful practically, since to definitively verify or refute both *S* and *T* may take longer than to definitively decide *S* or *T* alone, but it won't take an infinite amount of time. It might be thought that a statement like 'all swans are white' should be regarded as a *D*-statement, since it can be refuted in a finite period of time—namely by the observation of a non-white swan. But we cannot stipulate a time during which it will be refuted, if false. We can quite properly bet that it will be refuted during a certain sequence of observations—say 1000. But then we are dealing not with the *universal* generalization, but with the obviously determinable statement: 'each of the next 1000 swans will be white'.

We can thus restrict the domain of personal probability to the set of *D*-statements, and we can leave out of account, so far as action and decisions are concerned, the rest of the statements of science. De Finetti has argued this way in "Foresight." Although this seems reasonable from the point of view of the world in action, from the contemplative point of view, something seems fishy. Surely, general statements and theories, even though we cannot act *directly* on them or bet on their truth, seem to be appropriate objects for belief or doubt or perhaps even acceptance. But on the view under consideration, such statements don't even fall within the domain of the probability function.

The fishiness will be familiar to students of the philosophy of science. The same kind of oddness surrounds Ramsey's Theorem and Craig's Lemma which tell us that the observational content of any theory can be expressed in a theory in which no terms from a specified theoretical vocabulary appear. As in the personalistic treatment of general statements, there seems to be something very queer about the Ramsey-Craig treatment of statements containing theoretical terms. To be sure, the Craigian or Ramsified theory does have all the observational consequences of the original theory. In point of observational fact we can't tell the difference, and yet most of us feel that there really *is* a difference.

Not all of those statements that are retained as 'observation' statements under the Ramsey-Craig reforms are *D*-statements. Thus 'all swans are white' could perfectly well turn out to be a consequence of a Ramsified or Craigian theory, though this statement is not one in the domain of the personal probability function. Nevertheless we can combine the two approaches to get a perfectly practical, down to earth, system for action and decision which should be regarded as perfectly adequate from a purely activist point of view.

We begin with an ordinary scientific language *L*, containing both theoretical and observational terms (T_t and T_o). We accept certain theories within this language. Let us denote the set of axioms of these theories by A_t; they will in general involve theoretical as well as observational terms. A certain set of statements F in this language will be what I have called D-statements. We suppose also that a probability function P is provided whose domain includes F. We suppose (1) that F is a Boolean algebra, (2) that the members of F do not contain expressions from the vocabulary T_t. I shall call this a scientific framework, $< L,\ T_t,\ T_o,\ A_t,\ F,\ P >$. A *purification* of a scientific framework shall consist of the replacement of L by L', in which the set of theoretical terms is empty, the replacement of A_t by its Craigian form, CA_t, and the restriction of the domain of the probability function to F. Thus a purified scientific framework has the form $< L',\ O,\ T_{\bar{o}},\ CA_t,\ F,\ P|F >$. An obvious constraint to impose on the probability function is that for any statement S, if $S \in F$ and CA_t entails S, then $P(S) = 1$. But from the personalistic point of view, this is the *only* restriction to be imposed on P. If A_t happens to be empty (as may well be possible), even this constraint is vacuous. Some extreme personalistic views would suppose that any talk of accepting theories in the original framework was already elliptical, and that therefore no constraints whatever should be imposed on P.

The purified system is a complete system for action. That is, any problem of action or decision that can be handled within the original scientific framework, can also be handled in the purified framework. Nevertheless a lot of us have a strong and uncomfortable feeling that something important is left out of the purified framework. What is left out, of course, is just what is desired from the contemplative point of view. We suppose that there is more to knowing about the world than having the appropriate dispositions to act on D-statements. We suppose that there is more to knowing about the world than that knowledge that can be expressed in observational terms, even if we include statements that go beyond the determinable. To be sure, a vision of what the world is like may fall short in some respects as a program for action in the world; for example we can know that between a quarter and a half of the draws from an urn result in black balls, without knowing how to bet on the next draw, or without agreeing that the product of the odds on a black ball and the odds on a non-black ball ought to be unity. Indeed from the contemplative point of view, talk of action may be regarded as altogether extraneous to our true epistemological concerns.

6. From a general philosophical point of view, both the specialized world view which takes contemplation as fundamental and the specialized world view which takes action as fundamental seem too narrow. Both the man devoted to unadulterated action, and the man entowered in pure thought are seen as having shortcomings. What we have come up with is a general scientific framework, in which various hypotheses, statistical and otherwise, have come to be accepted, including general statements and theories. Classical statistics can be seen as one attempt to provide a logic for this sort of inductive acceptance; and recent

developments in philosophy can be understood the same way: for instance Levi's approach in *Gambling with Truth* and *The Enterprise of Knowledge*. We have also come up with a purified framework, consisting of an algebra of *D*-statements, together with a *P*-function defined over them. The former is science seen from the contemplative world view; the latter is science seen from the activist world view.

Is there some way to tie these two points of view together in theory as we all know perfectly well they are tied together in practice? I have already alluded to one constraint that is imposed on the *P*-function: namely that if *S* is in *F*, and *S* is entailed by the unpurified system, $P(S)$ must be equal to one. According to the personalistic doctrine, no further constraints are to be imposed on the *P*-function. A person who agrees that a certain coin is unbiased, that there is nothing peculiar about the mechanism by which it is being thrown, and yet who offers two to one odds on heads may have a perfect rationality score on the personalistic view, but he is somehow ignoring something important. There ought, it seems, to be some connection between the statistical hypotheses we accept in our unpurified scientific framework, and the set of dispositions we have to act, as reflected in our personal *P*-function.

The connection that seems natural to me is the following: when there is a statistical hypothesis in the unpurified framework according to which between *p* and *q* of the *A*'s are also *B*'s, then the statement that a particular *A* will be a *B* ought to have a *P*-value between *p* and *q*, unless there is a good reason to the contrary. One good reason to the contrary might consist in the fact that we've already observed that that *A* is a *B*; in that event the *P*-value in question should be 1. Another good reason might be that that particular *A* is also known to be a *C*, and we have in our unpurified framework a statistical hypothesis concerning the proportion (or measure) of *B*s among the members of $A \cap C$. It is not an easy matter to spell out these good reasons, or to see how they are related to each other. But that is not the task I've taken on here, though I have attempted it elsewhere (*The Logical Foundations of Statistical Inference*).

Assuming that some such connection can be established between the contents of the unpurified scientific structure and the *P*-function defined over the statements *F*, it is clear that the purified structure by itself is inadequate: there is nothing in the purified structure to embody those constraints on the *P*-function that are imposed by the accepted statistical hypotheses of the unpurified structure. On the other hand, those constraints are not sufficient to restrict dispositions to act to those which are acceptable; thus if we include dispositions to act as a part of our attitude toward the statements in *F*, then the constraints imposed by accepted statistical hypotheses do not determine adequately our attitudes toward these statements.

Putting these various comments together: the contemplative view leads to the original scientific structure, without the *P*-function. The active view focuses on the set of *D*-statements *F*, together with a *P*-function defined for these statements.

Statistics, construed as decision theory, is concerned with the elements of F, together with the P-function. Statistics, construed as the theory of testing hypotheses, or construed as a logic of induction, is concerned with the mechanisms by which the contents of the structure as a whole can be changed. The connection between the two consists in constraints imposed by the hypotheses we accept on the P-functions that characterize our dispositions to act. P-functions are also, of course, subject to the constraints imposed by the Dutch Book Theorem. Constraints imposed on P-functions are only misleadingly regarded as constraints on belief; belief belongs to the realm of contemplation, while P-functions belong to the realm of action. Constraints on P-functions are constraints on dispositions to act.

We need to be clear about our ideas, but it is also important to be clear about the purposes for which we want to make our ideas clear. To have a coherent approach to decision and action in the world which is not self-defeating is important and the personalistic approach to statistics provides an enormous amount of clarification in this regard. A strongly instrumentalist view of science is perfectly adequate to the design of experimental apparatus as well as to the creation of engineering wonders. But we want to understand the world, as well as to act in it, and it is in connection with the mechanisms for rejecting and accepting hypotheses that other approaches to statistics and to scientific theory are important. That we do not have to understand the world in order to act coherently in it is true but irrelevant. One might also claim that one need not act coherently in order to understand the world. In point of fact, we want both to act in the world and to understand it. I have been trying to show how both desires can be satisfied, and how, in the process, an important strand tying both the contemplative and active views of the world together is revealed.

3

Tyche and Athena

The study of the foundations of probability and statistical inference seems to be about as technical and abstract a topic as one can imagine. Even for a philsopher, in this age of technocracy and specialization, it seems a narrow specialized field, connected perhaps to the philosophy of science or perhaps to that somewhat disreputable poor relation of real logic, inductive logic. I think, however, that in reality this study is fundamental to a very wide variety of topics in philosophy, and that indeed many philosophical problems have been rendered nearly insoluble only by the lack of an adequate treatment of probability. In brief compass, I shall try here to indicate the various ways in which probability bears on other philosophical topics.[1]

1. Let us begin with a rough and intuitive discussion of probability itself.[2] I take probability to be fundamentally an epistemological concept: that is, the probability of something is what it is only relative to some body of knowledge. If we construe a body of knowledge as a set of statements of some language, then probability admits of a logical definition: probability becomes a logical concept. I take 'probability' to be univocal, and all probabilities to be single case probabilities. The probability of a statement S, relative to a set of statements T, is determined by logical considerations alone. Probability is thus *not* subjective, any more than deducibility is subjective, though the relations of probability and deducibility that usually *interest* us are the ones involving the body of knowledge we actually have, or the premises we actually accept. It does not seem plausible that in all cases our knowledge is such that there is exactly one real number representing the probability of the statement S relative to the body of knowledge T; it often seems that the best we can do on logical grounds is to say that the probability of S is *about p*, or greater than a half, or the like. Thus I take the range of the probability function to be intervals, rather than real numbers. Finally, it seems desirable that every probability should be based on a known statement of frequency or potential frequency. It turns out that these

Reprinted, with modifications and additions, from *Synthese*, no. 40 (1979), pp. 415-1436, by permission of the publisher.

constraints can be made to yield a plausible notion of probability. Specifically, we shall say that the probability of S, relative to the body of knowledge w in the language L, is the interval (p, q) just in case: there are terms of L, a, b, c, such that:

(1) w is a rational corpus or body of knowledge in L;
(2) '$S \equiv a \in b$' $\in w$ [S is known, in w, to be equivalent to '$a \in b$'] ;
(3) '$a \in c$' $\in w$ [a is known to belong to the reference class c in w] ;
(4) '$S(c, b, p, q)$' $\in w$ [In w it is known that the frequency of b's among c's is between p and q];
(5) $RAN_{w,L}(a, b, c)$ [Relative to the body of knowledge w, a is a random member of c with respect to b] .

Some comments are in order. First, what is a rational corpus? From the point of view of providing an analysis of probability, we want to put as few constraints on w as possible. The only two constraints it seems essential to impose are (a) that w not contain a contradiction '$s \wedge \sim s$', and (b) that it contain the logical consequences of any statement that appears in it. This means that a body of knowledge could contain an inconsistent set of statements; we do not stipulate that a body of knowledge must be logically closed, nor that it have a model. This is not to say that at some later point — say when we are doing epistemology — we might not impose further constraints which would lead to these consequences for rational corpora; it is merely to say that when we are analyzing probability we don't need them.

Second, by the use of '$\in$' it is clear that L is a relatively strong language. In point of fact we require that the language be strong enough to contain a reasonable amount of mathematics. In my formal work I have used a first order language to which axioms of set theory are added, so that the whole of mathematics is available. This is a matter of convenience rather than necessity; a much weaker mathematical base would suffice. What would not suffice are the languages considered by most of those who have explored the possibility of a logical conception of probability (Carnap [1], Hintikka [4], Hilpinen [3]), for these languages are too weak to express statements of proportionality.

On the other hand, the language employed is straightforwardly extensional. It may be the case (as I have admitted elsewhere [10]) that some specific *theories* require the use of modal locutions; but in general we need not suppose this.

Third, it is specified that c be one of a special class of terms qualifying as reference terms. It is well known (cf. 'More on Maximal Specificity', [7] and the references therein) that not every term will serve as an appropriate reference term. For example, 'the union of the prime numbered tosses of this coin and the tosses yielding heads' is a perfectly good term of ordinary language; we have good reason to believe that the frequency of heads in it is 1 or close to 1; if we want a reference class to be potentially infinite, this one is; and so on. It is clearly not an appropriate reference term. The specification of what terms of the language L will count as potential reference terms is to some extent arbitrary. But this arbitrariness does not seem to be of paramount importance, since the selection of a particular language L is also 'arbitrary' in some sense, and to provide criteria for selecting one language or another will implicitly provide criteria for selecting one set of reference terms or another. I do not think there is any way of avoiding the problem of choosing a language. If P is a primitive predicate of the language, I cannot imagine grounds on which 'the set of objects x such that Px' could be rejected as a potential reference term; and yet we can easily imagine a language in which this term denotes precisely the objects denoted by the awkward term considered earlier. Thus, for the purposes of analyzing probability, we suppose that there exists, for an arbitrary language L, a canonical list of the reference terms of L, RT_L. (The list is infinite, of course.)

Fourth, it is stipulated that in the rational corpus w it is known that the frequency of b's among c's is between p and q. This is what requires that the language L we consider be relatively powerful. It might alternatively be required that what is known is *not* merely a statement about frequencies in an extensional language, but a statement about chances in an intensional language. Note that *probability* in any case is intensional—it is a metalinguistic notion, like that of provability or validity—and thus probability statements are opaque to object language replacements. The possibility that the statistical statements on which probability is based might be construed as concerning propensities rather than frequencies is one we shall consider in each of the following sections. I shall claim that in almost no case do propensities offer an advantage over frequencies.

Fifth, there is the problem of randomness. This is a rather complicated matter, but essentially we say that relative to the body of knowledge w, a is a random member of c with respect to b just in case there is nothing in w which would yield a 'better' (more useful) probability for '$a \in b$'. Suffice it for our present purposes to observe that as a consequence of the analysis of randomness, if $RAN_{w,L}(a, b, c)$ and $RAN_{w,L}(a', b', c')$ and '$a' \in b' \equiv a \in b$' $\in w$, then what we know about the proportion of c's that are b's is just the same as what we know about the proportion of c''s that are b''s. Here, too, one may take a modal turn. It might be maintained that a is a random member of b just in case a is chosen by a method which has a propensity to select each member of b equally often. (Note that in this case the reference to c is vacuous; if a is a random member of b under this construal, it is so with respect to any property whatever.) We may still want to retain reference to the rational corpus w, since it may be that it is only *under a certain description* that a is a random member of b, and knowledge of that may be required to be a part of our body of knowledge. Again, in what follows, we shall continue to take account of this alternative, and to argue against it.

Sixth, it should be noted that on this construal *all* probabilities are single case probabilities. Consider the sort of statement that has been construed as a candidate for a frequency interpretation: 'The probability that an A is a B is p'. To begin with, it seems perfectly appropriate to interpret the indefinite article 'an' in such locutions as short for a condition involving randomness: for example, 'for every (term) x, if $RAN_{w,L}(x, A, B)$, then $PROB_{w,L}('x \in B') = (p, p)$'. But this will hold just in case the statement '$S(A, B, p, p)$' belongs to w. Thus to assert that the probability that an A is a B is p, is precisely to assert that the proportion of A's that are B's is p. But since x is a singular term (a metalinguistic variable), the probability itself is a single case probability. Of course there are all sorts of other propositional attitudes: one might wonder if it is true that the probability that an A is a B is p; one might counterfactually speculate about what would happen if the probability that an A is a B were p; one could claim it to be impossible that the probability that an A is a B is p; and so on. I would argue, though this is not the place to do it, that such locutions can be handled by considering rational corpora not specified as being the body of knowledge of an individual at a time, or of a group of individuals, but rather specified in some other way. Thus for example one might consider a set of statements w^* constrained to be true and general to account for such statements as: Although relative to Tom's rational corpus 'The probability of an A being a B is p' is true, it is not *really* true (i.e., relative to w^*) that the probability of an A being a B is p.

It turns out that for an arbitrary but sufficiently rich language, we can show that probabilities exist for almost all statements; that if '$S \equiv T$' $\in w$, then $PROB_{w,L}(S) = PROB_{w,L}(T)$, so that $PROB_{w,L}$ is indeed a function; and finally that these probabilities are coherent in the sense that there exists a function P, satisfying the axioms of the probability calculus, such that for every statement S of L, if there is an interval (p, q) such that $PROB_{w,L}(S) = (p, q)$, then $p \leqslant P(S) \leqslant q$.

Much has been written of probability as legislative for rational belief, as a degree of belief, as a rational betting coefficient, and so on. It is clear that if someone is going to post odds, and take any set of bets offered at those odds, his odds had better be such as to conform to the probability calculus. But there is nothing probabilistic about this: it is a straightforward matter of *deductive* logic (having nothing to do with probability at all) that if his posted odds do not conform to the probability calculus, a smart bettor can make a book against him. It is not at all clear, however, that one's degrees of belief come in real numbers and correspond to the odds that he is willing to post. It is true that you can force me to post odds on rain tomorrow; it does not follow that my degree of belief in rain tomorrow is exactly that indicated by the odds I post. I can post various odds (within limits) without feeling that my belief in rain tomorrow is different in the various cases.

In any event, while $PROB_{w,L}$ imposes constraints on the odds I can rationally post, it does not determine them uniquely. If there are degrees of belief, probability imposes constraints on them by demanding that they lie within certain intervals. In this sense, probability is legislative for rational belief. This is not to say that the person whose body of knowledge is w, and for whom $PROB_{w,L}(S) = (p, q)$, may not offer odds corresponding to a 'degree of belief' falling outside this interval; it is only to say that in so doing, he is being irrational.

2. The most straightforward application of probability is as a guide to action. Let us suppose we are contemplating an action that depends on whether a is a B. For example, we are going to make book on that eventuality, or we are contemplating a bet on it, or we are going to take out insurance against it, or we are contemplating two courses of action which will have very different utilities for us, depending on whether a is a B or not.

Suppose that for X the probability of '$a \in B$' is (p, q). On the interpretation of probability being considered, this means that the odds that X may accept or offer on a bet are rationally constrained only to correspond to a point in this interval. (Of course X will not allow a book to be made against him; but this has nothing to do with his degrees of rational belief—it is a matter of his not being willing to suffer a certain loss.) In general, the expected value of '$a \in B$' for X will be an interval (pV, qV), where V is the value of '$a \in B$' for certain. Although this introduces complications into our decision theory, they are complications which replace other difficulties: according to subjectivist approaches, if r is the subjective probability of '$a \in B$', the expected value of '$a \in B$' is rV, exactly, and the only rational rule to follow is that of maximizing expected subjective utility. But then r may have any value at all. On our view it is constrained. On objectivist views, '$a \in B$' will not generally have any probability at all, or its probability may well not be known, and we are then directed to follow such a rule as that of minimizing maximum possible losses. Again, this amounts to supposing that the probability of '$a \in B$' may have any value whatsoever. The attempt to follow both approaches leads to flat out contradiction.[3] The present approach saves what is reasonable in both of the other approaches.

Let us consider the constraints that an upholder of a propensity view of probability might want to impose. First, he might want to insist that the statement '$S(A, B, p, q)$' on which the probability is based be a genuine propensity statement, and not merely frequency statement. It is not hard to see that this requirement is misguided. Suppose that '$S(A^*, B, p^*, q^*)$' is a propensity statement, and that (p^*, q^*) differs from (p, q), and that X knows the propensity statement. For example, X might know of a certain coin, that it has a propensity of .6 to land heads when tossed on a standard apparatus; at the same time, he may know of the tosses of that coin performed yesterday that .4 of them yielded heads, but not which tosses yielded heads. Suppose a is 'the fifth toss performed yesterday'. It is perfectly clear that the probability he should use for alternatives that depend on whether or not the coin landed heads on its fifth toss yesterday is .4 rather than .6; he should use all the information he has available—in Reichenbach's words, he should use the narrowest reference class about which he has adequate statistics. (Of course this needs a lot of unpacking: 'narrowest' and 'adequate' are ambiguous; and the principle needs to be supplemented to take account of situations in which Bayesian arguments that depend on our knowledge of multidimensional reference classes are appropriate.) It thus seems flatly wrong that X should always be constrained to base his probability on a propensity statement rather than on a frequency statement, even if he does have propensity statements in his body of knowledge.

Second, the propensity theorist might demand that a be selected by a method that has the same chance of selecting any object in A. To this we may reply in two ways. Suppose that a, as before, is 'the fifth toss to be performed yesterday'. This toss could be selected by such a method: we might know that ten tosses were performed yesterday, and we might select one by consulting a table of random numbers, choosing a toss to be considered in such a way that any of the ten tosses has an equal chance of being selected. But it is hard to see why our epistemological attitude toward 'the fifth toss yields heads' should be any different in this instance than it is when that toss is selected by mutual agreement between X and Y. Furthermore, suppose that a is 'the next toss', and let A be the set of tosses. It is hard to see how it can be true (or even quite what it can mean) to assert that a has the same chance of being any one member of A as any other, or to say that it is 'selected' by a method which can be characterized in this way.

3. Perhaps the most direct and basic use of probability in epistemology is its application to statistical inference. On the view of probability being discussed, it is perfectly possible for statistical hypotheses (like any other statements) to be rendered highly probable. There are a number of issues in the theory of statistical inference that are illuminated by this view. For example, long-run frequencies of errors of various sorts may not turn out to be probabilities (because the randomness requirements are not met). Bayesian inference—particularly stable estimation—turns out to be rather widely applicable, despite the fact that probabilities are intervals. The result of an inference, however, is not that a statistical hypothesis has a certain real number probability, but that it has a probability which is an interval. If the interval is rather narrow and rather close to 1, then we say that the probability of that hypothesis is 'high'.

It is not only the fancy and technical statistical inferences that are of concern to us, however, but also the common, garden variety, inferences regarding our ordinary experience, or regarding the experience of someone who is put into the world with a language and no background knowledge. If I have often in the past caught fish at the south end of the lake, seldom in the past caught fish at the north end of the lake, though I have fished each end equally often, it is rational for me to think that I am more likely today to catch fish at the south end—other things being equal. The phrase, 'other things being equal' is precisely what embodies the conditions of randomness required for the probability statement. If

I imagine someone with no background knowledge of the world at all, but with a knowledge of the language L (if this is not already self-contradictory!), and he observes over and over that the sun rises after a certain intuitively assessable period, it is rational for him to have a relatively high degree of confidence that the sun will almost always appear after such a period.

The last example illustrates the most primitive form of direct statistical induction. Let us examine a more formal version of it. Consider a class C, and a property P. We suppose C finite, so that 'proportion' makes good sense. A certain proportion p of the objects in C, then, have the property P. Let us take a probability of 0.99 as corresponding to 'practical certainty'. Consider the set of subsets of C containing 10^6 members of C. (In doing philosophy the cost of sampling is negligible). If p is 1 or 0, the proportion of these samples that exactly reflect the composition of C is 1; but if p is between 1 and 0, any proportion less than 1 will provide an accurate picture of how often P occurs in C. The worst case is when $p = 1/2$: for a given level of accuracy, this proportion will yield the smallest frequency of 'representative' samples. If p is a half, we may compute that 99 percent of the samples of 10^6 we draw will exhibit a frequency of P that is within .00124 of the frequency of P in C. Thus before we draw a sample, the probability is (0.99, 1.0) that our sample will have a frequency of P within .00124 of that in C. This is because, relative to what we know (which we assume to be extremely little, for the purposes of this philosophical example), the sample we draw is a random member of the set of all such subsets of C with respect to revealing the true frequency of P. Now we draw the sample, and, lo and behold, every one of the C's in the sample has the property P. The sample is still a random member of set of all such subsets of C with respect to revealing the true frequency of P. (It wouldn't be if we *already knew* the true frequency of P—but by hypothesis we don't know that.) Therefore after our observation, the probability is still (.99, 1.00) that the sample has a frequency of P within 0.00124 of that in C. Therefore the probability is (0.99, 1.00) that at least 0.998 of the C's have the property P. Or, roughly speaking, it is practically certain that practically all of the C's have the property P.

Of course when our rational corpora are not so empty of empirical content as that of the hypothetical primitive inductivist, the assertions of randomness required for probability statements of the sort mentioned may not hold. But if they do not hold, it is because of the existence in our body of knowledge of empirical assertions that interfere with the metalinguistic assertions about randomness. In other words, to suppose that our body of knowledge is such that it is not probable to the degree (.99, 1.0) that at least 99 percent of the C's have the property P, is to suppose that there is *knowledge* in our rational corpus (for example, that the sample comes from a part of the universe of C's in which we might expect an unusually high frequency of P) which interfers with the assertion that our sample is a random member of the set of subsets of C containing 10^6 items.

It is in the context of statistical inference that the demand that the sample be selected by a method that yields an equal propensity for each possible equi-numerous sample to be selected is both the most common and the most plausible. It is this kind of demand that underlies the frequent statistical proviso that the sample be a *random* sample. This is often 'assured' by the employment of tables of random numbers, of randomizing devices, and the like.

Let us suppose that we are concerned with simple binomial inference, and that we want to assess the probability that the sample is *representative*. As we observed, a great majority of these possible samples are representative; the problem is to convert this 'great majority' into a probability. We consider two stages in our search for knowledge.

First, *before* we have drawn the sample, we may consider the probability that it will be representative. If we suppose our method of sample selection is such that the probability that a given sample is drawn equals the probability that any other sample is drawn — a state we can sometimes be in, in virtue of circumstances being so fortunate as to allow us to employ random numbers or randomizing devices in drawing our sample — the probability that our sample will be representative is precisely the proportion of representative samples. If, on the other hand, we do *not* employ randomization, whether or not the sample is random will depend in what we *do* know about the method of sampling. Thus if we are interested in the average size of rocks in a truck, and we propose to scoop some rocks off the top as a sample, we know (from physics) that the sample is not very likely to be representative — the large rocks will tend to end up on the top. On the other hand, there are non-random sampling techniques that seem perfectly all right. If we are sampling the set of outcomes of trials of a certain sort, there is often no reason not to regard the next n trials as a random sample of size n. If we are sampling fish, or insects, or people, the constraints imposed by availability preclude the possibility of 'random' sampling in the sense previously mentioned. What is at issue in each case is whether or not the sample is random, in the epistemological sense, with respect to being representative.

Second, we consider the probability that the sample is representative *after* we have selected it. This, of course, is what really interests us, for if the probability is high that the sample is representative, the probability is high that the population from which it is drawn is similar in composition to the sample — and to get information of this sort is what we are doing the sampling for. Now, after having obtained the sample, the situation with regard to a sample obtained by randomization is exactly the same as it is with regard to a sample obtained without randomization: what counts is what we know about the particular sample we have in fact obtained. In particular, if there is any deliberately selected sample which would not be regarded as random with respect to representativeness, then that sample cannot be regarded as random with respect to representativeness when it is the outcome of randomized selection. Whatever arguments there are for rejecting *that* sample as being probably representative when it is selected on purpose are equally good arguments for rejecting it as being probably representative when it is selected by randomization. And since randomization requires that each sample have the same chance of being selected, that particular sample must stand as good a chance of being selected as another. Randomization provides neither a necessary nor a sufficient condition for the sample to be random in the sense that interests us after it has been drawn.

The upshot of this discussion is that while randomization may play a reassuring role in the *design* of sampling experiments—it makes it possible to assert that the probability is high that a sample *will* be representative—it is quite irrelevant to the post-experimental analysis of data. What counts after the experiment is whether or not the sample is a random one in the epistemological sense: that is, we must have no reason to assign it to some subclass of the set of equinumerous samples in which the frequency of representativeness is known to be lower than it is in the set of all equinumerous samples. (It might belong to a subclass in which we have reason to *believe* that the frequency of representativeness is *higher*; that is the idea behind stratified sampling.)

4. How do items get into this rational corpus? This is a question that leads us into epistemology. High probability is certainly one of the things involved in the acceptance of statements. (Of course some people, Richard Jeffrey, for example, wish to deny that people ever accept statements; they may sometimes be *caused* to assign probability 1 to them, but that is a different matter.)[4] How high is 'high'? The difficulty of answering that question in general suggests that a rational corpus should be indexed by a number representing 'practical certainty'. A rational corpus with one index may be appropriate in one context, one with another may be appropriate in another context. One notion of practical certainty is appropriate when the stakes are low, a more rigorous (demanding) notion is appropriate for higher stakes.

A necessary condition for the acceptance of a statement S into a rational corpus of level k is that its minimum probability be at least k. It would be awkward to take this as a sufficient condition, because, given a body of statistical evidence concerning the frequency of P in C, for example, we want to accept (if any) only one strongest statement, although there are a whole set of statements of high probability. The strongest statement, the one with the most empirical content, is the one that assigns the shortest interval to the measure p. We thus build a condition of this form into the criteria of acceptance for statistical statements. It applies automatically to the acceptance of quantitative statements: to say that the length of a table is $m \pm d$, feet is to say that measurements of the table have a mean in the interval $m \pm d$, with probability at least k.

Beyond this, we allow high probability to function as both a necessary and sufficient condition of acceptance. This has the consequence that we must eschew deductive closure for rational corpora. This is a result of the lottery paradox:[5] Let k represent practical certainty. In a lottery of more than $1/(1-k)$ tickets and only one winner, the probability is at least k that a specified ticket will not win. Thus for every i we may accept the statement that that ticket i will not win. But to accept all these statements is inconsistent with accepting the statement, which we also suppose to be acceptable, that some ticket will win. Observe that there is no explicit contradiction here: no statement of the form 'A and not-A' is accepted, unless we allow deductive closure. Indeed, note that no fewer than $1/(1-k)$ statements must be conjoined to get contradictory statements. Many people regard this as unnatural: they think that a body of rational beliefs should at least have the property that there is a model in which all of the statements are true. But the lottery paradox—as well as more telling paradoxes regarding the acceptance of statistical statements—suggests that there is no natural way of picking one consistent set of statements as preferable to another contrary one. Two alternatives suggest themselves: first, that we abandon deductive closure, and strict consistency, and allow a body of beliefs which is not strictly consistent to be a rational corpus. This seems to me the most natural procedure, since I feel of my own body of beliefs that it is practically certain that some of them are false. This does not strike me as irrational, but on the contrary as rather well substantiated. The alternative is to say that any consistent subset of the former set of statements is a proper rational corpus. This has the disadvantage that it does not seem to conform to the way some people ordinarily think; and it has the added and philosophically more important disadvantage that a given body of evidence does not *uniquely* determine a rational corpus of a given level in a given language. Since interpersonal agreement about what beliefs are supported by given evidence is one of our strongest desiderata in setting forth criteria of rationality, it is a decided disadvantage to have to abandon it so early in the game.

In addition to accepting statistical statements (such as, 'practically all C's have P', 'the weights of this strain of mice are distributed approximately normally with mean m and standard deviation s', and the like) we accept universal generalizations (all mice are omnivorous) and theories (the genetic theory) and observation statements (the mouse is in the cage). Let us see how acceptances of these kinds fit into the framework outlined.

Consider first universal generalizations. Some philosophers have suggested that universal generlizations should be construed as 'inference tickets': that rather than having in our body of knowledge the statement 'All C's are P', we have, metalinguistically, the principle that from 'x is a C' we may infer 'x is a P'. Although this seems to be a distinction without a significant difference (whatever is problematic about a universal generalization is problematic about the corresponding inference ticket) it does provide a hint. We have already seen how it can become practically certain that practically all C's are P. Specifically, let us suppose that the statement 'Between 0.99 and 1.0 of the C's are P' is accepted in the body of knowledge of level 0.99. Consider an arbitrary C. If it is a random member of C with respect to the property P, then the probability that it has the property P is $(0.99, 1.0)$. In other words, it is practically certain, in the same sense, that it has P. Now consider all those terms t such that 't is a member of C' is known in the body of knowledge in question. (Observe that we presuppose a theory of definite descriptions such that 'the first C which fails to have P' is not *known* to be a member of C, unless we know that some C's are not P.) Suppose that every such t is a *random member* of C with respect to P, relative to the body of knowledge. This means that relative to that body of knowledge, for any term t whatsoever, if we have '$t \in C$' in that body of knowledge, then relative to that body of knowledge we shall have: the probability of 'Pt' is $(0.99, 1.0)$; this in turn means that 'Pt' itself will be probable enough to be accepted into any lower level body of knowledge. The effects, then are exactly the same as those of accepting the universal generalization into the body of knowledge of level 0.99. Thus I suggest:

'All C's are P's' is to be accepted in the body of knowledge of level k just in case (i) there is a body of knowledge of level $k + \epsilon$ relative to which the probability is $(k, 1.0)$ that at least a proportion k of C's have P, and (ii) for every term t such that '$t \in C$' belongs to the body of knowledge of level $k + \epsilon$, $RAN_{w, L}(t, P, C)$ where w is the body of knowledge of level $k + \epsilon$.

It is perfectly possible, of course, that we will be able to accept the statistical statement when we know of one or a few C's that lack P; it is perfectly possible that we will be able to accept the statistical statement when we have adequate ground for believing that some C's are not P, even if we have never seen one. But under either of these circumstances we shall have a term t (the first C lacking P) such that $RAN_{w, L}(t, P, C)$ is false.

In a primitive state of nature, employing a primitive language containing only observation terms, it is unlikely that there would be very many acceptable universal generalizations. That is, bears sometimes disappear into thin air, and sometimes turn into people, crows are usually black, but sometimes pink and orange; sticks that feel straight usually, but not always, look straight; and so on. No such primitive state and no such primitive language ever existed, of course, but if it did, there would be a natural way of introducing a new language, with a new vocabulary, that would be more interesting and useful. This process would be analogous to that by which theories are introduced in more usual kinds of language. In the hypothetical primitive state a necessary and sufficient condition for considering something to be a bear (for accepting 'a is a bear' in any rational corpus of whatever level) is that the observer whose rational corpus it is is appeared to in a bear-like manner by a. In this state one accepts, for example, 'practically all bears are corporeal.' But one cannot accept 'all bears are corporeal', because there are exceptions. There are bears, for example, through whom a spear will pass as though there were nothing there. Let us now introduce a change in the language: let us introduce a new term, 'real-bear', of which it is analytically true that it is corporeal. We now have the generalization: 'all real-bears are corporeal' in our body of knowledge, but it is, alas, without empirical content—it reflects part of the *meaning* of the term 'real-bear'.

Where has the empirical content of our original statistical generalization gone? It hasn't evaporated; it merely appears in a new guise: What used to be a bear has become an apparent real-bear; and now we say that practically all apparent real-bears are real-bears; i.e., corporeal. In other words, we achieve a universal generalization by introducing a distinction between appearance and reality, i.e., by introducing the possibility of error. The empirical content now connects appearance and reality. Were we only concerned with this one generalization, there would have been no gain: there is little difference between saying 'practically all bears are solid' and 'all bears are bears' and saying 'all (real) bears are solid' (in virtue of the meaning of the terms) and 'practically all apparent bears are bears'. But we are not concerned with this one generalization, but with a whole group of them: bears like honey, bears hibernate, bears have platulate feet, bears nurse their young, and so on. In the primitive hypothetical state, all of these would be represented by rough statistical generalizations. After the change from 'bear' to real-bear', many of these statements will be replaceable by universal generalizations; furthermore, *these* generalizations will have empirical content. Of course there are any number of alternative treatments of a given case such as this. For example, we may modify the language in such a way that real-bears have (analytically) a whole cluster of properties $P_1 \ldots P_n$. It is then a universal generalization with empirical content that bears have some further property P_{n+1}. Although it is now analytic that bears have the property P_1, it may turn out that everything with the property $P_1 \ldots P_n$ also has the property P_{n+1} and this is now also an empirical universal generalization.

If we regard a theoretical term as a term that cannot be applied without running the risk of error, practically all the terms of ordinary language turn out, on this view, to be theoretical. Furthermore, what we ordinarily regard as observation terms and statements, 'crow', 'this is a black crow', themselves turn out to be subject to error. There are two ways of treating this error. It is perhaps the most important theorem of epistemology to show that these two ways are equivalent.

(I) We retain the pair of terms, 'real-bear' and 'apparent-bear' in our language. We include in our body of knowledge incorrigible statements (such as 'α is an apparent-bear'), and infer (under the appropriate circumstances) that α is a real-bear, on the basis of the generalization that practically all apparent-bears are real-bears.

(II) We drop the term 'apparent-bear', at least for zoological purposes, and employ only the term 'real-bear', or 'bear' for short. On judging that α is a bear, we include 'α is a bear' directly in our rational corpus. But we recognize that error is possible; and thus we do not regard this statement as incorrigible. We therefore include it in a rational corpus of a certain level (the level corresponding to the highest level of rational corpus in which 'α is a bear' occurs under alternative (I)).

If we adopt alternative (II), which strikes me as a more realistic description of what scientists in fact do, observation statements, involving these somewhat theoretical terms, come to be incorporated *directly* into our rational corpora on the basis or our observational experience. They may, of course, have to be rejected later—that is what corrigibility is. When I observe that a spear passes through α without harming it, I must withdraw the assertion that α is a bear (or undertake a profound rearrangement of my rational corpus). We shall return to corrigibility in a moment.

The introduction of a term like 'electron' or 'field strength' is in principle no different from the introduction of the term 'real-bear,' except that the connection with observation is a little more indirect. There are certain analytic connections among such terms; there are certain empirical generalizations regarding such terms. As in the case of the bear, it is to some extent an arbitrary matter what shall be regarded as analytic of the meanings of the terms. What counts is that in a certain body of knowledge, a certain set of statements, either analytic or acceptable generalizations, appears. If we construe a theory as a language together with a set of axioms (ignoring the distinction between analytic and empirical axioms), what counts is that the set of axioms be acceptable and have empirical content. In order for that to be the case, they must be connected to low-level theoretical terms (like 'real-bear').

In the case of quantitative theories, such as those of physics, probabilitistic considerations play an especially pervasive and important role. (These considerations play a similar role in qualitative theories, but it is not so easy to see the role.) The theory predicts, say, that the angle between two trajectories will be θ. Furthermore, we perform the experiment a number of times, and not only is the angle not quite θ in any experiment, but it varies from experiment to experiment, while the theory asserts that it is always the same. We know perfectly well what is going on: our measurement of the angle is subject to error. Furthermore, we understand the character of the error: we have a theory which describes how these errors are distributed. The physical theory together with the theory of error yields a distribution for the observations of θ. If we observe something incredible (i.e., something whose probability on the theory is .001), we do not reject the observation, but rather the theory. We reject it only tentatively, and other things being equal. Statistically we know that if we make enough observations, some anomalous ones will occur. But if a given observation is a random one in the appropriate (epistemological) sense, the probability that it is anomalous will be so low that we may simply accept the assertion that it is not anomalous. Since that it is not anomalous entails the negation of the theory, we accept the negation of the theory. Note that if we have *accepted* the theory in that body of knowledge, the observation is not a random number of observations with respect to being anomalous: the theory entails that the deviant observation is anomalous. When the freshman gets a deviant result in his physics lab, we do not reject conventional physical theory, even if we cannot put our finger on what he did wrong.

The possibility or impossibility of a crucial experiment for a theory has been discussed extensively in philosophical literature. From the present point of view, a crucial experiment is clearly impossible. If the results are quantitative at all, the general theory of error applies, and we always must consider that the anomalous result may merely be one of the improbable ones whose occurrence (on rare occasions) is in fact *predicted* by the theory together with the standard theory of error. Even if the prediction is qualitative, the possibility of error is there: what appears to be a bear may not be a bear, but a mere bear appearance (hallucination, misinterpretation, or whatever). What counts in the assessment of an alleged crucial experiment is the evaluation of probabilities, just as that is what counts in the assessment of non-crucial experiments. The difference is one of degree (in the historical instances of allegedly crucial experiments, the probabilities are extremely large).

A theory construed as a language L together with a set of axioms A cannot simply be treated as 'probable'—to begin with, probability is only defined relative to a language, and so cannot directly determine the choice of a language. It should be observed, in the first place, that we are concerned not with how scientists or other people go about accepting theories, because the behavior of people is always more or less irrational, but with how people *ought* to decide to accept theories. Furthermore, one of the constraints is that the theories are there to be accepted: we are not concerned with how someone might go about making up a theory. We are concerned primarily with the choice between given theories.

Although two theories as potential candidates for inclusion in a rational corpus have different languages, this does not mean that they are probabilistically incomparable, as some recent writers seem to have maintained. Let two theories be (L, A) and (L', A'). (Often L and L' will contain the same terms; this does not mean that the languages are the same, for different 'meaning postulates' connecting the terms, and connecting those terms with the background language L^* may occur in A and in A'.) We are given a rational corpus w, in the background language L^*. Suppose that our language L^* is expanded by the addition of L, and that w is modified by the addition of the logical consequences of A, and the deletion of any negations of consequences of A that may occur in w. Let the result be w_T; let the result of doing the same thing with the theory (L', A') be $w_{T'}$. Theory (L, A) is preferable to theory (L', A') just in case the empirical content of w_T is greater than that of $w_{T'}$ (and it is preferable to do without either theory if the empirical content of w is greater than that of either w_T or $w_{T'}$). We accept a theory just in case it is preferable to any of its alternatives; if there are two theories that rank equally, it doesn't much matter which is accepted. To do all this we need a measure of empirical content; that in turn will be a matter of probability, though there are a large number of problems concerning the details.

This same procedure gives us a way of dealing with corrigibility of lower-level statements. For a statement to be corrigible is for it to be capable of correction; that is, we must be able, after accepting the statement, to turn around and reject it (on good enough evidence). In that rational corpus, this can't be done probabilistically, since the probability of the statement relative to a rational corpus in which it appears as a member is $1 -$ it could not be higher. But we may look instead at a higher-level rational corpus in which that statement doesn't appear: if, relative to that higher-level rational corpus as modified by the acquisition of new information, that statement is no longer so probable, then we reject it from the lower-level rational corpus. But there are also occasions when a theoretical (linguistic) modification is called for, and in those cases it may be the higher-level statement that gives way, rather than the lower-level statement.

All of the foregoing is problematic and programmatic in one degree or another. Nevertheless, if it can be carried through, the notion of an empirical body of knowledge, based on a body of experiential evidence, makes sense; and up to an arbitrary choice of theories of equal empirical content, that body of knowledge is uniquely rationally determined by that body of experiential evidence.

All the probabilities in this epistemological program are single case probabilities. Each is based on a known statistical statement, and on a statement of randomness. In the case of statistical statements based on observed samples, we have argued that neither the probability of that statement, nor the required notion of randomness, need be construed in terms of propensities. Things are not quite so clear when it comes to the interpretation of the statistical or universal statements in the rational corpus. I have argued elsewhere [10], however, that most of these statistical statements may be construed in terms of straightforward frequencies. The two significant exceptions concern mathematical probabilities (those involved in dropping lines on circles, or in selecting real numbers 'at random' from an interval, for example) and theoretical probabilities (those involved in quantum mechanics, or in the kinds of physical processes employed in gambling apparatus). As for the modalities perhaps involved in theoretical and universal generalizations, it seems to me that this necessity can often be construed as linguistic necessity. In any event, the most important sort of probability in this program of reconstruction is error-probability, and that, it seems to me, can only be construed in terms of frequencies in sets of events.

5. The concept of epistemological probability has a significant bearing on the theory of practical judgment. Faced with an alternative between two courses of action, what does the agent do? What makes his choice rational, if it is? It seems clear enough that this use of the word 'rational' is derivative from the preceding one: the agent is rational if his choice of a course of action is based on a rational corpus which is itself justifiable. Suppose that the agent prefers one outcome to another. Then, if his rational corpus is such that he *knows* that one action will

lead to the preferred outcome and the other to the outcome that is not preferred, all other things remaining the same, then clearly he is rational in his choice
just in case he chooses the first action. But this is not a realistic description of
the choice situation.

(i) Every action has a number of consequences more or less remote, more or
less predictable.

(ii) In many real situations, the agent cannot *know* that his action will lead to
a certain outcome, but will only know that his action will lead to one or another
outcome with certain probabilities.

With respect to (i) we must consider the outcome of an action to include its
more remote consequences. We can do this, because we take (ii) seriously: that
is, we must suppose that the outcome of an action is only known probabilistically, in general, anyway; therefore we might as well take account of the probabilistic elements of (i) at the same time. The preference ranking or utility function of
the agent then should be defined over future states of the world. Suppose that
he assigns a utility to each of the possible future states of the world. Then suppose that he has a choice of two actions: one of which yields one distribution of
probabilities over possible states of the world, the other yields a different distribution of probabilities over possible states of the world. If we were to adopt a
Bayesian-personalistic interpretation of probability, the problem of rational
choice would be solved: the agent should choose that action which yields the
maximum mathematical expectation—i.e., the maximum of the sum (or integral)
of values of states of the world multiplied by the corresponding probabilities (or
density function).

But from the present point of view, things are not quite this simple. In general, rather than a probability p that action A will yield state of the world W,
with value $V(W)$, we have an interval, (p, q). Thus the mathematical expectation,
too, turns out to be interval valued. If the expectation of action A is (v_1, v_2) and
the expectation of action B is (w_1, w_2) how does the agent choose between
them? There is one clear-cut case—when one of the intervals falls entirely to the
right of the other. If this is not the case, then various other principles of decision
under uncertainty may play a role. For example, one might adopt a minimax
principle: adopt that action (of the acceptable ones) whose *minimum* expected
value is the highest. Or an optimistic maximax principle: adopt the action with
the highest *upper* expectation. Or any of several other techniques. I would suggest that only the first principle—the principle that one action should be chosen
over another when its interval of expectation falls entirely to the right of the
interval of expectation of the other—is a *rational* constraint on choice.

But this is not the only way in which epistemological probability enters into
the theory of practical judgment. In assigning values to possible futures of the
world, I must not only take account of the facts (as best they are represented in
my body of knowledge) regarding the trajectory of the world, but I must take
account of such facts as I have regarding my own trajectory. What I am inter-

ested in now is not how satisfying a certain world a year from now would be to me now, but how satisfying that world would be to me a year from now. That is, I can be quite sure that my utility function will change over time, and though I may not have very good methods for predicting its changes, the methods are better than none. I can be quite certain, at any rate, that certain aspects of my utility function will not change drastically over the next year, but even this is a probabilistic question.

There may be categorical ethical imperatives to take account of as well as matters of practical judgment. Even if this be so, epistemological probability has a role to play. Under such an ethical theory, certain classes of actions are obligatory or proscribed absolutely, and without regard to present or future circumstances. But as has been pointed out often enough in the past, it is not always clear to an agent whether a proposed action of his is going to fall into one of those classes or not. Granted that X is absolutely forbidden, is it the case that what I am about to do is an instance of X or leads to an instance of X? Should I refrain, after all? It seems very likely that under ordinary circumstances it may be a matter of argument whether the agent's proposed action is or is not an instance of X; this being so, it seems reasonable to suppose that probabilistic considerations are appropriate for the agent—even though they are of course quite irrelevant to the rightness or wrongness of the act itself.

Again, all of these probabilities are single case probabilities; again none of them seems to need to be based on statements of propensities; again, they are more than subjective. In many instances, what we want to base our expectations on are frequencies in classes of events that extend into the future. But these frequencies need not be construed as propensities; on the contrary, if we know both a frequency in the actual world and a propensity reflecting frequencies in possible worlds, it is the former rather than the latter that provides the best foundation for the probaiblities that we should take as a guide in life.

6. There are metaphysical doctrines on which the concept of epistemological probability has a bearing, too. For example, the doctrine of universal causality is often called upon to glue together the realm of scientific theory and the domain of human experience. Causality is not something we observe directly in the world around us. What we experience, as Hume said, is merely constant conjunction. If causality is anything at all, then it is either a theoretical attribute —something we encounter in well-formulated scientific theories— or else it is something we require in order to understand how we can argue from instantial experience to universal scientific hypotheses. It is not the latter, according to the present epistemological theory, for we can explain how universal generalizations and even theories are rationally included in our bodies of empirical knowledge without calling on causes. Whether or not it is the former requires somewhat more careful argument. Within a theoretical framework, it is often said that one phenomenon causes another; in the Newtonian framework, the changing relative

positions of the earth, sun, and moon cause the tides. This is, indeed, to say more than that the tides are correlated with the positions of the sun and moon. In a medical theoretical framework, to say that a certain virus causes a certain disease is to say more than that they are found in constant conjunction. One way of treating causality in such contexts is to observe that the causal statement is so called because its universality follows from a general theory, together with some boundary conditions. Thus it seems plausible to regard attributions of causality as metalinguistic comments on the *source* of certain universal generalizations, rather than something embodied in those generalizations themselves. Thus while it is quite reasonable and comprehensible to say that we have discovered the cause of this or that, the metaphysical doctrine of universal causation seems quite another matter. What we find at the very foundations of the best understood parts of science are not statements about causality, but statements of universal (or in the case of quantum mechanics, statistical) association. It is from those statements that we (eventually) derive the much more specific statements that we call 'causal'. Furthermore, for the vast majority of phenomena, we have no causal account. We act as if we think there is one—that is, we look for ways in which to account for these phenomena under general theories— we look for the cause of cancer. But that does not mean that we have a warrant for thinking that we will succeed. Even in the case of quite simple phenomena: the tossing of coins, the balkiness of gasoline engines, the perversity of people, . . . , where we think that 'in principle' a causal explanation of what occurs could be found, we rarely find that explanation. Indeed, even in the paradigm case of law-like behavior, the behavior of the fulcrum balance, the causal account adds nothing of interest other than the indication of the source of the law. The pervasiveness of error prevents an exact confirmation of even the constant conjunction part of the law; and thus surely prevents confirmation of a law that purports to go beyond constant conjunction. Despite the evidence we have that many things happen in relatively orderly ways, we have very little evidence indeed that the universe, especially in detail, is not whimsical in character.

A recent replacement of the doctrine of universal causation is the doctrine of universal propensity. But we have already argued that in most applications of probability, frequencies in the real world are preferable to propensities in hypothetical possible worlds as a guide to action. If this is so, it is difficult to see why there is any more motivation for us to postulate the existence of real propensities to glue the events of the world together than there is for us to postulate a causal glue. The extent to which it is possible to characterize the world in terms of irreducible statistical statements, like the extent to which it is possible to characterize the world in universal statements, is a matter for scientific inquiry, rather than for metaphysical speculation. At the moment, as throughout the past, much of our knowledge is reflected in statistical statements. And now, as throughout the past, much of the progress of scientific inquiry consists in reducing those statistical statements to an ever more fine-grained, but always epistemologically relativized field of potential reference classes.

7. Epistemological probability has been defined in detail for very powerful and general languages. Many of the consequences of this conception of probability for statistical inference have been worked out. Some observations have been made regarding scientific inference in general. But the details concerning the acceptance of theories, of the development of an appropriate measure of empirical content applicable to large (infinite) sets of statements, remain to be developed. Some of the important consequences of the existence of error for the theory of measurement and the testing of scientific hypotheses have been mentioned, but more remains to be done in this area. The consequences for decision theory, in the relatively narrow framework treated by statistical decision theorists, have been considered in some detail, but the more general consequences require development. Finally, the general philosophical consequences of this approach to rational empirical knowledge, in ethics, metaphysics, ontology, and so on, have been no more than lightly touched upon. There is a fertile and virgin field here for further explanation.

NOTES

1. This paper is a translation, with modifications, of [8].
2. For more detail, see [9].
3. See Chapter VI of [9].
4. See [5].
5. The ramifications of this problem are discussed in [6] and [9].

BIBLIOGRAPHY

[1] Carnap, Rudolf, *The Logical Foundations of Probability*, 2nd ed., Chicago, University of Chicago Press, 1962.
[2] Fetzer, James, 'A World of Dispositions', *Synthese* 34 (1977), pp. 397-421.
[3] Hilpinen, Risto, 'Rules of Acceptance and Inductive Logic', *Acta Philosophical Fennica* 21, Amsterdam, North-Holland Publishing Co., 1968.
[4] Hintikka, Jaakko, 'A Two-Dimensional Continuum of Inductive Methods' in J. Hintikka and P. Suppes (eds.), *Aspects of Inductive Logic*, Amsterdam, North-Holland Publishing Co., 1966, pp. 113-132.
[5] Jeffrey, Richard, *The Logic of Decision*, New York, McGraw-Hill Book Co., 1965.
[6] Kyburg, Henry, 'Conjunctivitis' in Swain (ed.), *Induction, Acceptance, and Rational Belief*, Dordrecht, Holland, Reidel Publishing Co., 1969; this volume, Chapter 14.
[7] Kyburg, Henry, 'More on Maximal Specificity', *Philosophy of Science* 37 (1970), pp. 295-300.
[8] Kyburg, Henry, 'Tuche e Athena', (in Rumanian), *Logicieni si Filosofi Contemporani*, Bogdan (ed.), Bucharest, 1974.
[9] Kyburg, Henry, *The Logical Foundations of Statistical Inference*, Dordrecht, Holland, Reidel Publishing Co., 1974.
[10] Kyburg, Henry, 'Chance', *Journal of Philosophical Logic* 5 (1976), pp. 355-393; this volume, Chapter 7.

Part II. Critical Probability Papers

4

Probability and Decision

There is a double-barreled thesis I want to defend here: it is that on the one hand the theory of statistical inference gives us a great deal of knowledge about the process of drawing conclusions from evidence; and that on the other hand, the conclusions that one draws depend to a large extent on the philosophical conception of probability with which one starts. I shall conduct my argument on the supposition that a behavioristic analysis of believing and conclusion-drawing is appropriate. I'm not at all sure that this is the case; indeed, I'm pretty sure that with respect to believing, it isn't the case. But I am only going to deal with a very simple behavioristic situation: that in which we are called upon to make a decision under conditions of uncertainty. The analysis of this particular case will make both the points I want to make, and will make them in the strongest way I can make them.

There are three possible 'conditions of uncertainty' that we might want to deal with: in the first there is *no* uncertainty; in the second there is a known *statistical* uncertainty; and in the third there is what one might call an *epistemological* uncertainty. Each of these conditions (though only the last is realistic) will serve to suggest some of the factors that go into the basic problem of decision under uncertainty.

1. Values. When we can predict the most far-flung consequences of each of our actions, the problem of making a decision is relatively simple: we need merely choose that act that has the most valuable total set of consequences. We may put the matter another way. We may look at the problem as one of choosing a particular world, or a particular state of the world, which we assume to be completely known in all its details. In real life this simple picture is complicated by two kinds of uncertainty: we do not always know precisely what the consequences of our actions are going to be (what particular world it *is* that we are choosing); and neither do we know how much we are going to like even the

Reprinted from *Philosophy of Science* 33, no. 3, July (1966), pp. 250-261, by permission of the publisher.

predictable consequences of our acts.[1] There are certain steps we can take with respect to our ignorance of what will happen—the nature of these steps is precisely the subject of this paper. The second problem I propose (in the very best of company) to ignore. I shall simply suppose that the choosing agent has a clear-cut scale of values such that he knows which of any pair of possible worlds he would prefer (not only now, but in the future, when perhaps he has found himself inhabiting one of them), and such that he is able to relate their values quantitatively. This is required for our discussion, because we must be able in principle to answer such questions as: Is a choice that leads to world A with a probability of 0.9 and world C with a probability of 0.1 preferable to a choice that leads to world B with a probability of 0.5 and world C with a probability of 0.5? A solution to the problem that I am proposing to ignore here consists in a utility function (to use the jargon term), which assigns to each of the states of the world that *may* result from a given decision, a numerical value. Needless to say, we do not need to suppose that any two individuals have the same utility function. We simply suppose that when we consider the problem of choice for any agent, one of the factors that enters into our solution is his utility function, and we suppose that utility function to be defined over all the possible states of the world.

2. Uncertainty. Although it seems to me that people might find it far harder to know exactly what they want—and particularly what they will want after they've gotten what they thought they wanted—than to know exactly what will happen in the future, we shall take the first problem of decision as solved and turn our attention to the one that interests us here: namely, the problem raised by our lack of knowledge concerning the future. There are two kinds of ignorance I shall consider: the simplest sort of ignorance is that which makes lotteries exciting; the other is that which makes horse racing exciting.

A lottery is exciting because although we know that exactly one of a number of alternative states of the world will obtain, and although we know that everything possible is done to insure that one of these states won't have an unfair advantage over the others, we don't know which particular state will obtain. This is generally expressed by saying that the probability of any one state is the same as that of any other state: or, in the particular case of a lottery, that the probability of any one ticket winning is the same as the probability of any other ticket winning. This is not typically the case in a horse race; one cannot arrange horse races in such a way that each horse in the race has (by any sort of general consensus) an equal probability of winning. There is available a wealth of information about each horse which presumably has a bearing on the probability of that horse winning (if such a probability exists at all), and there is no acceptable way of modifying the circumstances—by handicapping, say—so that the probabilities come out equal. One would find it hard, perhaps, to construct a clear and definite distinction between these two kinds of situation that could not be attacked as artificial; and yet they do seem to differ in an important way. I shall regard the first situation as embodying statistical uncertainty; and the latter, where the probabilities depend so heavily on knowledge, as embodying epistemological uncertainty.[2]

3. Mathematical Expectation. To fix our ideas, and to make matters as clear as possible for those for whom this is an unfamiliar way of thinking, consider a lottery with one thousand tickets, numbered from 000 to 999. In this lottery there is only one prize, and it is $100.00. There are various alternative decisions we can consider in this context: the decision to buy a ticket or not to buy one at a given price; the decision to buy a ticket carrying a specific number; the decision to buy a certain number of tickets. The same classical analysis can be applied to each of these decisions. The key concept of this classical analysis is *mathematical expectation.* Mathematical expectation is defined in terms of probability and utility: we say that the mathematical expectation of an alternative (buying *a* ticket, buying ticket number *K*, buying three tickets, not buying any tickets) is the sum of the values of each of the possible ensuing states of affairs, each multiplied by the probability that the state of affairs will ensue. Thus the value of buying a ticket for five cents (disregarding all but monetary values) is $99.95, the value of the state of affairs in which that ticket wins, multiplied by the probability that that state of affairs will in fact be the case following that decision (0.001, since there are a thousand tickets and the lottery is run so as to be fair), plus −0.05, the value of the state of affairs in which the ticket does not win, multiplied by its probability, .999. The value of the decision to *buy* a ticket at 0.05 is thus

$$.001 \times 99.95 + .999 \times -.05 = +.05;$$

the tickets are underpriced.

More realistically, suppose the tickets are priced at fifteen cents. The people running the lottery are guaranteed a profit of $50.00, if they sell all the tickets. Now the mathematical expectation of the decision to buy a ticket is $99.85 \times .001 - .15 \times .999$, or $-.05$. The mathematical expectation of refraining from buying a ticket is $100.00 \times 0 + 0 \times 1.0$, or precisely 0.

We can formulate a perfectly classical rule for decision in these lottery cases:

RULE I. So act as to maximize your mathematical expectation; where the mathematical expectation of an act is simply the sum of the values of the alternative states of affairs that may follow upon that act (no imputation of any sort of causal relation being involved), each multiplied by its probability:

$$ME(A) = \sum_{\text{all outcomes}} V(O_A) \times P(O_A)$$

One more brief example. Suppose we are betting on the fall of a well-balanced, fair die. You agree to give me a dollar if the die does not land with the one spot up; I agree to give you ten dollars if it does. What is the mathematical expectation of this act of yours? It is minus a dollar, with a probability of 5/6, plus ten dollars, with a probability of $1/6$; $-1 \times (5/6) + 10 \times (1/6) = 4/6 = 2/3$ of a dollar. If we look at the bet as an act of mine, everything remains the same, except that the signs of the values are reversed; the expectation of the act is plus a dollar, with a probability of $5/6$, minus ten dollars, with a probability of $1/6$, or $-2/3$ of a dollar.

We do not, of course, fully understand Rule I, since we do not know just what probability is; indeed, my thesis is that the meaning of the rule and even the consequences of the rule will depend on the philosophical interpretation which is given to the concept of probability. Furthermore, there are interpretations of "probability" under which it makes sense to look for a justification of the rule (and there are corresponding probability-theorists who claim to have found such a justification), other interpretations under which the rule may be regarded as a part of the *definition* of "rationality," and still other interpretations (as we shall see) under which the rule is not always applicable.

4. The Calculus of Probability. At this point I shall present a fragment of an uninterpreted calculus of probability. Then I shall present three alternative interpretations of this probability calculus.

First of all, we suppose the probability calculus to be embedded in a system of logic and mathematics which provides us with the necessary machinery for calculating with real numbers. The ingredients of the calculus are four: primitive terms, formation rules, axioms, and rules of inference. The primitive terms will consist of the appropriate primitive terms of logic and mathematics, together with a function constant P, a set of terms A, B, C, . . . , and three operators: a one-place operator N and two two-place operators O_C and O_D. The formation rules of those of logic and mathematics, together with the added rule that $P(S)$ is a real number, provided that S is an expression in a sequence that contains A, B, C, . . . etc., and contains Nx, $x\,O_C y$, and $x\,O_D\,y$ only when x and y are expressions occuring earlier in the sequence.

The axioms are these (in addition to the logical and mathematical axioms):

    1. $0 \leqslant P(S) \leqslant 1$
    2. $P(NS) = 1 - P(S)$ [Thm: $P(NNS) = P(S)$]
    3. If $P(S_iO_CS_j) = 0$ for $i \neq j$, then $P(S_1O_D(S_2O_D(S_3O_D \ . \ . \ .))) = \sum P(S_i)$

If the operators O_C and O_D and N are given one of the usual interpretations, which presupposes that the terms A, B, C, . . . are interpreted in one of two ways, these are all the axioms we need. But since I wish to give an *uninterpreted* calculus here, I shall add axioms—actually more than need be added—that will allow the construction of the usual probability calculus *prior* to the provision of an interpretation. There are eight additional axioms:[3]

    4. $P(S1O_C(S_2O_CS_3)) = P((S_1O_CS_2)O_CS_3)$
    5. $P(S_1O_D(S_2O_DS_3)) = P((S_1O_DS_2)O_DS_3)$
    6. $P(S_1O_cS2)\ 0\ P(S2OCS1)$

7. $P(S_1 O_D S_2) = P(S_2 O_D S_1)$
8. $P(S_1 O_D(S_2 O_C S_3)) = P((S_1 O_D S_2) O_C(S_1 O_D S_3))$
9. $P(S_1 O_C(S_2 O_D S_1)) = P((S_1 O_C S_2) O_D(S_1 O_C S_2))$
10. $P(N(S_1 O_C S_2)) = P(NS_1 O_D NS_2)$
11. $P(N(S_1 O_D S_2)) = P(NS_1 O_C NS_2)$

The rules of inference are the standard logical rules.

Before passing on the three interpretations of the probability calculus which I wish to consider, I shall state and prove one theorem: Bayes's theorem. In order to state it, I must first introduce, not another concept, but merely a convenient abbreviation. Consider expressions of the form:

$$\frac{P(S_1 O_C S_2)}{P(S_1)}$$

They occur often enough that it is convenient to have an abbreviation for them; I shall use $P(S_2/S_1)$, which we read "The probability of S_2, given S_1."

Definition:

$$P(S_2/S_1) = \frac{P(S_1 O_C S_2)}{P(S_1)}$$

Bayes's theorem in its simplest form is just the following:

Theorem:
$$P(S_2/S_1) = \frac{P(S_2) \times P(S_1/S_2)}{P(S_1)}$$

The proof is obvious: apply the definition to $P(S_1 O_C S_2)$ and $P(S_2 O_C S_1)$, and then use Axiom 6.

5. Interpretations. There are three fairly standard interpretations of probability. There is a logical interpretation, a subjectivistic interpretation, and an empirical-frequency interpretation. These are all fairly well known, and each of them has been claimed to hold the key to the problem of decision under circumstances of uncertainty.

The most prevalent interpretation of probability, as well among philosophers as among statisticians, is one form or another of the empirical interpretation. This interpretation takes probability statements to be empirical statements that describe the behavior or characteristics of certain classes of objects or events encountered in the world. On this view, to say that the probability of heads on a toss of a coin is a half, is to say something that, whether it be true or false, purports to describe the potential behavior of the coin. One consequence of this approach to probability is that we don't generally know all the probability statements that we would like to know. A probability statement is a statement about a large, perhaps infinite, class of events in the world; it is a statistical hypothesis about the behavior of a *kind* of object or event or experiment. We can test a probability statement in various ways, and often confirm it to a high degree; but we may also be interested in probability statements that have never been tested at all, and may even be untestable, such as a statement about the probability of a particular horse winning a particular race.

A second interpretation of probability that is fairly common is that which takes it to be a logical relation between evidence and conclusion. This interpretation is rare among scientists (Harold Jeffreys being one of the few distinguished exceptions), but it is common among logicians; the chief modern proponent of this interpretation is Rudolf Carnap. According to this interpretation there is a logical relationship between one statement (regarded as hypothesis) and another statement (regarded as evidence) in virtue of which the first has a certain probability relative to the second. Sometimes it is claimed (as in the systems of Keynes, Koopman, and Jeffreys) that the numerical value of this relation, the actual degree of probability, must at times be intuited just as one intuits the validity of some simple deductive relations; in logical systems of probability that have been proposed recently, degrees of probability can always be calculated.

An important distinction between the logical view and the empirical view is that while every categorical probability statement on the empirical view is a statistical hypothesis, and thus *not* known with certainty, but, since empirical, subject to confirmation or disconfirmation, on the logical view this is not the case; indeed, on the logical view the only way in which a true probability statement might fail to be known is through logical ignorance or incompetence on the part of the knower. Probability statements on this view are, like the statements of logic, analytic and *a priori*. A true probability statement is always a logical truth.

There is usually held to be a connection between these logical probabilities and *degrees of belief*. If, relative to the statements expressing my knowledge, the probability of a certain statement, S, is p, then the degree of belief that it is rational for me to have in S is also p. *Probability is legislative for rational belief.*

The third interpretation I want to mention, the *subjectivistic* interpretation, is in many ways a weakened version of the logical interpretation. It is basically psychological rather than logical. Degree of belief is the fundamental concept of this interpretation: probability statements represent the degrees of belief of individuals. (Whence the adjective "subjectivistic.") But these degrees of belief are intended to be not so much the actual degrees of belief of a living individual as an idealized version of those actual degrees of belief. The actual degrees of belief may have to be modified in order that relations among them satisfy the probability calculus. Thus while someone might initially have a degree of belief equal to 1/4 in S, and a degree of belief equal to 1/4 in not-S, conformity to Axiom 2 of the probability calculus requires that he modify his degrees of belief so that the sum of the degrees of belief in S and in not-S will be one.

Like the logical interpretation, this interpretation makes it in general impossible not to know the probability of a given statement. In fact, it goes even further in that direction, for on the logical interpretation it was possible to be ignorant of the relevant logical relation, or to fail to perceive it, while on the subjectivistic interpretation it is supposed to be *impossible* to fail to have an opinion about a given statement—i.e., to fail to have a degree of belief in that statement.

This interpretation has become well known only in relatively recent years, since the publication in 1954 of Savage's book, *The Foundations of Statistics*, but the theory as a single articulated theory of probability and statistical inference dates back to the 1930s in the work of Bruno de Finetti and F. P. Ramsey.

I have spoken only of the interpretation of the function constant P, but there are also alternative interpretations of the terms A, B, C, etc., and of the operations N, O_C and O_D. The empirical interpretation generally interprets the terms A, B, etc. either as *sets*, or as *kinds* of events. In the former case N becomes complementation, O_C intersection, and O_D union. Axioms 4-11 may be eliminated. If A, B, C, etc. are interpreted as kinds of events, the operations must be interpreted appropriately, and axioms 4-11 must be kept. On both the logical and subjectivistic interpretations, the terms are usually taken to be sentences or propositions. The operation N is taken to be negation, O_C conjunction, and O_D disjunction. Axioms 4-11 are replaced by the stipulation that logically equivalent statements are to have the same probability.

These three interpretations of the one calculus of probability will now be applied to the problem of decision under uncertainty. Let me review the three interpretations briefly:

The Empirical Interpretation: Probability statements are statistical hypotheses, subject to confirmation and disconfirmation. They are often unknown. The arguments of the probability function (the kinds of things we speak of the probability of) are classes or kinds of events.

The Logical Interpretation: Probability statements are logical truths, if true, self-contradictory if false. They can only be unknown through ignorance or logical incompetence, and such cases don't interest us. The arguments of the probability function (the kinds of things we speak of the probability of) are statements.

The Subjectivistic Interpretation: Probability statements express personal opinions, subjective degrees of belief, subject to potential modification so as to conform to the rules (relations) of the probability calculus. They can in no event be unknown. The arguments of the probability function are usually taken to be statements, but they may be taken to be events.

6. Applications I. On any of these interpretations of probability, mathematical expectation may perfectly well be defined as we have defined it above: the mathematical expectation of an alternative is the sum, over all the possible states of the world that might ensue, of the relative value of that state of the world, multiplied by the probability of that state, (i.e., the probability of the event in question, or the class, or the relevant statement describing that state of the

world.) Rule I, which directs the decision maker to maximize his mathematical expectation, is perfectly applicable to many situations on any interpretation of probability.

The typical example is that of gambling, but much the same can be said concerning situations that arise in insurance, in quality control, and so on. Suppose that a gambler offers me a choice among three alternatives that depend on the outcome of a toss of a well-balanced die: A_1: to pay one dollar, and to receive back two dollars if a three turns up or if a four turns up, but to get nothing back otherwise. A_2: to play for free, and to receive four dollars if either a one or a two turns up, but to lose seven dollars if a five turns up. A_3: to refuse to play. We may calculate the mathematical expectation of each of the alternatives as follows:

$$ME(A_1) = (-1) + 2 \times {}^2\!/_6 = -1 + {}^4\!/_6 = -{}^1\!/_3$$
$$ME(A_2) = 4 \times {}^2\!/_6 - 7 \times {}^1\!/_6 = +{}^1\!/_6$$
$$ME(A_3) = 0$$

The recommendation would be the same on each interpretation of probability: adopt alternative A_2. In general, the relevant probabilities will be the same— or very nearly the same—however we interpret probability, just so long as we have excellent ground (as we have in the case of a well-balanced separate die) for supposing that we know about the statistical behavior of the objects with which we are dealing. Therefore the calculation of mathematical expectation yields the same results however we interpret probability. When we can foretell the future, at least in a statistical sense, different interpretations of probability will not lead to conflicting recommendations. What is the best course of action on one theory will also be the best course of action on the other two. These are the lottery-type situations I mentioned earlier; the problem is simply a problem in calculation.

The type of problem represented by a horse race is quite different. To calculate the mathematical expectation of betting at fixed odds on a given horse, one has to know the probability that that horse will win. For the subjectivist, there is no problem in calculating this probability: it is simply the degree of belief that that person has in the statement: "Horse A will win." On logical interpretation this probability will exist, though it may be difficult to calculate. On the frequency interpretation, it is generally held that the probability in such a case does not even exist: what is the set that the statistical hypothesis that *is* this probability statement is about? Frequentists often claim that "probability" here doesn't even have the same *meaning* that it has in ordinary probability statements. Therefore one cannot calculate mathematical expectations, and Rule I is no help at all.

7. Applications II. Now let me introduce a more realistic situation in which we may or may not be able to foretell the future in the required statistical sense.

Once upon a time there lived in a far away land a beautiful princess, named Sally, the daughter of one of the cleverest Kings of all time. Realizing that in these days of high taxes and vengeful relatives, the traditional trial by combat or test of strength for the joy of his daughter's hand and for half his Kingdom was rather out of place, and further realizing that his own treasury was seriously depleted, and yet being at heart a kind man and a good father, he caused to be published far and wide in his kingdom the following offer:

Attention Princes: I, King Osbert, offer half of my lands, and the hand of my beautiful daughter Sally, to that Prince who will predict correctly the number of white balls there will be among four drawn from an urn of black and white balls. As his stake, the applicant must put up his own principality, which must consist of at least 10,000 hectares, which shall be forfeited if his prediction fails.

A certain Prince, yclept Hogarth, whose scholarship was admired far and wide, decided to apply for Sally's hand. He compared the size of his own principality with that of the King, the fruitfulness of his vineyards with those of the King, and, finally, unromantically throwing the beautiful Sally into the scales, calculated that he would improve his lot twenty-fold if he won his bet with the King, but would be reduced to nothing if he lost. He went to the King to learn the details of the King's proposal.

The King agreed that the drawings would be conducted under circumstances insuring the strictest fairness to both parties. He further stipulated that the urn would be one of four kinds: it would either contain 25% white balls (Hypothesis H_1), or half white balls (Hypothesis H_2), or 90% white balls (Hypothesis H_3) or finally, only 10% white balls (Hypothesis H_4). Furthermore, the King (having taken rather a fancy to Hogarth) confided in him that the urn would be chosen at random from a storehouse, and that in the storehouse half the urns are of the first kind, a quarter of them are of the second kind, an eighth are of the third kind, and an eighth are of the fourth kind.

TABLE I

Hypothesis	% White	% of Urns
H_1	25	50
H_2	50	25
H_3	90	$12\frac{1}{2}$
H_4	10	$12\frac{1}{2}$

Hogarth the hero was not yet satisfied. He took the problem to the statistical institute of his own country. Now this is a problem whose solution is the same, whatever the interpretation of probability one adopts. It is a problem in which we have precise statistical knowledge, and when we have good statistical knowledge, logical and subjectivistic probabilities always fall into line. The solution to the problem is given by the following table, which presents, for each alternative open to the Prince, *its mathematical expectation.*

TABLE II

Alternative	Mathematical Expectation
A_0 (predict 0 white balls)	-0.248
A_1 (predict 1 white ball)	1.579
A_2 (predict 2 white balls)	3.441
A_3 (predict 3 white balls)	5.515
A_4 (predict 4 white balls)	2.937

The mathematical expectation of all the alternatives but one is positive; the alternative for which the mathematical expectaton is a maximum is A_3 — that of predicting that three of the four balls are white.

Hogarth was mightily pleased with the table: it not only told him which of the alternatives he should choose, but it also told him that his mathematical expectation in choosing that alternative was decidedly positive. But there is more to the story. The head of the statistical institute came to Hogarth and whispered to him that he could perhaps increase his mathematical expectation some more, if only he could persuade the King to let him sample the urn before making his prediction. Given the composition of a sample of balls from the urn, it is possible to use Bayes's theorem to derive new probabilities for the alternative hypotheses as to the composition, and thence new mathematical expectations for the alternatives that face the Prince. Suppose that the Prince were allowed to take a sample of two balls from the urn, and it turned out to consist of one white ball and one black ball. We could use Bayes's theorem to calculate the posterior probability of the first hypothesis, relative to the described event, as follows:

$$P(H_1/E) = \frac{P(H_1) \times P(E/H_1)}{P(E)} = \frac{((1/4) \times (.375))}{P(E)}$$

The quantity $P(E)$ may be computed as

$$P((EO_C H_1) O_D (EO_C H_2) \ldots O_D (EO_C H_4)) = P(EO_C H_1) +$$

$$P(EO_C H_2) + \ldots + P(EO_C H_4) = \sum_{i=1}^{4} P(H_i) \times P(E/H_i).$$

In the particular case at hand, $P(E) = .3573$.

We can now construct a new table. I shall present it in a different form: it will consist of an 4×5 rectangular array, consisting of four columns, one under each hypothesis, and five rows, one corresponding to each alternative action. The entries of the table are quantities $u_{ij} b_j e_j$, where u_{ij} is the utility of alternative A_i, given that hypothesis H_j is true, b_j is the probability of hypothesis H_j, and e_j is the probability of the evidence consisting of a white ball and a black ball, given that hypothesis H_j is true. The quantity $1/P(E)$ is factored out of each product, since it has no bearing on our description, but only changes utility scale. The sum of the entries in each row represents the utility of that alternative on the new utility scale.

TABLE III

	H_1	H_2	H_3	H_4	SUM
A_0	−.165	.039	.057	−.045	−.114
A_1	−.003	.531	.230	−.042	.716
A_2	−.640	.860	.001	.001	1.702
A_3	1.475	.531	−.042	.230	2.194 ←
A_4	1.060	.039	−.045	.057	1.156

The recommended alternative is again A_3; to compare utilities, we must divide by $P(E) = .3575$. Then the utility of A_3 (on the old scale) is 6.15 as opposed to 5.51. It would certainly be worthwhile, it seems, to be able to take a look at a sample.

So far every computation was a computation that would be made regardless of how the probability calculus were interpreted, and every recommendation was a recommendation that any statistician would have endorsed. Everything is very straightforward.

But now discord will raise her head. For when Hogarth went to the King with his request for permission to take a sample before making his prediction, the King flew into a rage. "Very well," he snapped, "If that's the kind of game you want to play, I'll go along with you. Oh yes, I know you have been consulting those *types* at the statistical institute. I'll let you have your sample, but instead of taking an urn *at random* from the storehouse, I'll *choose* one according to the composition it has. And I'll *fool* you!"

Poor Hogarth went back to the statistical institute to learn some more statistics. This time, however, there was no agreement about what he should do. There was agreement about the basis on which he should act: Somehow his action should be based on a 4 × 5 table of the form we have already looked at.

Let us leave aside the question of the h_i's for the moment, and compute those probabilities and utilities that are computable however we interpret the probability function. This gives rise to the accompanying table for the Prince's problem: Each entry is again of the form $u_{ij}e_jh_j$.

And now what? Suppose that we interpret probability as some kind of relative frequency. When the King was taking the urns at random from the storehouse, it made reasonably good sense to talk about the relative frequency with

TABLE IV

	H_1	H_2	H_3	H_4
A_0	$-.330h_1$	$.156h_2$	$.228h_3$	$-.179h_4$
A_1	$-.006h_1$	$2.125h_2$	$.922h_3$	$-.167h_4$
A_2	$1.280h_1$	$3.44h_2$	$.004h_3$	$.004h_4$
A_3	$2.950h_1$	$2.125h_2$	$-.167h_3$	$.922h_4$
A_4	$2.120h_1$	$.156h_2$	$-.179h_3$	$.228h_4$

which he would come up with an urn of type one or of type two. But now he is going to the storehouse with the deliberate intent of choosing an urn that will confuse Hogarth. There's no telling how his mind will work.[4] The so-called probabilities h_j, if they are probabilities at all, are most certainly unknown. How are we to fill out the table? Where are we to get the numbers h_j, and what are they to signify?

It is at this point that the theory of testing hypotheses comes to our aid with a new policy. This is minimax policy, developed by statisticians with an inclination to frequency interpretations of probability, precisely for the job of dealing with such situations as this. (It has been also discussed by Braithwaite who calls it, for reasons that will be obvious in a moment, the prudential rule.) The object of this rule is to minimize the maximum risk we run in making a decision under uncertainty. It is a conservative rule:

RULE II: Construct a table like Table III, but forget about the h_j's. For each alternative, select the minimum of the entries under the hypotheses. Then as your course of action, select that alternative for which this minimum is a maximum.

In plain language, the rule directs us to assume the worst, for each alternative open to us, and then to choose that alternative for which the worst is comparably least bad.

The Prince can apply this rule to his situation. Table V gives his computations. The final column of the table lists the *minimum* expectation under each of the hypotheses for the given alternative; and the rule will direct him to follow alternative A_2, for which this expectation is a maximum.

TABLE V

	H_1	H_2	H_3	H_4	MIN	
A_0	$-.330$	$.156$	$.228$	$-.179$	$-.330$	
A_1	$-.006$	2.125	$.922$	$-.167$	$-.167$	
A_2	1.28	3.44	$.004$	$.004$	$.004$	←
A_3	2.95	2.125	$-.167$	$.922$	$-.167$	
A_4	2.12	$.156$	$-.179$	$.228$	$-.179$	

But if the Prince doesn't happen to have committed himself to a frequency interpretation of probability, there are alternatives open to him. Suppose that he has accepted a logical interpretation of probability. Then the probabilities h_j certainly do exist, and he can perfectly well use the classical rule which tells him to maximize his mathematical expectation. What should he take the h_j to be? Well, since it is very hard to see what kind of reason could be adduced for taking them to be unequal, and since logical probability is supposed to be reasonable, the natural thing to do seems to be to take them to be equal. The result of taking them to be equal is Table VI.

TABLE VI

	H_1	H_2	H_3	H_4	SUM
A_0	$-.330 \times \frac{1}{4}$	$.156 \times \frac{1}{4}$	$.228 \times \frac{1}{4}$	$-.179 \times \frac{1}{4}$	$-.031$
A_1	$-.006 \times \frac{1}{4}$	$2.125 \times \frac{1}{4}$	$.922 \times \frac{1}{4}$	$-.167 \times \frac{1}{4}$	$.718$
A_2	$1.28 \times \frac{1}{4}$	$3.44 \times \frac{1}{4}$	$.0037 \times \frac{1}{4}$	$.0037 \times \frac{1}{4}$	1.182
A_3	$2.95 \times \frac{1}{4}$	$2.125 \times \frac{1}{4}$	$-.167 \times \frac{1}{4}$	$.922 \times \frac{1}{4}$	1.457 ←
A_4	$2.12 \times \frac{1}{4}$	$.156 \times \frac{1}{4}$	$-.179 \times \frac{1}{4}$	$.228 \times \frac{1}{4}$	$.581$

The classical rule directs him to adopt alternative A_3, since the sums of the rows are proportional to their mathematical expectations.

Finally, the Prince may have been swayed by the new subjectivistic approach to statistics and probability. (Indeed, this is not so implausible; the problem may be looked at as a psychological contest between the irrational King and the Prince.) On this view, as on the logical view, the h_j's always exist and are always known. But on the subjectivistic interpretation, they reflect the Prince's feelings about the likelihood of various hypotheses, whether these feelings are grounded in any rational structure or not. For one reason or another or none at all, let us suppose that the Prince comes to the belief that the third hypothesis is the most likely; in fact he comes to have a degree of belief equal to 0.7 in H_3, and to 1/10 in each of the other three hypotheses. Given that these are his degrees of belief, the table that provides the solution to the Prince's problem is the following.

TABLE VII

	H_1	H_2	H_3	H_4	SUM
A_0	$-.033$	$.016$	$.159$	$-.018$	$.124$
A_1	$-.001$	$.212$	$.645$	$-.017$	$.839$ ←
A_2	$.128$	$.344$	$.003$	$.000$	$.475$
A_3	$.295$	$.212$	$-.117$	$.092$	$.482$
A_4	$.212$	$.016$	$-.125$	$.023$	$.126$

The sums of the rows are again proportional to the mathematical expectations of the alternatives. According to this table, the Prince should adopt alternative A_1.

Poor Prince Hogarth! All that study, and he has been told only that if he thinks that probabilities are relative frequencies, and he wishes to minimize his maximim loss (or maximize his minimum gain) he should follow alternative A_2, but that if he thinks that probability is a logical relationship, then he should follow alternative A_3, or then again, if he takes probabilities to be rationalized and orderly degrees of belief, he should follow alternative A_1. In short, he has been shortchanged.

Is it really the case that all these conceptions of probability are on equal footing? Is there no *true* interpretation of probability? I don't know, although I am inclined to think that there is.

I have encountered many statisticians who know that there are a variety of interpretations of probability, and who think this is a good thing: it seems somehow broad-minded and generous to allow that probabilities might be regarded as frequencies, but perhaps on the other hand they might be taken as logical relations, and then again . . .

But here is Hogarth, in a definite statistical situation, almost classical in its simplicity; and each of the alternative conceptions of probability leads to a different recommendation. The problem is the same; the evidence is the same; the values involved are the same; the hypotheses have only the given logical structure that they have; the opinions of Hogarth are only those opinions that he actually has; and yet according to the *purely abstract* interpretation of probability he adopts there will be three contrary courses of action recommended to him. This is a situation that cries out for explanation. It is a problem worthy of the best study of both statisticians and logicians. [5]

NOTES

1. For want of a nail . . . the battle was lost.
2. I have argued elsewhere, ([1], [2]), that the distinction I am drawing here *is* an artificial one, and that indeed its artificiality is an important clue as to the meaning of "probability". But it is a commonplace distinction in the field of statistical inference.
3. The only author I know who has given axioms for an uninterpreted calculus in this sense is Karl Popper [4].
4. He is clearly not altogether rational; if he were, and he played the game according to the prescriptions of game theorists, then his behavior would be predictable. In this particular case it would be completely determined; but in any event it would be determined in a statistical sense. But we suppose that the King is not rational.
5. For bibliographical materials pertaining to these problems, see [3].

BIBLIOGRAPHY

[1] KYBURG, H. E., *Probability and the Logic of Rational Belief*, Wesleyan University Press, Middletown, 1961.
[2] KYBURG, H. E., "Probability and Randomness," *Theoria*, 1962, 29 (1963), pp. 27-55.
[3] KYBURG, H. E., "Recent Work in Inductive Logic," *American Philosophical Quarterly*, 4, (1963), pp. 249-287.
[4] POPPER, Karl, "Two Autonomous Axiom Systems for Probability," *British Journal for the Philosophy of Science*, 6, 1955.

5

Bets and Beliefs

The subjectivistic or personalistic interpretation of probability is playing a larger and larger role both in statistics and in philosophy these days. In statistics it is associated with the recent resurgence[1] of Bayesian techniques which began with the work of Bruno de Finetti,[2] and which has been enthusiastically championed in English-speaking statistical circles by L. J. Savage.[3] In philosophy the importance of this interpretation of probability has been felt in certain problems concerning induction, rationality, and decision-making, into which it has injected new spirit. It also has important connections with the (now) traditional logical approach of Carnap[4] and his followers. Most of those who hold a logical view of probability—that is, those who think that there is at least one sense in which probability statements reflect logical relationships—now find in the personalistic arguments first stated by Ramsey,[5] and developed and refined by Savage, Lehman,[6] Kemeny,[7] and Shimony[8] in recent years, a justification for the principles or axioms that any conventional logical probability theorist takes his logical probability relations to satisfy.

I think this subjectivistic interpretation of probability is mistaken, but I also think it is an important interpretation, and I think it is very important indeed to be very clear about why it is mistaken. A good part of this paper will be concerned therefore with a sympathetic presentation of the subjectivistic point of view, and a rebuttal of some common objections to it. The remainder will be concerned with what I take to be its serious drawbacks, which are also, in view of the fact that the subjectivistic theory may be regarded as merely a weakened form of the confirmation theories, drawbacks to those theories.

Just as we consider ordinary logic to be a logic of full belief, so let us consider an extension of it, probability logic, to be a logic of partial belief. Even a frequentist can agree to this, if he is willing to regard partial beliefs as *estimates* of relative frequencies. (Indeed this very approach is adopted by Reichenbach in

Reprinted, with modifications and additions, from *American Philosophical Quarterly* 5, no. 1 (January 1968), pp. 54-63 by permission of the publisher. Based on research supported by the National Science Foundation.

63

his *Theory of Probability.*[9]) If we believe that *a* is a crow, then we must (by ordinary logic) believe that *a* is a crow or *a* is black, and we must refrain from having the belief that *a* is not a crow. Ordinary logic is a logic of consistency in a very strong sense; in the sense that if my beliefs violate the laws or ordinary logic, some of those beliefs are flatly wrong.

Now if I am about to toss a coin, I can consider the statement that it will land heads. Do I believe this? It seems reasonable to want to avoid answering this question with either "Yes" or "No," and instead to say, "I believe it to a *certain degree*," or "I *partially* believe it." We can lay down criteria for partial beliefs on intuitive grounds—and this is very much what Keynes[10] and Koopman[11] have done—without specifying how these beliefs are to be measured or detected. For both Keynes and Koopman these partial beliefs represent probability relations that can be detected introspectively, and can even be compared with one another in certain (but not in all) cases. But there is no objective, interpersonal, way of measuring them. There are those, like Ramsey, who say that they simply cannot detect probability relations, however hard they introspect. I rather feel that I can, in certain special cases, and I gather that such intuitions were what provided the original basis for Carnap's confirmation functions. Yet even if Keynes is right and Ramsey wrong about being able to uncover certain simple probability relations introspectively, Ramsey is surely right in feeling that such introspective measures will not be sufficient as a basis for making the probability calculus into an instrument for achieving interpersonal agreement and for making decisions under circumstances of uncertainty. We need some way of determining when the beliefs of an individual conform to the conditions that we intend to lay down, and when they don't.

The time-honored way of finding out how seriously someone believes what he says he believes is to invite him to put his money where his mouth is.[12] Ramsey's proposal for measuring partial beliefs is simply a refinement of this technique. Because there is a considerable amount of misunderstanding concerning just what is presupposed by Ramsey's proposal to define degrees of belief behavioristically, it is worth while going into some detail.

Let us first define an ethically neutral proposition as one such that its truth or falsity is a matter of indifference—i.e., all other things being equal (everything that affects us), we do not care whether this proposition is true or false. (For example, the statement "The number of hairs on my head is odd" is surely an ethically neutral proposition.) We define belief of degree 1/2 in an ethically neutral position P as follows: Suppose a person is not indifferent between two states of affairs, say α and β; i.e., that he prefers the state of affairs represented by α to the state of affairs represented by β, or he prefers the state of affairs represented by β to the state of affairs represented by α. Suppose that he has no preference between (1) α-if-proposition-P-and-β-if-proposition-not-P, and (2) β-if-proposition-P-and-α-if-proposition-not-P. Then he believes P to the degree 1/2.

Given, now, an ethically neutral proposition, believed to degree 1/2, we need only an arbitrary starting point: say the value of the total situation, a-if-P, β-if-not-P. Take the value of this gamble to be 1/2. Now we need merely find a state of affairs γ which is just as desirable as this gamble: its value, too, must be 1/2. Consider the gamble γ-if-P-and-β-if-not-P. (where β is preferred to a); it has the value of 3/4. And the gamble a-if-P and γ-if-not-P, will have the value 1/4. If there are other states of affairs preferable to β or more detestable than a, the scale may be extended to include them as well. What matters is simply that the existence of this single ethically neutral proposition P, which is believed to the degree 1/2, suffices to determine the whole scale of values for possible states of affairs. [13]

We can now use these values of total states of affairs to determine degrees of belief in *any* proposition: including those that are *not* ethically neutral: if the option of a-for-sure has the same value for a person as the option β-if-S-and-γ-if-not-S then his degree of belief in S is the ratio of the difference in value between a and γ, to the difference in value between β and γ: $\dfrac{\gamma - a}{\beta - \gamma}$ (we suppose $\beta > a$).

On this basis it is possible to *prove* that the usual axioms of probability theory hold for degrees of belief. Ramsey (p. 181) proves as "fundamental laws of probable belief":

(1) The degree of belief in P, plus the degree of belief in not-P equals 1.

(2) The degree of belief in P given Q, plus the degree of belief in not-P given Q equals 1.

(3) The degree of belief in P and Q equals the degree of belief in P multiplied by the degree of belief in Q given P.

(4) The degree of belief in P and Q plus the degree of belief in P and not-Q equals the degree of belief in P.

Ramsey writes:

These are the laws of probability, which we have proved to be necessarily true of any consistent set of degrees of belief. Any definite set of degrees of belief which broke them would be inconsistent in the sense that it violated the laws of preference between options, such as that preferability is a transitive asymmetrical relation, and that if alpha is preferable to beta, beta for certain cannot be preferable to alpha if P, beta if not-P. If anyone's mental condition violated these laws, his choice would depend on the precise form in which the options were offered him, which is absurd. He could have a book made against him by a cunning bettor, and would then stand to lose in any event. (p. 182.)

This has been christened the Dutch Book Theorem, by Isaac Levi. [14]

This is as far as the formal logic of subjective probability takes us. From the point of view of the "logic of consistency" (which for Ramsey includes the probability calculus), no set of beliefs is more rational than any other, so long as they both satisfy the quantitative relationships expressed by the fundamental laws of probability. Thus I am free to assign the number 1/3 to the probability that the sun will rise tomorrow; or, more cheerfully, to take the probability to be 9/10 that I have a rich uncle in Australia who will send me a telegram tomorrow informing me that he has made me his sole heir. Neither Ramsey, nor Savage, nor de Finetti, to name three leading figures in the personalistic movement, can find it in his heart to detect any logical shortcomings in anyone, or to find anyone logically culpable, whose degrees of belief in various propositions satisfy the laws of the probability calculus, however odd those degrees of belief may otherwise be. Reasonableness, in which Ramsey was also much interested, he considered quite another matter.[15] The connection between rationality (in the sense of conformity to the rules of the probability calculus) and reasonableness (in the ordinary inductive sense) is much closer for Savage and de Finetti than it was for Ramsey, but it is still not a strict connection; one can still be wildly unreasonable without sinning against either logic or probability.

Now this seems patently absurd. It is to suppose that even the most simple statistical inferences have no logical weight where my beliefs are concerned. It is perfectly compatible with these laws that I should have a degree of belief equal to 1/4 that this coin will land heads when next I toss it; and that I should then perform a long series of tosses (say, 1,000), of which 3/4 should result in heads; and then that on the 1001st toss, my belief in heads should be unchanged at 1/4. It *could* increase to correspond to the relative frequency in the observed sample, or it could even, by the agency of some curious maturity-of-odds belief of mine, decrease to 1/8. I think we would all, or almost all, agree that anyone who altered his beliefs in the last-mentioned way should be regarded as irrational. The same is true, though perhaps not so seriously, of anyone who stuck to his beliefs in the face of what we would ordinarily call contrary evidence. It is surely a matter of simple *rationality* (and not merely a matter of instinct or convention) that we modify our beliefs, in some sense, some of the time, to conform to the observed frequencies of the corresponding events.

This sort of objection, which may have been responsible for the lack of attention Ramsey's theory received for over a decade, was partially met by the first statistician to promote the subjectivist cause, Bruno de Finetti. De Finetti's theorems concern sequences of events that he calls "equivalent" or "exchangeable." A sequence of exchangeable events is a sequence in which the probability of any particular distribution of a given property in a finite set of events of the sequence depends only on the *number* of events in that distribution that have that property. An easy way of characterizing sequences of exchangeable events is merely to say that they are sequences in which the indices are held to be irrelevant. "Held to be," because whether or not a particular sequence is regarded as being composed of exchangeable events is a subjective matter—one which might be determined, for a given person, by proposing bets à la Ramsey or Savage.

An illustration will make clear what I mean: consider an irregular die. One of the ways it can land is with a one-spot uppermost. Let us call this type of event a success. Now consider any throw of the die. The absolute, unconditional, prior (*a priori*, if you will) probability that this particular throw will yield a success may be anything you want, according to the judgment you form from the particular shape and feel of the die; but if you regard the throws of the sequence to be exchangeable, as most of would, you must attribute the same prior probability to success on the first throw, on the 7th throw, on the 300th throw, and in general on the *i*-th throw. This does not mean that you are prohibited from learning from experience; indeed it is precisely to allow for and to explain learning from experience that de Finetti introduces the concept of exchangeability, to take the place of the traditional independence and equiprobability. The *conditional* probability of success on the *n*-th throw, given knowledge of the results of the preceding *n*-1 throws, will *not* in general be the same as the prior probability of a success on the *n*-th throw. This conditional probability will generally reflect the frequency of past occurrences.

The "problem of induction" is solved for the subjectivist, with respect to sequences of exchangeable events, by various laws of large numbers which de Finetti has proved for these sequences. One pointed consequence of these theorems is the following: If two people agree that events of a certain sequence are exchangeable, then, with whatever opinions they start, given a long enough segment of the sequence as evidence, they will come arbitrarily close to agreement concerning the probability of *future* successes, provided that neither of them is so pigheaded that his probability evaluations are totally insensitive to evidence provided by frequencies.[16] This is to say, after they have both observed a sequence of *n* of the events under consideration, they will attribute probabilities that differ by at most ϵ to success on the $(n + 1)$-st event. And indeed, however small ϵ may be made, there is an *n* which will make this statement true.

There are two perverse ways of avoiding this natural result. One is to deny that the events are exchangeable; the other is to deny the influence of past observations on present probability assignments. Neither of these gambits is ruled out by the axioms developed by Ramsey and his successors. The present holders of subjectivistic views seem to feel that this is simply a fact of logic. This is all that logic can do for us, and that's that. (But as Professor Nagel has pointed out in discussion, a judgment of exchangeability amounts to a good old-fashioned *a priori* judgment of equiprobability: we judge every combination of *n* successes and *m* failures to be equiprobable.) Logic cannot determine our views, even relative to a body of evidence; it can only stipulate that certain combinations of statements are inconsistent (deductive logic) or that certain combinations of beliefs are inconsistent (the Dutch Book Theorem).

The typical response of the logical probability theorist, such as Carnap, is to argue that there are more standards of logical adequacy than those expressed by the standard axioms of the probability calculus. These logical theorists welcome the subjectivist approach as providing a *proof* of the soundness of the basic postulates of probability theory, but they do not think that these postulates go far enough. Carnap, for example, wishes to incorporate in his system postulates reflecting not only the symmetries corresponding to exchangeability, but also symmetries concerning predicates. But these refinements and developments would certainly be irrelevant if I could show that even the few axioms accepted by the subjectivists were inappropriate as guides to rational belief. This is precisely what I intend to do in the remainder of this paper. I shall try to point up those respects in which even the basic axioms accepted by the subjectivists seem to be too strong; in doing so, I shall at the same time be attacking both subjectivistic and logical points of view, and also attacking those relative frequency views in which *estimates* of relative frequencies play the same role as logical probabilities, and also satisfy the same axioms.

There are three respects in which I take these axioms to be defective: (1) in taking it to be possible to evaluate a degree of belief to any desired degree of accuracy; (2) in supposing it sufficient to characterize a degree of belief by a single number, thus disregarding considerations such as the weight of the evidence; and (3) in leading to very strong beliefs about matters of fact on purely *a priori* grounds. The first two of these points are well known and have been discussed by subjectivists.[17]

In the formalized systems of subjective probability — Savage's, for example — it is a theorem that the degree of a person's belief in any statement can be evaluated to any degree of accuracy whatever. A simple consequence of this theorem which will illustrate the point at issue is that my degree of belief in the statement, "The President of the United States in 1984 will be a Republican," is fixed with just the same precision as my degrees of belief in the various possible outcomes on tosses of a coin that I am fully convinced is fair. Thus the probability of the political statement in question may be just the same as the probability that between 456 and 489 tosses out of 1027 tosses of this coin will result in heads; or it may be a bit less, say, between the probability of this coin-tossing statement and the statement: Between 455 and 488 tosses out of 1027 tosses of this coin will result in heads. Now the subjectivist would argue that this is not altogether unrealistic; after all, if I were presented with the choice of a gain (to be paid in 1984) if there is a Republican president in 1984, or the same gain if between 456 and 489 of 1027 tosses result in heads, I might prefer to stake the gain on the coin tossing statement; and if I were presented with the choice between staking the gain on the political statement, or on the slightly less probable coin tossing statement that there will be between 455 and 488 heads on 1027 tries, I might prefer to stake the gain on the political statement. The point is that if I am *forced* to choose what event I shall stake a gain on, I shall make such a choice.

But it seems unreasonable to demand that such choices be *consistent* in the sense in which the subjectivist uses the term. Thus I see no reason why I should not stake my possible gain on the political statement in the first case, and then turn right around and stake my possible gain on the coin statement in the second case, despite the fact that I know perfectly well that the former coin statement is more probable than the second. It seems reasonable, because my opinions as to the probability of the President being Republican in 1984 simply aren't that definite.

The subjectivist can argue that my opinions have changed between the first choice and the second; and there is nothing wrong with that. But I don't *feel* as if my opinions have changed; I have acquired no new *evidence* that bears on the likelihood that the President in 1984 will be a Republican. *One* way of looking at the matter would be that my degree of belief has changed; but an equally good way of looking at it, I should think, would be that my degree of belief was simply *not* altogether definite. It might be that the best we could say was that it was on the same order of magnitude as the probability of either of the two coin-tossing statements.

How about what the subjectivist calls consistency? If my belief that the President in 1984 will be a Republican is characterized merely by a vague interval, say as falling between .3 and .4, and if I can appropriately accept odds corresponding to any real number within these limits, then why shouldn't I accept a bet that there will be a Republican president in 1984 at odds of 7:3 and simultaneously a bet that there will be a non-Republican president at odds of 4:6? If the bets are in dollars, and I make both of them, I can have a book made against me, and I shall lose a dollar in either event. It is only if beliefs correspond simply to real numbers (rather than to intervals, say) that we can formulate a condition that will preclude my having a book made against me; so the subjectivist argues.

But this argument for precision of beliefs is irrelevant. The fact that it is irrational to make both bets simultaneously (which fact depends on *no* probabilistic considerations at all) doesn't imply in the least that it is unreasonable to make either bet alone. The mere fact that I can be forced into making a choice upon which of two eventualities I would prefer to stake a gain does not really imply that my belief is best represented by a single real number.[18]

There is another argument against both subjectivistic and logical theories that depends on the fact that probabilities are represented by real numbers. This has been discussed here and there in the literature as the problem of total evidence. The point can be brought out by considering an old fashioned urn containing black and white balls. Suppose that we are in an appropriate state of ignorance, so that, on the logical view, as well as on the subjectivistic view, the probability that the first ball drawn will be black, is a half. Let us also assume that the draws (with replacement) are regarded as exchangeable events, so that the same will be true of the i-th ball drawn. Now suppose that we draw a thousand balls from this urn, and that half of them are black. Relative to this information both the subjectivistic and the logical theories would lead to the assignment of a conditional probability of $1/2$ to the statement that a black ball will be drawn on the 1001st draw. Nearly the same analysis would apply to those frequency theories which would attempt to deal with this problem at all.[19] Although there would be no posit appropriate before any balls had been drawn, we may suppose that of the first two balls one is black and one is white; thus the "posited" limiting relative frequency after two balls have been drawn is 1/2, and this is the weight to be assigned to the statement that the next ball will be black. Similarly, after 1000 balls have been drawn, of which half have been black, the appropriate posit is that the limiting frequency is one half, and the weight to be assigned to the statement that the next ball will be black is 1/2.

Although it does seem perfectly plausible that our bets concerning black balls and white balls should be offered at the same odds before and after the extensive sample, it surely does not seem plausible to characterize our beliefs in precisely the same way in the two cases.

To put the matter another way: If we say that we are going to take probability as legislative for rational belief (or even as legislative for relations among degrees of beliefs in related statements), then to say that the probability of statement S is 1/2 and that the same is true of statement T is simply to say that our epistemological attitude toward the two statements should be the same. But for the two statements in question, this is clearly wrong. The person who offers odds of two to one on the first ball is not at all out of his mind in the same sense as the person who offers odds of two to one on the 1001st ball. What is a permissible belief in the first case is not the same as what is a permissible belief in the second case.

This is a strong argument, I think, for considering the measure of rational belief to be two dimensional; and some writers on probability have come to the verge of this conclusion. Keynes, for example, considers an undefined quantity he calls "weight" to reflect the distinction between probability relations reflecting much relevant evidence, and those which reflect little evidence. Carnap considers a similar quantity when he suggests that we regard probabilities as estimates of relative frequencies, for we can distinguish between more and less *reliable* estimates. But it is still odd to think that "$c(h, e) = p$" is *logically true*, considered as a degree of confirmation statement, and at the same time only *more or less reliable* considered as an estimation statement.

Such curious gambits are not even open to the subjectivist. Though Savage distinguishes between these probabilities of which he is sure and those of which he is not so sure, there is no way for him to make this distinction within the theory; there is no internal way for him to reflect the distinction between probabilities which are based on many instances and those which are based on only a few instances, or none at all. The fact that corresponds to increase in weight for the logical theorist and the frequentist is the increasing uniformity of probability judgments of different individuals with an increase in the evidential basis for them, and the decreasing impact of new evidence. But this yields no reason, for example, for not gambling with people who have better information than you have. Nor does this give any reason for preferring to bet for large stakes when our beliefs are based on a large amount of information, than when we have only a little information. Or consider a case in which our degree of belief is 1/2, and the odds we are offered are 10:9. If our degree of belief is based on a good deal of information it makes good sense to take advantage of this positive mathematical expectation; but if our belief is based only on a small amount of information, it would surely be regarded as foolish to risk much, even though our expectation is quite positive. But on either subjectivistic or logical theories, strictly considered, it would be rational to bet any amount (subject to the limitations imposed by the fact that money is not the same as utility), simply because the mathematical expectation is positive.

I come now to the third sort of objection. This is the objection that *a priori* subjective or logical probabilities implicitly seem to contain information or predictions about future frequencies. It is a difficult objection to state, in its general form, for subjectivists and logical theorists are quick to point out that a prior probability does not constitute any sort of a prediction about long-range frequencies. It is true that if my (or the) prior probability of E is 1/4, I shall act in many ways just as I would if I knew that the long-run frequency of E's was 1/4. But this is not to say that the statements are equivalent in meaning, because there are also crucial differences. The one statement is logical or psychological; the other is an empirical statement about a certain sequence of events. Furthermore, the statement about the long-run frequency would not be changed as we observed members of the sequence: If we take the long-run frequency of heads on tosses of a particular coin to be 1/2, the observation of a dozen tosses, eight of which resulted in heads, will not make us assign a different probability to heads on the 13th toss. But the conditional probability that interests us when we have observed a number of elements of the sequence is generally quite different from the prior probability. There is no ground on which we can say that a prior probability gives us any *knowledge* about future frequencies. Put another way: a subjectivistic or logical probability statement does not *entail* any (empirical) statement about relative frequencies.

On the other hand, we may have a lingering feeling that the division between logical probabilities and relative frequencies is not quite as clean and sharp as Carnap would have us think. A clue to this fact lies before our eyes in de Finetti's laws of large numbers: if we can draw conclusions about subjective probabilities on the basis of relative frequencies, can't we perhaps draw some conclusions about relative frequencies on the basis of subjective (or logical) probabilities?

Although there is no relation of entailment between statements about subjective probabilities and statements about frequencies, we may consider a weaker relation. Thus if it were to follow from a statement about subjective or logical probabilities that a certain statement about frequencies was overwhelmingly probable, I would regard this as constituting a relationship between the subjectivistic statement and the empirical statement about frequencies only slightly less strong than the entailment relation. (After all, this is just what subjective and logical probabilities are supposed to reflect: a relation between evidence and conclusion that is weaker than the entailment relation.) Furthermore, if, from an *a priori* logical or subjectivistic probability statement based on (esentially) no evidence whatsoever, it followed that a certain empirical statement was overwhelmingly probable, and worthy of a very high degree of ration belief, I would take this as evidence of *a priorism* of the worst sort, and evidence that there was something seriously wrong with the theory. Surely we no longer expect, or even desire, to be able to draw conclusions about the world from statements which are not about the world (in the same sense). From statements which are logically true, and do not even *refer* to our evidence, we do not expect to be able to draw (even probabilistic) inferences about the relative frequency with which black balls are drawn from urns; and the same is surely true of psychological statements.

What I shall next do is show that in fact there is a broad class of cases in which just this occurs within the subjectivistic theory, and *a fortiori* within the logical theory. To do this, I must state and prove a theorem. It isn't very long or very complicated; it is quite closely connected to theorems of de Finetti.

Theorem: Let $E_1, E_2, \ldots$ be a sequence of exchangeable events with respect to some characteristic C, represented by a random quantity X_i which takes the value 1 if E_i has the characteristic C and the value 0 if E_i lacks the characteristic C. Define

$$Y_b = \frac{1}{h} \sum_{i=1}^{b} X_i;$$ Y_b is thus just the relative frequency of the characteristic in

question among the first b events. Let m_1 be the prior probability of $C:P$ $(X_i = 1) = m_1$, and let m_2 be the conditional probability $P(X_i = 1 \mid X_j = 1)$ for $i \neq j$. Then we have:

$$P\left(|Y_b - m_1| > k \sqrt{\frac{m_1}{b} + \frac{b-1}{b} m_1 m_2 - m_2{}^2}\right) < \frac{1}{k^2}$$

Proof:

1. It is easy to show that the mean of Y_b is just the prior probability of the characteristic in question,

$$m_1 = P(X_i = 1).$$

2. We calculate the variance of Y_b:

$$E(Y_b - m_1)^2 = E(Y_b{}^2 - 2m_1 Y_b + m_1{}^2) = \frac{1}{b^2}\,(bE(X_i{}^2) +$$
$$b(b-1)E(X_i X_j)) - 2m_1{}^2 + m_1{}^2$$

3. Since the random quantity X_i either has the value 0 or the value 1, $X_i^2 = X_i$ and $E(X_i{}^2) = E(X_i) = m_i$.

4. Since the events are regarded as exchangeable, $P(X_i = 1 \cdot X_j = 1)$ always has the same value when $i \neq j$; let us write it in the form

$$P(X_i = 1) \cdot P(X_j = 1 \,|\, X_i = 1), \, = m_1 m_2$$

5. Thus we have, finally,

$$E(Y_b - m_1)^2 = \frac{m_1}{b} + \left(\frac{b-1}{b}\right) m_1 m_2 - m_1{}^2$$

6. Tchebycheff's inequality gives us:

$$P\left(|Y_b - m_1| > k \sqrt{\frac{m_1}{b} + \frac{b-1}{b} \, m_1 m_2 - m_2{}^2}\right) < \frac{1}{k^2}$$

Q. E. D.

We now have an expression which gives us an upper limit for the probability of there existing more than a certain difference between a prior probability, m_1 and a relative frequency, Y_b. The difference itself involves both the prior probability m_1, and the conditional probability m_2. To fix our ideas, let us suppose that the prior probability of C is 1/100, and that the conditional probability of C_i given C_j is double that. For example, we might consider an urn filled with balls, and we might very well attribute a probability of 1/100 to the statement that the first ball to be drawn is purple. Then, given that one ball is purple, we might attribute the probability 2/100 to the statement that another ball is purple.

Now if b is very large—and there is no reason for not letting b approach infinity—the expression for the variance of Y_b boils down to:

$$m_1 (m_2 - m_1)$$

Taking advantage of the fact that in this particular case $m_1 = m_2 - m_1$, we have the further simplification,

$$E(Y_b - m_1)^2 = m_1{}^2$$

Using Tchebycheff's inequality, but reversing the inequality signs, we have:

$$P(|Y_b - m_1| < km_2) > 1 - \frac{1}{k^2}$$

Taking $k = 10$, for example, what we have just proved, in plain words, amounts to:

If the prior probability of getting a purple ball from this urn is 1/100, and if the conditional probability of getting a purple ball, given that one other ball is purple, is 2/100, and if we regard the sequence of draws as exchangeable, then the prior probability is at least .99 that in an *arbitrarily long run,* or in the limit, not more than 11% of the balls will turn out to be purple. The probability is at least .9996 that no more than half will be purple.

Here is a clear case in which we have arrived at a practical certainty — surely a probability of .99 may amount to practical certainty at times — that a certain relative frequency will hold (not more than 11%), for an indefinitely long sequence of events. It is a clear case, it seems to me, of claiming to obtain knowledge about the world from *a priori* premises. It is true that the claim is not a categorical one; we do not arrive at the conclusion that the relative frequency of purple balls *will* be less than 11% but only at the conclusion that it is *overwhelmingly probable* that this relative frequency will be less than 11%. But this does not save the plausibility of the theory, for almost all of our empirical knowledge is of this sort, particularly from the logical and subjectivistic point of view. Our scientific knowledge is not *certain* but is *overwhelmingly probable*. It is no more plausible to claim to be able to deduce on *a priori* grounds (from psychological or logically true premises) that the probability is .99 that no more than 11% of the balls drawn from an urn will be purple, than it is to claim to be able to deduce on similar *a priori* grounds that the probability is .99 that the number of planets is seven.

It may be wondered whether there is any difference *in principle* between being able to be 99% sure on *a priori* grounds that less than 11% of the balls will be purple, and being able to be 1% sure on *a priori* grounds that the first ball to be drawn will be purple. To this there are two answers: First, that there is no difference in principle, but a very great intuitive difference between being practically sure about a very general hypothesis, and just having a certain small degree of belief about a particular event. The subjectivist will be quick to point out that all the theorem says — all any subjectivistic theorem says — is that *if* you have such and such beliefs about individual draws and pairs of draws, *then* you ought to have such and such other beliefs about long sequences of draws. But there seems to me all the difference in the world, intuitively, between being pretty sure that a given ball in an urn is not purple, and being equally sure that in the next thousand, or ten thousand, or million(!) draws from the urn, not more than 11% will result in a purple ball. Both the "given ball" and the "million draws" are, strictly speaking, particulars; but the latter is just the sort of particular knowledge which is properly termed general scientific knowledge. Indeed knowledge about — i.e., in subjectivistic terms, very strong beliefs about — the statistical character of the next million draws is precisely the sort of thing we should expect to get only by painstaking research, sampling, etc., and not at all the sort of thing we should expect to be able to deduce from tautologies concerning logical ranges or from the data of introspection. The subjectivist will tell me that my belief about the simple event, together with the axioms of the probability calculus, simply *entails* my having such and such a belief about the complex event; to which I reply, so much the worse for the axioms.

The subjectivist may say that he proposes rather to rearrange his initial beliefs than to reject any axioms. As even a subjectivist must admit, this is a perilous practice. It also greatly reduces the regulative force of personalistic probability, for the whole point of de Finetti's laws of great numbers is to show how the theory is not subjective in a *bad* sense, because ordinary people whose opinions are not very extreme will eventually be forced into agreement with each other and with the empirical relative frequency. But if we can withdraw our judgments of exchangeability whenever we begin to feel uncomfortable—even in such straightforward cases as drawing balls out of urns or rolling dice—then our pet opinions need have nothing to fear from the evidence even if the opinions are not extreme.

The answer that the original opinion of the person will change as he makes draws from the urn is irrelevant: he has not made any draws from the urn, and if all he wants is to be sure (let us say) that less than half of the draws will result in a purple ball, he doesn't even have any motivation to make draws from the urn; he can be extremely sure *a priori.* The answer that prior probability assignments and beliefs about long-run relative frequencies go hand in hand is also not quite to the point. In a sense, that is just what has been shown above. But in another sense, one may find beliefs about long-run frequencies to be relatively inaccessible to behavioristic assessment, while such simple beliefs as those we started with are very easy to discover. It is the fact that those simple, accessible, natural prior beliefs entail, through the axioms of the probability calculus, such strangely strong beliefs about long-run frequencies, that seems counter-intuitive.

The second answer is more interesting and also more controversial. It is that if we have a rule of acceptance in inductive logic, it is very difficult to see how the case in question could be distinguished in point of generality or high probability from the most conventional acceptable statistical hypotheses. The distinction between a statistical hypothesis, for the subjectivist, and a statistical hypothesis as understood by an objectivist, is that the subjectivist (at least, de Finetti) wants to reject the whole notion of an unbounded or indefinite or completely general statistical hypothesis. According to this view, we have only to deal with specific propositions. But some of these propositions are statistical in form (e.g., about 51% of next year's births will be births of males), and do refer to rather large groups of instances (e.g., in the case in question, to millions). Let us leave entirely aside the question of the general statistical hypothesis (the *indefinitely* long run of births will produce just 51% males); whether such completely general hypotheses are ever accepted or not, there are many who would agree that hypotheses like the one about next year's births can, given a sufficiently cogent body of evidence, come to be reasonably accepted. The ground on which such a statement might come to be accepted is generally taken to be its probability, relative to a body of evidence. And in precisely the same way, a statement (such as, of the next million balls drawn from the urn, no more than 11% will be purple) may be highly probable relative to the evidence for it (even though that evidence be no more than tautologies or the results of introspection). This material statistical statement, then, making a specific assertion about the number of purple balls that will be encountered in a rather long future, may perfectly well come to be accepted on the basis of no empirical evidence at all. (Surely introspection does not provide *empirical evidence* for the statement.) We would then have to say that the statement was accepted on *a priori* grounds, in the sense that it was accepted independently of any empirical evidence for it. If we adopt both subjectivistic probabilties and a rule of detachment, we are committed to *a priori* synthetic knowledge.

One way out is to eschew a rule of acceptance for inductive logic. There are many who think that no such rule (rules) can be found. (But it is an interesting fact, I think, that the largest concentration of such people is to be found in the ranks of subjectivists!) Much has been made of the fact that no consistent (and otherwise adequate) rule has been proposed. There are plenty of consistent acceptance rules, such as "Accept anything you want, provided it doesn't conflict with what you've already accepted," "Accept anything entailed by observation statements that you can vouch for," "Accept the strongest hypotheses that you can think of that are consistent with your present body of beliefs, and accept them only so long as they are not refuted by observation." Indeed, the only subjectivist I know who allows no form of acceptance rule is Richard Jeffrey.[20] The problem of an inductive acceptance rule is the problem of spelling one out in practical detail; a purely probabilistic rule faces very serious difficulties, and these difficulties may either be solved by employing a probability concept for which they do not arise, or circumvented by proposing other criteria than probability as conditions of acceptance.

But whether or not one believes that a rule of acceptance can be formulated that is satisfactory, the consequences of the theorem are not satisfactory. If one has a probabilistic rule of acceptance, then one can be led to *accept* very far-reaching empirical statements, despite the fact that one has not a shred of empirical evidence for them; if one supposes there is no acceptance rule of this sort, one is still led to have very high degrees of belief in these far-reaching empirical statements on the basis of no empirical evidence whatsoever. It is one thing to have a degree of belief based on no evidence about the color of a certain ball; it is something else again to have a high degree of belief based on no evidence concerning a relative frequency in an enormous empirically given population.

The argument I have presented does depend on certain peculiarities of the case: we require that the events considered be exchangeable, in de Finetti's sense. But most of the sequences of events that we deal with are reasonably regarded as sequences of exchangeable events; it is only in virtue of this fact that de Finetti's laws of large numbers are interesting. We also require that the *a priori* probability of the characteristic in question be small; but surely we shall have no trouble finding sequences of events and characteristics for which the prior probability of the characteristic is small. Finally I made use of the supposition that the conditional probability would be conveniently double the prior probability. We need merely suppose that it be *no more than* double the prior probability. And surely we can find sequences for which this is true, too. The assumptions that I have made are not very special, or very farfetched. Further-more, we shall of course get very similar results in circumstances which are merely *quite* similar to those that I have described.

As providing grounds for rejecting subjectivistic theories of probability, how-ever, we do not have to suppose that situations like the one that I have described crop up all the time; the mere fact that they *can* crop up seems to me to provide good enough reason for abandoning the theory which allows them.

Now observe that we must also reject logical theories like Carnap's, for Car-nap's systems are essentially built on the subjectivistic theory by the addition of further conditions. These conditions not only do not interfere with the above argument, but would make it even easier to carry through. Symmetry conditions would allow us to *prove* that certain sets of individual events are exchangeable, for example.

Furthermore, frequency theories that are embellished with a superstructure of posits, like those of Salmon and Reichenbach, must also go by the board. If the posits are to serve as basis for determining betting quotients, they must satisfy the same axioms as the subjectivistic probabilities; and therefore the above proof will go through for them too.

Where do we go from here? At this place I can only hint at an answer. A probability concept which took "degrees" of rational belief to be measured by intervals, rather than by points, would avoid all of these difficulties. Although on this sort of theory, a belief, as reflected behavioristically, is still either ration-al or irrational (the betting ratio either corresponds to a point inside the allow-able interval, or it doesn't), there is nothing in the theory itself which demands that degrees of belief in a behavioristic sense be sharply defined. Secondly, the interval conception provides a very natural way of reflecting the weight of the evidence. The prior probability that a ball drawn from an urn of unknown com-position will be black could be the whole interval from 0 to 1. In a rational corpus (of a given level) based on a certain amount of evidence consisting of a sequence of draws from the urn, the probability may be narrowed down to the interval between 1/3 and 2/3; relative to a rational corpus (of the same level) based on a large amount of evidence of the same sort, the probability may be the interval between .45 and .55. Finally, if we take probabilities to be intervals, the theorem proved above simply will not work. Perhaps if one wishes to apply probabilities in the conduct of everyday life and in the evaluation of beliefs, one may simply have to put up with the inconvenience of an interval conception of probability.

NOTES

1. H. Jeffreys, long an enthusiastic champion of Bayesian statistical techniques, wrote from a logical rather than a subjectivistic point of view.

2. Bruno de Finetti, "Foresight: Its Logical Laws, Its Subjective Sources" in H. E.

Kyburg and H. Smokler (eds.), *Readings in Subjective Probability* (New York, John Wiley, 1964). This essay first appeared (in French) in 1937.

3. Leonard J. Savage, *Foundations of Statistics* (New York, John Wiley, 1954).

4. Rudolf Carnap, *The Logical Foundations of Probability* (Chicago, University of Chicago Press, 1950).

5. Frank P. Ramsey, *The Foundations of Mathematics and Other Essays* (New York, Humanities Press, 1950). First published, 1931.

6. R. Sherman Lehman, "On Confirmation and Rational Betting," *The Journal of Symbolic Logic*, vol. 20 (1955), pp. 251-262.

7. John G. Kemeny, "Fair Bets and Inductive Probabilities," *The Journal of Symbolic Logic*, vol. 20 (1955), pp. 263-273.

8. Abner Shimony, "Coherence and the Axioms of Confirmation," *The Journal of Symbolic Logic*, vol. 20 (1955), pp. 644-660.

9. Hans Reichenbach, *The Theory of Probability* (Berkeley and Los Angeles, University of California Press, 1949). First German edition, 1934.

10. John Maynard Keynes, *A Treatise on Probability* (London, Macmillan, 1921).

11. Bernard O. Koopman, "The Bases of Probability," *Bulletin of the American Mathematical Society*, vol. 46 (1940), pp. 763-774.

12. Folklore.

13. Ramsey actually employs seven other axioms; these concern only requirements of consistency in assigning values to total states of affairs.

14. Isaac Levi. Paper read at the 1965 meeting of the American Philosophical Association, Eastern Division.

15. Indeed, he suggests that sometimes it may be *reasonable* to sin against the probability calculus, or even against the standards of deductive logic (p. 191).

16. Strictly speaking, there are other pathological distributions of belief that must also be ruled out.

17. See, e.g., Savage, *Foundations*, p. 57; the third I take to be novel.

18. Savage considers this problem (p. 59), and is clearly made uncomfortable by it, but does not regard it as fatal to the theory.

19. Wesley Salmon, "The Predictive Inference," *Philosophy of Science*, vol. 24 (1957), pp. 180-190.

20. Richard Jeffrey, *The Logic of Decision* (New York, McGraw-Hill, 1965).

6

Subjective Probability: Criticisms, Reflections, and Problems

1. INTRODUCTION

The theory of subjective probability is certainly one of the most pervasively influential theories of anything to have arisen in many decades. It was developed first by probability theorists and philosophers (Koopman [12] and Ramsey [21], primarily), then by a few somewhat unconventional statisticians (De Finetti [4] and Savage [22]). Growth in interest in the topic among statisticians was slow at first, but turned out to be (it seems) exponential in character. From statistics it spread to economics, political science, and the social sciences in general. From philosophy it spread to psychology and decision theory, and thence again to economics and political science. Although one could not say that it was dominant in any of these fields, it occupies a respectable place, either as subject matter or as methodological doctrine, in each of them.

One reason for this spread is both cultural and practical. The theory of subjective probability is undogmatic and antiauthoritarian: one man's opinion is as good as another's. It imposes only relatively weak constraints on the beliefs that a man has; if two people disagree, their disagreement can be treated merely as a datum, rather than as a cause of conflict. The theory embodies a modern spirit of tolerance and democracy. At the same time, in many areas people's degrees of belief are in relatively close agreement. The theory can also simply accept this agreement as a datum, and go on from there.[1] There is no need to justify that agreement, or even to look into its source. We need not get hung up on deep and abstract (and possibly artificial) issues in order to proceed to use this theory of probability in testing hypotheses, in making statistical inferences, in formulating theories of rational decision, in describing choice behavior under uncertainty, and so on.

The reason for the philosophical popularity of the doctrine is that it appears to be minimally committal—that is, it is easy to say that whatever the true doctrine of probability may be, *at least* it requires that the ordinary axioms of

Reprinted, with modifications, from *Journal of Philosophical Logic*, no. 7 (1978), pp. 157-180, by permission of the publisher.

the probability calculus hold of it; and since it is just these axioms that are required by the subjective theory, anything we can establish using the subjective theory will, *a fortiori*, be established for a more demanding theory. The theory provides a good working basis for philosophical investigation because it is maximally tolerant and minimally restrictive.

In the pages that follow, I shall argue that although the theory appears to be all things to all people, in fact it is a snare and a delusion and is either vacuous and without systematic usefulness, or is simply false. Before charging off into the brush, however, let us get straight about the animal we are after. By 'the' theory of subjective probability, I mean any of quite a large group of interpretations of the probability calculus which lead to the assignment of a numerical probability to each sentence or proposition of a language (or event of a field of events), and in which these assignments do not reflect any known or hypothetical frequencies.

The language in question may be restricted to the part of a natural language in which sentences relevant to a given problem or decision may be formulated, or it may be a larger or smaller fragment of an explicitly formalized language. Sometimes (particularly in statistical applications) the propositions or sentences are parametrized, and we consider, not the assignment of probabilities to specific propositions, but rather the assignment of probability densities to the parameters.

What do the numbers represent? This depends on the way in which the theory is construed. It may be construed as a descriptive theory or as a normative theory; and it may be construed as a theory of decision under uncertainty, or as a theory concerned with degrees of belief. The interpretations offered by various authors may not always fall cleanly into one of the resulting four classifications, but if the theory does not work under any of the four pure interpretations, it is unlikely that it can be saved by ambiguity.

If the theory is construed as a descriptive theory of decision making under uncertainty, the numbers represent theoretical psychological characteristics (conveniently, if loosely, referred to as degrees of belief) which enter into a general descriptive theory of actual behavior under uncertainty. If the theory is construed as a descriptive theory of degrees of belief, the numbers represent actual degrees of belief, which we may attempt to measure by examining behavior under uncertainty. If the theory is construed as a normative theory of decision, the numbers represent parameters which *ought* to satisfy certain constraints. If the theory is construed as a normative theory of degrees of belief, then the numbers represent the measures assigned to sentences of a language, and *ought* to satisfy at least the constraints of the probability calculus. I include among the latter theories such 'logical' theories as that sought by the early Carnap [1], according to which on logical grounds alone we should be able to assign a probability measure to every sentence of the language, those discussed by the later Carnap [2], [3], in which the probability measures of the sentences of the language are determined by a few parameters that represent personal or subjective commitment, and those proposed by Hintikka, [10], Tuomela [18], Niiniluoto [17] and others in which the probability measures of the sentences are determined by a few parameters which reflect *empirical* 'judgments' about the actual nature of the world.

All of these interpretations impute the same structure to probabilities (relevant exceptions will be noted in due course):

$p(b)$ is a real number lying between 0 and 1.

$p(e \wedge b) = p(e) \cdot p(b/e)$, where $p(b/e)$ is the conditional probability of b, given e.

If b and g are logically exclusive, $p(b \vee g) = p(b) + p(g)$.

2. THE DUTCH BOOK ARGUMENT

In subjectivistic interpretations or probability, there is a fundamental nexus in which logic and behavior meet. It is the betting situation, first described with the intent of clarifying the relation between probability and belief by F. P. Ramsey [20]. Basically, the connection is this:

Step I: The more convinced I am that something is going to happen, the higher the odds I am willing to offer in a bet that it will occur. Ramsey's idea was to take the *least odds* at which an individual would accept a gamble on the occurrence of E to indicate his degree of belief in E. We assume that these least odds are well defined: that is, we assume that if the agent is willing to accept a gamble at $P{:}S$, then he will accept a gamble at $P'{:}S$ for any P' less than P. This can be made more precise and more plausible as follows.[2] Consider a gamble for a fixed-stake S where a price P is charged. The least odds at which the agent is willing to accept such a gamble is the least upper bound of the ratios $P/(S-P)$ representing the gambles the agent is willing to accept. We also assume that these least odds are independent of the size of the stake. We do not assume, yet, that the least odds will remain unchanged for a negative stake—i.e., for bets on the nonoccurrence of E. We do assume, however, that the individual has least odds for a whole algebra of events (or propositions), i.e., that if his least odds are well-defined for E and F, they are well defined for $\sim E$ and for $E \wedge F$.

Step II: We regard it as irrational for a person to have a book made against him—i.e., to accept a sequence of bets such that, no matter how events turn out, he loses.

Step III: We conclude that it is irrational for a person's beliefs to be represented by least odds such that the person can be the victim of a Dutch Book concocted by an unscrupulous bettor. (I don't know who first used the word 'unscrupulous' in this context, but it does create a persuasive image of the virtuous Rational Man protecting himself against the Forces of Evil.)[3] From this, in turn, it follows that those odds must be related in just the way that probabilities are related in the standard probability calculus. Whatever else is true about rational beliefs, then, (we might, for example, demand with Carnap that they reflect certain linguistic symmetries) they must at least satisfy the core axioms of the probability calculus. We have thus found, in the Dutch Book argument, a justification for the demand that rational degrees of belief satisfy these axioms. (If we are construing the subjectivistic interpretation of probability empirically, we have found in the Dutch Book argument *prima facie* warrant for taking the probability calculus as a plausible empirical hypothesis.)

Or have we? It is noteworthy that Carnap, in *The Logical Foundations of Probability* [1], does *not* employ these arguments to justify the axioms he lays down for degree of confirmation. He was perfectly aware of Ramsey's work, and devotes several pages to defending Ramsey against the charge of 'subjectivism', there construed as the denial that there is a difference between merely coherent degrees of belief and *rational* degrees of belief. Ramsey himself writes, "It is not enough to measure probability; in order to apportion correctly our belief to the probability, we must also be able to measure our belief." (Quoted by Carnap [1], p. 16.) Of course we know that Carnap was later persuaded that the Dutch Book argument was sound, and on a subjectivistic view it may very well turn out to make no sense to attempt to measure probability and belief independently. Nevertheless, let us begin by taking a close look at the argument.

We first note that Step II has nothing to do with degrees of belief or with probabilities. No rational person, whatever his degrees of belief, would accept a sequence of bets under which he would be bound to lose no matter what happens. No rational person will in fact have a book made against him. If we consider a sequence of bets, then quite independently of the odds at which the person is willing to bet, he will decline any bet that converts the sequence into a Dutch Book. His least odds on E, for example, may be $2:1$, while his least odds on E and F may be $4:1$; this violates the calculus, but is no Dutch Book. His least odds on E may be $2:1$, and his least odds on $\sim E$ may be $2:1$, there is not even a Dutch Book here, unless he accepts each bet—and, of course, being rational, he will accept no more than one bet, for otherwise, at the same amount on each bet, he would be bound to lose.

According to the subjectivistic theory, it is irrational to offer $2:1$ odds that a certain toss of a coin will land heads and to offer $1:1$ odds that it will land tails. But it is *not* unreasonable, on this view, to offer $2:1$ odds to A that the toss will land tails, and then to offer $2:1$ odds to B that the following toss will land heads. Nor is it irrational to make the following bet: I agree to draw a card from an ordinary deck, and if it is red offer you $2:1$ odds on heads, and if it is black, offer you $2:1$ odds on tails. In fact, however, so far as the Dutch Book argument goes, it would be perfectly rational for me to offer you $2:1$ odds on heads *and* $2:1$ odds on tails, provided I make it clear that I am offering only one bet. Note that this has nothing to do with my placing a value on gambling: If I *accepted* both bets, it would imply that I valued the gamble in itself; but my refusal to accept more than one bet precludes warrant for the assertion that I am assigning a high value to the utility of gambling.

The rational man will not actually have a book made against him; but this is a matter of deductive logic, and not of probability; a matter of certainties and not a matter of degrees of belief. Step II then is a heuristic device, or, to put it less charitably, a red herring.

The conclusion that a rational man's degrees of belief, as reflected in his least odds, must satisfy the axioms of the probability calculus does not follow from the assumptions thus far made.

What we require in order to capture the intent of the Dutch Book argument is an intermediate step:

Step I-A: We assume that the individual is willing to take any combination of bets, for any stakes, at the least odds that characterize his degrees of belief.

In effect, this step amounts to the demand that the individual post odds on a field of events or statements, and then *make book* according to the odds he has posted. Note how different this is from Step II: Step II points out that a rational man will not *actually* have a book made against him. But we already know that, and that has nothing to do with the 'least odds' at which he would bet on an event, or even on each event in a field of events. This consideration imposes no constraints on the numbers we assign to statements or events. Step I-A, on the other hand, imposes a constraint on the posted odds concerning a whole field of events, when the individual is required to accept all bets offered to him at those posted odds. The constraint here concerns *potential* sets of bets, not actual ones. The rational man, in posting his odds, protects himself against all possibilities; he must make book with all comers, as an equal opportunity bookie, according to the odds he has posted. Thus we must replace the assumption of Step II by the following assumption:

Step II-A: The rational man will not put himself in a position in which he can *potentially* have a book made against him.

Note, however, that the conclusion that these posted least odds can be converted into a set of numbers satisfying the axioms of the probability calculus still does not follow. The least odds the agent offers on E may be 2:5, and the least odds he offers on $\sim E$ may also be 2:5. In fact, if he is a professional gambler, the sum of the odds he offers on any two complementary bets will of course add up to less than 1; this is how he makes his money. And there is hardly anything irrational about this!

We may, however, arrive at the following conclusion: with every event or proposition we may associate two numbers, one representing the least odds at which the agent will bet *on* the event, the other representing the least odds at which the agent will bet *against* the event. We can now show that there exists a function P, satisfying the axioms of the probability calculus, such that for every event in our field of events the value of that function will belong to the closed interval determined by the corresponding numbers.

A number (a relatively small number) of writers follow the Dutch Book argument only this far; C. A. B. Smith [24], I. J. Good [8], P. Suppes [25], I. Levi [16], A. Dempster [5] are among them. It is possible then to take the set of functions P satisfying the posted odds to characterize an individual's degrees of belief. Note that in so doing we are abandoning the notion that there is a single real-valued degree of belief associated with each proposition in our algebra, determined by the least odds at which an individual will bet *on* that proposition.

What we require in order to obtain the conclusion of the Dutch Book argument is a stronger assumption by far than any we have made so far. It may be stated thus:

Step I-B: We assume that the individual is willing to take any combination of bets, for any stakes, *positive or negative*, at the least odds that characterize his degrees of belief.

To stipulate that the odds may be postive or negative has the effect of requiring that the agent be willing to take either side of a bet at his posted odds. Now, at last, the conclusion of Step III will follow from the assumptions of Steps I, I-B, and II-A. The posted odds can now be translated into numbers, associated with each member of the field in question, which satisfy the probability calculus. There are other ways to obtain such numbers which eliminate the need to be sloppy about the marginal utility of money and the desirability of gambling: for example we may force (or bribe) an individual to express a preference between acts that depend on the states of nature (the field of events). The best known approach along these lines is that of Savage [22] .

What is noteworthy is that we obtain a set of numbers satisfying the probability calculus only by *compelling* the individual to do something: to post odds on E and odds on $\sim E$ and then to accept bets, with positive or negative stakes, at these odds; or to express a preference between receiving a prize if it rains on March 3, 1986, and receiving a prize if between 1,456 and 1,603 heads appear on 3,341 tosses of a specific coin. It is only through this sort of compulsion that we can obtain a full set of numbers satisfying the probability calculus.

But now we see that the argument from Step I, Step I-B, and Step II-A, to Step III, while valid, is no longer sound: we have no reason to suppose that an individual would be willing to post odds under these conditions, or to take the time and effort to express a serious set of preferences. We must replace I-B by:

Step I-C: The individual can be *made* to post odds on which he will take any combination of bets, for any stakes, positive or negative.

It will follow that these odds will conform to the probability calculus. But now the connection between these odds and degrees of belief has become attenuated to the point of obscurity. However irrational and strange my degrees of belief, I will, under compulsion, post odds that are coherent (or publish a coherent preference ranking).

As I look out the window, it occurs to me that the least odds I would be comfortable about offering on rain today are about 3:7, and the least odds I would be comfortable about offering against rain are about 3:7. If I am forced, in accordance with Step I-C, to post odds and make book, I will pick a number between 0.3 and 0.7 to determine those odds. But I will be no more comfortable with 0.5 than with 0.4 or 0.6. The number I pick will depend on my mood and my circumstances. But it does not seem to me that my 'degree of belief' in rain is varying correspondingly according to my mood and circumstances.

There may indeed be a rough intuitive connection between my degree of belief in an event E and the least odds I am willing to offer in a bet on E. But this connection is much too loose to generate by itself a set of numbers conforming to the probability calculus. The Dutch Book argument gives excellent reasons for adopting a table of odds or publishing a list of preferences which conform to the basic core of the probability calculus, but it does so at the cost of severing the immediate and intuitive connection between odds and degrees of belief that the argument originally depended on. In fact, at this point, we may find ourselves wondering if there *is* any such thing as 'degree of belief'.

There are a number of directions we can go from here, and various theories of subjective probability have explored these various directions. We can regard 'degree of belief' as a kind of intervening variable in an empirical decision theory: that is, a psychological theory that accounts for the decisions that people actually make. The theory would assert that people act as if they had degrees of belief conforming to the probability calculus, and so acted as to maximize their expected utilities. Or we can regard 'degree of belief' as a kind of intervening variable in a normative decision theory: people *ought* to act as if they had degrees of belief conforming to the probability calculus, and were maximizing their expected utility. Or we can suppose that decisions and preferences just constitute a way of *getting at* degrees of belief (or that there is some other way of getting at degrees of belief), and construe the probability calculus as a theory of people's actual beliefs. Or, finally, we can suppose that decisions and preferences are just ways of getting at degrees of belief (or that there is some other way of getting at degrees of belief) and construe the theory of subjective probability as a normative theory of degrees of belief. In the sections that follow, we shall explore each of these four alternatives in turn.

3. EMPIRICAL DECISION THEORY

A number of investigators have taken subjectivistic probability as an ingredient in an empirical theory of how people actually make decisions. People's decisions, of course, are highly complex, and involve a number of factors that are extremely hard to evaluate. The theory is tested, therefore, under relatively simple and artificial circumstances. For example, subjects are presented with a board containing a large number of red and white thumbtacks. Although the subject is not given enough time to count the thumbtacks, it is found that usually his judgment of the proportion of red thumbtacks is quite accurate. The subject is offered a pair of bets on red against white. He chooses a bet. A row and column of the thumbtacks display are selected by a device which insures that each thumbtack will be selected equally often (and the subject knows this). The bet is then settled. The bet is sometimes a matter of real money; sometimes a matter of hypothetical real money bets; sometimes a matter of chips or counters [6].

There are a number of things to be noted about such experiments. First, subjective factors that might be regarded as extraneous to the probability-utility framework are excluded as rigorously as possible. Second, the amounts involved in the bets are arranged so that they are quite strictly linear in utility. Third, although the probabilities involved are 'subjective', they very closely reflect the frequencies of the various outcomes. Thus these experiments constitute a simple and direct test of the SEU (subjective expected utility) theory of decision under circumstances highly favorable to the theory. As Edwards remarks, if the theory is going to work for subjective probabilities in general, it should certainly work for subjective probabilities which simply reflect objective frequencies [6].

It turns out that while the theory predicts reasonably well for probabilities in the middle range, it goes awry for large or small probabilities, despite the fact that the utilities involved are well within the linear range. Furthermore, it goes awry in different ways for positive expected utilities and for negative expected utilities.

Even in these highly artificial and simple situations, people do not act in ways that are consonant with the assumption that their degrees of belief, as reflected in their choices between bets, satisfy the axioms of the probability calculus.

From a psychological point of view, one is interested in developing a theory of choice behavior under uncertainty which will enable one to predict and understand people's choices, not in devising a theory of belief that embodies certain *a priori* constraints. Psychologists therefore seem to have largely moved away from the SEU model. Much of the recent literature relevant to this development is cited in [23], especially pp. 9-11.

That psychologists are abandoning the SEU model does not mean in itself that subjective probability is being abandoned. One possibility is that "subjective probability' — i.e., degree of belief — may no longer be required to satisfy the axioms of the probability calculus. Edwards [6] suggests the possibility that the additive property be abandoned. The abandonment of any such property entails the rejection of the Dutch Book arguments as yielding a description of choice behavior even under ideal circumstances. It strongly suggests that it is inappropriate to call the 'subjective probabilities' that enter into such a revised empirical theory 'probabilities' at all.

Another possibility that is being actively pursued is that an accurate descriptive decision theory will involve not only expected gain, but other moments of the gain as well. Thus people might be concerned not only with their *expectation* in a gamble, but with the *variance* of the outcome, preferring, say, gambles with modest expectation and small variance to gambles with larger expectations but much larger variance. Here again, however, we find problems for the conventional subjectivistic interpretation of probability. The conventional interpretation supposes (as in the Dutch Book argument) that we can get at subjective probabilities in a straightforward way through compulsorily posted betting odds, or through the analysis of forced choices among alternatives. But this approach takes the SEU model for granted, and applies it inside out, so to speak, to determine subjective degrees of belief. If we suppose that preferences are not determined by subjective expected utility, but in some other more complicated way, it may be difficult to measure 'degrees of belief'.

In any event, the neat relations among 'degree of belief', and 'utility', and 'expected utility' that underly the Dutch Book argument are not reflected in people's actual choice behavior.

4. NORMATIVE DECISION THEORY

One response to this situation (I think it would have been Savage's, and it would certainly be that of a large number of philosophers and economists) is to say that the subjective expected utility model of decision was never intended to be an empirical description of how people actually make decisions, even under 'ideal' circumstances, but rather a normative prescription of how people ought, rationally, to make decisions. Of course we suppose that people by and large are relatively rational—and the evidence of the psychological experiments for the mid-range of probabilities provides gratifying confirmation of the general rationality of people. But the fact that when the probabilities become (according to the theory) large or small people cease somewhat to be rational should not be construed as *undermining* the normative theory.

Let us, then, confront this normative theory in its own terms, ignoring the fact that people are not always rational in their actual behavior. Indeed, were people always rational in their decisions, we would hardly be motivated (except perhaps as metaphysicians) to develop an elaborate theory of rationality. In point of fact, the main use of normative decision theory is in providing guidance under circumstances of uncertainty. Savage himself remarks that " . . . the main use I would make [of the axioms] is normative . . . " ([22], p. 20).

There are a number of ways of formalizing normative decision theory in a subjectivistic framework. The following, adapted from Savage [22], will suffice for our purposes. We need to get at both utilities and probabilities; the mechanism for doing so is to look at preference rankings. Preference rankings of what? Of *acts* construed as functions from states of affairs to consequences. We can choose our acts—that is what decision theory is all about—but we cannot choose the state of the world, nor can we choose the consequences of our acts. Normative decision theory is designed to guide our choices among acts.

The subjective approach supposes that on the basis of an individual's ranking of acts (functions, remember) we may infer both his probabilities and his utilities. It must be supposed that probabilities and utilities cannot be evaluated independently of the ranking of acts—else the agent might be in the position of ranking most highly an act whose mathematical expectation is not the highest, and this blatantly violates the basic thrust of the subjectivistic approach. On the other hand, if we begin with a complete preference ranking among acts, what is the point of the analysis into utilities and probabilities? The process seems obviously circular: we start with a preference ranking among acts, and by dint of careful analysis arrive at probabilities and utilities, and by computing mathematical expectations arrive at a ranking which (unless something has gone wrong) precisely matches the original one!

The point, however, is that the individual's initial preferences may be partly unknown and partly incoherent. For example, he may prefer act A to act B; act B to act C; and act C to act A. This is clearly irrational: preference should be transitive, and nothing should be preferred to itself. His preference ranking may be incoherent in a more sophisticated way: for example, he may prefer A if state X obtains and B if state not-X obtains to A if X, and he may prefer A if X to B if not-X. This set of preferences is incoherent because there is no assignment of probabilities and desirabilities that will lead to mathematical expectations that conform to this ranking. (Suppose that the probability of X is p; then the value of the first ranked alternative is p times the value of the second ranked alternative plus $(1-p)$ times the value of the third ranked alternative; the value of the mixed alternative must be between the values of the pure alternatives, since $0 < p < 1$; this contradicts our original stipulation.)

If such an incoherence is pointed out to a rational individual, he will presumably alter his preference ranking. Savage says that to be in this state is to be 'uncomfortable' in the same sense as to find oneself committed to a logical inconstency. But to be 'in this state' is to presuppose that one's preferences form a simple order, and as Savage himself recognizes, actual preferences form at best a partial ordering ([22], p. 21). It is precisely in the attempt to make one's preferences conform to the theory—that is, in the attempt to produce a simple order of preferences from one's actual partial order—that one stumbles on violations of the theory. It is these inadvertent violations of the theory that ought somehow to be rectified. The normative force of the theory, then, is that it says that the preference ranking of an individual *should* be such that there exists a probability function and a utility function for which the mathematical expectations computed in accordance with those functions agree with the preference ranking.

Axiomatizations of subjective theories generally require an assumption even stronger than that of simple order among preferences. Savage ([22], p. 6, p. 39) requires that there are states of the world with arbitrarily small probabilities. He is able to show that a preference ranking satisfying his postulates can be decomposed into a unique probability function and a unique desirability function. The desirability of an act can then be represented as its mathematical expectation.

Jeffrey [11] imposes a condition that is somewhat weaker on preference rankings: the 'splitting condition' requires that any (non-neutral) element of the preference ranking can be expressed as the disjunction of two equiprobable incompatible elements that are ranked together ([11], p. 104). Jeffrey's system does not entail that there are *unique* probability and desirability functions that expresses the preference ranking; it merely entails that there is a family of pairs of probability and desirability functions which will *fit* the preference ranking, in the sense that mathematical expectations computed in accord with any of them will yield rankings among elements that conform to the original rankings.

Now how do we use this normative decision theory? We begin with a partial preference ranking. The axioms of the theory help us to make our preference ranking more complete. That this sort of exercise can be very useful is clear; subjectivist decision theory has become entrenched in business schools precisely because of this usefulness. It is most useful when there are relatively standard measures of desirabilities (dollars) or of probabilities (frequencies) or both. There are often a fairly large number of fixed points in a preference ranking that can be established by such considerations; these can give some indication of how 'inconsistencies' are to be resolved. But the axioms cannot do the whole job; if we start with a partial ranking, there may well be acts whose relative positions in the preference ranking are not determined by the initial partial ranking and the axioms of the theory. We must then consult our intuitions to decide how those alternatives are to be ranked.

It may be the case that our initial partial preference ranking is incoherent — even though it is only partial, it may conflict with the axioms of the normative theory. As Savage points out on numerous occasions, the theory cannot tell us how to resolve that conflict. Again we must consult our intuitions. The theory tells us that some change must be made in our preference ranking, but it does not tell us what change. It will generally be the case that our preference ranking is incomplete in the sense that, given our initial preferences, there will be alternatives whose location is not determined by those preferences together with the axioms of the theory. Again, we must call on intuition to complete the preference ranking, to the extent that it needs to be completed. (In order to use the theory we need not always have a preference ranking complete in all detail.)

Once we have a preference ranking that satisfies the axioms of the theory, we can crank out at least one probability and desirability function, and perhaps a family of them. We can now use these probability and desirability functions to compute mathematical expectations. And we are then directed to perform that act with the greatest mathematical expectation. But of course that act is the act at the head of this coherent preference ranking. So if we've got a coherent preference ranking, we don't have to make any computations. On the other hand, if we don't have a coherent preference ranking, the theory won't tell us *how* to make it coherent. If we have a coherent but partial preference ranking, the theory may allow us to make it more complete. The theory thus functions as a heuristic device enabling us to specify our preference ranking in an organized way, and revealing incoherencies that require resolution.

We must now ask, however, how important the role of subjective probability is in enabling normative decision theory to perform its function. Our suspicions may be aroused by two facts: First, Jeffrey's form of the theory allows the derivation from the preference ranking of not one, but of a whole family of probability functions. If these functions are construed as yielding subjective probabilities—i.e., degrees of belief—this means that the preference ranking does not either yield or require a *unique* degree-of-belief function. Second, the most clear-cut and persuasive applications of the theory are those in which the subjective probability function simply mirrors well-established statistical frequencies. In these applications, then, we can construe the function whose combination with a utility function is to yield the coherent preference ranking as a perfectly straightforward frequency function, having no psychological import whatever. (It *may* be the case that there are such things as degrees of belief, and it *may* be that in certain situations these degrees of belief have the same magnitudes as certain relative frequencies, but in the applications we are discussing both of these assumptions are gratuitous and irrelevant.)

Many of the most interesting of the applications of the normative decision theory, however, are applications which do *not* involve well-tested roulette wheels or other apparatus yielding alternatives with well-known frequencies. The question now is whether or not the probability numbers that emerge from the analysis of the preference ranking can nevertheless be construed as known (or reasonably believed) frequencies. Certainly in many of the instances in which the normative decision theory is applied—in business decisions, for example—it is not hard to imagine that the probability numbers can plausibly be construed as estimates of the relative frequency with which a given sort of thing happens in given circumstances. Again, to the extent that this is plausible, there is no need to construe these numbers as reflecting subjective degrees of belief.

It may be questioned whether or not this is always the case. There are certainly applications of Normative Bayesian Decision Theory in which the probability numbers emerge from a dialogue between the decision theorist and the executive decision maker, rather than from any recorded tables of statistical data. But this does not settle the question of what the numbers that thus emerge represent. On the subjectivistic interpretation of probability, they represent degrees of belief; but we may also suppose that these numbers represent the executive's (possibly "subjective") estimates of *objective* frequencies. We might be hard put, on occasion, to formalize these intuitive judgments: it can be far from obvious what frequency in what reference class is being intuitively estimated when the decision maker says that he would just bet even money that the sales of product X in 1979 will exceed 145,500 units. Nevertheless, it is not implausible to suppose that there is some estimate of an objective frequency underlying such judgments.

It is worth remarking that the specification of a reference class is not a trivial problem even in the case of probabilities that are quite clearly related to frequencies: probabilities that arise in weather forecasting, in insurance, and the like. (See [14], [15].) For formal languages there is a mechanism that will yield a correct reference class, given a body of knowledge—see [14]. The extent to which this mechanism can be valuable heuristically in relatively informal contexts remains to be seen.

To sum up: If we suppose we begin with a full preference ranking among acts, there are two possibilities. Either the preference ranking is coherent, or it is not. If it is coherent, we are all set—we merely follow the dictates of our preference ranking with no further analysis. If it is not, then something must be changed; but as Savage never tired of pointing out, the subjectivistic theory will not tell you what to change. Subjectivistically interpreted, Normative Bayesian Decision Theory, whatever its heuristic virutes, is either philosophically vacuous or impotent: vacuous if our preferences are already coherent, impotent if our preferences are not coherent and we want to know how to change them. What has made the theory attractive to non-philosophers—to psychologists and economists and businessmen—is of course precisely its heuristic virtues. But as I have tried to point out, *these* virtues are preserved—and quite possibly enhanced— by adopting a point of view in which probabilities are given an interpretation which rests ultimately on frequencies rather than on degrees of belief. Finally, since Jeffrey can achieve a representation of coherent preferences through the use of a whole family of pairs of utility and probability functions, it seems clear that it is unnecessary and perhaps ill-advised to hypostatize these probabilities as 'degrees of belief' in even an idealized psychological sense.

5. EMPIRICAL THEORY OF DEGREES OF BELIEF

Can we construe the subjectivistic theory of probability as an empirical theory of degrees of belief? We note that the failure of the theory as an empirical theory of decision does not entail its failure as a theory of degrees of belief. The subjectivistic theory construed as a theory of decision making involves two other ingredients besides degrees of belief: it involves utilities, and it involves the acceptance by the individual of the principle of maximizing mathematical expectation. Thus the kinds of experiments that psychologists have performed to test the subjectivistic theory of decision are not really decisive with regard to a subjectivistic theory of degrees of belief. But then in order to test the latter theory we must find some way—preferably more direct—to measure degrees of belief than that to which we are led by the full blown subjective expected utility theory.

One way would be to inquire of people what their degrees of belief in various propositions are. This is a very unlikely approach: people will often say they don't know, and they will often announce numbers that do not fit into the calculus of probability. We must assume—if the theory is to have a chance at all —that people have no very clear access to their degrees of belief.

Furthermore, it is not altogether clear that there are degrees of belief. We can introspectively distinguish a number of qualities of our beliefs: confidence, enthusiasm, intensity, but it is not so easy to sort our beliefs out along the linear array that we want to think of as representing degrees of belief. It is particularly difficult to do this introspectively.

Savage has suggested a number of ingenious ways to get at degrees of belief which do not involve the entire subjectivistic theory of decision. For example, one could discover the maximum amount that a person would pay for a ticket that would return him a dollar if S is true; that amount would represent his degree of belief in S. But this will not do for several reasons. First of all, the prices a person offers for tickets on a number of related propositions may well not satisfy the axioms of the probability calculus. In fact this will quite generally be the case, since there are traditional probability calculations (the birthday problem, for example) that most people find surprising. Second, on the subjectivistic view, a person may change his opinions at any time, for good reason or for no reason. To discover whether or not a person's degrees of belief satisfied the axioms of the probability calculus would require that we test all of his beliefs—or a large set of them—simultaneously. But of course we can't actually do this. Finally, it is difficult to see how in *this* program of measurement we can eliminate the influence of risk: a conservative sort would, I imagine, discount his tickets (say, offering $p - \epsilon$ for a dollar ticket on S, and $1 - p - \epsilon$ for a dollar ticket on $\sim S$), and an enthusiastic gambler might well offer a little extra for the fun of gambling. The same sorts of problems arise here as arise in the general attempt to assess probabilities by gambling behavior discussed in Section 2.

Another device proposed by Savage, and endorsed by a number of writers on subjective probability, is the forced choice: the subject is asked to choose between receiving a substantial prize if it rains in Los Angeles three weeks from today, and receiving the same prize if a sequence of 15 coin tosses contains 12 heads. Although no finite number of such forced choices can show that his degrees of belief *do* obey the probability calculus, a finite number of them can show that they don't. If the forced choices yield an ordering of propositions that can be explained by a set of degrees of belief satisfying the calculus, that is certainly evidence that the theory has something to it.

But we have every reason to expect that such a test would fail to support the theory. Just as the degrees of belief that people claim will not satisfy the probability calculus (else they would not be surprised by probability calculations), so their choices, which no doubt come close to reflecting the degrees of belief they would claim, will not be consistent with the probability calculus. And we have the same temporal problem as before: since on the subjective view, degrees of belief may change freely, we must measure a number of related degrees of belief simultaneously, and the proposed technique does not allow us to do that.

Finally, we may suppose that someone invents an epistemeter which will measure a thousand degrees of belief simultaneously through electrodes wired to the head of an individual. If there were such a device, it could put our theory to relatively direct test. The device would have to be tuned and standardized, of course, but that could perhaps be done by means of some of the techniques mentioned earlier. Now if we had such a machine, it is conceivable that then we could discover something much like degrees of belief that characterizes people's brains, and which does indeed satisfy the axioms of the probability calculus. But I wouldn't bet on it. At any rate, so far as *present* evidence is concerned, we have no evidence that people's degrees of belief satisfy the probability calculus, and considerable evidence to the effect that they do not.

6. NORMATIVE THEORY OF DEGREES OF BELIEF

Relatively few people, I assume, have seriously proposed that the subjective theory of probability be construed as an empirical theory of degrees of actual belief. They have said, rather, that the subjective theory is ideal or normative: should an individual discover that his degrees of belief do not conform to the probability calculus, he will just by that very fact be motivated to change them in such a way that they do conform. When someone shows me the calculation which establishes that the odds are better than even that that two people in a room of twenty-one people will have the same birthday, I revise my degree of belief accordingly. According to the introspective testimony of some, the feeling is much like that of being caught in a logical contradiction.

It is difficult to make much out of this introspective feeling; not all individuals testify to having felt it, and it hardly seems a firm enough foundation to build a normative theory of degrees of belief on. Ramsey [20] pointed out long ago that there was no point in a normative theory of belief if there were to be no way of measuring beliefs.

If we had an epistemeter, of course, we could apply the normative theory: we could take an individual, wire him up, and see whether or not his momentary degrees of belief conformed to the probability calculus; if they did, we could give him a gold star. Science fiction aside, however, there seems to be no behavioral way to get at degrees of belief. Even in the most persuasive case, when we demand that an individual post odds representing his degrees of belief, and take all bets offered, we have no assurance whatever that his degrees of belief will conform to the probability calculus, precisely because of the fact that if he is *deductively* rational, he will not post incoherent odds, however incoherent his degrees of belief may be.

At the moment, then, there is no way of getting at a person's degrees of belief which is dependable enough that it could serve as a ground for asserting that he is or is not rational in his degrees of belief, as opposed to his preferences. But we may nevertheless consider the subjectivistic theory as a standard of rationality that we are simply not in a position to *apply* practically at the moment. It may still be important theoretically and philosophically, and it may in fact turn out to be feasible to apply it practically some day. Indeed, this is the way in which most philosophers who take the subjectivistic theory of probability as a standard of rationality, more or less without argument, seem to look on it. It is simply assumed that whatever else may be said about rationality, at any rate one's degrees of belief should conform to the probability calculus.

There are several things to be said about this. The first and most obvious is that it is not at all clear that there *are* degrees of belief in the sense required by the demand that they conform to the probability calculus. The calculus requires that with each proposition there be associated a real number, and that these real numbers be related in certain ways. But there may be nothing that corresponds to the term 'degree of belief'; or if there is it may need to be measured by an interval, or by an n-dimensional vector. It seems reasonable to suppose that 'degree of belief' is a psychological concept which depends for its usefulness on the psychological theory in which it appears. But at the moment, there is no such psychological theory.

Second, this construal of the subjective theory entails that one should be very certain indeed of propositions that seem both very powerful and empirical. Thus if one has a degree of belief equal to p in a certain relatively rare kind of event (e.g., that the next ball drawn from an urn will be purple), and if one supposes that one's degree of belief that the second ball is purple, given that the first one is purple is not more than $2p$, and if one regards the draws as exchangeable in the subjectivist's sense, then one should be 99% sure that no more than 11% of the draws, in the long run, will yield purple balls. (For details of such arguments, see [13].)

This is, indeed, what one's initial beliefs commit one to, if they conform to the probability calculus. On the other hand, most of us would regard the consequence as unintuitive. The moral, I believe, is that there is no way to make one's beliefs conform to the probability calculus—on the assumption that they are real numbers—without doing violence to some rational intuitions. To reject the consequence requires—essentially—rejecting the supposition that there are any exchangeable sequences of events, which would undermine the usefulness of the subjectivistic theory.

Finally, we may ask what functions this normative theory of degrees of belief performs. It is clear that it serves no function for non-philosophers. But is it possible that it performs a function for philosophers—can we get some mileage out of a theory which supposes that there are degrees of belief, and demands that they conform to the usual probability axioms?

We consider two cases. First, suppose that these are all the constraints there are on rational belief. Then any distribution of degrees of belief over the propositions of a language is as good as—as rational as—any other, provided the axioms of the probability calculus are satisfied. But the axioms are compatible with any degree of belief in any individual (nonlogical) statement. No degree of belief in any nonlogical proposition can, by itself, be ruled irrational. The set of degrees of belief in a number of related propositions are constrained, on this view, by the requirements of rationality. But what does this constraint tell us? It does not tell us that the rational individual will not in fact have a book made against him, for if we grant him deductive rationality we already know that he won't actually allow a book to be made against him, regardless of what his degrees of belief are.

It might be maintained, and would be by anyone who regarded the theory of subjective probability as providing insights into scientific inference, that its main function is dynamic; it is the changes in the probability function that are wrought by empirical evidence, through the mediation of Bayes's theorem (or a generalization thereof) that give the theory its philosophical importance. The most frequently cited examples are the convergence theorems: Given that two people have degrees of belief that satisfy the probability calculus, and given that their degrees of belief satisfy some relatively mild constraints in addition to the coherence constraints, then, as empirical evidence accumulates, their distributions of beliefs will become more and more nearly the same. Of course there is nothing *in the theory* that requires that even the mild constraints will be satisfied for a rational person. But the really serious problem is that there is nothing in the theory that says that a person should *change* his beliefs in response to evidence in accordance with Bayes's theorem. On the contrary, the whole thrust of the subjectivistic theory is to claim that the history of the individual's beliefs is irrelevant to their rationality: all that counts at a given time is that they conform to the requirements of coherence. It is certainly not required that the person got to the state that he is in by applying Bayes's theorem to the coherent degrees of belief he had in some previous state. No more, then, is it required that a rational individual pass from his present coherent state to a new coherent state by conditionalization. Just as he may have got to his original coherent state by intuition, whimsey, imagination, evidence processed through Bayes's theorem, or any combination thereof, so he may with perfect rationality pass from his present coherent state to a future coherent state through any of these mechanisms. If he depends on Bayes's theorem, it is a matter of predilection, not of rationality. For all the subjectivistic theory has to say, he may with equal justification pass from one coherent state to another by free association, reading tea leaves, or consulting his parrot.

This leads us to the second and more interesting case, in which the subjectivistic theory of degrees of belief embodies more than the constraint of coherence. The most obvious addition will be a principle that directs us to change our beliefs in accordance with Bayes's theorem: When we pass from one coherent epistemic state to another, as a result of acquiring evidence e, the probability function that describes our new state *should* be the conditional-on-e probability function of the old state. This is the principle of epistemic conditionalization, and is accepted, at least implicitly, by almost all writers who employ the subjectivistic theory.

The principle of conditionalization puts the theory in a new light. Thus supplemented, the theory makes the rationality of my beliefs at a future time depend not only on their coherence, but on their history. My beliefs at that time will be rational only if they are derived from my present beliefs by conditionalizing on the evidence that becomes available to me between now and then.

But if the rationality of my beliefs tomorrow depends on my having rational beliefs today, and conditionalizing to reach tomorrow's beliefs, it follows by the Relativity of Time that the rationality of my beliefs today depends on my having had rational beliefs yesterday, and having conditionalized on them to reach today's beliefs, or else that I can start being rational at any time—in particular, tomorrow, so that tomorrow's beliefs need not, after all, be based on applying conditionalization to today's beliefs. In the latter case we are back to pure subjectivism. But in the former case we are in Carnap's old position—the one he occupied before being seduced by the siren song of subjectivism: in theory and in principle a rational being would have beliefs that are precisely determined by his total body of evidental knowledge as accumulated from time zero to present, and by the language he uses. Probabilities—degrees of belief— are logically determinate, and quite independent of what degrees of belief any actual person happens to have. The problem, then, as Carnap saw, is to determine the values of the absolutely prior probabilities—the probabilities that should be assigned to the statements of the language prior to any experience at all. Carnap's view was that we should assign these probabilities on the basis of *rational intuition.* It turned out that this was extremely difficult to do, and even Carnap, in his later years, began to doubt its possibility. The demands such a program imposes on rational intuition are simply too great.

Harper [9] treats the degree-of-belief function as an abstract theoretical object in an epistemological framework. The point is to explore the philosophical character of epistemic changes, and for these purposes we need be concerned neither with evaluating nor interpreting the function in question.

A middle position is defended by Hintikka and some members of his school [10, 17, 18, 19]. We define a logical probability measure on the sentences of a language, and assert conditionally that *if* this measure represents our prior belief, and *if* the principle of epistemic conditionalization is accepted, *then* such and such interesting results follow. But no attempt is made either to defend the prior measure assignment as demanded by rational intuition or to defend it as corresponding to anybody's actual beliefs. It is sometimes said that (if it did represent someone's beliefs) it would represent a 'presupposition' about the nature of the universe. Since no attempt is made to defend these presuppositions as rational, we would seem to be back in the realm of purely subjective theory; and since it is not argued that the measures in fact represent anyone's beliefs, we seem to be in a realm both hypothetical and subjective, from which we can learn little of either philosophical or practical import.[4]

7.

Despite the fact that subjectivistic probability is highly fashionable both in statistics and in philosophy, it appears to have serious shortcomings. We may account for its popularity in statistics by its heuristic role in teasing out the commitments that are implicit in an agent's preference ranking; but its role there is purely heuristic, and we need not assume that there is anything psychological that corresponds to the 'degrees of belief' that emerge from certain of those analyses. And note that in some analyses—Jeffrey's for example—a unique probability function doesn't even emerge as an auxiliary notion from the analysis. We may account for the popularity of subjective probability in philosophy in part by fashion, in part by laziness (it is easy to manipulate), and in part by the fact that it has few viable competitors. Nevertheless it is poor philosophy to adopt a false theory to achieve a certain end just because one doesn't know of a true theory that will achieve that end.

I conclude that the theory of subjective probability is psychologically false, decision-theoretically vacuous, and philosophically bankrupt: its account is overdrawn.

NOTES

1. In some cases this agreement can be explained by convergence theorems.

2. This formulation is due to Levi, [15], pp. 413-414.

3. It is interesting to note, as pointed out to me by Teddy Seidenfeld, that the Dutch Book against the irrational agent can only be constructed by an irrational (whether unscrupulous or not) opponent. Suppose that the Agent offers odds of 2:1 on heads and odds of 2:1 on tails on the toss of a coin. If the opponent is rational, according to the theory under examination, there will be a number p that represents his degree of belief in the occurrence of heads. If p is less than a half, the opponent will maximize his expectation by staking his entire stake on tails in accordance with the first odds posted by the Agent. But then the Agent need not lose. Similarly, if p is greater than a half. But if p is exactly a half, then the rational opponent should be indifferent between dividing his stake (to make the Dutch Book) and putting his entire stake on one outcome: the expectation in any case will be the same.

4. It is worth noting, however, that Levi's proposals in [15] and [16] escape these criticisms, and most of those that follow. He supposes that the epistemic state of the agent is represented by a convex set of coherent probability functions, thus escaping criticism based on the alleged exactness of so-called "degrees of belief". More important, as a good pragmatist he does not demand that the rationality of an epistemic state depend on its history; he is concerned mainly with the rationality of changes from one epistemic state to another, and while he takes some of these changes to depend on conditionalization, he also admits changes that do not depend on conditionalization.

BIBLIOGRAPHY

[1] Carnap, Rudolf, 1950, *Logical Foundations of Probability,* The University of Chicago Press, Chicago.

[2] Carnap, Rudolf, 1968, 'Inductive Logic and Inductive Intuition', *The Problem of Inductive Logic,* Lakatos (ed.), pp. 258-267.

[3] Carnap, Rudolf, 1961, 'Inductive Logic and Rational Decisions', *Studies in Inductive Logic and Probability I*, Carnap and Jeffrey (eds.), pp. 5-31.

[4] De Finetti, Bruno, 1973, "La Prevision," *Annales de l'Institute Henry Poincaré* 7, pp. 1-68.

[5] Demster, A., 1961, 'Upper and Lower Probabilities induced by a Multivalued Mapping', *Annals of Mathematical Statistics* 38, pp. 325-339.

[6] Edwards, Ward, 1960, 'Measurement of Utility and Subjective Probability', in Gulliksen & Messick, pp. 109-128.

[7] Edwards, Ward, 1962, 'Subjective Probabilities Inferred from Decisions', *Psychological Review* 69, pp. 109-135.

[8] Good, I. J., 1962, 'Subjective Probability as a Measure of a Non-Measurable Set', in Nagel, Suppes and Tarski, *Logic, Methodology and Philosophy of Science*, Stanford University Press, pp. 319-329.

[9] Harper, William L., 1975, 'Rational Belief Change, Popper Functions, and Counterfactuals', *Synthese* 30, pp. 221-262.

[10] Hintikka, Jaakko, 1971, 'Unknown Probabilities, Bayesianism and De Finetti's Representation Theorem', *Boston Studies in the Philosophy of Science* VIII, Buck and Cohen (eds.), D. Reidel, Dordrecht.

[11] Jeffrey, Richard C., 1965, *The Logic of Decision*, McGraw-Hill Book Co., New York.

[12] Koopman, B. O., 1940, "The Bases of Probability," *Bulletin of the American Mathematical Society* 46, pp. 763-774.

[13] Kyburg, H. E., 1968, 'Bets and Beliefs', *American Philosophical Quarterly* 5, 54-63.

[14] Kyburg, H. E., 1974, *The Logical Foundations of Statistical Inference*, Reidel, Dordrecht and Boston.

[15] Levi, Isaac, 1977, 'Direct Inference', *Journal of Philosophy* 74, pp. 5-29.

[16] Levi, Isac, 1974, 'On Indeterminate Probabilities', *Journal of Philosophy* 71, pp. 391-418.

[17] Niiniluoto, Ilkka, 1972-73, 'Inductive Systematization: Definition and a Critical Survey', *Synthese* 25, pp. 25-81.

[18] Niiniluoto, Ilkka, and Raimo Tuomela, 1973, *Theoretical Concepts and Hypothetical-Inductive Inference*, Reidel, Dordrecht.

[19] Pietarinen, Juhani, 1972, *Lawlikeness, Analogy, and Inductive Logic*, North Holland, Amsterdam.

[20] Ramsey, Frank P., 'Probability and Partial Belief', in Ramsey, *The Foundations of Mathematics*, pp. 256-257.

[21] Ramsey, Frank P., 1950, *The Foundations of Mathematics*, Braithwaite (ed.), Routledge & Kegan Paul Ltd., London.

[22] Savage, Leonard J., 1954, *Foundations of Statistics*, John Wiley, New York.

[23] Slovic, Paul, Fischhoff, Baruch, and Lichtenstein, Sarah, 1977, 'Behavioral Decision Theory', *Annual Review of Psychology* 28, pp. 1-39.

[24] Smith, Cedric A. B., 1961, 'Consistency in Statistical Inference and Decision', *The Journal of the Royal Statistical Society*, Series B (Methodological), Vol. 23, No. 1, pp. 1-37.

[25] Suppes, Patrick, 1974, 'The Measurement of Belief', *Journal of the Royal Statistical Society*, Series B (Methodological), Vol. 36, pp. 160-191.

7

Chance

1. INTRODUCTION

In a number of bodies of scientific knowledge there are laws and theories which, when applied in particular circumstances, give rise to statements that are not categorical but stochastic in character. In physics: quantum theory, statistical mechanics. In biology: genetic theory. In sociology and psychology: laws that express not an invariable relation between quantities, but a variable stochastic relation. This fact has called forth in recent years a variety of what purport to be analyses of the 'use of probability in scientific theories'. These analyses are usually expressed in terms of 'chance' or 'propensity'. It is argued (or, anyway, stated) that these are 'intensional' notions, and that they are not reducible to frequencies.[1]

I wish to argue here that 'probability' occurs but rarely and peripherally in scientific theories; that an adequate account of the use of stochastic laws in science need not make use of any such concept as propensity or chance; that indeed the latter concepts add nothing to what is provided by our knowledge of frequencies; and that while there is in a certain sense an intensional aspect of some of our knowledge of frequencies, it is far too weak an aspect to provide grounds for any interesting or profound conclusions—for example about the need for a new logic.

2. PROBABILITY AND SCIENCE

That the word 'probability' appears but rarely or not at all in bodies of scientific law or theory is hardly arguable. Laws and theories are generally expressed mathematically, and in mathematical expressions eleven-letter English words are not typographically popular. What those who refer to the use of probability in science have in mind is something like the following: There occur in these bodies of science certain expressions whose English rendering would be sentences such

Reprinted, with modifications, from *Journal of Philosophical Logic*, no. 5 (1976), pp. 355-393, by permission of the publisher.

as the following: The probability of an atom of X, in state S, under circumstances C, undergoing a transition to state S' is p. The probability that the offspring of an individual of genotype g_1 and an individual of genotype g_2 will be of genotype g_3 is q. The probability that at temperature T a molecule will have a velocity between v_1 and v_2 is r. The probability that a blue-collar worker of Irish descent living in the Greater Boston area will vote Democratic is s.

Some such sentences are encountered in applications of science — though perhaps even then not so often as in philosophical analyses of the sciences. But they are not encountered in the principles or axioms or laws of the special sciences. What we encounter there are general statements expressing stochastic relations among random quantities. Thus in the quantum-mechanical case what we find are functions representing certain distributions or densities of the values of certain quantities under certain circumstances. What we find in statistical mechanics is a distribution function giving a distribution of velocities as a function of temperature. What we find in genetics is a distribution of the genotype as a function of locus and linkage of contributing genes. What we find, even in the rawest sociological case, is a distribution of voting behavior as a function of such variables as income, ethnic group, residence, etc. Even here, in most cases, we have not pushed matters back to the axioms and principles of the science; the point is that one need not push things very far back in order that there be nothing left that can be interpreted in English as 'the probability that an A is a B is p'.

This is not to say that in informal descriptions of what is going on, the word 'probability' will not occur. It might occur in statistical mechanics, for example, in the context: 'Let us define a phase space in the following way, and assume that each molecule has the same probability of being in each cell of the phase space'. But this does not have the form of an assertion: 'The probability of an A being a B is p', in the body of the science, and it is offered, not as a part of the science standing by itself, but rather as a way of characterizing the distribution function which will be offered on the next page as part of the body of the science.

None of this is very startling. Everybody knows that what one encounters in the sciences that involve stochastic laws and theories has the form, not of 'probability' statements, but of mathematical distribution and density functions. The question is whether the way to approach these stochastic elements is through the concept of probability, and particularly through a concept of probability in which propensity or chance plays an important role. It is not at all obvious that such a circuitous and indirect approach to the analysis of distribution and density statements is the most appropriate.

Suppose, however, that we had at hand an interpretation of statements of the form 'The probability that an A is a B is p'. Would this not suggest that the route might not be circuitous after all? Let us suppose we have our corpus of scientific knowledge a statement to the effect that the distribution of the random quantity X (weight, say) in the population P (frogs of a certain species, say) is given by the distribution function F (the normal distribution with mean m and variance s^2, say). We might attempt to provide a probabilistic interpretation of this statement along the following lines: Given any real number x, the probability that a member of P will have a weight less than x is $F(x)$. When we are given a standard real number designator (6.578, say), this will have just the form that we can (supposedly) interpret: 'The probability that a member of P will have a weight less than 6.578 is $F(6.578)$'. Or: 'The chance that a member of P will have a weight less than 6.578 is $F(6.578)$'. Or: 'The propensity . . . '. Two difficulties loom: First, of course, 'chance' and 'propensity' are no more transparent than 'probability'; we must go on to give some sort of account of these new terms, perhaps in the form of a semantics for them. Such a semantics must be tied to frequencies, either from the outset, if we give an account of propensities in terms of frequencies in hypothetical infinite populations, or indirectly, through Bernoulli's theorem, if we give a 'single case' account of propensities.[2] Second, if we follow this route it will take a non-denumerable set of analyses to provide the interpretation for a single distribution statement: in the case at hand, one for each real number. It would be tempting to do it wholesale: 'For every real number x, the chance that a member of P will have a weight less than x is $F(x)$'. But this surely will not do: no one has offered a propensity interpretation of probability statements that involve a free numerical variable, and it is hard to see how one *could* be offered. It would, at any rate, not be an 'analysis' or 'interpretation' in any usual sense.

Another, and more down to earth, difficulty arises. We are required to suppose (if we take the distribution statement literally) that there is a finite chance that a frog will have a large negative weight. We are required to suppose that what is being characterized is not, as it seems, the population P, which of course is finite, but some other, hypothetical, population. But surely we would be better off, scientifically, if we knew the *exact* distribution of weights in the (finite) population P. We would, at least, know more about frogs.

3. TERMINOLOGICAL CONVENTIONS

Before we embark on an analysis of stochastic laws in science, let us make some terminological conventions.

'Probability' will be used in the sense that I have given it elsewhere. It will be construed, that is, as a logical relation holding between a sentence and a set of sentences construed as a body of knowledge or rational corpus, and having as its range subintervals of the interval $[0, 1]$. The probability of a statement S, relative to a body of knowledge K, will be the interval $[p, q]$ just in case:

(a) S is known (in K) to be equivalent to a statement of the form '$a \in A$'.

(b) There is a term C, such that:

    (i) a is a random member of C, with respect to belonging to A, relative to K,

    (ii)   there is in K a statistical statement asserting that the measure of A in C lies between p and q.

The relation of being a random member is explicated, not in terms of probability, but in terms of what else is known in K about a. It does entail, of course, that a is known (in K) to be a member of C. It is unnecessary, for our purposes here, to go into further detail concerning the randomness relation, except to remark that variable C is constrained to belong to a recursively characterized set of terms characteristic of the language; not all expressions are potentially capable of serving as reference terms.

Controversial though this analysis of 'probability' may be, it will not beg any important questions here. There are three issues, however, which require resolution: (1) Is the 'statistical statement' mentioned in (b) (ii) a statement specifying that the proportion or measure of A's that are B's lies between p and q, or is it a statement of empirical non-epistemological probability, or chance, where the terms 'A' and 'B' occur in a nonextensional context? (2) is the credal state of a rational agent X whose body of knowledge is K and which meets the conditions (a) and (b) to be characterized (with respect to S) by the assignment of the whole interval $[p, q]$, or might his credal state be characterized by a subinterval $[p, q]$ or even a point in $[p, q]$? What is the appropriate explication of the random-member-of relation? A full resolution of these issues, and hence a complete analysis of 'probability' along the lines I have suggested, has important bearings on the question of direct inference in which the credal state of a rational agent is derived from, or constrained by, premises which include a 'statistical statement' of one of the varieties cited under (1).[3]

Although I shall be arguing against the importance of the special sense that 'chance' has been given by some writers, I shall use the word in the statistical statements mentioned in (b) (ii). Thus I shall refer to such statements as 'The chance that an A is a B lies between p and q' rather than to statements that use the word 'measure' or 'frequency' since the latter may be thought question-begging. In fact, the very word 'statistical' used to characterize these statements may already be thought to be question-begging. In my previous analyses I have left more or less open the question of the interpretation of the chance statements on which probabilities are to be based—though I have intimated that they should be construed in relatively extensional terms.

I shall use the phrases 'strict chance' and 'strict chance interpretation' to express the view that chances are *not* reducible to frequencies—even hypothetically and in the long run.

I shall use the terms 'distribution' and 'frequency' in a directly extensional way, to reflect the actual distributions and actual frequencies in an actual population, or, if some other population is specified, in that specified population.

I use the word 'population' to mean either a specified set of objects, or in the case of infinite populations, a specified sequence of objects.

4. INTUITIONS ABOUT CHANCES

There are a number of examples designed to appeal to intuition that are alleged to show the necessity of distinguishing between chances and frequencies. Consider a coin, newly minted, that is to be tossed but once and then destroyed: the frequency with which it will land heads is either 0 or 1; yet we want to say that the chance of its landing heads is a half. Or consider a bottle struck by a hammer. There is a certain chance that it will shatter into exactly ten pieces; this chance is perfectly well determined; but there is no way of repeating this experiment, and thus no frequency (other than 0 and 1) to which we can refer.

In general, the scheme is this: we consider a definite description (the a such that F) or an indefinite description (an H) where the definite description entails that the object described belongs to H; we set things up so that H seems to be a perfectly appropriate class on which to base a 'chance' or a 'probability', and furthermore, one in which we know the value of the chance or probability; and yet (by the description of the circumstances) the frequency in H (if it exists, since H may be empty), is either 0 or 1 (if H has but one member) or, at any rate, known to be different from the intuitive 'probability' or 'chance'. These examples are intended to show that repeatability, and therefore frequency, has nothing to do with chance (or probability, as it is usually put), and thus that chance cannot be reduced to frequency but must be considered an independent concept in its own right.

On my view of probability *these* arguments cut no ice. That is because probabilities are defined essentially for equivalence classes of statements, and we can generally find a statement which will yield the appropriate 'chance'. There are any number of classes, to which the next toss of a coin a, soon to be destroyed, belongs: for example it is a toss of a newly minted coin, it is a toss of a coin, it is a toss of a penny (say), it is a toss of a roughly symmetrical metal disc whose two sides are distinguished as 'heads' and 'tails', it is (to push even further back in the direction of generality) an event of kind K, where events of kind K are events whose initiating conditions vary (almost) continuously over a certain range, which have two outcomes, and which are such that very small variations in the initiating conditions may lead to a reversal of the outcomes. (We can characterize events of kind K in quite specific physical detail.) In any event, there is no dearth of possible reference sets on my view, even for the 'unique' event. (After all, is not *every* event unique?)

Again, suppose that in fact we did have in our body of knowledge a fair amount of data concerning the particular newly minted coin a that is the subject of discussion. Suppose it has been tossed a hundred times and has yielded fifty-three heads. Under ordinary circumstances this fact will have no special place in our scientific body of coin-tossing lore; the hypothesis that governs our probability, the 'chance' hypothesis, is the general one to the effect that half the tosses of coins in general yield heads. In either event (when a is tossed but once, or when a is tossed a hundred times) we have no reason whatever to include in our body of coin-tossing lore a chance statement regarding this particular newly minted coin.

How about the broken bottle? There we don't know what the chance is that it will shatter into ten pieces, but we are invited to suppose that there is such a chance. (I suppose, for example, that we might say that it is more probable that it will break into exactly ten pieces than that it will break into exactly ten thousand pieces.) If one were to analyze this case, one might do so along the lines of 'events of kind K' above, with the exception that instead of two outcomes, there are N, where N is the maximum number of pieces the bottle might be shattered into. (Surely 10^5 is an adequate upper bound for N.) But we would not suppose that a minor variation in initial conditions would be capable of producing a completely different outcome. We may, nevertheless, be able to impose some bounds on the distribution of the random quantity 'number of pieces' even in this barely described instance — e.g., that the corresponding frequency function has a maximum somewhere between 5 and 100; that it decreases on each side of its maximum, and so on.

None of this goes to show that there is no such thing as chance. We might still want to interpret the statistical or chance statements on which (in my view) probabilities are based as requiring a non-frequency interpretation. It may be that we would not want to say that the probability of heads on the toss of a coin was a half unless we could say, not merely that half the tosses of coins land heads, but that the *chance* of a toss of a coin landing heads was a half.

One argument that we do not always require strict (intensional) chance statements to found our probabilities on, but may sometimes be satisfied with frequencies, comes from the use of actuarial data as the basis for our probabilities. We do not talk of the chance that fire will strike our house; of the probability that Aunt Martha will live for ten more years; of the likelihood that our car will be stolen. It is difficult to imagine what the chance mechanisms are in these cases; the probabilities seem to be based on straight-forward actuarial statistics. Now of course it might be maintained that what is based on the statistics is just an inference to a chance mechanism; so this is not really a knockout argument for frequencies, although it is hard to see what would motivate one to introduce a chance mechanism in these cases except a prior commitment to the thesis that all probabilities must be based on chance. I do not know how such a mechanism would go: 'In 43.14% of the worlds just like this one, except . . . (except what?), Aunt Martha dies within ten years'.

A more serious argument against frequencies arises from considering counterfactual cases: If this coin (which never has been, never will be tossed) were to be tossed, the probability is a half that it would land heads. Can we say that the hypothetical event is a (hypothetical) member of the set of tosses of coins, and thus that the frequency in that set determines the probability? This invites the response that the whole set of coin tosses may be considered hypothetical: suppose that there were no tosses of coins at all in this world; would we not still want to say that the probability of a toss of a coin resulting in heads is a half? It seems that we would. But can we simply say then that the hypothetical coin tosses are instances of mechanisms of type K alluded to earlier? And thus that they have one outcome or another with equal frequency? This invites the response that the set of mechanisms of kind K may be considered hypothetical: suppose there were no mechanisms of that sort in the world; would we not still want to say that the chance of one of the two possible outcomes on a trial of such a mechanism would be a half? We could, I suppose, imagine such mechanisms, even if none existed. But if the mechanisms are merely hypothetical, merely imagined, then they will have just the characteristics we decide to attribute to them. Unicorns have the properties that we decide the unicorns have. And what seems to be built in here is that the frequencies of the two alternatives are equal.

Nevertheless, there does seem to be something intensional built into the statements we accept as bases for probabilities. They do support counterfactuals. They do not appear to be extensional: if the set of A's is in fact identical to the set of B's, it may yet happen that the chance that an A is a C is different from the chance that a B is a C; and that the chance that a D is an A is different from the chance that a D is a B. If a and b are two definite descriptions (or proper names), the probability that a is F may differ from the probability that b is F, even if $a = b$ is true. All of these things are reflected in ordinary probability talk. All of them are not only taken account of, but made much of, by those who offer strict-chance interpretations of statistical statements.

5. THE INTENSIONALITY OF PROBABILITY

On the view that I have defended elsewhere in a number of places, *probability* is indeed intensional: the probability relation is like the deducibility relation, and failures of the substitutivity of identity and the like are only to be expected. But since I take probability to be metalinguistic—to represent a relation between a sentence and a set of sentences—we have here what Quine would regard as merely the second grade of modal involvement. Even if $a = b$, we cannot deduce Fa from Fb—unless we take as a premise '$a = b$'. Similarly, even if $a = b$, we cannot say that the probability of 'Fa' relative to the set of sentences constituting our rational corpus is the same as that of 'Fb' unless we have in our rational corpus the sentence '$a = b$'.

A similar analysis will do for certain cases of failure of substitutivity of identity in chance or statistical statements. To have reason (inductive reasons or other reasons) to accept into your rational corpus 'The chance that an A is a C is p', is not to have reasons to accept 'The chance that a B is a C is p, even though in point of fact $A = B$, unless we also have reason to accept '$A = B$'. Here again the inductive or deductive 'reasons for accepting' are naturally and unsurprisingly intensional.

But the proponents of strict-chance interpretations of statistical statements want more intensionality than this: they want to regard the chance statements themselves, as statements in the object language, to be intensional. To give an example borrowed from Levi,[4] suppose that a coin producing machine produces coins, fifty percent of which have a 0.4 chance of landing heads, and fifty percent of which have a 0.6 chance of landing heads. S consists of a tossing of a coin obtained from the machine. T consists of a tossing of a coin which has a 0.4 chance of landing heads which is obtained from the machine. It may in fact happen that the set of events of kind S is identical to the set of events of kind T. But we want to distinguish between the chance of an event of kind T yielding heads (0.4) and the chance of an event of kind S yielding heads (0.5). Therefore substitutivity of identity *in the chance statement,* and not merely in a probability statement, fails, and the chance statements themselves must be construed as non-extensional.

The argument is perfectly valid, and it does show that under certain circumstances there may be a non-extensional element in chance statements. The circumstances will be discussed at length later on. But there is also the question of what to make of the argument. Suppose that we know that $S = T$. Then to base probabilities on the chance statement concerning S would conflict with our interest in using probabilities for informing and guiding our choices and actions in the actual world. Suppose that in fact $S = T$, but that we don't know it. Then knowing of a certain trial only that it was an event of kind S, we would quite properly assign a probability of 0.5 to the occurrence of heads on it. If we knew more, we would assign a different probability to heads. But we don't know all about the actual world; we don't know a lot of things, such as whether that particular trial will yield a head or not. Did we know this, we would have no use for probability.[5] To know that $S = T$ is to have knowledge of a certain frequency: that 100% of trials of kind S are trials of kind T. Knowing this, even if we also know that the *chance* that a trial of kind S is a trial of kind T is only a half, we would be well-advised to take it into account. Thus that chance statements can be non-extensional should not be taken to imply that our assignments of probabilities should be based on facts about the world, rather than our knowledge of facts about the world.

A rather nice illustration of a related conflict of intuitions is provided by an example in a paper of van Fraassen.[6] Consider an infinite sequence of rolls of a *fair* die, of which (miraculously) exactly ten turn up with an even number. Assuming that we know that half of these tosses resulted in twos, it is obvious, according to van Fraassen, that the conditional probability of a two in this sequence, given an even number, is just the proportion of two's among the ten even tosses. It is perfectly obvious, according to some chance theorists, that even in this sequence, the conditional probability of a two, given an even number, is a third; the die is fair. Even if we know the frequency, even if there is no question, as in this example, of expanding the sequence (it is already infinite), still the chance in question is a third. My intuitions here are fully on van Fraassen's side: if we know the frequency of two's among the even numbers in the *actual* sequence, then whatever the conditional chance in principle and in general, it is *that* frequency that I would want to use as a guide to action. If I happened to know that five of those ten tosses yielded two's, I would not be willing (as it seems I should be on the strict-chance interpretation) to offer two-to-one odds against a specified one of those tosses yielding a two.

I am not concerned here to argue for correct intuitions, but simply to show that there is an honest conflict of intuition involved. In the cases to be discussed below, I shall attempt to clarify the points at issue. Since it is the uses of probability that lead to this conflict of intuitions, and since these uses are related to the grounds that we have for accepting chance statements, I shall classify the cases to be considered according to the source of the chance statement. Although the meaning of a chance statement is a question of its semantics, rather than its source, it will not undermine our analysis to look at the sources of these statements, providing we can do so in a fairly exhaustive way.

6. CASE I

We may have complete knowledge of a frequency in a finite and completely examined class, or of a distribution in such a class. The paradigm case is the knowledge of the frequency of white balls in an urn containing black and white balls in known numbers. A less trivial example would be the distribution of shoe sizes in an inventory of a shoe store. A less useless example would be the distribution of weights in a certain herd of cattle.

In the first example, that frequency will be the chance that a ball in the urn is white. It will sometimes be the chance that a ball *drawn* from the urn is white—that is, when we have no grounds for supposing the drawing biased.[7] In the second example, we could use that knowledge as the basis of a probability statement concerning the probability that a given shoe was size 7B. In the third example, we could use the knowledge to found the probability that a certain steer—say the first one through the loading chute—will weigh over a thousand pounds.

Many writers—Levi among them—would say that there was no question of chance at all in any of these examples. According to these writers, in order to arrive at a chance statement concerning the urn, we must specify *how* the ball is to be selected; but then the chance statement will not concern the contents of the urn, but rather the character of selections *from* the urn. But is it not conceivable that we should be invited to bet on the color of a specified ball *in* the urn? The one next to be drawn, or the one nearest the top, say? And wouldn't the *known* frequency be an appropriate basis for computing odds? Levi, as I understand him, would say that in these circumstances there is no appropriate basis for computing odds.

The intuitions of the chance theorist are clearest in the shoe store example. Shoes are not just thrown around in the shoe store, as balls may be in the urn, and it is hard to conceive of being in a position to bet on the size of any object merely identified as a specified shoe in the store. But we could make up a story that would make sense out of this: suppose, just after the inventory is taken, the shoe store is hit by a bomb. Wearing a size 7B, and requiring new shoes, we wonder how long it will take (how many pairs we will have to examine) before we can expect to come up with the right size.

Finally, it is quite realistic to be concerned with the probability that the next steer through the chute will weigh over a thousand pounds (for example, it is relevant to determining what to offer to pay for the steer). Even in this case it is not hard to imagine a hard-line chance-theorist insisting that there are no chances and thus no probabilities involved—at least not without a theory concerning the pushiness of steers of various sizes. The frequency statements and distribution statements that concern these finite sets are simply not chance statements, and will not support (or be) probabilities. He will insist that only when we consider *selections* by a given *method* from these sets are we concerned with chance statements and probabilities—and in certain cases, of course, these statements will give chances and distributions that reflect the composition of the finite classes. For this to be the case, we must know something about the method of selection—for example, that it is fair or 'random'. I shall return to this question later (in Section 9); for the moment I am supposing that we don't know anything about the properties of the method of selection, or that there just is no question of selection. Under this circumstance, Levi, for example, will insist that rationality imposes no constraints on our degrees of belief: we have no usable chance statements regarding the white balls, the shoes, or the steers.

We have here a simple conflict of intuitions, and in the last analysis it may be that you pays your money and you takes your choice. It seems quite clear to me that if you really don't know anything about the way the ball, the pair of shoes, or the steer is selected, you are rationally bound to have degrees of belief that reflect the relevant proportions. The opposite is quite clear to Levi.

In any event, *if* these are to be construed as the sort of statements on which probabilities can be based (as I construe them), it is clear that they are perfectly extensional. No modalities or possibilities or possible worlds are involved; substitutivity of identity is preserved; however the urn is described or identified, it has the proportion of white balls in that it has, and there's an end of the matter. Chance statements of this sort, if statements of this sort are chance statements, are perfectly extensional and unmysterious. (Recall, however, that the *probabilities* based on them are intensional; the probability that a specified ball is white, relative to my body of knowledge, depends, obviously, on *how* it is specified.)

7. CASE II

A rather more common case is that in which the grounds for accepting a distribution statement or statistical statement about a spatio-temporally limited class are actuarial. As in the first case, our statistical or distribution statement concerns a finite specified class, but now our knowledge about this class derives from our having examined a sample of it and drawn a conclusion by statistical inference. How statistical inference works is not to the point here; what is to the point is that we have acquired knowledge about a distribution or a frequency in a finite class of which we have examined only a fraction. For example, we may have examined a sample of balls from a very large urn, and concluded that a fraction p of the balls in the urn are white. Or we may have tested a sample of radio sets from a production line, and concluded that the proportion of defective radios in the day's run is q. Or we may have examined a sample of steers from the herd, and concluded that weight is distributed roughly normally with a mean of m and standard deviation d in the herd.

Clearly, in this sort of case, the same analysis as before is appropriate; and equally clearly the devout chance theorist will insist (with, I think, less plausibility this time) that our conclusions are not chance statements at all. He will argue that strict chance statements will concern *selections* from the classes by a specified method. But it seems to me even clearer than in the examples of Case I that these statements can be, and are, and ought to be used directly as a basis for probability assessments.

Whether or not these are to be counted as chance statements, they are statements on which probabilities can usefully be based; and whether or not they are to be counted as chance statements they are unmysteriously extensional and nonmodal.

8. CASE III

A still more common case is that in which the grounds for accepting a distribution statement or statistical statement are actuarial, and again the statistical or distribution statement concerns a finite specified class—but in which we do not assume that the subject class is narrowly limited in space and time. Thus, on the basis of an observed sample, we may infer that the mean wingspan of a certain species of mosquito is w; or that the mean feed requirement of a thousand-pound Black Angus steer is f; or that the frequency of death among 65-year-old white females in our society is t. As the last example suggests, there may in these cases be a certain amount of vagueness in the specification of the class.

There is implicit a certain vagueness in the specification of the classes in the other two examples as well: we suppose that wingspan is characteristic of the *species* of mosquito; but we do not suppose that evolution has come to a halt. We suppose that the group of mosquitos we are talking about extends into the past for a good long time and will, in the absence of strong selective pressures, extend into the future for a good long time. If we want to be precise, we can be: we can stipulate that we are speaking of examples of this species as they exist on earth between 1900 and 2000. In the case of longevity, we can specify a smaller period of time—say 1970-1980—because we know that longevity is subject to secular trends. (Better, of course, we can perhaps say something about the secular trend, and thus free ourselves from the restriction to a rather short timespan.) Note, however, that even in the longevity example we are *not* talking about the death rate that applies merely to the past year, for which the statistics are in. If we are an insurance company, we don't care about last year—that is all water over the dam. We care about death rates over the next five years, and we care about it in order to fix realistic premiums.

In this case I am no longer confident about predicting the reactions of the strict-chance theorist. Will he maintain that the statistical and distribution statements we obtain concerning such classes are not chance statements? If so, it would seem to be a *reductio* of his position, for it is hard to imagine more clear-cut paradigms of the statistical and distribution statements we use as a foundation for the probabilities that we must take account of in practice. He may indeed *say* that what we are inferring in these cases are not frequency or distribution statements but statements of chances. But if this is to be more than an empty form of words, we must be able to distinguish the inferred frequencies from the inferred chances. Or, let us be generous, and let us suppose that the chances need not be 'inferred' but may be simply 'given' in some way. Suppose that it is given that the *chance* of survival for a year of a 65-year-old American female is q, where the *frequency* of survival for a year in the same class is p, and that p is significantly different from q. Suppose you are an insurance company competitively betting on the survival of a given candidate for insurance. Would you use p or q to determine your odds?

It seems patent that if you knew the frequency, you would use that to determine your odds.

Nevertheless, the chance or statistical statement that we come to accept on the basis of the data (to use a more neutral locution than 'infer') does go beyond the data. Does it go beyond the actual world? The answer seems to be 'yes', but only in a very attenuated sense. It is worth being quite specific about this attenuated sense.

Let us suppose that we look at a large number of A's, and conclude that the chance of an A being a C is about p. The chance statement, we suppose, concerns a large number of A's, past, present, and future. It is perfectly consistent both with our data and with the chance statement we come to accept that there should have been either more or less A's in the past and that there should be more or less A's in the future. We can distinguish three interestingly different kinds of worlds that are possible relative to what we know. Most naturally, there is a set of possible worlds just like the present one, except that various numbers of A's occur in the future. Any one of these, for all we know, may be the actual world.

There is also a set of possible worlds just like the present one, except that various numbers of A's occur in the past. We may or may not be in a position to say which of these is actual. There is a certain sense in which we cannot regard the possibility of there having been more or less A's in the past than there actually were as a 'real' possibility in the sense in which we can regard it as a 'real' possibility that more or less A's will occur in the future. But, again, there is nothing inconsistent with our knowledge of the sample we have observed, and nothing inconsistent with the chance statement, about supposing that there were more or less A's in the past.

Finally, there is a set of possible worlds like the present one, except that it lacks the sample of A's we actually took. These worlds are inconsistent with our body of knowledge in that our body of knowledge contains knowledge of these A's; but it is perfectly consistent with a body of knowledge containing the chance statement we have accepted.

The chance statement we accept about A's imposes constraints on all these possible worlds; it thus enables the statement to support counterfactuals (if more children had been born in the eighteenth century, roughly half of them would have been males), and it accounts generally for their limited appearance of intensionality.

It is worth comparing chance statements of this sort with acceptable empirical universal generalizations (if there are any).[8] Suppose we find the empirical generalization, 'All A's are B's' acceptable, where the set of A's is large and extends both into the past and into the future. We may use such statements as warrants for subjunctives and counterfactuals: If x should turn out to be an A, it will be a B. Were y to have been an A, it would have been a B as well. But we need not attribute any non-extensional content to the generalization itself; it may represent no more than the brute extensional fact that in the actual world (whichever among the for-all-we-know-possible worlds it may be) it is true the set of A's is included in the set of B's.[9]

Does it make sense, in this case, to distinguish between chance and frequency statements—that is, to suppose that although the *chance* of an A's being a C is p, the proportion of A's that are C's in the actual world is q, where q is different from p?[10] Consider the possible worlds in which the number of A's is different from the actual number of A's. First, to have reason to believe that the chance of an A being a C is p, is to have reason to believe that the frequency, in any of these worlds, is p. Second, suppose that in fact it turns out that the frequency of C's among A's in the future is such that the overall frequency of C's among A's is q rather than p. This does not show that our original statement concerning the chance of an A being a C was unwarranted; but it does show that it was wrong. Given our original statement asserting that the chance is p, such a world is not among the possible ones. Note that this is an impossibility—not an improbability via Bernoulli's theorem. What we infer (*in this actuarial case*) is just that the frequency is (about) p. If the frequency turns out to be other than (about) p, we have simply been wrong—however sound our original statistical inference.

Despite the fact that the chance statement can be used to support counterfactuals, there is no ground here for distinguishing between chance and frequency. The content of the statement we infer from the sample is precisely that in all the worlds construed as possible (relative to that statement) the frequency with which A's are C's is about p. Again, whether these statements are to be considered 'chance' statements, they certainly are statements that can serve to found probabilities; and whether or not they are considered 'chance' statements, they are straightforwardly extensional.

9. SAMPLING

It might be maintained that statistical knowledge of the sort we have been considering is simply not 'science' at all, and that a bare frequency, unfounded by any theoretical account, is too crude, too 'empirical' to deserve the honorific title of 'science'. This suggestion is unhelpful for two reasons, one controversial and one obvious. The controversial reason is that (at least, so I believe) at the heart of every theoretical structure is a set of brute empirical frequencies which themselves have no further theoretical underpinnings. If nowhere else, it lies in the theory of error which allows us to form a connection between a body of scientific doctrine and the real world of actual observation and experience. The obvious reason is that even if we restrict 'science' in the suggested way, a great deal of what we know about the world—including much that is of paramount importance in guiding our day-to-day decisions—will fall outside the domain of 'science', and will nevertheless be codified in chance statements that are, like those we have just been considering, based relatively directly on observed frequencies.

Whether they are science or not, then, we must account for the kinds of statements we have been discussing. One attempt to assimilate them to more 'scientific' statements is to argue that in these cases, although we are looking directly at frequencies, we are supposing that there is some genuine theoretical chance mechanism underlying the frequencies.[11] The argument that this 'must' be the case hinges on the assumption that chance statements must be interpreted in some deep nomological sense. Since I see no necessity for making that assumption, nor see any ground for making it, the argument never gets off the ground.

The best attempt (although it fails, too) to assimilate the kinds of cases we have been talking about the strict chance statements is that provided by Isaac Levi.[12] Consider (writes Levi) the simple direct inference: 90 percent of Swedes are Protestant; Peterson is a Swede, and that is all X knows about him; therefore X should take probability that Peterson is a Protestant to be 0.9. This argument fails, according to Levi: "I see no compelling reason why rational X should be obliged to make a credence judgment of that sort on the basis of the knowledge given. X does not know whether the way in which Peterson came to be selected for presentation to him is, or is not, in some way, biased in favor of selecting more Swedish Catholics than are represented in the Swedish population as a whole." For the argument to go through: "X should know that Peterson has been selected from the Swedish population according to some procedure F and also know that the chance of obtaining a Protestant on selecting a Swede according to procedure F is equal to the percentage of Swedes who are Protestants." And, regarding the procedure: "In practice, methods of selecting members of some population having the required property involve using tables of random numbers or some stochastic device."

First, let us suppose that percentage of Protestants is 90, and let us suppose that the population of Sweden has been carefully numbered, and that Peterson has been chosen with the help of a table of random numbers. The method F, then, by which Peterson is chosen is indeed a method which, to the best of our knowledge, would choose each member of the population with equal frequency in the long run. I claim that this is neither necessary nor sufficient for X to be rationally bound to have a degree of belief of 0.90 in Peterson's Protestantism. For the lack of necessity, I can only confront Levi's intuitions with my own: it seems plain to me that if all X knows about Peterson is that he is a Swede it would be utterly whimsical and irrational of him to pick some number out of the air (0.5, say) and take that as his degree of credence. As for the lack of sufficiency, there is nothing in our story that prevents X from being Peterson himself. There is nothing that prevents the method from picking out a village priest who is well known to X. Under either of these circumstances (and under as many more as you would like to make up) it is clearly inappropriate and irrational for X's credence in the proposition that Peterson is a Protestant to be 0.9. One way to save the sufficiency of the condition that Peterson be selected by a random method as grounds for X's credence judgment would be to add the requirement that that is *all* X knows about Peterson—i.e., that he is a Swede selected by method F. I do not know whether Levi would endorse this requirement, however, and even if he did, to spell it out in detail would seem to amount to much the same thing as spelling out in detail the requirement that Levi dismissed earlier as inadequate: that all X knows about Peterson is that he is a Swede. Knowing that the *chance* that method F will select a Protestant is 0.9, and that Peterson was selected by method F seems to me quite analogous, for all epistemological and decision-theoretic purposes, to knowing that 90% of Swedes are Protestant, and that Peterson is a Swede, and nothing else about him.

Second, there is a lurking, and, to my mind vicious, circularity or regress in the requirement that the method F be random, or have the property that each Swede have the same chance of being selected by it. Levi mentions tables of random numbers of stochastic devices. We must, of course, be quite sure that each digit (and each pair of digits, etc.) in the table occurs equally *often* in the long run, and we must be quite sure that each outcome of the stochastic device occurs equally often in the long run. (Or, 'with the same chance'.) If the grounds on which we were sure of these things were statistical—inference from a sample of the numbers or from a sample of trials of the stochastic device—we might well be faced with a vicious circularity of one sort: what chance mechanism can we use for taking the sample of random numbers, or the sample of trials of the stochastic device, when we have to have the well-constructed table of random numbers or the fair stochastic device to take samples in the correct way?

But let us suppose that we don't have to learn about the table of random numbers or the stochastic device inductively. Let us suppose that we simply construct the table of random numbers (in actual fact such tables are edited to remove any digits or combinations of digits that occur with excessive frequency), or that we can come to know about the random device on purely theoretical grounds. *Even so,* a vicious circularity or regress is ready to pounce. Suppose that the method F, as required, uses a table of random numbers or a stochastic device to pick out a Swede. Described more fully, the method F constitutes a function from *outcomes* (of selecting a number from the table, or conducting a trial with the stochastic device) to *Swedes*. Given the outcome, we have obtained our Swede. Whatever reasons we have for wanting to put constraints on the method of selecting a Swede in the first place, will therefore be reasons for wanting to put constraints on the selection of a random number or a trial of the stochastic device. Consider the table of random numbers. It is a finite collection of numbers, just as the population of Swedes is a finite collection of Swedes. In order for X to have a basis for his judgment about Peterson, he must know that Peterson was 'selected for presentation to him' by a method F that gives to each Swede an equal chance of selection. Since F is simply a function from the table of random numbers to Swedes, X must know that the *number* that is *selected* from the table of random numbers is selected by a method F', which gives to each Swede an equal chance of being selected. This will be assured, if F' gives to each number in the table an equal chance of being selected. It will surely *not* be assured (on Levi's view) if it is merely the case that 'all we know' about the number is that it comes from the table. The use of tables of random numbers thus invites infinite regress that can only be terminated by the use of a stochastic device.

How about the outcome of a stochastic device? The trial and its outcome are not 'selected' at all, but merely *given*. But if this is acceptable, it is unclear why Peterson himself, who is also 'merely given', is not acceptable in the first place. If he is not acceptable, it is because we know something special about the trial—for example that its outcome is mapped into a Swede we happen to know to be a Catholic. It is hard to see, in principle, what we have accomplished by the introduction of the stochastic device.

A favorite stochastic device for selecting a sample—e.g., for deciding in an experiment which subjects are to be the experimental group and which the control group—is a deck of red and black cards in the appropriate numbers. If m out of N are to be in the experimental group, the deck will consist of m red cards and $N - m$ black cards. The candidates are ordered (quite arbitrarily); the deck is *then* shuffled; and candidates are put into one group or another according to whether the card that corresponds to their place in the arbitrary order is red or black. The principle is the same as that of drawing straws. We might say that the credence, for X, that Peterson is a Protestant is 0.9 only if X knows that Peterson got the short straw.

In this instance the regress is patent. As Levi has said on many occasions, (what is in fact but a paraphrase of his assertions about Peterson): the chance of drawing a black card is *not* the same thing as the proportion of black cards in the deck, even though it *may* under certain circumstances, have the same value. It will in fact have the same value, only when the drawing is done by a certain procedure P, which is such that . . . .

In practice, of course, it is another matter. Confronted by a roomful of Swedes—tall ones and short ones, skinny ones and fat ones, men and women— it would be very hard to pick one at 'random' in such a way as to justify the credence judgment about Protestantism. One would be pulled in various directions: the dark haired fellow? No, he might have Mediterranean ancestry; but that tall one with the broad head may be more likely to be Protestant; and . . . So it is vastly simpler and more agreeable to everyone to use a table of random numbers, or to draw lots. But the argument for this is *not* that it is a way of insuring the operation of a chance element; it is that at the stage of drawing a number it is easier to be in a state of adequate ignorance so that the passage from frequency to probability not be disturbed.

I conclude, then, that nothing stands in the way of basing probabilities on simple frequencies in certain cases; the efforts to assimilate frequency and distribution statements that concern finite populations to more theoretical strict chance statements are, at least in these simple situations about which I have been speaking, misguided and ineffective.

It should be observed that this is not either a trivial or a small number of cases: it includes the probabilities based on actuarial and demographic statistics; many of the probabilities encountered in biology; most of the probabilities encountered in the social sciences; most of the probabilities encountered in medicine, and so on. In short, it covers the probabilities that are based on the statistical and distribution statements that apply, to the best of our belief, to actual large populations in this world. In these cases, even if we had knowledge concerning populations in possible worlds, our knowledge about the actual world would be a better guide to action and belief in the actual world.

I have argued that from an epistemological point of view—from the point of view which demands of probability that it function as a guide in life—the interpolation of a 'chance method' between a population of known characteristics and a probability judgment is neither necessary nor sufficient for the validity of the 'direct inference'. One further difficulty should be noted. (Though it pertains only to inferences from infinite populations, this seems to be the appropriate place for it.) Suppose that we know that X is normally distributed in a certain population, with an unknown mean μ and variance 1. We select a sample of 10, by whatever method is taken to suffice to insure the validity of the direct inference. We know that the difference between the sample mean, $\bar{x}$, and μ, is distributed normally with mean 0 and variance 1/10. Since conditions for the direct inference are satisfied, we may infer that the probability that this difference falls in any interval is given by the integral of the normal distribution of mean 0 and variance 1/10, taken over that interval. But similarly, we know that the difference between the sample median, m, and μ is distributed normally with mean 0 and variance $\pi/20$. We may therefore also infer that the probability that *this* difference falls in any interval is given by the integral of the normal distribution of mean 0 and variance $\pi/20$—since we are still assuming that the conditions for direct inference are satisfied. But let us suppose in a particular case that we in fact observe that $\bar{x}$ and m are both equal to 3. We will, if the conditions for direct inference are still satisfied, be led to contrary probability judgments. Since the sample is the same sample, from the same population, it is hard to see how conditions for direct inference that merely pertain to the method by which the sample is selected can be of help. In particular, the inclusion of a 'chance' element clearly will not help us to choose between the two conflicting probabilities.

10. CASE IV

Let us consider trials on a chance setup and suppose that the grounds we have for accepting a frequency or distribution statement characterizing outcomes on that chance set-up are actuarial—that is, that we have made a large number of trials on that chance setup and have inferred those distribution or frequency statements. For example, we might have drawn balls from the urn of Case I by a certain method M, and inferred that under that method each ball has an equal chance of being *drawn*. Or we have rolled a die with a certain device, and concluded that the distribution of points is thus and so. Or (more realistically) we have produced a series of items on a certain machine, and concluded that the distribution of diameters is such and such.

What distinguishes this case from the previous ones is that the population is under our control, and our results seem to be independent of the size of that population. Thus in drawing balls from the urn by method M, we may infer, after a certain number of trials, that the chance that M will select a given ball is the same for each ball. When we have done our experiment, we conclude that the same holds for all applications of method M—by which we mean all possible applications, and not merely those that we happen to have made in gathering our data. And we suppose that this is so, even if we never use method M again. In a certain sense our conclusion seems to go beyond not only our data, but beyond any actual set of trials. It seems to concern possible trials, and thus to launch us irrevocably into the marvelous realm of possible worlds, modalities, intensions, and the like. The same is true of our rolls of a die; the same is true of the production of a given machine.

Let us suppose that our chance set-up is self-actuated, and goes on clicking away, turning out results of trials for year after year for (let us say) a hundred years. Then we could easily assimilate Case IV to Case III; the population we are interested in is the set of results produced by the setup; we have observed a sample of those results; and we have concluded that certain frequencies or certain distributions are characteristic of the population as a whole. But this is not the case: the chance setup operates only when we operate it, and, after we have obtained our 'sample', we can pull the plug, destroy the apparatus, and never again perform a trial on it.

We *might* not. We might, if we wished, and time and money sufficed, go on and perform 10^{10} trials on the apparatus, or $10^{(10^{10})}$ trials. The sample of trials that we did perform gives us perfectly good information about the characteristics that this long series would have were it to be performed. The only trouble is that it is not performed. But is this a trouble? Surely if we wish to form a proper degree of belief concerning an outcome of a trial that was actually made, but of which we have no detailed knowledge, the statistics of those trials are precisely what we should depend on.

The difficulty becomes a difficulty only if we want to consider some more trials that *will* be performed, or if we want to say what *would* be the case if more trials *were* to be performed.

Before discussing this question, let us look back at Case III. There we considered frequency and distribution statements which pertained to the actual world, but which were realistic in the sense that they were about classes whose extensions were, though specified, specified with a margin of vagueness. We don't know exactly how many mosquitoes of the species in question there are; nor how many thousand-pound Black Angus steers we are talking about, nor (exactly) how many 65-year-old ladies we are talking about. And it doesn't matter. The inference is just as sound, the frequency or distribution statement just as good a basis for probability statements, regardless of whether there are a few more or a few less individuals in the subject class, indeed whether there are a lot more or less. Our inference, and our inferred statement, though it is about the actual world, is about a world we do not thoroughly know. One must be very cautious, especially nowadays, in talking about possible worlds; but it is tempting to say that in Case III examples, our inference is good for any one of a number of possible worlds that, for all we know, might be actual. If there were a few more mosquitoes, we could swallow them without straining. Does this way of talking commit us to intensionality for distribution and frequency statements? Surely not. Our statements are intended to apply to the actual world—whichever one of those possible actual worlds it may be.

Now let us look back at the trials of the chance setup. Suppose that it is not we, but a friend of a friend who operates the chance setup. We do not know what his plans are—perhaps he will quit once he has accumulated enough evidence for us to make an inference, or perhaps he won't; perhaps he will keep on while breath yet remains. Under *these* circumstances it seems that we can assimilate Case IV to Case III. We don't know exactly how many trials will be run on the setup, but, however many, we have adequate evidence to suppose that the frequencies or distributions are what we inferred them to be from our sample. The actual size of the population has very little bearing on the soundness of the inference. The statements we infer are intended to apply to the actual world, which is one of the possible worlds in which $E + n$ trials are made on the setup, where E is the number of trials we have used as evidence, and n is any integer whatever. Of course if we know that $n = 0$, we have very precise information indeed about the frequencies and distributions; but if n is larger than (say) k, it won't make much difference how much larger it is. Since we don't know how large n is, and since our knowledge of the frequencies and distributions is simply a bit vaguer when n is larger than when n is 0, what we properly claim as knowledge about that actual world is the (set of) distributions that apply to large values of n.

What we can say when the chance setup is operated by a friend of a friend we can say when we operate it ourselves, so long as we haven't made up our minds how often to conduct trials on it. Again we are in Case III: the distribution statements we accept and use as a basis for direct inference, or for calculating probabilities, are straightforwardly extensional, objective statements about the actual world.

This is no longer the case when we decide to smash the apparatus after conducting E trials. This cruel and wanton *act* of ours throws a monkey wrench into the analysis. We have two alternatives: first, we can simply take into account that those are all the trials there are of that apparatus, give the explicit enumeration of the results as our distribution, and suppose that we are in Case I. This is not always implausible. It provides, for example, the correct distribution and the correct probabilities if we are interested in the outcomes of trials that have actually been performed and we have thrown away or forgotten the list of specific outcomes of each trial. (Thus if R occurs a fraction p of the time among the E trials, the probability is p that trial number m produced R, so long as we have no special knowledge about m.) Alternatively, if our interest extends to trials that we might have but did not perform, then we need merely *pretend* that we are in a world in which at least $E + k$ trials are performed. What kind of a locution is this? It means that we regard the actual set of trials as a truncation of a set of $E + k$ trials. To be on the safe side, let us suppose the actual set of trials is regarded as a truncation of a set of 10^{10} trials. This represents, to be sure, a merely possible world, at best. But it is a specific possible world: it is a world which was kept from being actual only by our *decision* to cut off the experiments on the chance setup. The frequency and distribution statements that characterize the outcomes in the large set of trials also characterize the outcomes in the actual set of trials. (If 45% of the results in the actual set of trials are of type R, then, say, between 44% and 46% of the results in the hypothetical set are of type R, and this interval statement is what we take to be our knowledge. But it is still true that in the actual set of trials between 44% and 46% are of type R; and it is only as a result of a decision on our part to break the machine that we know that the stronger statement is true of actual trials.)

This is not significantly different from our treatment of Case III. The distribution statement we come to make about the mosquitoes characterizes the actual population, but also some nearby hypothetical ones. The distribution statement we accept about the outcomes of the chance setup characterized not only the actual set of trials, but also some hypothetical ones. It is this latter fact that allows us to use our statistical knowledge counterfactually: if we *had* run another trial, the probability *is* (0.44, 0.46) that we would have gotten a result R.

Let T be the (generic) set of trials of the chance setup. We can say that our knowledge of distributions and frequencies applies to any truncation (of which the actual set of trials is a part) of any set of 10^{10} trials. Let us call such a world a T-ful world. If we know that only E trials are made, we know something more; but what we know is in a sense accidental. The *general* knowledge we have obtained applies to any truncation of a T-ful world, and thus may serve to support counterfactuals involving possible trials, as well as to characterize the actual set of trials.

At this point we have, indeed, gone off the deep end. Construed this way frequency and distribution statements do have an intensional component: they do concern other worlds than this one. But these other worlds are very much like this one—in fact they all include this world as an initial part. Furthermore, in the T-ful worlds, containing 10^{10} trials, of which the actual set of trials is a truncation, the frequency and distribution statements are again perfectly extensional. Of course there are a number of T-ful worlds—there are, so far as we know, after we have obtained the evidence of E trials, a lot of ways in which the 10^{10} trials *might* turn out, although they all have in common the *same* distributions and frequencies.

Note that we are not here inferring the chance that the frequency in the large class is p from the premise that the chance in a single case is p; we are not using Bernoulli's theorem here, any more than we use it when we are making an inference from a sample to a distribution in a finite actual population. What we infer is that the frequency *is* p. To accept that is to rule out worlds in which the frequency differs from p as impossible, not merely as improbable.

When we have covered the next two cases, we shall return, in more detail, to the question of the semantics of chance statements, and in particular to the question of their intensionality.

11. CASE V

Let us once again consider trials on a chance setup, but let us suppose that the grounds we have for accepting a frequency or distribution statement characterizing outcomes of the chance setup are not actuarial, but theoretical. Thus, for example, we might consider throws of a icosahedron performed on a machine which is such that on general physical grounds we could infer that the frequency with which each side results is equal. Furthermore, we can suppose that in this case, there are *no* trials made, so that the set of trials, in the actual word, is extensionally identical to the set of trials made on some other kind of chance setup (say, one with a loaded icosahedron) on which no trials are made either. Here there seems to be an obvious and serious failure of extensionality.

In Case II, we supposed that we were sampling from a larger population, and that the inference which resulted in the addition to our body of knowledge of the chance statement in question was a straightforward statement about that large population, even though the boundaries of membership in that population might be a bit vague or imprecise. In Case IV, in which again the basis of our knowledge of chances was assumed to be actuarial, we found it natural to expand our interpretation of the chance statements slightly in order to take account of *possible* populations. But even here there was assumed to be an actual population (of trials) in the actual world, of which the inferred chance statement was true, and which could be considered a truncation of any of a number of large possible populations. In the present case we can come to accept the chance statement in the *absence* of a large amount of actuarial data, and thus without being assured of a large population in the actual world of which the chance statement is true. Indeed, we may assume that in the actual world there are *no* members of the population that the chance statement is about.

Nevertheless, much the same gambit will work. A population of trials containing no instances, after all, can be construed as a (rather severe) truncation of a population of possible trials. But we must still specify what this possible population is, and what its properties are. Let us take the population to consist of a large number (say, 10^{10}) of trials on the specified chance setup. The chance setup must be specified: it must be a chance setup of a specified kind K, or we would not be able to infer on the basis of a general theory what the distribution or frequency characterizing the chance on that setup should be. Futhermore, we must have in our body of knowledge both some sort of theory, and some sort of boundary conditions connecting the theory to the kind K, which will enable us to derive the chance statement we suppose to have been admitted into our body of knowledge on theoretical grounds. Two examples will help to indicate what I have in mind.

Consider first the icosahedron. We may suppose that no icosahedron has ever been or ever will be manufactured. The chance setup consists of taking a hard, elastic icosahedron, rattling it about in a cup, and throwing it onto a hard, elastic, surface. The sides are numbered from 1 to 20. The 'outcome' is the number of the side on which the icosahedron comes to rest. We would naturally suppose that the chance of its landing on each side was roughly equal. The grounds for this supposition are: that a hard elastic body thrown onto a hard elastic surface will bounce around a lot, and that very small differences between the sets of momenta characterizing one throw and those characterizing another throw will lead to different outcomes, and that this will be so over quite a wide range of initial momenta. (I am supposing we are taking account of all six independent momenta in three-dimensional space.) A boundary condition that enables us to compute chances (roughly) from these theoretical considerations is that under the circumstances described there will indeed be a fairly wide range of momenta on any set of trials. It might be a little hard to show, but it would be possible to show, on this basis, that in any reasonably large set of trials, whatever (within reasonable limits) the distribution of initial momenta, the distribution of outcomes would be relatively uniform. Note that we are *not* assuming here anything about chances of the outcomes on single throws: we consider a large set of initial momenta having a distribution that satisfied our boundary conditions, and is otherwise undetermined.[13] (In practice, of course, we would simplify the argument and the calculations by supposing that this distribution is continuous and relatively smooth; but this is just a way of making the argument easier.)

Note also that the argument does *not* require Bernoulli's theorem, unless we suppose (what I am saving for the next case) that there is a probabilistic element within the theory itself—for example, if we assumed that there were only a probabilistic connection between the fully specified momenta, distances, coefficients of elasticity, masses, temperatures, and so on, and the outcome of a single trial. We do not have to assume that there is no probabilistic element, either; all we have to assume is that relatively small changes in momenta will be accompanied by different outcomes.

Consider, at the other end of the extreme, a chance setup like Levi's,[14] which involves hitting a bottle with a hammer. The outcome is the number of pieces the bottle breaks into. We don't have any very clear idea of the chance that the bottle will break into ten pieces—which is as it should be. We do have a rather loose theory of material failure, according to which the force and angle and place of the hammer blow will determine how a bottle with a certain internal structure (of thickness, etc.) will break. We do not have, as we had in the previous example, a fairly clear and precise idea of how variations in these factors will produce variations in the outcomes. We might be able to say that on a large number of trials, in which the hammer blows are directed at the same place on the bottle, and the bottles are fairly uniform, that there would be a most frequent outcome and that outcomes increasingly far removed from that outcome will occur with decreasing frequency. We might thus be able to say that on a large number (say 10^{10}) of trials, the frequency function describing the distribution of outcomes would be any one of a large class having the properties that it has a maximum (say) somewhere between $N = 5$ and $N = 50$ and that its value for N less than or equal to 0 is 0, and for N greater than 10,000 is 0, and that it is steadily decreasing for values of N on either side of its maximum.

Again this is not a matter of applying Bernoulli's theorem, or any probabilistic argument, but of making deductive inferences according to a theory of material failure, on the basis of some assumptions regarding the distribution of the relevant physical characteristics of the hammer blows. We come to a conclusion about the distribution of outcomes in a possible population of trials. It is not a very definite conclusion; but how could it be, on the basis of such a loosely specified trial? This is to be contrasted with Levi's treatment of the bottle-breaking problem: he claims that the chance of Pepsi bottle *b* breaking into ten pieces when hit with a hammer 'will be well defined'. He does not suggest *how* it could be defined. Nor does he suggest any way (nor even that he believes there is any way) to discover the values of such chances. If they exist, they are certainly practically useless, and, so far as I can tell, metaphysically useless as well.

What we know in these cases, then, is a distribution in a large possible population. We do not know the distribution precisely, even though it is known on theoretical grounds. What we know is that one of a number of distributions (which may, as in the case of the Pepsi bottle, cover quite a wide range) characterizes this possible population. Even in the case in which the computation of the distribution is based on quite simple and clear-cut theories and boundary conditions, there will be a certain looseness of fit: a chance setup, specified in empirical terms, cannot be so precisely specified, and the boundary conditions cannot be so precisely specified, that a theory will lead to exactly one distribution in the corresponding possible population. The possible population is determined by the specification of the chance setup and its boundary conditions. We take the actual population to be a truncation of this possible population.

12. CASE VI

Here we are concerned, not with a chance setup characterized empirically, but with an idealized chance setup. We consider, for example, the chance of a perfectly fair coin landing heads, tossed under ideally randomized circumstances; the chance of an atom in a certain state undergoing a transition to another state; the chance of a line, dropped at random on a unit circle, cutting off a chord of length less than $\pi/2$. Many writers, even down-to-earth empirical fellows like van Fraassen, seem to take this to be the special paradigm case of all talk of probabilities and chances.[15] But these are not the ordinary cases. The ordinary cases are those like the first three we discussed. (Talk of chances in relation to *ordin-*

ary gambling apparatus, for example, falls under Case III; what interests poker players as a basis for their probability judgments is the question of what proportion of one-card draws in the past and future history of poker will result in the completing of a flush. If there were an official 'chance' which differed from that frequency, I can see no reason why they should be interested in it.)

It is only with the development of relatively sophisticated physical theories, and relatively sophisticated mathematical apparatus for dealing with them, that cases like Case V become of interest; they have been of interest, then, for only a few hundred years. And most of the cases like our present case are of even more recent vintage. There is an exception, not among common folk, but among mathematicians and natural philosophers. Any of the cases that are like our Case V can be idealized. To idealize such a case sufficiently, to idealize it to the point where no actual chance setup could ever satisfy the description, to consider a sequence of trials that could never be performed, under conditions that could never be established, and which, if established, could never be known to be established, would, of course, lead us directly to a case of type VI. And mathematicians and natural philosophers are, as we all know, prone to just this kind of idealization. So among that relatively select group Case VI chances have been considered for as long as Case V chances.

It appears to be the case that many of the applications of probability theory in the sciences can only be construed as examples of Case VI chances. This appearance is misleading. There is no room for continuous distributions, for example, in any case we have considered before; yet most of the distributions that are discussed in scientific texts and papers are continuous. Even in the standard, commonplace, Gaussian theory of error, it is assumed that in the absence of systematic error, errors will be distributed normally about a mean of 0. Nothing can be distributed normally in a finite class. It is supposed that the diameters of ball bearings produced by a certain machine are distributed normally about a designed diameter (say); but for this to be true of the actual product of the machine would require the machine to be eternal and indestructible. Obviously all such assertions as these are intended to hold only approximately. For errors of measurement of the weight of a penny to be distributed normally entails that there is a finite chance that the measurement will be in error by a thousand pounds; and indeed with half that chance that the observation will yield a negative weight of about half a ton. Similarly, there will be a finite chance that the ball-bearing machine will produce a ball bearing of negative diameter. Thus in considering the frequency and importance of Case VI chances, one should not be misled by the frequency with which continuous distribution functions are used to characterize *approximately* those distributions in populations that are acknowledged to be finite. In such instances the continuous distributions are no more than convenient approximations to what we really have grounds for believing.

The genuine case of this sort is one in which there is in our body of knowledge a theory that contains among its primitive assertions statements of chances (in the form of density functions or distribution functions) and which yields the chance statement in question.

It is characteristic of such chance statements that they must be construed as being about an infinite possible population; but the chance statements themselves contain an implicit characterization of that population. Consider, as an elementary example, the assertion that the chance of heads on an ideal toss of a an ideal coin on an ideal surface is a half. The population on which the chance distribution is to hold is no longer even a possible population: it is an impossibly ideal population, to start with, and needs to be countably infinite, to boot. What makes the coin ideal is that it is perfectly elastic, has a perfectly even, radial distribution of mass, and yet has distinguishable sides. What makes the surface ideal is its flatness and elasticity. (Scratch 'perfectly'—we don't want the coin bouncing ideally forever!) None of this requires an infinite population. But we also require that the tossing mechanism be such as to provide the coin with a continuous, smooth distribution of momenta. It doesn't matter what shape this distribution is, so long as it contains no very sudden changes. The ideality of the coin and the surface, then, amount to the condition that *arbitrarily* small changes in momenta will reverse the outcome from heads to tails and vice versa. It is not hard to show that the smallest set of objects which can have a continuous distribution of a random quantity is a countably infinite set (and futher, that any continuous distributions can be modeled in a countable set). This possible population (which indeed has a frequency of heads exactly equal to a half [with probability 1] as we can easily show deductively) is generated (in imagination) by the ideal tossings of the ideal coin. It is thus *given* as ordered. Indeed, it is composed of the very same sequence of objects (trials) as is characterized by the assumed (arbitrary) distribution of momenta.

Since the population is not really possible (ideal coins don't exist) we need not construe any actual population as a truncation of it. But ideal cases do have functions—in simplifying computations, in providing insights that in fact may have actual applications, in providing an approximation to the actual. The connection between this case, and that of the chance that a real coin will land heads as might have been considered under Case V, is the following: In the case of the possible population of tossing of a real coin, our knowledge is only approximate: all we can plausibly claim to know is that the frequency of heads is *about* a half. But we can in a number of ways measure how closely a real coin and tossing apparatus approximates the imaginary ideal case we have been discussing; and we can assert that the closer the real coin and tossing apparatus approximates the ideal imaginary one, the closer will the frequency of heads in the possible population (of which the actual population is a truncation), approximate a half.

Let us now turn to the quantum mechanical case. For the sake of constructing a more informative example (though at the risk of getting out of my depth in physics) let me suppose that the chance statement we are concerned with gives the chance of an atom of A, in state S_1 undergoing a transition to state S_2 is $1/\sqrt{2}$. This is not a statement about an imaginary population of atoms, as the preceding statement was about an imaginary population of tosses; on the other hand, the *value* of the chance has been cleverly chosen so that only an infinite population can have a frequency corresponding to that chance. We may be further puzzled by the fact that there seems to be no natural order (as there was in the previous example) in which the infinite population might be generated. And we may be quite baffled by the further reflection that (on the latest picture of things) there are only a finite number of atoms in the universe anyway.

But we can give a model of the theory in the same spirit as our previous models. Suppose that the set of such atoms is finite, or that we restrict our concerns to some finite portion of the universe. At any given time, then, only a finite number of atoms of A are in S_1. Assuming that things don't happen infinitely rapidly, so that (let us say) during an interval of time Δt, there are more than a finite number of atoms in S_1, the temporal order will give us a segment of our countable sequence. What the chance statement tells us is that in this possibly hypothetical infinite sequence, the limiting frequency of transitions is $1/\sqrt{2}$.

I call the sequence 'possibly hypothetical' because it does depend on a temporal order, and although the theory does not allow changes in the laws (its says what the laws are) it need not entail the sequence is infinite. In fact, it might entail that it is not—it might deny the creation of atoms A in state S_1, or predict that at some point in time there will be no atoms of A left at all. Or it might concern, not atoms, but artifically created particles of which, we may suppose, that no more than a handful ever come to exist. And therefore, as before, we conclude that what the chance statement says about the actual sequence is that it is a truncation of a possible population characterized by a certain frequency—the difference being that in this case the possible population must be construed as an infinite sequence. But the infinitude of the sequence is all right, because it is the theory itself—and not any inference for actuarial data —that tells us what its properties are.

Actually, there are any number of infinite sequences of which the actual population (if it is finite) may be the initial segment. But what the theory says is that all of these infinite sequences are characterized by the same limiting frequency.

Bas van Fraassen makes much of the conflict between limiting frequencies (in general) and countable additivity (in general).[16] Countable additivity is a generally assumed property in stochastic theories, or theories in which (as I would prefer to put it) chance statements occur fundamentally. But on the present analysis there is no question of providing a *general* limiting frequency interpretation of chances *in general.* We are forced to consider limiting frequencies only in the context of theories; and the theories which force us to consider limiting frequencies specify (as they clearly must) what quantities are to be construed as countably additive. The same theories specify (implicitly) the (set of) infinite sequences that are intended to be models of the theories, and of which the actual sequence is to be a (possibly improper) initial segment or truncation. And it is hardly plausible to suppose that there can be a conflict or inconsistency between an acceptable theory and its models!

The lesson to be learned from van Fraassen's examples and arguments is not that the frequencies and countable additivity conflict, but that, *if* a stochastic theory fails to specify exactly what properties, sets, random quantities it is concerned with measuring, *then* it jolly well ought to, since we cannot assume that every definable thing is countably additive. This applies only to *theories* — our Case VI; for only there do we have infinite sequences at all, and so only there does the question of countable additivity even come up.

Let us now look at the geometrical example. There are two classical analyses of this problem; they are jointly known as Bertrand's paradox, because they are inconsistent, yet both perfectly plausible.

Analysis One: The line will fall on the circle a certain distance X from the center of the circle. If we suppose that X is simply chosen at random between 0 and r, the radius of the circle, we may compute that the chance that the line will cut off a chord longer than the side of the inscribed equilateral triangle will be a half.

Analysis Two: Consider the central angle Y made by the radii intersecting the ends of the chord. This angle varies between 0 (when the line is tangent to the circle) and 2π (when the line cuts the center of the circle). Assume that Y is evenly distributed between 0 and 2π, and it is easy to compute that the chance that the line will cut off a chord longer than the side of the inscribed equilateral triangle will be 2/3.

Both arguments are completely hypothetical, and both concern imaginary populations. The populations are different, for in one we suppose that X has a uniform distribution, and in the other we suppose that Y has a uniform distribution. (Note that in the coin example, and in the icosahedron example, we only obtained a chance statement about one quantity by making certain assumptions regarding the distribution of another quantity — the momenta. In that case, subject to some smoothness conditions, it didn't matter what that distribution was. In this case it does.) Furthermore, the populations (infinite sequences) are determined by (in fact are the same as) the populations for which the respective distributions of X and Y are supposed to hold. (The assumption that X has a uniform distribution between 0 and r entails that the population over which X has this distribution be at least countably infinite.)

As a mathematical curiosity, this is an end of the matter. But if, as in the example of the imaginary coin, it is supposed that the analysis of this problem can throw some light on physical events, we must be a little more careful. It was pretty clear how a real coin and tossing apparatus could approximate the ideal coin and ideal tossing apparatus. If we are throwing a two-by-four at a manhole cover, it is not clear which of the two analyses of the chord and the circle problem should be regarded as yielding on approximation. If either! (If we are really throwing the two-by-four at the center of the manhole cover the chances will approximate those of neither analysis, if the usual, approximately normal, distribution of error obtains. But of course all this puts us squarely in the actuarial realm of Cases III or IV.)

13. THE SEMANTICS AND INTENSIONALITY OF CHANCE

The cases I have considered are relatively exhaustive as far as statements of chance that we can ever have reason to accept are concerned. There may well be chance statements which we could never have reason to accept which would fail to fall into any of these categories. I leave them out of account, as being of interest only to theologians. I will be satisfied to have made sense of the chance statements we need for conducting human affairs and for understanding human science.

In Cases I, II, and III, we are considering actual populations. The chances are determined by the frequencies or distributions in those actual populations. In these cases, chance statements are perfectly extensional and not at all modal. This is not to say, even here, that they cannot support counterfactuals: If the tallest woman in England in 1851 had had one more child than she did, the chances are about even it would have been a boy. But if we have a true chance statement in our body of knowledge about the population A, and A and B have exactly the same members, then the corresponding chance statement about B will be true. The frequency of C, or the distribution of the random quantity X, will be the same in A as in B simply because it will have the same set of values: A and B *are* the same set. We can *suppose* that that A has some more (or some less) members than in fact it has without disturbing the chance statement; but this merely reflects the fact that when the chance statement is based on statistical inference, a minor change in the composition of the parent population would have no effect on the soundness of our inference. If we can draw a conclusion about a 10,000-member set on the basis of a sample of 1,000, we can draw the same conclusion about a 100,000 member set on the basis of the same sample. (Note that in Case I, where the populations are small and known by complete enumeration, this does not hold.)

We must, of course, be a little careful concerning the population that a casually enunciated chance statement is about. Thus Levi considers "The chance that a toss of coin a performed by Sidney Morgenbesser yields heads is a half,"[17] and ponders the paradox that this can be true even when we know that Sidney Morgenbesser tosses this coin only once. According to Levi this shows that chances can't be identified with frequencies. I consider this just a consequence of a loose way of speaking. Both Levi and I would agree that the probability that the toss in question landed heads is a half, and that is one of the ways in which the quoted sentence might be interpreted. The probability statement, however, is (on my view) based on a chance statement, and in this case the chance statement concerns the very large population of coins tossed in general (not as Levi suggests the population of tosses of coin a, which may itself be rather small). Thus it is not always the case that in any statement of the form 'The chance that an A is a C is p' the occurrence of A is extensional; but that is because such locutions are often used to express probabilities, and probability is no more extensional than provability. It is when the chance statement is one that we have reason to accept (reasons of the sort cited in Cases I, II, and III) and is not intended as a probability statement, but as the (potential) *ground* for a probability statement, that the occurrences of A and B are perfectly extensional .

Cases IV, V and VI are somewhat different, since in a certain sense they are about possible rather than actual populations. This is not troublesome in Case IV, for there we are assured of a fairly large actual population, and we *cannot* have grounds for supposing that the chances—the frequencies and distributions—in the large possible distribution are *different* from the frequencies and distributions in the actual populations we have taken for evidence. This can be true in Cases V and VI. But even in these cases, the chance statement is *about* a possible population (or an infinite sequence) and in this population is perfectly extensional. Thus when we have theoretical grounds for asserting that the chance that an A is a C is p (interpreted seriously as a real chance statement, rather than as one of the infinitely many ways of expressing probabilities), those very theoretical grounds determine the set A^* of which A is an improper, or proper, or total truncation. Now if B^* is in fact identical to A^*, the same frequencies will hold of B^* as of A^*. Frequency and distribution statements about the full populations are (obviously) perfectly extensional. In the truncations A and B this need not be so, since we can have $A = B$ without $A^* = B^*$. In these cases, the occurrence of A in 'The chance that an A is a C is p' is not extensional. But this failure of extensionality is limited. In an A-ful world—a world in which a full possible population of A's is present—there would not be a failure of extensionality.

If we construe chance statements as being about the full populations, there is no failure of extensionality at all. If A^* and B^* are both full populations, as specified earlier, and if $A^* = B^*$, then any distribution statement about A^* implies the corresponding distribution statement about B^*. The truth conditions are given for the full populations, and not for the truncation that happens to occur in the actual world.

In short: If the basis for our accepting a chance statement is actuarial—i.e., a statistical argument from a sample to a population—the population in question may be construed as a full one. If the basis for our accepting a chance statement is theoretical, then the population in question must be construed as being a full one.

The element of intensionality lies in the fact that A and B may be identical in this world, (particularly when both are empty) while a B-ful and an A-ful population may not be identical. To accept a chance statement $C(A)$ about A is to accept a statement with subjunctive overtones: *Should* this be a world full of A's, certain frequencies *will* obtain. Note that the degree of modal involvement is relatively minimal: If it is a theorem of our language that $A = B$, we will have $C(A)$ if and only if $C(B)$. If we accept a theory one of whose consequences is that $A = B$, we will have $C(A)$ if and only if $C(B)$. If our grounds for accepting $C(A)$ consist of a large sample of A's; if all the A's we encounter are also B's, and vice versa; and if both A and B are acceptable as reference classes, then we will have equal grounds for accepting $C(B)$: if $C(A)$ is acceptable, so is $C(B)$.

Chance statements are thus not mere codifications of statistical data; they go beyond the data on which they are based, and in some cases they are based on accepted theories rather than on any data. In almost all cases, if we focus on the right reference class (tosses of coins in general, rather than tosses of *this* coin *now*), the chance statement on which a probability is based can be construed as a purely extensional frequency. There may nevertheless be some chance statements based on accepted theories that are not fully extensional. The question is, what are we to make of their intensionality when it does exist? The answer, as I see it, is that we are to make relatively little of it.

NOTES

1. Among those who have offered one form or another of propensity or chance interpretation of 'probability' as it is allegedly used in scientific theories are Popper [18, 19]. Hacking [8], Levi [13], Giere [4], Fetzer [3], Mellor [16], Gillies [6], Smokler [20], Pollock [17], and van Fraassen [21]. Each has a theory somewhat different from that of the others (and some might even object to being put in this general group). I do not propose to attend to any of these approaches in analytic detail, though I shall mention Levi and van Fraassen later on.

2. Thus we might say, directly, that in the world we consider in Section 5 a chance of a half for landing heads is attributed to coins in general (of which there aren't any) and a chance of greater than a half is attributed to coins biased in favor of heads. I do not seriously doubt that some metaphysical sense could be made of such attributions. I do not, however, think that they constitute any sort of *analysis;* nor do I see any way in which we can have grounds for such attributions in that world. I thus regard such a semantics as a copout and a dead end.

3. Isaac Levi provides a treatment of inferences of this sort in 'Direct Inference'. His analysis differs from mine in three ways, corresponding to the three issues cited in the text: (1) He insists that the underlying statistical statement should be *strictly* a chance statement, and not reducible to any sort of extensional frequency statement; (2) He construes the 'probability' of the conclusion of a Direct Inference to reflect the credal state of the rational agent whose corpus is K, and thus allows it to be a subinterval of $[p, q]$, whereas I take the conclusion to be an objective logical probability which merely imposes constraints on the credal state of the rational agent; and (3) He takes the satisfaction of confirmational conditionalization to be a constraint that the conclusions of such inferences must satisfy, and rejects my explication of randomness because it leads to a violation of this constraint. The conflict between us concerning (3) is clearly more fundamental and more

important than the others; indeed, (2) might be construed as a terminological dispute. Nevertheless, it is our disagreement over (1) that constitutes an instance of the controversy under examination here. This footnote and the paragraph to which it is appended have emerged from a detailed correspondence with Levi, who endorses the substance, while deploring the terminology.

4. Levi [14].

5. And of course this is quite independent of questions of determinism and the like; even if the world is a chance mechanism in the strongest and most metaphysical sense, there is still a set of sentences that I would take (if only I could know them) as characterizing that part of the future of the world that concerns me.

6. van Fraassen [21].

7. But see Section 9 on the relevance of the method by which individuals are selected from classes.

8. It is tentatively argued that there aren't any in my paper, 'All Generalizations Are Analytic' (Chapter 19, this volume), and a similarly titled paper [10].

9. It is true that puzzles may be generated for this treatment. I think they can be handled. This is not the place to attempt to treat either the puzzles or the solutions.

10. Note that if the connection is given by Bernoulli's theorem, there would be nothing wrong with supposing that p and q were different, even though it would be very improbable that they should turn out to be significantly different.

11. This is the view, I take it, of Mellor [16] and Fetzer [3], for example.

12. Levi [14].

13. This is very hypothetical, because it may be that to have information about the possible distribution of momenta, we might have had to make an actuarial inference at some point, and this might provide us with a large actual population, and put us back into Case IV.

14. Levi [14].

15. van Fraassen [21].

16. van Fraassen [21].

17. Levi [14].

BIBLIOGRAPHY

[1] Fetzer, James H., 'Dispositional Probabilities', *Boston Studies in Philosophy of Science* 8 1970, ed. by Buck and Cohen, Reidel, Dordrecht, 1970, pp. 473-482.

[2] Fetzer, James H., 'Statistical Explanations', *PSA 1972*, ed by Schaffner and Cohen, Reidel, Dordrecht, 1974, pp. 337-347.

[3] Fetzer, James H., 'Statistical Probabilities: Single Case Propensities vs Long Run Frequencies', in Leinfellner and Kohler (eds.), *Developments in the Methodology of Social Science*, Reidel, Dordrecht, 1974, pp. 387-397.

[4] Giere, Ronald N., 'Objective Single Case Probabilities and the Foundations of Statistics', *Proceedings of the Fourth International Congress on Logic, Methodology and Philosophy of Science*, Bucharest, 1971.

[5] Giere, Ronald, '*The Matter of Chance*, by D. H. Mellor', (review), *Ratio* 15 (1973), pp. 149-155.

[6] Gillies, D. A., *An Objective Theory of Probability*, Methuen and Co., London, 1973.

[7] Hacking, Ian, 'On the Foundations of Statistics', *British Journal for the Philosophy of Science* 15 (1964-65), pp. 1-26.

[8] Hacking, Ian, *Logic of Statistical Inference*, Cambridge University Press, Cambridge, 1965.

[9] Hacking, Ian, 'Guessing by Frequency', *Proceedings of the Aristotelian Society*, New Series, LXIV, 1963-64, pp. 55-70.

[10] Kyburg, Henry E., 'All Acceptable Generalizations are Analytic', *American Philosophical Quarterly* 14 (1977), pp. 201-210.

[11] Levi, Isaac, *Gambling with the Truth: An Essay on Induction and the Aims of Science*, Alfred A. Knopf, New York, 1967.

[12] Levi, Isaac, 'The Matter of Chance, by D. H. Mellor', *The Philosophical Review* 82 (1973), pp. 524-530.

[13] Levi, Isaac, 'On Indeterminate Probabilities', *Journal of Philosophy* 71 (1974), pp. 391-418.

[14] Levi, Isaac, 'Direct Inference', *Journal of Philosophy* 74 (1977), pp. 5-29.

[15] Mellor, D. H., 'Connectivity, Chance and Ignorance', *British Journal for the Philosophy of Science* 16 (1965-66), pp. 209-225.

[16] Mellor, D. H., *The Matter of Chance*, Cambridge University Press, Cambridge, 1971.

[17] Pollock, John, 'Probabilities', Ch. VIII of *Subjunctive Reasoning*, Reidel, Dordrecht, 1976.

[18] Popper, Karl R., 'The Propensity Interpretation of the Calculus of Probability and the Quantum Theory', *The Colston Papers*, ed by Korner, pp. 65-70.

[19] Popper, Karl, R., 'The Propensity Interpretation of Probability', *British Journal for the Philosophy of Science* 10 (1959-60), pp. 25-42.

[20] Smokler, Howard E., personal correspondence.

[21] van Fraassen, Bas, 'Relative Frequencies' *Hans Reichenbach: Logical Empiricist*, ed. by Salmon, pp. 129-167.

8

Logical and Fiducial Probability

1.

Of most intellectual disciplines it is possible to take a very optimistic view: where there is agreement we may congratulate ourselves on the fact that we have discovered something that approaches truth, and where there is controversy we may remind ourselves that it is only through the conflict of ideas that people are stimulated to create new approaches, to invent new concepts, and thus, eventually, to approach a new state of agreement. The Foundations of Statistical Inference is a field in which there has for some time been more controversy than unanimity. That this controversy has been productive can hardly be denied; yet I do not think that many statisticians or philosophers would argue that it would be unwise or irrational to hope to find more unanimity than now exists. I hope that I have found grounds for expecting some progress in this direction.

One reason for our difficulties is the ambiguity of many of the terms that are used centrally in the theory of statistical inference. When I refer to ambiguity here, I refer not only to the fact that some terms are used casually, being introduced without any sort of definition at all, even though they are words deserving definition. I refer also to words, recognized as troublesome, which are explicitly defined; but which are then used with an altogether different meaning from that with which they were formally endowed. In particular this is the case with the word "probability."

The concept of probability is central to the theory of statistical inference. For this reason, writers on the foundations of statistical inference are generally careful to give the word an explicit definition, or at least to characterize it very carefully. One reason that there are a number of different philosophies of statistical inference is that writers have worked on the basis of a number of different conceptions of probability. We have, for example, Jeffreys, adopting one logical

An invited paper reprinted from the *Bulletin of the International Statistical Institute: Proceedings of the 34th Session* (University of Toronto Press, Toronto, 1964), pp. 844-901, by permission of the publisher. The meeting was in Ottawa, Canada, in 1963.

conception of probability; Carnap, adopting another; de Finetti taking a subjectivistic view of probability; Neyman and Fisher working on the basis of distinct empirical theories.

I shall argue, first, that the conception of probability with which we start makes a difference not only with respect to our theory of statistical inference, but also with respect to the actual results that given evidence leads us to; second, that the ways in which various writers use the concept of probability are not so divergent as the definitions they give of it; third, that my own conception of probability is quite close to that *used* (not necessarily that defined) by a number of writers (and is nearly identical with Fisher's concept of fiducial probability), and, finally that my conception of probability *may* lead to a considerable unification of statistical methods.

2.

To show that the concept of probability one adopts has a serious effect in statistical inference—and not only in informative inference, but in simple decision procedures—I shall draw on the work of D. V. Lindley.[1] Lindley is writing from an extreme point of view; he says: "The purpose of experimentation is to enable one to decide between courses of action" (p. 31). It is interesting, and I think significant, that even within such a restricted framework ambiguity about the meaning of probability can lead to difficulties.

Suppose that there are n possible measures, $p_1 \ldots p_n$; and that we are to make a choice among m possible decisions $d_1 \ldots d_m$ on the basis of empirical evidence a. We construct an $n \times m$ matrix of the products $a_{ij} \, l_j(a)$ in which $l_j(a)$ is the likelihood of observing a if the probability distribution is indeed p_j and the a_{ij} are a set of non-negative constants ($1 < i < m; \ 1 \leqslant j \leqslant n; \ a_{ij} = 0$). There are various policies which one may employ in arriving at a decision. The extremes range from a game-theoretic procedure which would minimize the *maximum* of the expected losses $a_{ij} \, l_j(a)$ by selecting that row of the matrix in which the largest value of $a_{ij} \, l_j(a)$ is smaller than the largest value of $a_{ij} \, l_j(a)$ in any other row, to a Bayesian approach which would take the sum of the losses of a given row as the expectation of loss, and would select that row in which the sum is a minimum. We might say that there are a number of general techniques that can be employed here, and that all the statistician can do is to make them clear. But before we let matters go at that, we must look more closely at the constants a_{ij}. Lindley considers several possibilities. There is the possibility that the a_{ij} may be regarded as prior probabilities, though this leads to an incomplete class of decision functions. (One cannot decide what to *do* without taking utilities into account.) A natural way to complete the class of decision functions is to regard all errors on a par. Second, we can regard the a_{ij} as pure utilities: a_{ij} representing the *cost* of choosing d_i when p_j obtains. And third, we can regard them as expectations, combining both views. Some philosophers, notably Braithwaite,[2] regard this as a great unification of views on statistical inference. If A believes in prior probabilities he can introduce them into the factors a_{ij} and if B doesn't, he can regard the factors a_{ij} as pure utilities. Lindley himself suggests the following "solution to the decision problem." "Assign weights W_{ij} representing the seriousness of saying d_i when p_j obtains, all available evidence including losses and beliefs to enter into the evaluation of the weights, and then make the decision on the basis of the evidence a by the method of minimum unlikelihood with $a_{ij} = W_{ij}$" (p. 46).

But this leads to the following problem: If the weights W_{ij} contain any mixture of probability at all—i.e., if they can be factored into products of the form $u_{ij}q_j$, where u_{ij} is the cost of choosing decision d_i when the distribution p_j obtains, and q_j is the prior probability that p_j obtains—then there is generally a policy which will demonstrably yield the best results, namely, the Bayesian policy.

This policy, which simply chooses that decision for which the sum of the expected losses

$$\left(\sum_{j=1}^{n} u_{ij}q_j l_i(a) = \sum_{j=1}^{n} W_{ij}l_j(a) \right)$$

is a minimum, yields the decision procedure that has the highest mathematical expecation. Observe, in fact, that we do not even have to know anything about the magnitudes of the q_j's; all we have to do is *assume* the existence of the prior probabilities and have on hand the values of the weighting factors W_{ij}. Even if a minimax policy provides a rational way of choosing among decisions when the weighting factors W_{ij} contain no admixture of probability but are pure utilities it certainly is not rational when the weighting factors represent expectations.

Thus we are led to the conclusion that even in a concrete situation where we choose between decisions for practical purposes the decision we make will depend on our view of probability. On a subjectivistic or logical view the weighting factors will be expectations and to be reasonable we *must* use a Bayesian form of inference. On the classical frequency view these factors are utilities and a strong case can be made for a minimax method. On given evidence these two methods may, of course, lead to contrary conclusions.

3.

It is well known that (in principle) most of our troubles are over if we can become Bayesians in statistical inference. The philosophical difficulty and the point at which the various views of probability diverge is the question of the justification and evaluation of the prior probabilities or prior probability distributions required.

The original recommendation concerning *a priori* probability distributions was Laplace's: it was the principle of insufficient reason. This principle was quite soon seen (for example, by Boole) to lead to contradiction. For a while, however, there was no useful alternative. In 1921 Keynes offered a logical conception of probability which, through a requirement of total evidence and a requirement of symmetry, succeeds in avoiding the paradoxes to which the simpleminded principle of indifference led. But Keynes's principle of indifference fails to provide what we need most for the procedures of science, namely, a way of arriving at *a priori* continuous probability distributions. Jeffreys, in far closer touch with the actual problems and procedures of the physical sciences, has made many practical proposals regarding *a priori* distributions. These proposals have been adopted by some (perhaps many?) working scientists, but they lack the sort of logical justification which philosophers generally insist on. An answer to this shortcoming is attempted by Carnap and members of his school.

There seems to be a curious law of compensation operating here: a solution to the problem of uncovering *a priori* probabilities that is rigorous and precise— such as Carnap's—turns out to be quite useless to scientists who really need to have the *a priori* probabilities for their computations, while the practical means of providing these probabilities offered by such people as Jeffreys are so arbitrary as to be repugnant to most philosophical minds. We might wonder if this apparent law really holds, and we might test it by bending all of our energies to finding arguments for the derivation of *a priori* probabilities at once rigorous enough for the philosopher (and we are all philosophers to some extent) and at the same time powerful enough for the practicing scientist.

Unfortunately, any such attempt misses the point. The contradictions can be done away with, as Keynes and Jeffreys did largely do away with them; the *a priori* probabilities to which any arbitrary rule will lead us may be made as plausible as we want; but the difficulty remains that what is plausible to one may be implausible to another, and when we have guarded against one class of contradictions, we may yet be vulnerable to another. No general principle for computing *a priori* probabilities has yet received anything like universal acceptance, nor does such a principle seem likely to gain such acceptance.

In recent years, one ingenious attempt to circumvent these difficulties has attracted much attention. This is the attempt to found statistical inference on admittedly *subjective* assignments of probability. The basis of such attempts is the fact that in many cases a very wide range of initial *a priori* probability assignments lead to very nearly the same *a posteriori* probability distributions in the light of a given reasonable amount of evidence. One of the most outspoken champions of this approach to statistical inference is L. J. Savage. In a paper written by Edwards, and Lindeman, and Savage[3] we find the following illustration.

If you are taking your temperature with a thermometer that you are convinced is accurate, one reading will suffice to make you very sure that your temperature is very close to the temperature registered on the thermometer. It can be shown, as it is shown by Edwards, Lindeman, and Savage, that this is the case even if you are quite convinced that you have a slight temperature. There is a wide range of *a priori* distributions for your temperature that will all lead to essentially the same posterior distribution.

This is all very true, but it is also still rather bothersome philosophically. If it could be shown that such and such a conclusion followed, *regardless* of the particular *a priori* probability distribution with which we started, that would be one thing. But this is not the case on the personalistic view. It is perfectly possible to start with such an extreme distribution that the evidence can only modify it slightly. The hypochondriac, sure that he has a fever, throws the thermometer away when it registers normal, and, on the subjectivistic view, rightly and rationally so.

From a philosophical and logical standpoint the subjectivists may be caricatured as abandoning all prescriptions for *a priori* probabilities, on the grounds that none seems to be justified, and then turning right about face to say that *all* assignments of *a priori* probabilities are justified. If the former procedure of justifying *a priori* probabilities by a rule is unjustified however, surely the latter, which substitutes idiosyncratic whim for rule, is also unjustifiable. As Fisher says, "If the justification for any particular form of $f(x)$ is merely that it makes no difference whether the form is right or wrong, we may as well ask what the expression is doing in our reasoning at all . . . ."[4]

4.

We are thus led to look for alternatives to the use of Bayes's theorem. The best known of such alternative approaches is that of Neyman and Pearson. On this view the fundamental statistical problem is that of choosing between alternative courses of action on the basis of limited (inconclusive) evidence. A statistical test is a rule which yields, for every possible empirical outcome e, a decision d: $\delta(e)$ $= d$. On such a view *informative inference* — in which a decision means to *accept* a hypothesis or family of hypotheses — is a special case of statistical testing.

I shall mention two specific kinds of tests that are particularly interesting. Consider first the testing of a specific simple statistical hypothesis against a specific simple alternative. Classically such a test is described by two numbers, α for level, β for power. α is the probability — *in a frequency sense* — of rejecting the hypothesis being tested when it is in fact true (i.e., the probability of error of the first kind) and β the probability of the other kind of error (i.e., the [frequency] probability of accepting the hypothesis being tested when in point of fact the alternative hypothesis is true). Savage (1962) has shown that the characteristics of the test of such alternatives is determined by a single number, which can be regarded as reflecting the relative *a priori* probabilities of the two alternatives. Similarly, Birnbaum (1961) shows that binary experiments testing two alternatives can be characterized by a single number in accord with the likelihood principle; this number is α; β is taken to be equal to α. This corresponds on Bayesian principles to accepting both hypotheses as equally probable *a priori.*

The other kind of test I shall consider is that which leads to an interval estimate. This is the method of confidence-intervals, and it is applicable to the estimation of the value of a real-valued parameter θ. The results it leads to are of the form: whatever be the value of θ (or if there are nuisance parameters η, whatever be the values of θ and η) the probability is *at least* p that the experimental data will have the property π, where the experimental data e will have the property π if and only if $l(e) \leqslant \theta \leqslant u(e)$.

5.

Under special circumstances the method of confidence limits coincides with Fisher's fiducial inference. The best-known application of the fiducial argument (and one which coincides with confidence–interval arguments) is that of forming an interval estimate of the mean of a normal population with unknown variance. The conclusion of the fiducial inference is a probability distribution for the unknown parameter.

Both Birnbaum and Savage, again, have shown the existence of intimate connections between the theory of fiducial probability and Bayesian methods. The Bayesian theory of precise measurement provides a solution to the Behrens-Fisher problem that coincides with the solution proposed by Fisher; it leads to a "good understanding"[5] of the problem of estimating the ratio of two means, and this again agrees with the answer produced by the fiducial argument. In general, Savage says, "In many cases the theory of precise measurement tends to coincide in this way with the theory of fiducial probability,"[6] but the theory of precise measurement goes beyond the theory of fiducial probability because it is not dependent on the existence of sufficient statistics, and it is competent to handle discrete distributions. So far as it goes, however, the theory of fiducial probability seems to agree precisely with the theory of stable estimation (or theory of precise measurement) established by the Bayesian approach. Birnbaum speculates that "fiducial probability methods may in general coincide in form as well as in general intention with intrinsic confidence methods . . . ."[7]

6.

I have spent this long on background material because there is a really amazing web of interlocking relationships that exists among the various viewpoints on the foundations of statistical inference. In the background lie two distinct conceptions of probability. The subjectivists' approach to statistical inference is essentially Bayesian; but it leads to methods formally identical with methods put forward from a frequentist point of view by Fisher and with methods adopted by Neyman for testing hypotheses. In some cases the identity is nearly complete:

for example, in the case of binary experiments to choose the level and power of a test (α and β) is exactly the same as to choose the relative *a priori* likelihood of the hypotheses. In some cases the frequentist method of confidence intervals (particularly Birnbaum's method of intrinsic confidence intervals) coincides with the frequentist method of fiducial inference. The most adamant decision-theoretic school, Neyman's, has recently turned its attention to Bayesian inferences of a special kind investigated by Herbert Robbins and his students: empirical Bayes methods. These methods are Bayesian in the sense that they use Bayes's theorem; but they use past frequencies rather than *a priori* probabilities as data to feed into the theorem.

In spite of all these complicated connections, we are left with fundamental problems such as the one with which I started this paper: if probabilities are only frequencies, one procedure is called for; if there is an admixture of *a priori* probability in them, a contrary procedure may be called for. Furthermore, though there are surprising cases of agreement among the various points of view, there are also many cases of disagreement.

7.

My own conception of probability is, like Keynes's and Carnap's, a logical one. Probability statements are logically true, if they are true at all. A probability is asserted always relative to a body of evidence; relative to different bodies of evidence different probability statements will be true. This need cause us no concern, however, for as scientists we are all willing to share information with each other, and it is no real stretching of terms to speak of the body of general evidence in an entire field as the body of evidence relative to which we shall make our probability statements. I do not want to regard this body of knowledge as fixed in any absolute sense; over a period of time, however brief, it changes. But in order to clarify the process of inference we introduce the logician's standard idealization and regard the inference as taking place at a timeless moment. In this moment there are statements that are open to question and statements that are not open to question—though in another moment, or from another point of view, they could of course be questioned. In performing a t-test for the mean of a normally distributed quantity, for example, the fact that the quantity is normally distributed is not open to question; it is part of our body of evidence even though in another context it may be subject to test by just the same collection of data we are using for the t-test.

Let us refer to this body of general evidence as G. Formally, I shall regard G as a set of statements, and I shall suppose that G includes not only "observation statements" and the like, but also statistical statements and scientific laws and theories that are so probable (relative to other statements in G) as to be *practically certain*.

To say that the probability of the statement S is p, on this view is to say that

(1) S is equivalent to a statement of the form $a \in A$, (2) that relative to the body of general knowledge G, a is a random member of some class B, with respect to membership in A, and (3) that it is known in G that the proportion of members of B which are also members of A is p. For example, we can be practically certain that half the tosses of a well-tested coin result in heads; this is a statistical statement which we may include in our background knowledge G. Relative to this background knowledge, the next toss I make with this coin is a *random member* of the class of all tosses made with it; and I may therefore say, now, that the probability that the next toss I make with this coin results in heads is one half. If I am tossing the coin to decide whether to study some more tonight or to go out for a beer before retiring, and I stipulate that I shall have a beer if and only if the coin lands heads, then I may say, in view of the fact that my going to have a beer is materially *equivalent* to the statement that the next toss of this coin belongs to the class of tosses that yield heads, that the probability that I shall have a beer is one half. Furthermore I am under no obligation to suppose that the proportion p that gives rise to a probability is a real number; indeed, since I am supposed to *know* its value, it is more plausible to say that p represents an interval (p', p'').

There is one crucial notion to be explained: that of randomness. Since I have defined probability in terms of randomness, it is obvious that I cannot on pain of circularity define randomness in terms of probability. I have offered rather extensive discussions of this very complicated notion elsewhere;[8] here it must suffice to offer a few essential characteristics of randomness, and to leave it up to our intuitive understanding of the notion to guide us out of any difficulties we may get into.

To say that object a is a random member of the set B with respect to membership in the set A, is surely to say that we know that a belongs to B—that is, the statement, "a belongs to B" is an ingredient of our body of general knowledge G. The object a is a random member of the set B with respect to membership in the set A, also, only when there is no other set B^*, such that (1) we know that a belongs to B^*, (2) we know that B^* is included in B, and (3) we know the proportion of B^*'s that are A's. Indeed, it is tempting to take this stipulation concerning randomness, turn it about by rephrasing it in positive terms, and look at it as a *definition* of randomness. Why can't we say that a is a random member of B with respect to A when B is the *smallest* class to which a is known to belong about which we have statistical information? There are two serious difficulties with this proposal, which I shall mention only to show that no simpleminded and obvious solution to the problem of defining randomness is available. First is the fact that we must, if we are to be realistic at all, deal with statistical statements that are only approximate; but once we admit that to know that the proportion of B's that are A's is between 0.4 and 0.6 is to know *something* about this proportion, we are faced with the problem of what constitutes *knowledge* about a set. Let B_1 be a set that contains only the object a; B_2 a set about which we know only that the proportion of A's lies between 0.1 and 0.9; B_3 a set that includes B_2, but about which we know that the proportion of A's lies between 0.45 and 0.55. Clearly here we would like to say that a is a random member of B_3 with respect to A. We can arrange for this, with a few extra stipulations, but then we must also adjudicate, somehow, between B_3 and B_4, where neither B_3 nor B_4 is known to be included in the other, and where we know that the proportion of A's in B_4 is between 0.50 and 0.60.

The other serious problem is this: we want to define probability in such a way that statements that are known to be equivalent have the same probability. Let S be known to be equivalent to $a \in C$ and to $a^* \in C^*$. Our definition of randomness must be such that if a is a random member of B with respect to C, and if a^* is a random member of B^* with respect to C^*, then our knowledge about the sets B and C must be just the same as our knowledge about the sets B^* and C^*. That is, if we know that the proportion of B's that are C's is between p and q, we must also know that the proportion of B^*'s that are C^*'s is between p and q.

In simple cases, however, the suggestions that I have given work well enough; there are real-life situations in which they do not suffice to lead us to acceptable statements about randomness, but such situations are fairly rare. The extension of this notion of randomness to cases in which we are talking about general probability distributions rather than simple binomial probabilities is immediate, though when several parameters are involved in a distribution it may be the case that we run into a few novel difficulties.

Let me summarize now, as though we had a clear notion of randomness: we will say that the probability of a statement S is the interval $(p;q)$, when we *know*, in our general body of knowledge G, (1) that S is equivalent to a statement of the form $a \in C$; (2) that a is a random member of B with respect to C; and (3) that the proportion of B's that are C's lies in the interval $(p;q)$. Furthermore, to know that a is a random member of B with respect to C, is to have in our general body of knowledge G the statement "$a \in B$," but not to have simultaneously in G any triplet of statements "$a \in B^*$," "B^* is included in B," and "the proportion of B^*'s that are C's does not lie in the interval (p,q)."

8.

As a next step, on the way to showing that this very peculiar notion of probability does have consequences for the theory of statistical inference, I shall show that it appears to be precisely the notion of probability that Fisher has held for some years. I realize that this is a rather shocking thing to say, particularly in the light of Fisher's constantly reiterated insistence that probability statements must be testable, but let us look at some of the other things he says.

The most explicit definition of probability I have encountered in Fisher's writings is the following, from his recent book, *Statistical Methods and Scientific Inference*:

In a statement of probability the predicand, which may be conceived as an object, as an event, or as a proposition, is asserted to be one of a set of a number, however large of like entities of which a known proportion, *P*, have some relevant characteristic, not possessed by the remainder. It is further asserted that no subset of the entire set, having a different proportion, can be recognized.

If, therefore, any portion of the data were to allow of the recognition of such a subset, to which the predicand belongs, a different probability would be asserted using the smallest such subset recognizable.

When no further subset is recognizable, which can be known only by an exhaustive scrutiny of the data, the predicand is spoken of as a random member of the ultimate set to which it belongs.[9]

Earlier in the same book he writes, "The *knowledge* required for such a probability statement refers to a well-defined aggregate, or population of possibilities within which the limiting frequency ratio must be exactly known. The necessary *ignorance* is specified by our inability to discriminate any of the different sub-aggregates having different limiting frequency ratios, such as must always exist."[10]

The translation from Fisher's terminology to my own is almost trivial. I state explicitly a principle that Fisher uses: the principle that equivalent statements must have the same probability. I also generalize on the notion of probability to the extent that I allow probabilities to be based on *approximate* statistical knowledge. The problem that remains is that of showing that Fisher's conception of probability, like mine, is a logical one. Fisher claims that probability statements must be testable: " . . . any statement of probability to be objective must be verifiable as a prediction of frequency . . . ,"[11] and he refers to the "factual content" of probability statements. If probability is a logical concept, probability statements must be *logically* true if true at all, and will at any rate be immune to empirical test; and if these statements are logically true, they are, of course, empty of factual content. How could Fisher possibly be mistaken about something like this?

Let us go back to the probability statement about the coin: the probability of heads on the next toss is (about) one-half. If this statement has factual content, surely it can be refuted by experience. But does the occurrence of heads on the next toss refute this statement? Does the occurrence of tails refute it? Obviously not. What would refute it? I think Fisher would argue that a long sequence of tosses of which one-quarter resulted in heads would refute the statement. But in this he is clearly wrong. The statement says nothing about a sequence of tosses; it talks only about one particular toss. In just the same way, a statement of fiducial probability does not refer to a sequence of experiments concerning different parameters, but gives a probability distribution for a single, fixed parameter. On Fisher's own interpretation of probability, what is required is (1) *knowledge* of a proportion in a population and (2) lack of ability to *discriminate* subsets of that population in which the relevant proportion is different. If these requirements are met when we make the probability statement about the coin (or the statement of fiducial probability) then they are met once and for all, and no amount of future testing is going to give us any more information about whether or not these conditions were fulfilled *at the time we made the statement*. Indeed, as soon as the next toss of the coin has been performed and we know for certain that it resulted in heads or tails as the case may be, the probability statement is no longer *correct* in the sense that we can *then* discriminate a special subclass of the class of coin tosses to which the toss under discussion belongs: namely the set of tosses resulting in heads or the set of tosses resulting in tails, according to the result of that toss.

What *is* the effect of a long sequence of tosses of which one-fourth yield heads? It is not to refute the probability statements we made before, but to refute—to cause us to reject—the statistical statement on which the probability statement was based. When we made the original probability statement we knew (i.e., we presumably had adequate evidence to accept the proposition) that half the tosses of this coin result in heads. Now, on the basis of further evidence, we know better. Now we would assign a different probability to the event of heads on a given (future) toss of the coin; but this does not mean that our first assignment was wrong in any useful sense of the word "wrong." All it means is that our body of knowledge has changed.

This is certainly clear enough when it comes to a probability statement like "the probability that I shall get heads the next time I toss this coin is one-half"; what *can* we base such a probability on but the best estimate we can form of the relative frequency of heads? But there is a very similar statement whose analysis is more ambiguous: "the probability of heads on *a* toss of this coin is one-half." Notice the presence of the indefinite article "a." I think we may interpret its indefiniteness to signal randomness, so that an equivalent rendering of this statement is: "the probability of heads on *any* (every) *random* toss of this coin is one-half." On the analysis of probability that I gave and on the view that Fisher suggests, this statement will be true *if* and *only if* we *know* a statistical statement to the effect that half of the tosses of the coin yield heads. This is where Fisher has gotten confused about the factual content of probability statements as, I suspect, have most of those who hold a frequency view of probability. The only sense in which "the probability of heads on *a* toss of this coin is one-half" has factual content is that it says that as a matter of fact a certain statistical statement is in my rational corpus. This is a very weak sort of factual content. But the statistical statement itself has genuine factual content. When I *assert* the probability statement in question, I am directly asserting only that in my general body of knowledge G I have a particular statistical statement. But indirectly and implicitly I am also asserting that this statistical statement is true, well grounded, acceptable. It is this duality of assertion that has led to argument and confusion about the factual content of probability statements.

Evidence of this confusion can be found in Fisher's discussion of fiducial probability in the book I have been quoting from. Fisher is concerned at one point to answer the objection that his fiducial probability statements are not testable. He writes, "However, the aggregate of cases of which the particular experimental case is one, for which the relative frequency of satisfying the inequality statement is known to be P . . . could certainly be sampled indefinitely to demonstrate the correct frequency."[12] The aggregate of cases, though, is entirely hypothetical—it includes all possible values of the parameter under test, for example—and we can only sample from a real population. Furthermore, the probability P in question is derived from a statistical statement which is analytic; analytic in just the sense that the vague statement, "most large subclasses from a population represent the statistical makeup of that population," is analytic. What Fisher is *trying* to defend—the empirical testability of statements of fiducial probability—is not defensible at all. What he *should* be defending—the possible logical validity of such statements—he inadvertently defends perfectly adequately on the same page: "In the absence of a prior distribution of population values there is no meaning to be attached to the demand for calculating the results of random sampling among *populations,* and it is just this absence which completes the demonstration that samples giving a particular value T, arising from a particular but unknown value of θ, do not constitute a distinguishable sub-aggregate to which a different probability should be assigned."[13]

The fact that fiducial probability statements cannot be given the kind of empirical content that most statisticians still like to attribute to probability statements has led some writers to insist that there is a difference between fiducial probability and other kinds of probability. Even writers who are decidedly on Fisher's side take this view; for example, the biographical introduction to the collection of Fisher's papers, *Contributions to Mathematical Statistics,* contains the statement: "Fisher has laid emphasis on the fact that the concept of fiducial probability, *though entirely different from ordinary probability,* is equally rigorous."[14] But two years earlier, Fisher himself had written, "This distinctive terminology is not intended to suggest that fiducial probability is not in the strictest sense a mathematical probability, like that of any other to which the term ought to be applied."[15] And in 1956 he wrote, "Probabilities obtained by a fiducial argument are objectively verifiable in exactly the same sense as are the probabilities assigned in games of chance."[16] Fisher's instinct here is perfectly sound; the two kinds of statements employ precisely the same notion of probability. He is wrong only in believing (despite his careful analysis which brought him to the verge of recognizing probability as a logical relation) that it is an empirical notion.

9.

The most important concept for statistical inference to emerge from either Fisher's analysis or mine, is that of randomness. Fisher looks at the problem as one of finding an appropriate reference set, but an appropriate reference set is clearly (in this context) one of which the sample in hand is a random member with respect to the properties relevant to statistical inference. ("Random" here has only a peripheral connection with *randomization* in experiments.) A few examples will show this. In making a fiducial inference about a parameter θ, whose maximum likelihood estimate is T, we take our reference set to be the set of all pairs (T, θ). Within this set we can show that the proportion of pairs satisfying a certain inequality is P. Fisher goes on to write:

It might, however, have been true . . . that in some recognizable subset,
. . . the proportion of cases in which the inequality was satisfied should
have some value other than P. It is the stipulated absence of knowledge *a
priori* of the distribution of θ, together with the exhaustive character of the
statistic T, that makes the recognition of any such subset impossible, and so
guarantees that in this particular case . . . the general probability is applicable . . .
" . . . had there been knowledge *a priori,* the argument of Bayes could
have been developed, which would have utilized all the data, and which
would in general have led to a distribution *a posteriori* different from that to
which the fiducial argument leads. Bayes' method in fact calculates the distribution of θ in a particular subset of pairs of values (T, θ). . . .[17]

Similar considerations are expressed in his discussion of "student's" t test. The application of "student's" test "is more simple than will generally be the case in statistical work, for in this case no characteristic of the sample (i.e., of the whole body of observations available) can be found to define a subset to which our sample belongs, and which might exhibit a different, and more rele-vant, frequency distribution."[18]

It is not only in connection with inferences of the fiducial type that the question of the selection of a reference set — or what is the same thing, the question of randomness — comes up. In discussing tests of significance applied to a 2×2 table, Fisher argues that we need consider only possible tables having the same marginal totals, rather than all possible totals. In the particular case he considers, Neyman and Pearson enumerate 64 cases, as opposed to Fisher's 20.[19] I am not competent to settle the dispute, but I think the nature of the dispute provides further evidence for the adequacy of my conception of probability. What is at issue here is just this: is the 2×2 table arising from the experiment in question a random member of the set of all possible 2×2 tables or is it a ran-dom member of the subset of possible 2×2 tables that has given marginal totals? In view of the fact that it is not quite clear what property it is that the table is supposed to be random with respect to, it is hard to judge those rival claims, but *prima facie* the smaller reference set seems to be preferable.

Before going on to see to what extent the concept of probability I have offered here is able to resolve the conflicts and explain the connections among the various views of statistical inference I have mentioned, I shall look briefly at the relationships between my concept of probability and the frequency and subjectivistic concepts.

10.

The most popular view of probability among statistians is the relative frequency view. By this view I do not mean a formal and sophisticated identification of probabilities with limiting frequencies in infinite reference classes; I mean only the general view that probability statements entail assertions about long-run relative frequencies, and conversely. I have denied that this is an appropriate conception of probability, but there is obviously a close connection between statements about probability and statements about relative frequencies. On my view the connection is the following: to *assert* a probability statement, it is necessary that our body of knowledge *contain* a statistical statement. To assert that the probability of heads on the next toss of this coin is one-half, requires that we have in our general rational corpus the statement: the proportion of heads in tosses of this coin is one-half. When the frequency theorist says to me, in a shocked tone of voice, "Surely you can't say that the probability that an A will be a B is p, unless you know that the proportion of A's that are B's is p" — I agree with him. But the assertion depends on what I *know* or have reason to believe, and not on what happens to be the case; and knowledge about a relative frequency, while *necessary* for a probability assertion, is not sufficient: the condition of randomness must also be met.

The essential differences between my view and relative frequency views are (1) that on my view probability can be applied to individual events and propositions, and indeed my view contains explicit criteria for these applications, and (2) that the correctness of a probability statement demands only that the corresponding statistical statement be known — i.e., *reasonably believed* — rather than that it be true.

It is in recognizing the necessity of knowledge concerning relative frequencies that my view of probability differs from other logical views. The probability that an A will be a B may not exist, on my view — or rather, it may be represented by the completely uninformative interval $(0, 1)$. The only *a priori* probabilities other than these are those which admit of rigorous mathematical deduction — as in Bernoulli's theorem, for example, where we may consider the least favorable case of $p = \frac{1}{2}$, and on that basis calculate the proportion of samples that are approximately representative.

This lack of *a priori* probabilities precludes the general use of Bayes's theorem and marks one of the greatest distinctions between my conception of probability and that of the subjectivists. Another distinction lies in the fact that every probability is based on an explicit statistical statement; this leads to the elimination of every element of subjectivity, except that involved in setting the odds for bets in situations in which little knowledge exists. It can be shown, indeed, that probabilities defined as I have defined them (subject, of course, to a complete definition of randomness) are uniquely determined in the sense that, given a body of experience, there is one and only one pair of numbers $(p;q)$ for each statement such that the probability of that statement is that interval.

There is one connection between my logical probability and the probability of the subjectivists that is extremely important. It can be shown that there exists a set of real numbers satisfying both my conditions about probability and those of the subjectivists. Put another way, we can say that there is a function whose domain is the set of all statements in our language, whose range included in the set of real numbers, which is a *coherent* probability function in the subjectivists' sense, and which *also* satisfies my conception of probability in the sense that if the probability of the statement S is (p, q) on my view, this function will have a value in the interval (p, q) for the argument S.

This is extremely important for the following reason. Since my probabilities are intervals, there is no convenient way of developing a calculus of probability. (For many purposes none is necessary; we can do our calculating on the class ratio statements on which we base our probability statements.) In view of the existence of the function described above, we can often employ Bayesian computations to obtain limits (though perhaps wider ones than might be obtained in other ways) for probability intervals. This will be illustrated in the discussion of stable estimation below.

11.

Now let us see what light this new theory of probability throws on classical modes of statistical inference. Let us begin with the method of confidence intervals. Everyone is very clear about the fact that individual confidence-interval estimates carry coefficients (like 0.95 or 0.98) with them that cannot be regarded as probabilities of the estimates. On the standard view, these numbers are not probabilities because there is no random variable for them to be the probability of. The statement $\theta_1 < \theta < \theta_2$ is not a statement about a random variable; θ is a fixed but unknown constant characterizing a population, and it either lies between the two numbers in question or it does not. It makes no sense to talk — as one would have to talk on the classical frequency view of probability — of the relative frequency with which it fell between the two numbers. On Fisher's view we can come closer to giving the confidence limit statement a probabilistic meaning, but we still do not obtain probability statements, since confidence-limit methods only supply statements of inequality.

On the view of probability I have sketched, the inexactness of our knowledge of the proportion in question is irrelevant, and we obtain perfectly respectable probability statements from confidence-limit methods, provided that the conditions for valid probability statements are met at all. Consider, for example the confidence-limit estimate of a binomial probability parameter p on the basis of an observed relative frequency in a sample of size n, Given ϵ and p we can compute the proportion of n-fold samples from a population that are representative in the sense that $p - \epsilon < r < p + \epsilon$. This will be a minimum for $p = \frac{1}{2}$ and a maximum for $p = 0$ or $p = 1$. Say the minimum is P; the maximum of course, is 1. Thus whatever be the true value of p, the proportion of samples that are representative in the sense at hand lies between P and 1. If the sample we draw is a random member of the set of all possible samples with respect to membership in the set of representative samples, then we have all the ingredients of a probability statement: the probability that the sample we have drawn is representative is the interval $(P, 1)$. If, on the other hand, the sample is *not* a random member of the set of all possible samples, it is because we know that it is a member of a distinguished subset of this set, in which the proportion of representative samples differs from that in the original reference set. Thus we may have an even stronger statement about the parameter p, or we may have a weaker one, if, for example, we know that the sample was drawn by a method that only rarely yields representative samples. In any case, however, we have a perfectly respectable probability statement about the "unknown" parameter p.

The method of "intrinsic confidence limits" developed by Alan Birnbaum also leads to probability statements about the values of parameters. These statements are again subject to the usual conditions regarding randomness. There are circumstances in which the fiducial inference leads to results that conflict with classical confidence methods (but not with the method of intrinsic confidence limits, which is based on the likelihood principle). Under these circumstances it is the confidence-limit method that must give way.

The connections between my conception of probability and the Bayesian practice of statistics are far more complicated than those between my conception and the usual relative-frequency-decision-theoretic point of view.

"Reflection shows that any policy that pretends to ignore prior opinion will be acceptable only insofar as it is actually justified by prior opinion."[20] This may be true enough, but I think it is also true that any policy based on prior opinion will be acceptable only insofar as the prior opinion is justifiable. While the theory of probability that I have been offering does not provide *a priori* probabilities for use in Bayes's theorem, it does lead to the existence of very broad probabilities of the form (p, q), where p is close to 0 and q is close to 1, on the basis of relatively little evidence. These initial probabilities are based, not on whim, but on sound, if limited, evidence and precisely the standards of statistical inference with which we have been dealing all along. In view of the fact that p may be close to 0 and q close to 1, these initial probabilities may be pretty useless as guides to action; but combined with specific relevant evidence they may lead, through Bayes's theorem, to strong conclusions.

This comes about in the following way: write Bayes's theorem in the form $P(b,e) = (P(e,b)P(b))/P(e)$. Whatever intervals these probabilities may be, on my interpretation, we know that there exists a function f from statements to real numbers which satisfies both my system of probabilities and the axioms of personalistic probability.[21] The extension of this function to conditional probabilities is trivial. We find a function f which satisfies the conditions of both systems for the statements b, e, and the conditional statement e given b. Compute $(f(e,b) \cdot f(b))/f(e)$; this yields $f(b,e)$. But in view of the fact that f satisfies both systems and in view of the fact that e is part of our general body of knowledge, $f(b,e)$ must lie between the upper and lower limits of the probability of the hypothesis b. If we pick the "worst" possible function f, we will be led to a minimum probability for the hypothesis b. It can perfectly well happen that even this "worst" function yields, through Bayes's theorem, very respectably high probabilities. It is the theory of stable estimation that leads to this conclusion. Indeed, the tremendous importance of the Bayesian theory of stable estimation is precisely that it shows how far you can go on the basis of very general background information. It takes very little evidence (but it *is* a question of evidence) to limit the bounding distributions of a probability distribution enough so that the theory of stable estimation applies and leads to very precise results. (Not so precise, of course, as the Bayesians would like to make out.)

This brings me, finally, to the problem with which I started. What kind of a decision policy should we adopt when we are confronted with a matrix of numbers that are utilities, likelihoods, and probabilities in some unknown combination? The answer is not simple; it depends on the particular mixture with which we are confronted. If the alternatives have reasonably sharp probabilities, in my sense, then the Bayesian solution is the only rational one. If the probabilities of the alternatives are diffuse, it may be that we should adopt a different policy.

To put the matter more precisely, we should clearly make our decisions in accordance with mathematical expectation. On the Bayesian view, this is always possible. On the classical view, it is almost never possible, except when there is background information that gives rise to initial (frequency) probabilities. On my view, we must begin by noticing that when probabilities become intervals, mathematical expectations must also become intervals. The entries in the Lindley matrix, then will be of the form $(u_{ij}p_jl_j(a), u_{ij}q_jl_j(a))$, where u_{ij} represents the cost of making decision i when hypothesis j is true, $l_j(a)$ is the likelihood of a on hypothesis j, and (p_j, q_j) is the initial probability of the hypothesis j. In the situation of absolutely no initial knowledge at all, we will have $(p_j, q_j) = (0, 1)$, and a minimax solution is perhaps quite reasonable. On the other hand, it may very well be that the sum of the expected costs in one row is less, under all possible circumstances, than the sum in any other row; if that is the case, that row obviously represents the best possible decision procedure. There may also be intermediate cases, for which an argument might be presented for the minimax approach. What I *am* confident of, however, is that the rule of eliminating from consideration possible decision procedures that are demonstrably inferior to others in terms of mathematical expectation will eliminate the paradoxes of minimax decision theory.

The extent to which the view I have outlined will throw light on the problems of statistical inference remains to be seen. Superficially it looks as though the theory would go a long way to helping resolve some of the noisiest conflicts. I shall be very interested to see if it will lead to useful results when it is carefully applied to particular types of inference.

There is one more point to which this analysis has led us, and that concerns the cogency of evidence to control our beliefs. On the classical decision-theoretic point of view, we do not need to *have* beliefs at all, and our decisions are controlled by the selection of decision policies in conjunction with empirical evidence. This strikes me as rather too arbitrary, and I would prefer to side with the Bayesians who say that "in principle the solution of every decision problem is simply to maximize expected income with respect to the subjective probability that applies at the moment of making the decision."[22] But the Bayesian position is no less arbitrary. "We have had a slogan about letting the data speak for themselves, but when they do, they tell us only how to modify our opinions, not what opinion is justifiable." In view of the complete license the Bayesians have in assigning prior probabilities, we are just as badly off in this camp as in the decision-theoretic camp. Fisher's point of view on this matter strikes a responsive chord in me when he writes, " . . . there is something rather horrifying in the idealogical movement represented by the doctrine that reasoning, properly speaking, cannot be applied to empirical data to lead to inferences valid in the real world. It is undeniable that the intellectual freedom that we in the West have taken for granted is now successfully denied over a great part of the earth's surface. The validity of the logical steps by which we can still dare to draw our own conclusions cannot, therefore, in these days, be too clearly expounded, or too strongly affirmed."[23] I have written from the same conviction, and I would like to hope that my theory of probability will help to provide a basis for the clarification and unification of existing philosophies of statistical inference. I hope that it will help to make explicit the standards according to which there is after all a rational distinction between opinions that are justifiable and opinions which are not justifiable.

NOTES

1. D. V. Lindley, "Statistical Inference," *J. R. Statist. Soc.* 15 (1953), 30-65.

2. R. B. Braithwaite, "The Role of Values in Scientific Inference," in Kyburg and Nagel, eds., *Induction: Some Current Issues* (Middletown, Conn., 1963).

3. Edwards, Lindeman, and Savage, "Bayesian Statistical Inference for Psychological Research," *Psychological Review* 70 (1963), 193-242.

4. "Two New Properties of Mathematical Likelihood," *Proc. Roy. Soc. London, A,* *144* (1934), 287.

5. Savage, "Subjective Probability and Statistical Practise," *The Foundations of Statistical Inference,* Barnard and Cox (eds.), John Wiley and Sons, New York, 1962, p. 24.

6. *Ibid.*

7. "On the Foundations of Statistical Inference," *J. Amer. Statist. Ass.,* 57 (1962), 269-306; p. 302.

8. Probability and Randomness, *Theoria,* 1963; *Probability and the Logic of Rational Belief* (Middletown, Conn., 1961).

9. R. A. Fisher, *Statistical Methods and Scientific Inference* (New York, 1956), 109-10.

10. *Ibid.,* 33.

11. *Ibid.,* 59.

12. *Ibid.,* 59.

13. *Ibid.,* 59.

14. P. C. Mahalanobis, "Professor Ronald Aylmer Fisher," *Sankhya* 4 (1938), 270.

15. R. A. Fisher, Uncertain Inference, *Proc. Amer. Acad. Arts Sci.,* 71, no. 4 (1936), 253.

16. Fisher, *Statistical Methods,* 59.

17. *Ibid.,* 55.

18. *Ibid.,* 82.

19. *Ibid.* 87-88.

20. Edwards, Lindeman, and Savage, p. 31.

21. At the time of writing this essay, I thought that my probabilities satisfied the principle of conditionalization. It now appears that this is not the case. Nevertheless Bayesian inferences can often be represented in my system.

22. Savage, "Subjective Probability and Statistical Practise," p. 15.

23. Fisher, *Statistical Methods,* p. 7.

Part III. Constructive Probability Papers

9

The Nature of
Epistemological Probability

A number of people have asked about the nature of epistemological probability. Since presentations of epistemological probability involve a fair amount of technical complexity, it is natural to want a description of what it is all about to serve as a basis for making the decision about whether or not to invest the time and effort required to go into the system in detail. These notes are designed to provide that description.

1. Location in "probability" space

NOT empirical: Probabilities are not frequencies, measures on events or sets of events or sequences; they are not propensities or chances.

NOT subjective: Probabilities are not opinions, or beliefs, or degrees of belief, or dispositions to bet or act. Probabilities are not even *rational* degrees of belief.

BUT *logical:* Probabilities reflect an objective logical relation between sets of statements (real or hypothetical bodies of knowledge) and statements. The probability of S given K is what it is regardless of whether or not K is, has ever been, or will be, anybody's actual body of knowledge. Probability is a syntactical, metalinguistic notion analogous to that of provability. The ancestors of this view may be found in Keynes (1921) and Carnap (1951).

Comment: a) Probabilities reflect our knowledge of frequencies, measures, etc. They are thus always *related* to (based on) frequency or chance statements in K.

b) The epistemological import of probability is that it is *legislative* for rational belief: if K is the set of statements corresponding to my body of knowledge, my degree of belief in a statement S *should* reflect the probability of S relative to K.

2. Probability

Probability is defined relative to a corpus K of statements in a language L. The probability of S relative to K in language L, P_L (S, K), is the interval (p, q), if and only if:

There exist expressions x, y, z, and w in L such that

(a) w is a purely mathematical term denoting a Borel set,

(b) z is a random variable in L. (A random *variable* is a linguistic entity; a random *quantity* is a function whose range is included in the reals, or in a set of vectors whose components are reals. There is no real difference between a random quantity and a quantity.)

(c) "$S \equiv z(x) \in w$" is a member of K

(d) the proportion (or measure) of y that have z-values in w is *known* to be in the interval (p, q); i.e., the statement "$M(y, z \in w) = (p, q)$" is in K.

(e) x is a *random member* of y with respect to having a z-value in w, relative to K.

Comment: As a common special case, take w to be the characteristic function of the set v—i.e., suppose that we know: "$(x)((w(x) \in [1] \wedge x \in v) \vee (w(x) \in [0] \wedge {\sim}x \in v))$". Then if there exist expressions x, y, and v in L such that

(a$'$) "$S \equiv x \in v$" is in K

(b$'$) the proportion (measure) of y that is v is known in K to be in (p, q)

(c$'$) x is a random member of y with respect to v, relative to K,

then $P_L(S, K) = (p, q)$

3. The Corpus K

This represents what is "accepted" in a given context—both observational data that are practically certain, the theories, generalizations, and statistical statements that are practically certain or logically true. "Practical certainty" is characterized by a number r, close to l, which may be different in different contexts. Only statements whose lower probability, relative to a more demanding corpus, is greater than r may be accepted in the corpus of level r.

Since the rule of acceptance for a corpus K is essentially a probabilistic one, we should not expect deductive closure: it may be that both S and T are highly probable relative to K', but that their conjunction is not. On the other hand, this should not lead us to think of K as containing only atomic statements: there may well be quite long conjunctions probable enough to relative to K' for inclusion in K. The principle is that in order to accept a conjunction, that conjunction, and not merely its components, must be highly probable. Nor are we without deductive resources: it is a theorem that if S is acceptable in K, and the conditional $\ulcorner S \to T \urcorner$ is in K' (*a fortiori*, if it is a logical truth) then T is also acceptable in K. Putting both observations together, it follows that we can accept the logical consequences of any set of premises whose conjunction we can accept.

Comment: For certain philosophical purposes, the value of r may be taken to be 1. Then the observational data must be construed as phenomenological and therefore incorrigible; and only L-true theories and generalizations and statistical statements may be accepted. (E.g., the logically true statement that most subsets of A have roughly the same frequency of B's as A itself.) In general, however, r is less than 1, and K may contain uncertain statistical statements as well as corrigible data—for example, measurement statements.

4. The Language L

It is proposed to offer criteria (in terms of corpus content) for replacing one language by another. This is an incomplete project, but if it can be carried out will provide a resolution of the problem that $P_L(S,K)$ may not be the same as $P_L'(S',K')$, where S is the "translation" of S into L', K' is the translation of K into L', and K and K' represent roughly the "same" body of experience and acceptance. That is, probabilities do depend on the language in which our bodies of knowledge are formulated, but if we can provide rational grounds for choosing between two languages in terms of corpus content, then probability can still be legislative for rational belief.

Comment: We only need to have criteria for choosing between *two* languages, since we need only be concerned with *actual* alternatives.

5. Equivalence

We require that "$S \equiv z(x) \in w$" be a sentence in K. This is just truth-functional equivalence. It is knowing in K that the sentences S and "$z(x) \in w$" have the same truth value. If I know that "the last toss of this coin yielded heads" has the same truth value as "the first toss of this die performed after its manufacture yielded an ace," then I should assign both the same probability, despite the fact that considered alone, in the absence of the stipulated knowledge, the relevant statistical statements would involve different parameters.

6. Proportion

I use "proportion" loosely. I generally intend "frequency" in a real or hypothetical population. But this should not prejudice the issue of the semantic interpretation of statistical statements in physics and quantum mechanics. Whatever the analysis of such statements may be, however, they do lead to frequency statements in K.

To use Bertrand's example: Suppose we accept in K that a line is thrown on a circle in such a way that the angle subtended by the chord is uniformly distributed between 0 and π. If this represents a close approximation to some physical setup, we may accept that in a long sequence of trials on that setup, the frequency with which the length of the chord is greater than the length of the inscribed triangle is approximately p. If the conditions of randomness are met for a given trial, this will in turn justify the claim that the probability that the chord will exceed the side of the triangle on *that* trial is also p.

7. Reference Terms

Not all terms of a rich language can serve as reference terms: the assumption that any term may be a reference term quickly leads to paradox. Originally I attempted to provide a recursive characterization of reference terms that involved both the language L and the corpus K. (Note that this can be done without circularity: the set of potential reference terms relative to one level of corpus need not be the same as that relative to another level of corpus.) I gave this up in the face of complications, in favor of a syntactic characterization of the set of potential reference terms that depended only on the language L. Now complicatons in that characterization of the set of potential reference terms suggest that a second look at the possibility of having them depend on both L and K might be advisable.

8. Random Variables

Similarly, in a rich language, not all functors can be construed as random variables. I have offered a recursive characterization of a set of random variables dependent on the language L alone; it may be that these, too, should be relativized to K.

9. Randomness

Like probability itself, randomness is a metalinguistic logical relation. Properly we speak of a *term* x standing in this relation of randomness to another *term* y (one of the potential reference terms), relative to a random *variable* z (one of the canonical list of functors), an explicit mathematical term w denoting a Borel set, and relative to a body of sentences K in a language L.

The essential idea behind the definition of randomness is that given a sentence S and a body of knowledge K, rules are to be given which will pick out a set of terms x, y, z, and w such that the relation of randomness will hold for those terms. We do not require that that set of terms be unique: it is required only that for any two sets of quadruples, (x,y,z,w) and (x',y',z',w') picked out for S by the rules, our knowledge about the frequency with which the quantity z has values in w for y be the same as our knowledge about the frequency with which the quantity z' has values in w' for y'.

The two considerations on which the notion of randomness is built are the following: There are two kinds of conflict between two potential reference classes R and R' for determining the probability of S. Our knowledge about R may be represented by an interval that is properly included in the interval representing our knowledge of R' (or vice versa). Or neither interval may be included in the other. In the latter case, at least one of the potential reference sets must be eliminated. (For example, if we know that R is a subset of R', we will eliminate R'.) Having eliminated this sort of conflict among potential reference classes, we want to choose that reference class that gives us the most precise probability: if neither R nor R' is eliminated, but the interval associated with R is included in the interval associated with R', we should take R as the reference set.

10. The Calculus of Probability

The calculus of probability is just what follows from the foregoing—there are no further axioms.

(a) Complementation holds: $P_L(S,K) = (p,q)$ if and only if P_L (" $\sim S$", K) = $(1\text{-}q, 1\text{-}p)$

(b) Finite subadditivity holds: if for every i less than n, $P_L(S_i, K) = (p_i, q_i)$, and "$S_0 \vee S_1 \vee \ldots \vee S_{i-1} \rightarrow \sim S_i$" belongs to K, and P_L ("$S_0 \vee S_1 \vee \ldots S_{n-1}$", K) = (r, s), then

$$\sum_{i=0}^{n-1} p_i \leqslant r \leqslant s \leqslant \sum_{i=0}^{n-1} q_i$$

(c) Given any finite set of statements S_i, there is a coherent measure function B such that for all i,

$$B(S_i) \in P_L(S_i, K)$$

(d) Conditionalization fails, in the sense that if $P("S \wedge R", K) = (p, q)$ $P_L(S, K) = (p', q')$, and $P_L(T, K_S) = (p'', q'')$, where K_S is the corpus obtained by *accepting* S when the original corpus is K, then there *may* be no coherent measure function B such that $B("S \wedge T") \in (p, q)$, $B(S) \in (p', q')$ and $[B("S \wedge T")] / [B(S)]$ $\in (p'', q'')$. This implies that there is a difference between bets made *now* conditional on S and bets contemplated conditional on the *acceptance* of S.

10

Probability and Randomness

1. The difficulties that surround the notion of randomness are becoming quite well known.[1] Most contemporary treatments of probability attempt to define randomness in terms of probability, and most of them fail. Most contemporary treatments of probability have other shortcomings as well.[2] This paper is an attempt to support the conjecture that the horse has been put behind the cart; that the best notion to take as primitive is that of randomness; and that it may even be possible to define the notion of randomness first, and then that of probability in terms of randomness.

The paper is divided into three parts. First I shall introduce the concept of a rational corpus (formalized as a set of statements); set down some properties that we might expect the randomness relation to obey, and define probability accordingly. The concept of probability, so defined, turns out to be plausible in some respects, implausible in others. I then shall proceed to consider a very special case—which corresponds to the ordinary statistical conception of probability—in the hope that principles that will guide us to a sound definition of randomness will come to light. The third section will explore the question of how far these principles take us in the direction of generality.

I

2. Randomness, and hence probability, will be defined syntactically. I shall therefore take a rational corpus—relative to which all assertions of randomness and probability will be made—to be simply a set of statements having certain formal properties. To fix our ideas, we may take Quine's system of *Mathematical Logic* as legislative for logical truth. I shall take this system, supplemented by a

Reprinted from *Theoria*, no. 29 (1963), pp. 27-55, by permission of the publisher. Based on papers delivered at the 1959 meeting of the Association for Symbolic Logic and the 1960 International Congress for the History and Philosophy of Science. A more detailed treatment appears in my book, *Probability and the Logic of Rational Belief* (Middletown: Wesleyan University Press, 1961).

finite number of primitive predicates (of arbitrary type-relationship) to be the language of rational belief.

The first requirement of any set of statements that is going to be construed as a rational corpus is that it shall not contain contradictions: If a statement S belongs to it, then the statement nS—the denial of S—should not belong to it. Let us denote the rational corpus we are considering by $\mathcal{L}$. (I confine the use of the ordinary logical symbols to the metalanguage, employing Quine's protosyntactical notation to name, in the metalanguage, the logical symbols of the object language.) This gives us Axiom I:

I $$S \in \mathcal{L} \supset {\sim}nS \in \mathcal{L}.$$

This axiom is already somewhat questionable; it might come into conflict with the other axioms, should Quine's ML turn out to be inconsistent. But I shall merely suppose that if this should turn out to be the case, we would simply alter the system of ML.

The second (and rather trivial requirement) I shall impose on $\mathcal{L}$, is that it not be empty:

II $$(\exists x)(x \in \mathcal{L}).$$

A third requirement will be that of logical closure; but there are good reasons for wanting to use a rather weak form of logical closure.

A rational corpus may be construed as representing a body of beliefs of a person, or of a group of people, or of a society, or of God; it may be construed as a set of statements that are true, or it may be construed as a bare, simple set of statements whose relations to other statements interest us. Most important of all, I think, it may be understood as a set of statements that are overwhelmingly probable relative to some other set of statements. In the contexts in which we are most interested, a statement gets into $\mathcal{L}$ by being worthy of rational belief, which is to say, by virtue of its probability. One ought to believe what is probable, not what is true. How probable should these probable statements be? They should be practically certain. A degree of probability corresponding to practical certainty in one context may not in another context; but we can have a general theory by considering a sequence of rational corpora, of different levels, corresponding to different senses of "practical certainty." A rational corpus of the highest level would contain no probable statements at all, but only logical truths and (perhaps) some kind of sense data statements or protocol statements. A lower level rational corpus—say the level characterized by the ratio .99, which would correspond to the body of beliefs based on the association of "practical certainty" with the probability 0.99—would contain just those statements whose probability, relative to the set of statements constituting the next higher level of rational corpus, was at least 0.99.

Why consider rational corpora containing statements that are not known, but only probable? Because most of the statements that function as premises or even as data in scientific inferences, as well as in ordinary day-to-day assignments of probability, are themselves only probable. But these statements are simply *accepted;* they are not, in the context in which they serve as data or as the basis for other probability statements, merely regarded as probable. I do not regard the statistical hypothesis that this coin will land heads a fifth of the time in the long run as "improbable' in the same sense that I regard it as improbable that the next ten tosses of this coin will all land heads. In most contexts I would simply accept the hypothesis that the relative frequency of heads will be around a half, and I would simply reject any conflicting hypothesis; though all these hypotheses (relative to a philosophical corpus of the highest degree) are only probable in varying degrees. On the other hand, I would regard the chances of heads ten times in a row as one in a thousand — in most ordinary contexts.

But if we accept merely probable statements into $\mathcal{I}$, then we must reject complete logical closure of the sort that says: If S_1, S_2, . . . S_n belong to $\mathcal{I}$, and if the conditional whose antecedent is the conjunction of S_1 . . . S_n, and whose consequent is T, $S_1 \mathrm{cj} S_2 \mathrm{cj}$ . . . $S_n \mathrm{cd} T$, is a logical truth, then T will belong to $\mathcal{I}$. The following example will illustrate the need for this rejection.

Just as we would accept (in many contexts) a statistical hypothesis that had only one chance in a million of being false, so we should accept (before the drawing) the statement, "Ticket 456-357 will not win the one prize in a million-ticket lottery." The same thing is true of the statement, "Ticket 386-952 will not win the prize," and in general of every statement of the form, "Ticket i will not win the prize, where i is an integer between 0 and 1,000,000.

The following statement is logically true: "Ticket 000-001 will not win the prize $\supset$ (ticket 000-002 will not win the prize $\supset$ ticket 000-001 will not win the prize *and* ticket 000-002 will not win the lottery." In any rational corpus in which a million-to-one shot consitutes a practical impossibility, the two statements, "Ticket 000-001 will not win the lottery," and "Ticket 000-002 will not win the lottery," will appear. By the above principle of complete logical closure, we will therefore have the statement, "Ticket 000-001 will not win the lottery, *and* ticket 000-002 will not win the lottery," in the rational corpus. It is easy to see how this process may be carried on to the point where we have in the rational corpus the conjunction of a million statements, "Ticket 000-001 will not win and ticket 000-002 will not win and . . . and ticket 999-999 will not win the lottery." Together with the statement "there are exactly a million tickets in the lottery," we will be able to have in our rational corpus, "No ticket will win the lottery." But by hypothesis, we already have the statement, "Exactly one ticket will win the lottery." Thus we have a contradiction, in direct violation of Axiom I.

If the set of statements we are going to call a rational corpus is going to deserve the epithet 'rational', we clearly cannot abandon Axiom I. We must therefore weaken the notion of logical closure, or else abandon the hope that it will turn out to be rational to believe what is only probable. I shall weaken the notion of logical closure, and I shall do it by limiting to one the number of premises that may serve as basis for an argument justifying the inclusion of a statement in $\mathcal{L}$. I shall say that if $S \in \mathcal{L}$, and if S cd T is *logicaly true*, then T will belong to $\mathcal{L}$. ('X is logically true' will be written 'Thm X')

III $\qquad\qquad S \in \mathcal{L} \cdot \text{Thm } (S \text{ cd } T) \cdot \supset T \in \mathcal{L}.$

3. We shall need (in virtue of our limited form of logical closure) the notion of a biconditional chain. It is perfectly possible that S_1 b S_2 and S_2 b S_3 can both belong to $\mathcal{L}$, while S_1 b S_3 does not. (I denote the biconditional whose components are S and T by 'S b T'.) There is still an important relationship between S_1 and S_3, even though the statement S_1 b S_3 does not belong to $\mathcal{L}$. I shall say that S_1 and S_3 are connected by a *biconditional chain*. In general, if there is a sequence of biconditionals each of which is either an element of $\mathcal{L}$, or is S_i b T_i, where there is a statement R_i such that S_i b R_i and R_i b T_i both occur earlier in the sequence, and to which S b T belongs, then I shall say that S and T are connected by a biconditional chain. Following Quine, I shall write '$x \text{Pr}_z y$' to mean that the expression x is prior to the expression y, in the sequence of expressions z; this relationship among expressions is defined formally by Quine. I shall write 'S $\mathcal{L}$-B T' to mean that S is connected by a biconditional chain to T, in the rational corpus $\mathcal{L}$. I use 'y Ing z' to mean that expression y is in the sequence of expressions z.

Definition 1:

$\qquad$ "S $\mathcal{L}$-B T" *for* "$(\exists x)\,((y)\,(z)\,(y \text{ b } z \text{ Ing } x \supset \cdot y \text{ b } z \in \mathcal{L} \vee$
$\qquad (\exists w)\,(y \text{ b } w \text{ Pr}_x\, y \text{ b } z \cdot w \text{ b } z \text{ Pr}_x\, y \text{ b } z)) \cdot S \text{ b } T \text{ Ing } x)$".

The following six theorems, which show, first, that 'being connected in $\mathcal{L}$ by a biconditional chain' is an equivalence relation, and, second, that the existence of some biconditional chains assure us of the existence of others, can be proved with the help of sentential tautologies, and Axiom III.

$\qquad$ *Theorem 1:* S $\mathcal{L}$-B S.
$\qquad$ *Theorem 2:* S $\mathcal{L}$-B T if and only if T $\mathcal{L}$-B S.
$\qquad$ *Theorem 3:* If S $\mathcal{L}$-B T and T $\mathcal{L}$-B R, then S $\mathcal{L}$-B R.
$\qquad$ *Theorem 4:* If S $\mathcal{L}$-B T, then nS $\mathcal{L}$-B nT.
$\qquad$ *Theorem 5:* If S_1 $\mathcal{L}$-B T_1 and S_2 $\mathcal{L}$-B T_2, then S_1 cj S_2 $\mathcal{L}$-B T_1 cj T_2 ('T cj S' denotes the conjunction of T and S. The theorem may be proved using the tautology '$p \equiv q \cdot \supset : p \cdot t_1 \cdot \equiv \cdot q \cdot t_1$', and the tautology '$p \equiv q \cdot \supset : s_n \cdot p \cdot \equiv s_n \cdot q$', and Theorem 3).
$\qquad$ *Theorem 6:* If S_1 $\mathcal{L}$-B T_1 and S_2 $\mathcal{L}$-B T_2, then S_1 al S_2 $\mathcal{L}$-B T_1 al T_2. ('T al S' denotes the alternation of T and S. The theorem may be proved using the tautologies,

$\qquad$ "$p \equiv q \cdot \supset : p \vee r \cdot \equiv \cdot q \vee r$" and "$p \equiv q \cdot \supset : r \vee p \cdot \equiv \cdot r \vee q$".)

4. Among the statements in $\mathcal{L}$ that will particularly interest us will be statis-

tical statements. By a statistical statement, I mean a statement which states that the proportion of members of a class A that are also member of a class B, lies between the bounds p and q, where $p \leqslant q$; or, more generally, that the probability measure of the elements of $A \cap B$ in the set A lies between these bounds. Symbolically, I shall render such a statement thus:

$$\%(A, B, (p; q))$$

Its name will be rendered:

$$\text{``}\%(A, B, (p; q))\text{''}$$

The following is to be regarded as a logical truth:

$$\text{``}p \geqslant p' \cdot q \leqslant q' \cdot \% (A, B, (p; q)) \cdot \supset \% (A, B, (p'; q'))\text{''}$$

Where p, p', q, and q' are real numbers, statements such as "$p \geqslant p'$" are logically true, if true at all, so that whenever "$p \geqslant p'$" and "$q \leqslant q'$" are true, "$\% (A, B, (p; q)) \supset \% (A, B, (p'; q'))$" is logically true, and when "$\% (A, B, (p; q))$" belongs to $\mathcal{1}$, so (by Axiom III) does "$\% (A, B, (p'; q'))$". It seems reasonable to call the former statement *stronger* than the latter. A strongest statement is simply one which logically implies every other statement in $\mathcal{1}$ about the same subject matter, and which is implied only by statements equally strong. (Note that

$$\text{``}\% (A, B, (1/4; 3/4))\text{''} \quad \text{and} \quad \text{``}\% (A, B, (2/8; 6/8))\text{''}$$

are different statements of equal strength.) The following definitions define 'stronger than' as applied to statistical statements in $\mathcal{1}$, and 'strongest'. In these defintions—and in some of those to follow—I shall quantify into expressions in quotation marks. I shall not do this, however, except in contexts that could be reforumulated in syntax to require quantification only over strictly extensional contexts.

Definition 2:

$$\text{`` `}\% (A, B, (p; q))\text{' } \mathcal{1}\text{-Str `}\% (C, D, (s; t))\text{' ''} \textit{ for}$$
$$\text{``Thm `}p \geqslant s \cdot q \leqslant t\text{' ''}.$$

Definition 3:

$$\text{`` `}\% (A, B, (p; q))\text{' Str*}\mathcal{1}\text{'' } for \text{ `` `}\% (A, B, (p; q))\text{' } \in \mathcal{1}.$$
$$(r) (s) (\text{`}\% (A, B, (r; s))\text{'} \in \mathcal{1} \supset \text{`}\% (A, B, (p; q))\text{'}$$
$$\mathcal{1}\text{-Str `}\% (A, B, (r; s))\text{' ''}.$$

My reason for putting down definition 2 will be apparent later, when I shall introduce definitions for 'differs from' and 'is exactly the same as' as applied to statistical statements belonging to $\mathcal{1}$.

A condition I should like to impose on a rational set of statements is that it should be possible to find a *strongest* statistical statement about any subject matter about which there is a statistical statement in $\mathcal{1}$ at all. This condition is imposed by the following axiom:

IV   If   '% $(y, z, (p; q))$' $\in \mathcal{1}$,
          then $(\exists r) (\exists s) ($'% $(y, z, (r; s))$' Str*$\mathcal{1}$).

Axiom IV not only precludes the possibility of an unending sequence of statistical statements, each stronger than the preceding ones, which does not lead to a limiting statement that belongs to $\mathcal{1}$, but it also precludes the possibility of having statements in $\mathcal{1}$ which assign conflicting probability measures to the same sets.

There is one other small problem connected with statistical statements that I shall take care of by mortal fiat: it is perfectly possible for a probability measure to assign a measure 0 to a set $A \cap C$ in A, even if $A \cap C$ is not empty, but if we want to get probabilities from probability measures, this possibility should not be fulfilled. A slightly weaker condition fulfills the requirements of plausibility; this condition is embodied in Axiom V:

V   If '% $(A, B, (0; 0))$' $\in \mathcal{1}$ then $(x) (\sim'x \in A \cap B' \in \mathcal{1})$.

5. I now introduce a primitive relation, holding among three terms and a set of statements, which is to have an intuitive meaning roughly equivalent to Keynes's concept of randomness. I shall say that the term x is a random member of (bears the random-member-relation to) y, with respect to membership in z, relative to the set of statements $\mathcal{1}$, symbolically, x $\mathcal{1}$-Ran (y, z), only when certain conditions, embodied in further axioms, are met. Note that the reference to z and to $\mathcal{1}$ is required if we are to represent adequately the intuitive notion of randomness. The term x may bear the random-member-realtion to the term y relative to one set of statements $\mathcal{1}$, but not relative to another set of statements $\mathcal{1}$* (new information may cause us to reject an assertion of randomness). The term x may bear the random-member-relationship to the term y, with respect to the term z, but not with respect to the term z* ("the next ball to be drawn from this urn" may bear the random-member-relationship to "the set of balls in the urn" with respect to "the set of red balls," but not with respect to "the set of balls drawn from the urn.") The rest of this paper will be devoted to a search for an adequate characterization of this fundamental relationship.

The definition of probability in terms of randomness is of course rather trivial for us, given the randomness relation. I shall say that the probability of a statement S, relative to the rational set of statements $\mathcal{1}$, is the pair of numbers $(p; q)$, in symbols, S $\mathcal{1}$-Prob $(p; q)$, when there are terms x, y, and z, such that (a) x is a random member of y with respect to z, relative to $\mathcal{1}$, (b) x e z is connected to S by a biconditional chain in $\mathcal{1}$, and (c) there is a strongest statistical statement in $\mathcal{1}$ asserting that the proportion of y's that are z's (or the measure of z in y) falls in the interval $(p; q)$. In the following definition I use the convention that if y and z are terms, the sets that they denote (if any) are Y and Z. Again, it should be observed that the statistical statement mentioned in the definition could be spelled out syntactically in such a way as to avoid reference to the sets themselves.

Definition 4:

"S $\mathcal{1}$-Prob $(p; q)$" *for* "$(\exists x)\,(\exists y)\,(\exists z)\,(S\ \mathcal{1}\text{-B}\ x\ e\ z\ \cdot$
$x\ \mathcal{1}\text{-Ran}\ (y, z)\ \cdot\ \text{'\%}\,(Y, Z, (p; q)))'\ \text{Str*}\ \mathcal{1})$"

("$x\ e\ z$" denotes the statement formed by putting the term x in the first and the term z in the second blank of: "$(\ \in\ )$".)

There are certain characteristics that we may demand the random-member-relation to have. For the remainder of this first part of the paper, I shall follow the natural path and assume (in a sequence of provisional axioms labeled with the letter 'R') the random-member-relation to have characteristics analogous to those generally attributed to the probability relation. I shall also show that ultimately the natural path leads to difficulties.

The following two axioms are minimal. The first embodies the natural requirement that if the terms x, y, and z, and the set of statements $\mathcal{1}$, satisfy the randomness relationship, then the set of statements $\mathcal{1}$ must include the statement $x\ e\ y$. To say that x is a random member of y is at least to say that x is a member of y. The second is a meaty axiom, required for the proof the Theorem 7, which establishes uniqueness for probabilities. The axiom says that if two statements, $x_1\ e\ z_1$ and $x_2\ e\ z_2$ are connected by a biconditional chain, and x_1 is a random member of y_1 with respect to z_1 relative to $\mathcal{1}$, and x_2 is a random member of y_2 with respect to z_2, relative to $\mathcal{1}$, then a strongest statement in $\mathcal{1}$ about y_1 and z_1 will mention the pair of numbers $(p; q)$ if and only if a strongest statement about y_2 and z_2 mentions this pair of numbers.

R I   If x $\mathcal{1}$-Ran (y, z), then $x\ e\ y \in \mathcal{1}$.

R II   If $x_1\ e\ z_1$ $\mathcal{1}$-B $x_2\ e\ z_2$, x_1 $\mathcal{1}$-Ran (y_1, z_1), and x_2 $\mathcal{1}$-Ran (y_2, z_2),
       then '% $(Y_1, Z_1, (p; q))$' Str*$\mathcal{1}$ if and only if
       '% $(Y_2, Z_2, (p; q)))$' Str* $\mathcal{1}$.

The next three axioms are those which are the analogues of ordinary probability axioms. They lead to a calculus of probability, and to difficulties.

R III x $\mathcal{1}$-Ran (y, z) only if x $\mathcal{1}$-Ran $(y, \text{compl}\ z)$
(compl z is the term denoting the complement of the set denoted by z.)

R IV   If x_1 $\mathcal{1}$-Ran (y_1, z_1) and x_2 $\mathcal{1}$-Ran (y_2, z_2), then
               $(x_1\ Px_2)$ $\mathcal{1}$-Ran $(y_1\ \text{cp}\ y_2, z_1\ \text{cp}\ z_2)$
($y_1\ \text{cp}\ y_2$ is a term denoting the Cartesian product of Y_1 and Y_2; $x_1\ Px_2$ is a term denoting the ordered pair $(X_1; X_2)$.)

R V   If x_1 $\mathcal{1}$-Ran (y_1, z_1) and x_2 $\mathcal{1}$-Ran (y_2, z_2), then
               $(x_1\ Px_2)\mathcal{1}$-Ran $(y_1\ \text{cp}\ y_2, (z_1\ \text{cp}\ y_2)\ \text{un}\ (y_1\ \text{cp}\ z_2))$
($x\ \text{un}\ y$ is a term denoting the union of X and Y.)

These axioms provide for a number of properties that we expect any explicatum for probability to have. One of these properties is uniqueness: a given statement should have only one probability in a given context. Furthermore, statements that are equivalent should have the same probability. Both of these properties are immediate consequences of the following theorem, which establishes that any two statements connected by a biconditional chain in $\mathcal{L}$, have precisely one probability.

Theorem 7: If S_1 $\mathcal{L}$-B S_2 and S_1 $\mathcal{L}$-Prob $(p; q)$, then S_2 $\mathcal{L}$-Prob $(r; s)$ if and only if $p = r$ and $q = s$.

Proof: By definition 4, if S_1 $\mathcal{L}$-Prob $(p; q)$, there exist an x, a y, and a z, such that S_1 $\mathcal{L}$-B x e z, x $\mathcal{L}$-Ran (y, z), and '% $(Y, Z, (p; q))$' Str* $\mathcal{L}$. If $p = r$ and $q = s$, '% $(Y, Z, (p; q)) \supset$ % $(Y, Z, (r; s))$' is a theorem, so that (by Axiom III) '% $(Y, Z, (r; s))$' Str* $\mathcal{L}$. Since being connected by a biconditional chain is an equivalence relation, we also have S_2 $\mathcal{L}$-B x e z, and thus all the ingredients of S_2 $\mathcal{L}$-Prob $(r; s)$.

On the other hand, if S_2 $\mathcal{L}$-Prob $(r; s)$, there must exist an x^*, a y^*, and a z^* such that S_2 $\mathcal{L}$-B x^* e z^*, x^* $\mathcal{L}$-Ran (y^*, z^*) and '% $(Y^*, Z^*, (r; s))$' Str* $\mathcal{L}$. According to R II, under these circumstances, '% $(Y^*, Z^*, (r; s))$' Str* $\mathcal{L}$ if and only if '% $(Y, Z, (r; s))$' Str* $\mathcal{L}$, and '% $(Y, Z, (p; q))$' Str* $\mathcal{L}$ if and only if '% $(Y^*, Z^*, (p; q))$' Str* $\mathcal{L}$. In short, we must have both '% $(Y, Z, (r; s))$' Str*$\mathcal{L}$ and '% $(Y, Z, (p; q))$' Str* $\mathcal{L}$, which implies, according to Definitions 2 and 3, Thm '$p \geqslant r \cdot q \leqslant s$' and Thm '$p \leqslant r \cdot q \geqslant s$'; and these two statements can be theorems only when $p = r$ and $q = s$, or when our mathematics in inconsistent. We have ruled the latter possibility out of consideraton by Axioms I and II.

The following three theorems provide the background for a calculus of probability; they correspond to the law of negation, the general addition law, and the special multiplication law.

Theorem 8: If S $\mathcal{L}$-Prob $(p; q)$, then nS $\mathcal{L}$-Prob $(1-q; 1-p)$.

Lemma: If '% $(y, z, (p; q))$' Str* $\mathcal{L}$, then '% $(y, \bar{z}, (1-q; 1-p))$' Str* $\mathcal{L}$.

Proof: "% $(y, z, (p; q)) \equiv$ % $(y, \bar{z}, (1-q; 1-p))$" is a theorem, so that '% $(y, \bar{z}, (1-q; 1-p))$' $\in \mathcal{L}$. Let '% $(y, \bar{z}, (s; t))$' be any other statistical statement about y and z, in the set of statements $\mathcal{L}$; with the help of the foregoing theorem , we have '% $(y, z, (1-t; 1-s))$' $\in \mathcal{L}$. But Definition 3 then provides that Thm '$1-t \leqslant p \cdot 1-s \geqslant q$'. But this is just to say, Thm '$s \leqslant 1-q \cdot t \geqslant 1-p$', so that '% $(y, \bar{z}, (1-q; 1-p))$' Str* $\mathcal{L}$.

Proof of Theorem 8: Theorem 4, Axiom R III, and the above Lemma, yield Theorem 8 directly.

Theorem 9: If S_1 $\mathcal{L}$-Prob $(p_1; q_1)$ and S_2 $\mathcal{L}$-Prob $(p_2; q_2)$, then S_1 cj S_2 $\mathcal{L}$-Prob $(r; s)$ only if $r \geqslant p_1 \times p_2$ and $s \leqslant q_1 \times q_2$, provided that the conjunction of the two statistical statements required for the hypothesis appears in $\mathcal{L}$.

Lemma: If '% $(y_1, z_1, (p_1; q_1))$' Str* $\mathcal{L}$ and '% $(y_2, z_2, (p_2; q_2))$' Str* $\mathcal{L}$ and the conjunction of these two statements is in $\mathcal{L}$, then '% $(y_1 \times y_2, z_1 \times z_2 (p_1 \times p_2; q_1 \times q_2))$' will appear in $\mathcal{L}$.

Proof: III and the fact that '% $(y_1, z_1, (p_1; q_1)) \cdot$ % $(y_2, z_2, (p_2; q_2)) \cdot \supset$ % $(y_1 \times y_2, z_1 \times z_2, (p_1 \times p_2; q_1 \times q_2))$' is a logical truth.

Proof of Theorem 9: Either '% $(y_1 \times y_2, z_1 \times z_2, (p_1 \times p_2; q_1 \times q_2))$' Str* $\mathcal{L}$ or else there exists a statistical statement about $y_1 \times y_2$ and $z_1 \times z_2$ which is stronger than the one just mentioned. By Axiom IV, there is a strongest statement about these sets; i.e., there is a pair of numbers $(r; s)$ such that: '% $(y_1 \times y_2, z_1 \times z_2, (r; s))$' Str* $\mathcal{1}$ and $r \geqslant p_1 \times p_2$ and $s \leqslant q_1 \times q_2$. Using Axiom R IV, Theorem 5, and Definition 4, we have Theorem 9. Before commenting on this 'theorem', I shall give one more lemma and theorem, corresponding to the addition rule for probabilities.

Theorem 10. If S_1 $\mathcal{1}$-Prob $(p_1; q_1)$ and S_2 $\mathcal{1}$-Prob $(p_2; q_2)$, then S_1 al S_2 $\mathcal{1}$-Prob $(r; s)$ only if $r \geqslant p_1 + p_2 - p_1 p_2$ and $s \leqslant q_1 + q_2 - q_1 q_2$, provided that the conjunction of the two statistical statements relevant to the hypothesis appears in $\mathcal{1}$.

Lemma: If '% $(y_1, z_1, (p_1; q_1))$' Str* $\mathcal{1}$ and '% $(y_2, z_2, (p_2; q_2))$' Str* $\mathcal{1}$, and the conjunction of these two statistical statements also belongs to $\mathcal{1}$, then '% $(y_1 \times y_2, (z_1 \times y_2) \cup (y_1 \times z_2), (p_1 + p_2 - p_1 p_2; q_1 + q_2 - q_1 q_2))$' $\in \mathcal{1}$.

Proof of the lemma: Axiom III, and the fact that '% $(y_1, z_1, (p_1; q_1))$ · % $(y_2, z_2, (p_2; q_2))$ · $\supset$ % $(y_1 \times y_2, (z_1 \times y_2) \cup (y_1 \times z_2), (p_1 + p_2 - p_1 p_2; q_1 + q_2 - q_1 q_2))$' is a logical truth.

Proof of Theorem 10: Let y_1, y_2, z_1, and z_2 be the sets determined by the hypothesis (and definition 4); then, by the lemma, '% $(y_1 \times y_2, (z_1 \times y_2) \cup (y_1 \times z_2), (p_1 + p_2 - p_1 p_2; q_1 + q_2 - q_1 q_2))$' $\in \mathcal{1}$. By Axiom IV, there is a strongest statement in $\mathcal{1}$ about $y_1 \times y_2$ and $(z_1 \times y_2) \cup (y_1 \times z_2)$, say '% $(y_1 \times y_2, (z_1 \times y_2) \cup (y_1 \times z_2), (r; s))$' Str* $\mathcal{1}$, with $q_1 + q_2 - q_1 q_2 \leqslant s$ and $r \geqslant p_1 + p_2 - p_1 p_2$. Theorem 6, Axiom R V, and the lemma, then yield Theorem 10.

6. That we do not want to regard Theorem 9 as generally true is obvious from the fact that it corresponds to the special rather than to the general multiplication rule in ordinary probability calculi. If we draw balls, without replacement, from an urn containing two white balls and a black one, we should say that the probability of getting a black ball on the first draw is 1/3; the probability of getting a black ball on the second draw is 1/3; but the probability of getting both a black ball on the first draw and a black ball on the second draw is 0. In the ordinary way of looking at the matter, we say that the draws are not *independent,* and that the special multiplication rule therefore does not apply.

I would rather look at the matter in a different way. I would say that the difficulty lay in the implicit use of R IV, that this axiom was not true in some special cases, and hence should be rejected as characteristic of randomness. I should interpret the three foregoing statements about probability as follows: 'The ball to be drawn first' is a definite description; taking $\mathcal{1}$ as a set of statements I have good reason to believe, the ball it describes, is, relative to $\mathcal{1}$, a random member of the set of three balls in the urn, with respect to having the color black. Since I know that 1/3 of the balls are black, the probability that this ball is black is 1/3. The second statement means the same kind of thing: 'the ball to be drawn second' is simply another definite description, and the ball it describes is, relative to $\mathcal{1}$, a random member of the set of three balls in the urn with respect to having the color black. Note that on my interpretation, both of these statements hold without regard to the manner of drawing: with or without replacement, with or without statistical independence (since no statement about statistical dependence among the draws is included in $\mathcal{L}$). According to Theorem 9, we should therefore have: "The probability is 1/9 that the first ball to be drawn is black and the second ball to be drawn is black," and this clearly will not do. But the proof of Theorem 9 makes use of R IV, which say that if the first ball is a random member of the set of all three balls, and if the second ball is a random member of the set of all three balls, then the pair consisting of the first ball and the second ball is a random member of the Cartesian product of these two sets. This situation does obtain sometimes—for example, if we make the draws with replacement, or from two urns. But it does not hold always, as our example shows. If we make draws without replacement, we do not want to say that the pair of draws is a random member of the Cartesian product of the set of three balls with itself. Why not? Because *we know in advance that there is a proper subset of this set into which the pair of draws must fall;* the pair cannot fall into the diagonal. The pair of draws is, presumably, a random member of the remainder of the Cartesian product; in this remainder, the proportion of pairs of black balls is 0, so that the probability of a pair of black balls being drawn is just what we expect: 0. Since we are dealing in this case with a subset of the general Cartesian product, I feel somewhat justified in regarding this as the special case, rather than that in which R IV, and hence Theorem 9, corresponding to the 'special multiplication rule', holds.

I mentioned that something corresponding to R IV was sometimes illegitimately presupposed in discussions of random sampling. It is often said that a random n-fold sample from a population is one consisting of n objects, each of which is a random member of the population. But this is not the case; consider a population S, of which some elements have the property P. Draw one object; if it has the property P, then the n-fold sample is to consist of this object, together with the next $n-1$ objects drawn at random that have the property P; if the first object lacks the property P, then the n-fold sample is to consist of the first object, together with the next $n-1$ objects drawn at random that lack the property P. On nearly any interpretation of probability and on nearly any understanding of randomness, the i'th object in the n objects constituting our sample is a random member of the population S with respect to exhibiting the property P. But the sample as a whole is clearly not a random member of the n'th power product of the population with itself with respect to the property of representing the relative frequency of P in S. To detail the circumstances under which something like R IV does hold would require an explicit definition of randomness, to which I shall turn later. The italicized line, however, may provide a clue.

Again, in Theorem 10, we have proved something as a theorem which we should prefer not to regard as true in general. We wish to be able to say that the probability of getting a three on a roll of a die is 1/6; that the probability of getting a four on a roll of a die is 1/6; and at the same time that the probability of getting either a three or a four is 2/6, and not 2/6-1/36. The ordinary explanation of the value 2/6 for the probability is that the events of getting a three and of getting a four on a roll of a die are mutually exclusive.

Again, I would prefer to say that the difficulty lies in the general conditional concerning randomness, R V. Although it may be true that the n'th roll of this die is a random member of the set of all its rolls with respect to the property of showing a three, and that the n'th roll is a random member of the set of all its rolls with respect to the property of showing a four, it is not true that the n'th roll, paired with the n'th roll, is a random member of the Cartesian product of the set of rolls of the die with itself, with respect to the property of showing a three *or* a four. It is not a random member of this set because we know that the only set of pairs in the Cartesian product that the n'th roll with the n'th roll can belong to, are those in the diagonal; and here, of course, the proportion of elements that belong to the class we are interested in is 1/3.

There are, of course, circumstances in which R V, and hence Theorem 10, do apply. The easiest to visualize is that in which we have two bags, B_1 and B_2, where B_1 contains a ratio of white balls to black ones of p_1, and B_2 contains a ratio of white balls to black ones of p_2. Then, under ordinary circumstances, a ball drawn at random from B_1 may be combined with one drawn at random from B_2 to give a pair which is a random member of the set of all pairs of balls, the first of which is from B_1 and the second of which is from B_2.

It is worth noting that we cannot even be sure that either R V or the conventional special-addition theorem, adapted to my system, will apply. It may be that the pair we are considering is a random member of neither the whole Cartesian product of the basic reference classes, nor of the diagonal, but may be a random member of some other subset of the general Cartesian product. Suppose we are playing a special game with a pair of dice, in which a *play* consists of a throw of the dice in which the two dice show different numbers of dots. The probability that the first die will show a three is 1/6; the probability that the second die will show a four is 1/6; but the probability that the first will show a three or the second a four, on a given play, will be neither 1/3 nor 11/36, but 3/10.

On the basis of the definition of probability given here, in terms of randomness and a set of statements representing a hypothetical rational corpus or body of knowledge, we can thus establish an analogue only of the conventional rule for the probability of the denial of a proposition or the complement of an event. The special multiplication rule and the general addition rule for probabilities, in a suitably modified form, can be derived if we are willing to add Axioms R IV and R V to our system; but there are good reasons for refusing to make these additions: they preclude the possibility of interpreting 'Prob' in the formal system as the 'probability' of ordinary discourse. A different and more complicated characterization of randomness is required.

II

7. I shall now impose very severe restrictions on the set of statements $\mathcal{L}$, relative to which probability statements will be asserted, and I shall show that under these restrictions we can define randomness in such a way that we not only get the ordinary calculus of probability, but that if we regard this set of statements in a certain light—as containing only statements that are both true and worthy of belief—my (potentially) syntactical defintion of probability will perform all the functions that are ordinarily performed by frequency (or abstract-analogue-of-frequency) definitions, in addition to some other functions. Furthermore, in this special case it is easy to provide a simple, constructive, explicit definition of randomness.

First of all I shall restrict the relevant statistical statements that appear in $\mathcal{L}$ to statements about subsets of a given set K; furthermore I shall suppose that these statistical statements are perfectly precise; and I shall suppose that this set of subsets of K constitutes a field of sets. Finally I shall suppose that if a statement S is connected to a statement "$x \in y$" by a biconditional chain, where y belongs to the set of subsets mentioned above, and S is also connected to "$x_1 \in y_1$" by a biconditional chain, and y_1 also belongs to this set of subsets, then x and x_1 denote the same object. All this is embodied in the following additional axioms. It amounts to this: we restrict our probabilistic considerations to a fixed reference class K, and in fact we concern ourselves only with a definite field of subsets of K. This is essentially the case when we are considering only the outcomes of a definite game of chance; and, as may well be expected, the situation is not as complicated in such circumstances as this as it is in general. Statements R I-R V, which were treated as axioms in Section 5, are now to be replaced by the following: (IK denotes a set of terms, whose extension is the field of subsets of K described above.)

K I   If $x \in IK$, then "$X \subset K$" $\in \mathcal{L}$.

K II   If $x, y \in IK$, then $(\exists p) (\exists q)$ ('% $(K, X, (p; p))$.
                % $(K, Y, (q; q))$)' $\in \mathcal{L}$).

K III   If $x \in IK$ and $y \in IK$, then x un $y \in IK$, x int $y \in IK$,
                and compl x int 'K' $\in IK$

(x int y is a term denoting the intersection of X and Y; x un y is a term denoting the union of X and Y).

K IV   If S $\mathcal{L}$-B x e y and S $\mathcal{L}$-B z e w and $w \in IK$ and $y \in IK$,
                then (v) $(x$ e $v \in \mathcal{L} \supset z$ e $v \in \mathcal{L})$.

(Observe that I have substituted indistinguishability in the rational corpus for actual identity. As far as the *calculus ratiocinator* is concerned, it seems that Leibniz was right!)

K V   If y incl $z \in \mathcal{L}$ and z incl $y \in \mathcal{L}$ and x_1 e w_1 $\mathcal{L}$-B x_2 e w_2,

then   '% $(Y, W_1, (p; p))$' Str*$\mathcal{L}$ if and only if '% $(Z, W_2, (p; p))$'
Str*$\mathcal{L}$, where y, z, w_1, and $w_2 \in IK$.

I now come to four theorems establishing the completeness of our knowledge about the field of interesting subsets of K.

Theorem 11: If $y \in IK$ and $z \in IK$ and $(\exists q)$ $(q \neq 0 \cdot$ '% $(K, Y, (q; q)$' $\in \mathcal{L})$ then $(\exists p)$ ('% $(Y, Z, (p; p))$' $\in \mathcal{L})$.

Proof: By K III, the intersection term y int z will belong to IK, since y and z do. Thus, by K II, we not only have '% $(K, Y \cap Z, (r; r))$' $\in$ for some r, but we also have '% $(K, Y \cap Z, (r; r))$ $\cdot$ % $(K, Y, (q; q))$' $\in \mathcal{L}$. But with the help of the theorem, '% $(K, Y \cap Z, (r; r))$ $\cdot$ % $(K, Y, (q; q))$ $\supset$ % $(Y, Z, (r/q; r/q))$', Axiom III assures us that '% $(Y, Z, (r/q; r/q))$' $\in \mathcal{L}$.

Theorem 12: If $(\exists p)$ $(p \neq 0 \cdot$ '% $(K, X, (p; p))$' $\in \mathcal{L})$ and $(\exists p)$ $(p \neq 0 \cdot$ '% $(K, X \cap Y, (p; p))$' $\in \mathcal{L})$, then: if x, y, and z belong to IK, '% $(X, Y, (p; p))$' $\in \mathcal{L} \cdot$ '% $(X \cap Y, Z, (q; q))$' $\in \mathcal{L} \cdot \supset$ '% $(X, Y \cap Z, (pq; pq))$' $\in \mathcal{L}$.

Proof: The sets x int y, y int z, and x int y int z all belong to IK, in virtue of K III. Let p_1, p_2, and p_3 be the numbers asserted to exist by axiom K II, so that '% $(K, X, (p_1; p_1))$' $\in \mathcal{L}$, '% $(K, X \cap Y, (p_2; p_2))$' $\in \mathcal{L}$, and '% $(K, X \cap Y \cap Z, (p_3; p_3))$' $\in \mathcal{L}$. By Theorem 11, we have: '% $(X, Y, (p_2/p_1; p_2/p_1))$' $\in \mathcal{L}$, '% $(X \cap Y, Z, (p_3/p_2; p_3/p_2))$' $\in \mathcal{L}$. Since '$r \neq s \cdot$ % $(A, B, (r; r)) \cdot \supset \sim$ % $(A, B, (s; s))$' is a logical truth, we have, by Axioms I and III (and the hypothesis of Theorem 12): $p = p_2/p_1$, and $q = p_3/p_2$. But, again by Theorem 11, we have '% $(X, Y \cap Z, (p_3/p_1; p_3/p_1))$' $\in \mathcal{L}$.

Theorem 13: If $(\exists p)$ ('% $(K, X, (p; p))$' $\in \mathcal{L} \cdot p \neq 0)$ and x, y, $z \in IK$ then '% $(X, Y, (p; p))$' $\in \mathcal{L} \cdot$ '% $(X, Z, (q; q))$' $\in \mathcal{L} \cdot$ '% $(X, Z \cap Y, (r; r))$' $\in \mathcal{L} \cdot \supset$ '% $(X, Z \cup Y, (p + q - r; p + q - r))$' $\in \mathcal{L}$.

Proof: By K III, each of the terms involved belongs to IK; so that, by Axiom K II, there exist numbers p_1, p_2, p_3, and p_4, such that '% $(K, X, (p_1; p_1))$' $\in \mathcal{L}$ and '% $(K, X \cap Y, (p_2; p_2))$' $\in \mathcal{L}$ and '% $(K, X \cap Z, (p_3; p_3))$' $\in \mathcal{L}$ and '% $(K, X \cap Y \cap Z, (p_4; p_4))$' $\in \mathcal{L}$. The last two statistical statements logically imply '% $(K, X \cap Z \cap \bar{Y}, (p_3 - p_4; p_3 - p_4))$', so that it will appear in $\mathcal{L}$, and by Axiom K II, its conjunction with '% $(K, X \cap Y, (p_2; p_2))$' will appear in $\mathcal{L}$. In virtue of the theoremhood of '% $(K, X \cap Z \cap \bar{Y}, (p_3 - p_4; p_3 - p_4)) \cdot$ % $(K, X \cap Y, (p_2, p_2)) \cdot \supset$ % $(K, X \cap (Y \cup Z), (p_2 + p_3 - p_4; p_2 + p_3 - p_4))$', we have '% $(K, X \cap (Y \cup Z), (p_2 + p_3 - p_4; p_2 + p_3 - p_4))$' $\in \mathcal{L}$ and hence, by Theorem 11, we have the consequent of Theorem 13.

Theorem 14: If $(\exists p)$ $(p \neq 0 \cdot$ '% $(K, X, (p; p))$' $\in \mathcal{L})$ and $(\exists p)$ $(p \neq 0 \cdot$ '% $(K, X \cap Y, (p; p))$' $\in \mathcal{L})$, and x, y, $z \in IK$, then '% $(X, Y, (p; p))$' $\in \mathcal{L} \cdot$ '% $(X, Y \cap Z, (q; q))$' $\in \mathcal{L} \cdot \supset$ '% $(X \cap Y, Z, (q/p; q/p))$' $\in \mathcal{L}$.

Proof: This is simply an extension of Theorem 11; it can be proved in a manner similar to that in which Theorems 12 and 13 were proved.

8. I am now in a position to give an explicit definition of randomness. There is a general heuristic rule for selecting a reference class in applications of statis-

tics, and it is that we should select the *smallest* possible reference class. I shall use this rule: I shall say that x is a random member of y with respect to z (in the master set K), relative to $\mathcal{L}$—in symbols, x $\mathcal{L}$-Ran-K (y, z)—when Y is the smallest subset of K to which the object denoted by x is known to belong.

Definition 5:

$$\text{``}x \ \mathcal{L}\text{-Ran-}K \ (y, z)\text{''} \ for \ \text{``}y \in IK \cdot z \in IK \cdot (w) \ (w \in IK \cdot$$
$$x \ e \ w \in \mathcal{L} \cdot \supset y \ \text{incl} \ w \in \mathcal{L})\text{''}.$$

(I write y incl w for "$Y \subset W$".)

First I shall establish the existence of strongest statistical statements about the elements of IK—henceforth referred to as the interesting subsets of K:

Theorem 15: '% $(Y, Z, (p; p))$' $\in \mathcal{L} \cdot \supset \cdot$ '% $(Y, Z, (p; p))$' Str* $\mathcal{L}$.

Proof: Let '% $(Y, Z, (r; s))$' $\in \mathcal{L}$. If $r > p$ or $s < p$, we would have '% $(Y, Z, (r; s))$' $\supset \sim$ % $(Y, Z, (p; p))$' as a logical truth , and hence, by Axiom III, we would violate Axiom I. But if $r \leqslant p$ and $s \geqslant p$, we have '% $(Y, Z, (p; p))$' $\supset$ % $(Y, Z, (r; s))$' as a logical truth, and the consequent of Theorem 15 is satisfied.

Corollary: If y, $z \in IK$, and $(\exists p)$ $(p \neq 0 \cdot$ '% $(K, Y, (p; p))$' $\in \mathcal{L})$, then $(\exists q)$ ('% $(Y, Z, (q; q))$' Str* $\mathcal{L})$.

The first three statements I listed in Section 6 as axioms governing randomness turn out to be theorems under the conventions of the present section.

Theorem 16: If x $\mathcal{L}$-Ran-K (y, z), then $x \ e \ y \in \mathcal{L}$.

Proof: Definition 5.

Theorem 17: If x_1 e z_1 $\mathcal{L}$-B x_2 e z_2, x_1 $\mathcal{L}$-Ran-K (y_1, z_1) and x_2 $\mathcal{L}$-Ran-K (y_2, z_2), then '% $(Y_1, Z_1 \ (p; q))$' Str*$\mathcal{L}$ if and only if '% $(Y_2, Z_2, (p; q))$' Str* $\mathcal{L}$.

Proof: If x_1 $\mathcal{L}$-Ran-K (y_1, z_1) and x_2 $\mathcal{L}$-Ran-K (y_2, z_2), then by Definition 5, we have y_1 z_1, y_2, and $z_2 \in IK$. Then by Axiom K IV, we have (v) $(x_1 \ e \ v \in \mathcal{L} \equiv x_2 \ e \ v \in \mathcal{L})$. In particular, we have x_1 e $y_2 \in \mathcal{L}$ and x_2 e $y_1 \in \mathcal{L}$. Again referring to Definition 5, we have y_1 incl $y_2 \in \mathcal{L}$ and y_2 incl $y_1 \in \mathcal{L}$; by K V, '% $(Y_1, Z_1 \ (p; p))$' Str* $\mathcal{L}$ if and only if '% $(Y_2, Z_2, (p; p))$' Str* $\mathcal{L}$.

Theorem 18: x $\mathcal{L}$-Ran-K (y, z) only if x $\mathcal{L}$-Ran-K $(y, \text{compl } z)$.

Proof: Axiom K III and Defintion 5.

In this system, due to the highly restrictive definition of randomness, there is only a relatively small class of statements that have probabilities. Only statements connected by biconditional chains in $\mathcal{L}$ to statements of the form "$x \in z$", where z is an interesting subset of K, have probabilities; and even then, "$x \in z$" has a probability only when x is known to belong to a *smallest* interesting subset of K. This might not be the case, even when x is known to belong to K; we might have "$x \in y_1$" and "$x \in y_2$" each belonging to $\mathcal{L}$, where y_1 and y_2 are interesting subsets of K, without having "$x \in y_1 \cap y_2$" in $\mathcal{L}$. But there is one thing we can be sure of, and that is that if S_1 and S_2 are connected by a biconditional chain, and one of them has a probability, the other has the same probability.

Theorem 19: If S_1 $\mathcal{1}$-B S_2 and S_1 $\mathcal{1}$-Prob $(p; p)$, then S_2 $\mathcal{1}$-Prob $(p; p)$.
Proof: Definition 4, the corollary to Theorem 15, and Theorem 17.
Furthermore a statement can have only one probability.
Theorem 20: If S_1 $\mathcal{1}$-Prob $(p; p)$ and S_1 $\mathcal{1}$-Prob $(q; q)$, then $p = q$.
Proof: Definition 4 and Theorem 17.

The next three theorems concern maximum and minimum probabilities and the relation between the probability of a statement and the probability of its negation. The first theorem states that if a statement *x* e *z* appears in $\mathcal{1}$, where $z \in IK$, its probability is unity:

Theorem 21: If *x* e *z* $\in$ $\mathcal{1}$ and $z \in IK$, then *x* e *z* $\mathcal{1}$-Prob $(p; p) \supset p = 1$.

Proof: Let *y* be such that *x* $\mathcal{1}$-Ran-*K* (y, z), as required by Definition 4. Then by Definition 5, *x* e *z* $\in \mathcal{1} \supset y$ incl *z* $\in$ $\mathcal{1}$. But the following is a logical truth: "$Y \subset Z \cdot \supset \% (Y, Z, (1; 1))$". Thus *x* e *z* $\in \mathcal{1} \cdot x$ -Ran-*K* $(y, z) \supset$ '% $(Y, Z, (1; 1))$' Str* $\mathcal{1}$, and hence x e z $\mathcal{1}$-Prob $(1; 1)$. If there is no such y, there is no such probability.

Theorem 22: If *S* $\mathcal{1}$-Prob $(p; p)$, then n*S* $\mathcal{1}$-Prob $(1-p; 1-p)$.
Proof: Like the proof of Theorem 8, using Theorem 18 in place of R III.
Theorem 23: If *x* e compl*z* $\in \mathcal{1}$ and $z \in IK$, then *x* e *z* $\mathcal{1}$-Prob $(p; p) \supset p = 0$.
Proof: Theorems 21 and 22.

9. Now I shall establish the ordinary calculus of probability as it applies to a special class of the probability statements of this system. The first thing we need is the notion of independence; I shall say that two statements of the form *x* e *y* and *x* e *z* are independent if the probability of *x* e *y*, given *x* e *z*, is just the same as that of *x* e *z* alone. The probability of *x* e *y*, *given* *x* e *z*, is simply the probability of *x* e *y* relative to a rational corpus which has been extended by the inclusion of the statement *x* e *z* and its logical implicates. The following pair of definitions defines both conditional probabilities and independence of statements.

Definition 6:

"$\mathcal{1}$ [*x* e *z*]" *for* "$\hat{y}(y \in \mathcal{1}$ V Thm *x* e *z* cd *y* V $(\exists w)(x$ e $w \in \mathcal{1} \cdot$
Thm $(x$ e w cj *x* e *z*) cd *y*) V$(\exists w_1)(\exists w_2)(\exists x_2)(x$ e w_1 $\mathcal{1}$-B x_2 e w_2 .
Thm x_2 e *z* cd *y*)).

Definition 7:

"*x* e *y* $\mathcal{1}$-Indep *x* e *z*" *for* "*x* e *y* $\mathcal{1}$-Prob $(p; q) \equiv$
x e *y* $\mathcal{1}$ [*x* e *z*]-Prob $(p; q)$".

Theorem 23: If $z \in IK$ and $\sim x$ e *z* $\mathcal{1}$-Prob $(0; 0)$, then $\mathcal{1}$ [*x* e *z*] is a rational corpus satisfying Axioms I-V and K I-K V.

Proof: Axiom I. Consider the clauses of Definition 6: clearly the first clause cannot introduce a statement n*S* into $\mathcal{1}$ [*x* e *z*], where *S* is in $\mathcal{1}$, because it introduces nothing new. By the second clause, *x* e *z* and all its logical implicates belong to $\mathcal{1}$ [*x* e *z*]. Can one of these implicates have the form n*S*, where $S \in \mathcal{1}$?

No, since if x e z cd nS is a theorem, so is S cd n x e z, and we would have n x e $z \in \mathbf{\mathit{1}}$, and x e z $\mathbf{\mathit{1}}$-Prob $(0; 0)$. A similar analysis may be applied to the third clause. If the fourth clause introduced a contradiction, we would have to have n x_2 e $z \in \mathbf{\mathit{1}}$; but under the hypothesis of the clause, and K IV, this would imply x e compl $z \in \mathbf{\mathit{1}}$, which is ruled out by the hypothesis of the theorem. Axioms II, III, and IV are unaffected; Axiom V holds because of the hypothesis of the theorem. Axioms K I-K III are unaffected; the final clause of Definition 6 gives us K IV. Axiom K V remains unaffected.

The whole calculus of probability, so far as it applies to statements of the form '$x \in y$', where y is one of the interesting subsets of K now falls out of the following four simple theorems.

Theorem 24: $p \neq 0 \cdot x$ e y $\mathbf{\mathit{1}}$-Prob $(p; p) \cdot y \in IK \cdot z \in IK \cdot x$ e z $\mathbf{\mathit{1}}$ [x e y]-Prob $(q; q) \cdot \supset x$ e y int z $\mathbf{\mathit{1}}$-Prob $(pq; pq)$.

Proof: Let w be a term such that x $\mathbf{\mathit{1}}$-Ran-K (w, y) and (by Definition 5) x $\mathbf{\mathit{1}}$-Ran-K $(w, y$ int $z)$. We also have x $\mathbf{\mathit{1}}$[x e y]-Ran-K $(w$ int $y, z)$. By K IV and K V, we need consider only these terms. By Definition 4, '% $(W, Y, (p; p))' \in \mathbf{\mathit{1}}$ and '% $(W \cap Y, Z, (q; q))' \in \mathbf{\mathit{1}}$ [x e y], and thus '% $(W, Y \cap Z, (pq; pq))' \in \mathbf{\mathit{1}}$ [x e y], and in fact '% $(W, Y \cap Z, (pq; pq))' \in \mathbf{\mathit{1}}$, yielding the desired conclusion.

Theorem 25: If x e y $\mathbf{\mathit{1}}$-Indep x e z, then x e z $\mathbf{\mathit{1}}$-Indep x e y, provided neither x e z $\mathbf{\mathit{1}}$-Prob $(0; 0)$ nor x e y $\mathbf{\mathit{1}}$-Prob $(0; 0)$.

Proof: Definition 7 and the logical truth that holds for any term w: "% $(W, Y, (p; p)) \supset$ % $(W \cap Z, Y, (p; p)) \cdot \equiv \cdot$ % $(W, Z, (q; q)) \supset$ % $(W \cap Y, Z, (q; q))$"

Theorem 26: If '% $(Y, Z, (0; 0))' \in \mathbf{\mathit{1}}$ and $y, z, \in IK$, then x e y $\mathbf{\mathit{1}}$-Prob $(p; p) \cdot x$ e z $\mathbf{\mathit{1}}$-Prob $(q; q) \cdot \supset x$ e y un z $\mathbf{\mathit{1}}$-Prob $(p + q; p + q)$.

Proof: Axiom K IV and Theorem 13.

Theorem 27: If x e y $\mathbf{\mathit{1}}$-Indep x e z, and $y, z, \in IK$, then x e y $\mathbf{\mathit{1}}$-Prob $(p; p) \cdot x$ e z $\mathbf{\mathit{1}}$-Prob $(q; q) \cdot \supset x$ e y int z $\mathbf{\mathit{1}}$-Prob $(pq; pq)$.

Proof: Definition 7, Theorem 24.

The foregoing theorems suffice to establish the ordinary calculus of probability as it applies to statements of the simple form '$x \in y$', where x is a free variable or a proper name, and y is one of the interesting subsets of K. The extension of this system to include probabilities based on measure functions defined for a continuum of subsets of the master-set K is fairly obvious: We depend from a frequency function defined for all Borel sets in K. The above theorems in no way depend on the class-ratio interpretation of '%'.

In the foregoing system there is no natural way of relating the probabilities of statements like x_1 e z_1 and x_2 e z_2, even when x_1 e K_1 and x_2 e K_2 are members of $\mathbf{\mathit{1}}$. But we can (often simply on the basis of our knowledge about the interesting subsets of K) construct a new rational set of statements about a new master-set: the Cartesian product $K_1 \times K_2$. The original set of statistical statements in $\mathbf{\mathit{1}}$, about the interesting subsets of K_1 is now a set of marginal statistical statements about a projection of $K_1 \times K_2$. Suppose that x_1 $\mathbf{\mathit{1}}$-Ran-$K_1 \times$

K_2 (y_1, z_1), and that '% $(Y_1, Z_1, (p; p))$' is a marginal statistical statement about a one-dimensional projection of $K_1 \times K_2$. Then we have x_1 e z_1 $\mathcal{1}$-Prob $(p; p)$, just as we would have had, had we been dealing merely with the master set K_1. In the same way, we might have x_2 e z_2 $\mathcal{1}$-Prob $(q; q)$, where $z_2 \in IK_2$. Now we can compute that % $(Y_1 \times Y_2, Z_1 \times Z_2, (pq; pq))$, so that under the foregoing axioms, extended to $K_1 \times K_2$, we would have x_1 e z_1 cj x_2 e z_2 $\mathcal{1}$-Prob $(pq; pq)$, provided we had $(x_1$ pr $x_2)$ $\mathcal{1}$-Ran-$K_1 \times K_2$ $(y_1$ cp y_2, z_1 cp $z_2)$.

In principle there is no more difficulty in passing from a complete set of statistical statements about K^m to a set of statistical statements about K^n than there is in passing from statements about the master set $K_1 \times K_2$ to the master set K_1. Thus we may begin with as general and fancy a set as we wish, $K_1{}^m \times K_2{}^n \times \ldots \times K_3{}^r$, say, and base our assertions of randomness and our probability statements on a rational set of statements about a field of subsets of this set.

The net result of all this is that a rational set of statements has many of the properties that we associate with rational corpora, and the system of probability statements we come up with has much in common with a frequency theory of probability. When we say that the probability that a birth will be the birth of a male is about 0.51, we mean, first, that we think we have reason to believe the statistical statement "% (human births, births of males, (.50; .52))", and second, that this birth is a random member of the set of human births, relative to what we know, with respect to the property of being the birth of a male. We might properly regard the expression 'a birth' in this context as being replacable by a free variable 'x', restricted to the set of human births. This much of the foregoing theory corresponds precisely to the usual frequency — or frequency-oriented — theory.

The most telling objection to this statistical theory of probability has been that you cannot talk about the probability that some *particular* object — the *next* toss of this die, the sample to be drawn *tomorrow*, the birth of Sally's *first child* — will have a given property. People do apply probability to particular events, but this application has been left in the realm of intuition and common sense. In the above system the probability of a statement using a proper name to refer to an object is just as well-defined as the probability of a statement using a free variable to refer to no object in particular, but simply to an unspecified member of a class — *a* toss of the coin, *a* sample of measurements, etc. I maintain that the theory underlying the manipulation of statistical statements and the theory of probability are distinct: that the theory of probability is of interest primarily for its applications in particular proper-name situations in which we do not have detailed knowledge; that there is a right and a wrong in the application of the theory; and that the criteria of rightness and wrongness are — or should be — embodied in the theory itself. In the above system, I believe I have accomplished this for the very particular case in which we are concerned only with probability statements that can be reduced to statements about the membership of objects in sets belonging to a field of subsets of a master set K about which we have perfect statistical knowledge.

III

10. I shall now attempt to explore some of the difficulties in the way of removing the restrictions adopted in the last sections. The fundamental restriction we would like to remove, because it is so blatantly counterfactual, is that embodied in K II; we wish to allow approximate statistical statements to play a role in our theory of probability. Since, if we are going to allow approximate statistical statements to play a role in our probability theory, every non-empty subset of K may serve as the basis for a statistical statement (in virtue of the theorem: "$B \neq \emptyset \supset \% (B, C, (0; 1))$"), there seems to be no reason, *prima facie*, for selecting a particular set of subsets of K to function as the ground of every probability statement. Therefore let us take the set of *all* subsets of K to serve in place of the interesting subsets we considered before. For the sake of simplicity, I shall retain K IV and K V as axioms; K I-K III will be dropped. In K IV, replace $w \in IK$ and $y \in IK$ by "$W \subset K$" $\in \mathcal{I}$ and "$Y \subset K$" $\in \mathcal{I}$, respectively.

Definition 5 of randomness cannot simply be changed in the way we changed K IV, however, since the following theorem would lead to the conclusion that only unit classes would qualify as reference classes, and that the only probabilities that exist would be $(0; 0)$, $(0; 1)$, and $(1; 1)$:

$$(x) (x \in K \supset [x] \subset K)$$

Clearly, we must modify Definition 5 drastically.

The fundamental idea behind Definition 5 is this: we will deny that x is a random member of y with respect to z, relative to the rational corpus $\mathcal{I}$, when we don't know that x is a member of y at all, or when we know that x is a member of w and that w is included in y. Now the latter alternative is only siginficant when we know that the proportion of objects belonging to z in w is *different from* the proportion of z's in y. We can see this best, perhaps, in a concrete example. If we know that on the whole, half the balls drawn from a certain urn are red, but that in the long run, three-fourths of the balls drawn by person P from the urn will be red, we shall deny that the next ball drawn by P from that urn is a random member of the set of balls drawn from that urn with respect to the property of being red. The crucial facts in our denial of this assertion of randomness are two: the proportions of red balls in the two different candidates for reference class are known to differ; and the one class is known to be a subclass of the other. It is the latter fact which allows the next ball drawn by P to be a random member of the set of balls drawn from the urn, by him, with respect to the property of being red, despite the fact that, on the whole, the proportion of red balls differs from 3/4. What is the fact that allows the next ball drawn by P to be a random member of the set of balls drawn by him, with respect to the property of being red, even though we know that it belongs to its unit class, and that the proportion of red balls in that unit class lies between 0 and 1? It is the fact that our statistical information about the set of balls drawn by *P* is more *precise* than our statistical information about the unit class of the next ball drawn by *P*. Suppose that we know that between 6/10 and 8/10 of the balls drawn by *P* today are red, and that the next ball to be drawn by *P* will be drawn today. Still we shall say that this ball is a random member of the set of balls drawn by *P*, on the grounds that our knowledge of this set is more precise than our knowledge of the set of balls drawn by *P* today.

There are thus two ways in which the knowledge that *X* belongs to *W* can prevent *X* from being a random member of *y* with respect to *Z*: by difference and by strength. I shall begin by defining a relationship between statistical statements which holds when the statements *differ* in the sense required here.

Definition 8:

$$\text{" '\% } (A, B, (p; q))\text{' } \mathbf{1}\text{-Dif '\% } (C, D, (r; s))\text{' " } \textit{for}$$
$$\text{"Thm } 'p < r \cdot q < s \cdot \mathsf{V} \cdot p > r \cdot q > s' \text{".}$$

I shall say that the set *W* prevents *X* from being a random member of *Y* with respect to *Z*, by difference, relative to $\mathbf{1}$ (or more precisely, that the term *w* prevents, by difference, the randomness relation from holding for the terms *x*, *y*, and *z*, and the set of statements $\mathbf{1}$), when we know that *W* is a subset of *K*, and that *X* belongs to *W*, when strongest statements about *W* and *Z* and about *Y* and *Z* differ, in the sense of Definition 8, and when *Y* is not known to be included in *W*.

Definition 9:

$$\text{"}w \; \mathbf{1}\,\mathrm{PD}(x, y, z)\text{" } \textit{for} \text{ "}x \text{ e } w \in \mathbf{1} \cdot w \text{ incl } K \in \mathbf{1} \cdot \sim y \text{ incl } w \in \mathbf{1}.$$
$$(p) \, (q) \, (r) \, (s) \, (\text{'\% } (W, Z, (p, q))\text{' } \mathrm{Str}^* \, \mathbf{1} \cdot \text{'\% } (Y, Z, (r; s))\text{'}$$
$$\mathrm{Str}^* \mathbf{1} \cdot \supset \mathrm{Thm} \, 'p < r \cdot s < q \cdot \mathsf{V} \cdot p > r \cdot s > q'.)\text{"}$$

Similarly, I shall say that *W* prevents *X* from being a random member of *Y* with respect to *Z* by strength, when *X* is known to belong to *W*, *W* is known to be included in *K*, when strongest statements about *W* and *Z* are stronger than strongest statements about *Y* and *Z* but not vice versa, in the sense of Definition 2, and when there is no set *Y'* which prevents *X* from being a random member of *W* with respect to *Z*, by difference.

Definition 10:

$$\text{"}w \; \mathbf{1}\text{-PS } (x, y, z)\text{" } \textit{for} \text{ "}x \text{ e } w \in \mathbf{1} \cdot w \text{ incl } K \in \mathbf{1}.$$
$$\sim(\exists \, y') \, (y' \; \mathbf{1}\text{-PD } (x, w, z)) \cdot (r) \, (s) \, (p) \, (q) \, (\text{'\%}(W, Z, (p; q))\text{'}$$
$$\mathrm{Str}^* \mathbf{1} \cdot \text{'\% } (Y, Z, (r; s))\text{' } \mathrm{Str}^* \mathbf{1} \cdot \supset$$
$$\mathrm{Thm} \, 'p \geqslant r \cdot q < s : \mathsf{V} : p > r \cdot q \leqslant s')\text{".}$$

The definition of randomness is now straightforward, if a bit complicated. I shall say that the randomness relation holds among the terms *x*, *y*, and *z*, relative to the set of statements $\mathcal{L}$, when y incl K and x e y are members of $\mathcal{L}$, and when there is no term w which prevents (x, y, z) in the sense of Definitions 9 or 10.

Definition 11:

> $"x\ \mathcal{L}\text{-Ran}\ (y, z)"\ for\ "x$ e $y \in \mathcal{L} \cdot\ y$ incl $K \in \mathcal{L}$.
> $\sim(\exists w)\ (w\ \mathcal{L}\text{-PD}\ (x, y, z)\ V\ w\ \mathcal{L}\text{-PS}\ (x, y, z))".$

Let us try this definition out on the litmus of a concrete example. Consider an urn containing red and black balls; let D be the next ball to be drawn from the urn, and suppose we know that D is a draw made by a left-handed young man. Let K_1 be the set of draws made by young people, K_2 the set of draws made by men, K_3 the set of draws made by left-handed men, K_4 the set of draws made by left-handed people, K_5 the set of draws made by young men, and K_6 the set of draws made by left-handed young men. Let R be the set of draws resulting in a red ball, and suppose that the following six statements are strongest statistical statements about their respective subject-matters in our rational corpus:

(1)   % $(K_1, R, (.35; .45))$
(2)   % $(K_2, R, (.40; .50))$
(3)   % $(K_3, R, (.35; .50))$
(4)   % $(K_4, R, (.30; .40))$
(5)   % $(K_5, R, (.30; .60))$
(6)   % $(K_6, R, (0.0; 1.0))$

We would like to have 'D' $\mathcal{L}$-Ran ('K_3', 'R'), and hence '$D \in R$' $\mathcal{L}$-Prob $(.35; .50)$. Statistical statements about both K_1 and K_2 are stronger than the statement about K_3, but they conflict with each other so that neither K_1 nor K_2 can serve as a plausible reference class. K_5 and K_6 aren't plausible reference classes because we know more about K_1 than we know about K_5 or K_6. Our statistical knowledge about left-handed people (K_3) conflicts with our knowledge about K_3; but we say that D is a random member of K_3 rather than of K_4 because we know that K_3 is included in K_4. It is here, and only here, that the classical maxim of choosing the smallest possible reference class applies.

But under Definition 11, we still don't have 'D' $\mathcal{L}$-Ran ('K_3', 'R'). This may be seen as follows: Let the whole set of draws by left-handed men K_6 be very numerous. Then the proportion of the members of $((K_5 \cap R) \cup [D]$ that belong to R will be very close to 1; we will include in our rational corpus the statement

> "% $(((K_6 \cap R) \cup [D], R, (1 - \epsilon; 1.0)))".$

Clearly,

> '$((K_5 \cap R) \cup [D]$' $\mathcal{L}$-PD ('D', 'K_3', 'R').

Next, observe that the proportion of members of $((K_5 \cap R) \cup [D])$ that belong to R will be very close to 0: we will include in our rational corpus the statement,

> '% $(((K_6 \cap \bar{R}) \cup [D]\ R, (0; \epsilon))$'.

Thus

$$\text{`}((K_6 \cap \bar{R}) \cup [D] \;\mathcal{L}\text{-PD (`}D\text{', `}((K_6 \cap R) \cup [D] \text{ `}R\text{')'}$$

as well as

$$\text{`}((K_6 \cap R) \cup [D] \;\mathcal{L}\text{-PD (`}D\text{', `}((K_6 \cap R) \cup [D], \text{ `}R\text{').}$$

The only set known to be included in each of these two descriptive sets is $[D]$ the unit class of D. Thus we are right back where we were before with

$$\text{`}D\text{' }\mathcal{L}\text{-Ran (`}[D], \text{ `}R\text{')}$$

and

$$\text{`}D \in R\text{' }\mathcal{L}\text{-Prob (0; 1).}$$

We could prevent this by selecting a field of subsets of K, as we did before, which would not include such strange sets as those I have been talking about, and by restricting possible reference classes to elements in this field. But this seems arbitrary: how, in general, would we defend the selection of one set of subsets of K as opposed to another?

It would be sufficient if strange sets like $((K \cap R) \cup [D]$ could be excluded as possible reference classes. To exclude these sets is somewhat less restrictive than excluding all sets but those in a definite pre-selected field of subsets of K. It would be gratifying to find a general criterion that would eliminate the strange sets. One possibility suggests itself. There seems to be a very strong connection between the classes mentioned above, and Nelson Goodman's odd predicates "Grue" and "Bleen." My classes are not time- or place-divided, as Goodman's predicates are, but a solution to the grue and bleen problem could perhaps be generalized into a solution to my problem.

Lacking a general criterion, the solution to my problem that is most attractive to me is the following rather *ad hoc* one: Suppose that we start with an arbitrary, finite, list of subsets of K—just as, in point of fact, we start a scientific inquiry with a finite list of properties. Then we define the set of subsets of K that are going to be allowed to function as reference classes in the following way: it is to consist of sets named in the original list, complements of those sets (in K), and intersections of any number of sets from the augmented group. In effect, this definition precludes the possibility of making the unions of sets on which $((K_6 \cap R) \cup [D]$ and its ilk depend for their construction. We no longer have a field of sets, but this constitutes no difficulty; all we need is the freedom to make whatever intersections we want. We want the intersection of two reference classes to be a reference class. There is only one more difficulty. Why shouldn't the set $((K_6 \cap R) \cup [D]$ be among the subsets of K with which we start? One answer is the pragmatic one: if we had a language with primitive predicates corresponding to such classes, we would give it up and choose a new set of primitive predicates. Another answer might be that no natural language can have terms denoting classes of this sort, because a natural language must be learned inductively, and terms of this sort cannot be learned inductively.

NOTES

1. See, for example, G. Spencer Brown's little book, *Probability and Scientific Inference,* Longmans Green and Col., New York, 1957.

2. As proponents of any given theory will not hesitate to point out with respect to other theories.

11

Probability
and Informative Inference

1. INTRODUCTION

There are a lot of ways of skinning the statistical cat and there are a lot of ways of classifying those techniques. One way is to distinguish between those approaches which stem from an epistemological stance and those approaches which are pragmatic in character. Alan Birnbaum[1] has characterized the problem with which the epistemological approach has been concerned as the problem of *informative inference*. The kind of problem with which the pragmatic approach is concerned might be characterized as a decision problem; but if we so characterize it, we must beware of supposing that decision theory is concerned merely with the theory of decision. The words that statisticians use in their professional activities must be treated with circumspection.

To talk about accepting or rejecting hypotheses, for example, is *prima facie* to talk epistemologically; and yet in statistical literature to accept the hypothesis that the parameter θ is less than θ^* is often merely a fancy and roundabout way of saying that Mr. Doe should offer no more than $36.52 for a certain bag of bolts. Neyman[2] talks, or used to talk, about rejecting hypotheses; however, he made it very clear that this sort of talk was not to be interpreted epistemologically, but only as a kind of shorthand way of talking about inductive behavior—i.e., of making choices among courses of action on the basis of statistical evidence. On such a purely pragmatic approach, there seems to be no point in speaking of *accepting hypotheses* at all; it would be better and clearer simply to say what one means—to talk of buying the bag of bolts or not buying it.

As a general approach to statistics, however, this seems too narrow. It is, one might say, a function of engineering and not of science, to determine whether or not the evidence warrants buying a certain bag of bolts as a certain price. When it comes to general scientific hypotheses (e.g., that $f(x)$ represents the distribution of

Reprinted, with modifications and additions, from V. P. Godambe and D. A. Sprott, eds., *Foundations of Statistical Inference* (Toronto: Holt, Rinehart, and Winston, 1971), pp. 82-107, by permission of the publisher.

weights in a certain species of fish, or that a binomial distribution with a parameter of ½ represents the behavior of a certain coin in a certain tossing machine) then the purely pragmatic, decision theoretic, approach has nothing to offer us. The classical statistical testing procedures, derived from this viewpoint, are nevertheless employed in the sciences—psychological, social, medical, etc. They result in such statements as: *the null hypothesis is rejected at the 2% level of significance.* The import of such a statement is that such and such an empirical hypothesis is (for the time being, pending new evidence) acceptable. It would be a rare and foolish scientist who would claim that a certain hypothesis was acceptable, given certain evidence now, and that that hypothesis would continue to be acceptable regardless of what new evidence came to light. Acceptance is of course tentative, and of course subject to change. Nevertheless, the common-sense import of a scientific paper is generally that A causes B, or that the incidence of X is higher among C's than among D's, or that the distribution of the quantity Y among the members of P is approximately normal with mean m and standard deviation s. We use such hypotheses to guide our decisions in a wide variety of circumstances; we use them also as background information in further inquiries. Unless there are very good reasons to the contrary, it seems to me that we ought to try to accommodate this common sense view of the results of scientific inquiry in our theory of statistics. Therefore in what follows, I shall suppose that we do in fact accept some scientific hypotheses (if only tentatively) some of the time.

The main alternative to the hypothesis-testing approach is the Bayesian approach. Here again it is by no means clear from the way people talk and the words that they use whether they are concerned with informative inference or practical decision. The prior probabilities required for the Bayesian framework (and thus the framework itself) may be taken in three ways. First, the prior probabilities it requires may be taken as mere opinions—as reflecting psychological states of the decision maker or inferrer. This is the way in which it is taken by Jeffrey[3], de Finetti[4], and Savage [5]. It might be thought that this would lead to a purely pragmatic statistics in which both the input and the output reflect the propensities of individuals to make certain sorts of decisions in certain sorts of circumstances. Although this approach in general eschews the acceptance of hypotheses, it may nevertheless be regarded as a species of informative inference if we construe the outcome of the inference as, not the acceptance of a hypothesis, but the adoption a posterior conditional probability function $P(H/E)$ characterizing epistemologically the relevant hypotheses. Second, the prior probabilities the Bayesian approach requires may be taken as reflecting purely logical relations: this is the hopeful approach of Harold Jeffreys[6] and Rudolf Carnap[7], and it leads to a similar epistemological approach to satistical inference. What one obtains, for example, is a posterior distribution which is represented by a function $F(x)$ which, relative to a total body of evidence legislatively characterizes one's epistemological attitude toward a certain parameter in a binomial distribution; i.e., one's degree of belief, under those circumstances, that the parameter lies between a and b

should be $\int_a^b dF(x)$. The third way in which the Bayesian framework may be taken is that in which the prior probabilities are taken to represent known (or reasonably believed!) empirical frequencies. Here again we have an epistemological sort of statistics. But here we are definitely and explicitly committed to accepting at least tentatively at least some statistical hypotheses.

A brief tabular summary of this very sketchy characterization may come in handy later. We may organize it by conceptions of probability; techniques of inference, and results of inference. Under frequency or empirical conceptions of probability, we find non-Bayesian techniques of inference, except when there are empirical prior probabilities to be fed into Bayes's theorem. The results, so far as informative inference are concerned, are generally *reject H;* under the circumstances that there exist prior probabilities, there may emerge as a result a posterior distribution, *P(H/E)*. Subjective conceptions of probability employ only Bayesian techniques of inference; the outcome is always a posterior distribution *P(H/E)*, or the choice of an action. Logical conceptions of probability also employ Bayesian techniques of inference; one outcome is always a posterior distribution *P(H/E)*, but on some views (such as those of Hintikka and his students[8]) it is sometimes possible to detach a hypothesis *H* from its evidence and to accept *H*. This depends not only on *P(H/E)* but also on the internal character of *H* and of *E*. A fourth conception of probability, and its implications for statistical inference, will be discussed later.

Types of Probability, Inference and Results

Concepts of Probability	Techniques of Inference	Form of Result

empirical	Non-Bayesian
	Bayesian based on
	   accepted statistical
	   knowledge
		reject *H*
		posterior
		   distribution

subjectivist	Bayesian	posterior distribution for *H*; an action
logical	Bayesian	posterior distribution for *H*

2. PROBABILITY

The crucial concept in statistical inference is that of probability. The interpretation I am about to offer is not new—I have offered it before[9]—but I hope to make clear how it leads to a unified approach to inference.

Probabilities concern statements. The probability of a certain statement is an interval (the endpoints of which constitute the upper and lower probabilities that some people refer to). The statement S has the probability (a,b), roughly speaking, if and only if S is known to be equivalent to a certain statement of the form "$x \in z$," x is known to belong to an appropriate reference class y, x is a random member of y with respect to belonging to z, relative to all that we know about it, it is known that the measure of z in y is in the interval (a,b), and there is no proper subinterval of (a,b) into which this measure is known to fall.

This rough characterization refers constantly to what is known. The easiest way to formalize the reference to what is known is to refer to the statements that embody that knowledge: thus instead of saying that it is known that x belongs to y, to say that the statement, "$x \in y$," belongs to a certain set of statements. It may be objected that one cannot expect universal agreement about what is known—i.e., about what statements may be taken to belong to our body of knowledge and what cannot. This difficulty may arise in two ways. First, different people have had different experiences, different educations, etc., so that what is known to one person may not be known to another. Second, given the same data and background knowledge, two people may still disagree on whether or not some new hypothesis is so well-supported that it should be included in their collective body of knowledge. The first source of difficulty is not serious: one of the first requisites of the scientific enterprise is the willingness to share data; and one of the first consequences of the openness with which scientific investigation is conducted is that scientific data are highly accurate and dependable. Thus so far as data are concerned—that is, the down to earth particulars that constitute our evidence in scientific investigation—there is no reason to suppose that two people may not share a common body of knowledge.

The second source of difficulty—that people may not agree on what hypotheses to accept—has in turn two sources. (Recall that I am speaking of intellectual acceptance; acceptance on the basis of what Birnbaum calls *informative inference*. I am not talking about acceptance in the sense of performing some particular action, in which, of course, ordinary utilities, which might differ from person to person, are involved.) One source is that one person may have a higher standard of rigor than another: what is well enough demonstrated for one person, another may regard as insufficiently demonstrated, simply because the second person has higher standards in general. One person may be willing to accept a psychological hypothesis that is *not rejected at the .05 level*, while a fellow psychologist would not want to regard it as a part of his body of knowledge unless it were *not rejected at the .01 level*. Rejection levels provide a rather crude way of indicating the concept of rigor I have in mind, but they suffice to show how that there is no real difficulty here: although two people may not agree on what is an appropriate degree of rigor in a given context (i.e., what is an appropriate rejection level) they may be expected to agree on what is acceptable as knowledge at a *given* degree of rigor.

The other source of difficulty concerning the acceptance of hypotheses as parts or ingredients of our bodies of knowledge is that there simply is no general body of agreement on the logical question of what constitutes cogent evidence, even for a given degree of rigor. By calling it a logical question, I am of course presupposing that standards compelling essentially universal agreement can be given, and that these are standards of the same general character as those standards of deductive cogency that have so profoundly changed the character of mathematics in the past seventy-five years. Perhaps I am wrong about this. I hope not, for it is one of the more attractive myths about science that it sooner or later compels universal agreement. This has not happened yet, particularly when science touches on personal predilections, preferences, or prejudices. Some scientists, in the view of others, have a tendency to leap to conclusions, accepting hypotheses long before there is an adequate amount of evidence supporting them. Some scientists, in the view of others, tend stubbornly to resist new hypotheses, despite the overwhelming evidence in their favor. If such notions as *adequate evidence, overwhelming evidence* and the like are as objective as they pretend to be and as they should be, it should be possible to formalize them. At any rate, that is my goal.

Thus we shall construe a body of knowledge as a set of statements—much easier things to represent than propositions or facts, and of course we know a lot about sets. It should be observed that we do not know very much about bodies of knowledge, however. For example, it is not at all clear whether bodies of knowledge should be construed as being closed under conjunction; if s_1, and s_2, and . . . and s_n are all statements that belong to the set of statements comprising our body of knowledge, will the statement consisting of the conjunction of these n statements also belong to it? I would answer *no* on the grounds that I feel practically certain that at least one of the things that I am practically certain is true, is in fact false. Others feel that bodies of knowledge should be circumscribed in such a way that this kind of thing does not happen. Their grounds are that they would not want the set of statements they accept to entail a contradiction.[10] Such issues will not concern us here. We shall take the set of statements representing a body of knowledge as given, and make explicit any assumptions we make about it.

The first step is to introduce a distinction between statistical hypotheses and probability statements. It is the distinction, familiar to logicians, between object language and metalanguage. Statistical hypotheses are statements in the language of science—the object language—and concern the world out there: the stochastic behavior of dice, the distribution of telephone calls at an exchange, the behavior of radioactive substances, the distribution of shoe sizes in an army, and the like. Probability statements, on the other hand, *reflect* our knowledge about that world out there: and that knowledge, as I have suggested, is best reprresented by the statements in the object language of science. To talk *about* that knowledge therefore requires that we talk about statements in the object language (and indeed about sets of such statements) and that requires what the logicians call a metalanguage. Fortunately we can for many purposes (and at the cost of a little sloppiness) get by with the first and most common technique for mentioning and talking about statements, namely, quotation.

Statistical hypotheses are among the most important ingredients of a body of knowledge. They represent our general scientific knowledge about the world—that knowledge which guides our future actions and choices. Not all statistical statements are equally significant and interesting, however. For example, let S be the set of throws of a certain die that land with the six up, and let T be the unit set consisting of the next throw. It is perfectly true that a plausible measure of the set of sixes among the union of S and T is one or close to one; but this statement cannot be of scientific interest to us. To avoid having to consider such irrelevant statements, let us restrict the set of statistical hypotheses in the following way.

We begin with a set of potentially acceptable reference clases R, subject to the following conditions. These conditions are designed to eliminate from our considerations not only such oddly inappropriate reference classes as the one just mentioned, but also perhaps what Fisher has referred to as "artificially constructed pivotal elements"[11] which he took to lead to inconsistency through "false applications" of the fiducial method. The construction of R on the basis of a formal scientific language we leave for the appendix that follows the notes to this chapter.

Condition 1. $x, y, \in R \supset x \cap y \in R$
Condition 2. $x, y \in R \supset x \times y \in R$
Condition 3. $x \in R \supset x^n \in R$ (where x^n is taken as the set of functions from the first n ordinal numbers to R).

We now consider a set of sets D_F. The subscript F suggests that these sets arise from the result of applying functions to objects belonging to reference classes. The construction is again relegated to the appendix. We suppose,

Condition 4. $R \subset D_F$
Condition 5. $x, y \in D_F \supset x \cap y \in D_F$
Condition 6. $x, y \in D_F \supset x \times y \in D_F$
Condition 7. $x \in D_F \supset x^n \in D_F$

In addition, we suppose what must *not* hold in general for R,

Condition 8. $x, y \in D_F \supset x \cup y \in D_F$
Condition 9. $x, y \in D_F \supset x - y \in D_F$

A statistical statement is a statement of the form "$H(x, y, p, q)$" where $x \in R$, $y \in D_F$, and $0 \leq p \leq q \leq 1$. The statement "$H(x, y, p, q)$" is true if and only if the proportion of the members of x that are members of y lies between the limits p and q, or when there is an agreed upon standard measure and x is infinite, when the measure of y in x lies between these limits.

When we talk about a statistical hypothesis belonging to K we shall mean a strongest statistical hypothesis; i.e., if "$H(x, y, p, q)$" is a statistical hypothesis belonging to K, then if "$H(x, y, r, s)$" is also a statement belonging to K, "$H(x, y, p, q)$" entails "$H(x, y, r, s)$."

Although we do not suppose that K is closed under logical deduction—i.e., contains all of the consequences of all of its elements—we shall suppose that its unit subsets are closed under logical deduction. Thus if $S \in K$ and S entails T, then $T \in K$.

It should be observed that statistical statements do not by any means embody all of our statistical knowledge. Even a distribution function or a density function would not, according to the definition, constitute a statistical statement. But of course any such function would constitute, so to speak, shorthand for an infinitely large set of statistical statements of the form specified earlier. Thus if $y(z)$ is a set of objects such that their weight is less than z pounds, and weight in x is distributed normally with unit variance and mean m then "$(z)(H(x,y(z)), \Phi(z-m), \Phi(z-m)))$" is a statement, and a true one, but not a statistical statement as construed above, though it becomes one when we replace the variable z by a constant, e.g., "$H(x,y(5), \Phi(5-m), \Phi(5-m))$."

Now how about probability? I shall take probability to be an attribute of statements, as statistical hypotheses represent attributes of sets. Probability will be relative to a body of knowledge: that is, the probability of a given statement may have one value or another, depending on the body of knowledge relative to which that probabilty is taken. Furthermore, probabilities of statements will be directly related to statistical hypotheses in the following way: the probability of a statement S, relative to a body of knowledge K, will be the interval (p,q), under the following circumstances:

(a) S is known to be equivalent to a statement of the form, $a \in C$; formally, this is to say that the biconditional, "$S \equiv a \in C$" is to be a member of the set of statements K, where a and C are such that

(b) there exists a B, such that it is known that the measure of C in B is the interval (p,q)—i.e., such that "$H(B,C,p,q)$" is a statistical hypothesis in K about B and C—and such that

(c) a is (relative to K) a *random member* of B with respect to C. This condition is not to be construed (as is traditionally the case) as a new statistical hypothesis: it is *not* to be interpreted as asserting that a is as likely to be a as any other member of B, or that a is selected by a method which will produce each member of B equally often in the long run, or any such thing.

I shall refer to these three conditions as, respectively, the equivalence condition, the statistical condition, and the randomness condition. Each of them, and particularly the third, requires elucidation. The first condition stipulates that S is known to be equivalent to a statement of the form "$a \in C$," i.e., that the biconditional "$S \equiv a \in C$" must be a member of the set of statements constituting our body of knowledge. Of course if the biconditional is logically true—if S is *logically equivalent* to "$a \in C$"—then the biconditional will belong to our body of knowledge. (This follows from the unit set closure condition on K, for every statement entails every logical truth.) Such biconditionals may also belong to our body of knowledge on empirical grounds; they may even be quite accidental. Thus we may be interested in the probability that a green ball was drawn from urn number 1 and we may be informed (reliably) that a green ball was drawn from urn number 1 if and only if a black ball was drawn from urn number 2. If we happen to know nothing about the proportion of green balls in urn 1, but we do happen to know that half the balls in urn two are black, this will be a help. If we also happen to know that only ¼ of the balls in urn 1 are green, it will be less than no help. In general, of course, there will be a number of statements of the form, $a \in C$, that S is known to be equivalent to, and we require some means of picking out the (or an) appropriate one.

The second requirement spells out the necessity for the probability interval to be based solidly on *knowledge*, i.e., on a statistical hypothesis in the set of statements we take to represent our body of knowledge.

The third condition is the hardest to be explicit about. Indeed, a full treatment of this condition is beyond the scope of this paper, and possibly beyond that of its author. Nevertheless, there is one clear-cut circumstance under which we wish to deny that, relative to what we know, a is a random member of B with respect to C: namely, when we also know that a is a member of B^*, when we know that B^* is a subset of B, and when we have non-trivial statistical knowledge of B^* and C (i.e., knowledge not of the tautologous form "$H(B^*,C,0,1))$") that conflicts with the knowledge we have of B. This condition for the application of statistical knowledge has been pointed out explicitly by Reichenbach[12]; it is also mentioned explicitly by Fisher[13] (p. 32); and is indeed either implicit or explicit in most discussions of the *application* of statistical knowledge. This single condition for rejecting the randomness of an individual as a member of one class with respect to belonging to another will take us a long way, whether or not it can be made formally sufficient. At any rate, it will suffice for the developments to follow.

We must also define conditional probability. It cannot have the conventional definition, for there is, on the scheme being outlined here, no calculus of probability, other than that yielded as a pale reflection of the measure theoretic calculus of statistical hypotheses. The probability of a statement S, given a statement T, must clearly be understood as the probability of S, relative to a body of knowledge just like the one we are employing now, except that T is added to it, and all of those individual statements inconsistent with T are deleted from it. The problem then is one of specifying how our body of knowledge is to be modified in the process of adding T to it.

Let "$Cn(X)$" denote the set of consequences of a statement X. We must first free the body of knowledge K of any statements which contradict T; that is, we must delete from K all those statements P, such that P entails the denial of T, or what is the same thing, such that T entails the denial of P. Or, finally, the set of all those P such that $\sim P \in Cn(T)$. Then we add the consequences of T (since these will not contradict any statements in K), and we have our new, conditional, body of knowledge K^*. We might conceivably want to add more elements: thus we might want to add the consequents of all those conditionals that have consequences of T as antecedents to our new K—but we have enough to keep track of at the moment without considering such refinements, and in order to prepare the way for this we would have to first delete all the negations of such statements from K—and so on....

The body of knowledge that is like the body of knowledge K, but for containing T, we denote by $K + T$. According to the discussion just completed,

$$K + T = (K - \{P: \sim P \in Cn(T)\}) \cup Cn(T).$$

The conditional probability of S, given T, relative to the body of knowledge K, is therefore simply the probability of S, relative to the body of knowledge $K + T$.

3. AN EXAMPLE

To fix our ideas, let us take a very careful look at a very simple problem in informative inference. Let us suppose that in a certain population R, either ¼ or ⅔ of the individuals have a certain property P. Then we know that either ¼ or ⅔ of R is P, i.e., we contain in our body of knowledge the statement "$H(R,P,¼,¼)vH(R,P,⅔,⅔)$." This statement in turn entails the statistical hypothesis, "$H(R,P,¼,⅔)$"—in this oversimplified example we suppose we know no more about the measure of P in R than is embodied in the disjunction of the two statistical statements.

We wish to achieve greater knowledge of R and P; one way of expressing our desire is to say we wish to choose between the two statements; another way of expressing it is as the desire to test one hypothesis against the other; yet another way of expressing it is as the desire to use evidence to modify our present opinions through the application of Bayes's theorem. Let $H_1 = $ "$H(R,P,¼,¼)$" and let H_2 be the alternative. One way to get an enlightening comparison among all these ways of looking at the problem of increasing our knowledge is to look at it as a fixed-sample-size problem, and to compute the long run errors involved in various rejection rules. A rejection rule will have the form: reject H_1 if there are more than n P's in the sample, where n may vary from zero to the sample size. The rule will be denoted by S_n. Each rule will have two errors associated with it: that of erroneously rejecting H_1, and that of erroneously failing to reject H_1. Given the truth of H_1, we may calculate the long-run frequency of error of the first kind, and similarly, we may calculate the long-run frequency of error of the second kind. These errors are plotted against each other, for samples of size six and twelve, for all the relevant rules, on the accompanying graphs.

It should be noticed that before sampling (at least under most circumstances) these long-run conditional frequencies of error are genuine conditional probabilities of error. There is nothing in K, our body of knowledge, inconsistent with H_1; if

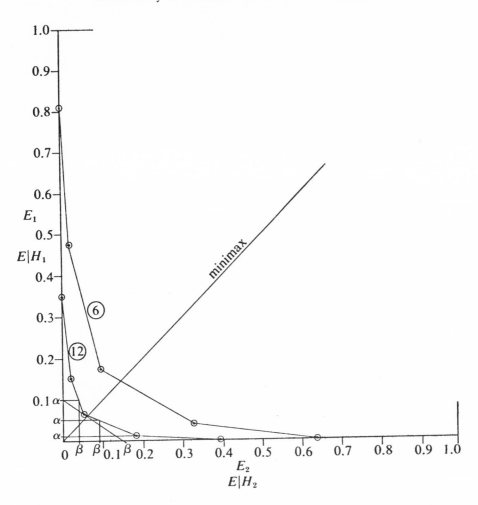

we add H_1 to our body of knowledge, we add its consequence, that the frequency with which sets of twelve R's contain more than five P's is (say) f. Assuming that the sample to be drawn is a random member of the set of all sets of 12 P's with respect to containing more than five P's, the conditional probability that it will contain more than five P's is exactly f. If we are following a rule, S_5, which says that we should reject H_1 if and only if there are more than five P's in the sample, we will be led to error (assuming the truth of H_1) if and only if there are more than five P's in the sample, and thus the conditional probability of our being led into error is also exactly f.

On these figures we can represent various statistical philosophies. A Bayesian choice of strategy, for example, can be indicated graphically by the point at which

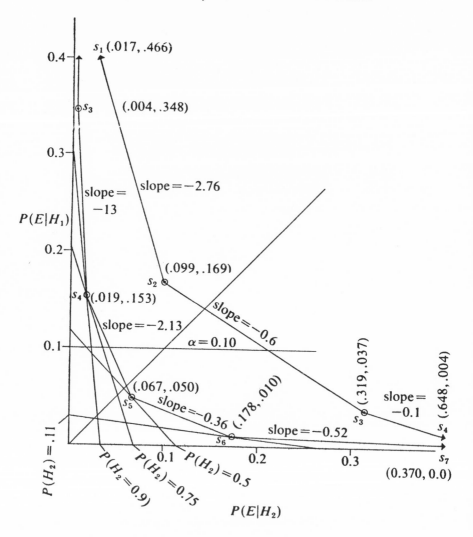

a line of slope $-\dfrac{w}{1-w}$ first touches the convex set representing all possible mixed and pure strategies, where w is the prior probability of H_2 and $1-w$ the prior probability of H_1. A minimax choice of strategy attributing equal importance to both sorts of errors would be indicated by the point at which the boundary of the convex set is intersected by a 45° line through the origin. A test level α and maximum power, is indicated by the intersection of the horizontal line representing an error of the first kind equal to α, and the boundary of the convex set.

Such a diagram can be used (and perhaps most often is used) to exhibit the consistency of these philosophies. There is no conflict among them, so the argument runs, because (for example) to choose S_i as a result of attributing a prior probability of w to H_2 is pragmatically indistinguishable from choosing S_i as a result of deciding to use the most powerful test of level α_w. More generally, let S_M be the strategy selected by the minimax method, and characterized by long-run frequencies of errors of either kind equal to (say) ϵ: $f(E_1) = f(E_2) = \epsilon$. Either S_M will be a pure strategy, or a mixed one. If it is a pure strategy, then there will exist a bundle of lines of negative slope touching the convex set at that point: say the bundle of lines whose slopes lie between $-m_1$ and $-m_2$. These lines correspond to prior probabilities of H_2 in the range between $\dfrac{m_1}{1+m_1}$ and $\dfrac{m_2}{1+m_2}$. In this case, to choose S_M on minimax grounds is just to take the prior probability of H_2 to be between these limits. If S_M is a mixed strategy, it is a mixture of two pure strategies $S_{M'}$ and $S_{M''}$, and there is just one straight line of negative slope (say, m) touching the convex set at S_M. This corresponds to assigning a prior probability of $m/(1+m)$ to H_2; under this assignment the best Bayesian strategy is $S_{M'}$ or $S_{M''}$ or any mixture of the two, including S_M.

In a similar fashion, to adopt the strategy S_M on the basis of a minimax philosophy amounts to the same thing in classical terms as deciding that a significance level of ϵ is satisfactory, and choosing the most powerful test of that size: it turns out to be S_M, and its power, of course, is $1-\epsilon$.

Or let us begin from the classical testing point of view, and choose the most powerful test of size α. This will lead to a strategy S_C. As before, we can find Bayesian arguments which will also justify the choice of S_C. Furthermore, S_C will be the minimax strategy for the case in which we attribute unequal importance to errors of the two sorts: namely in which we regard an error of the first kind as k times as important as an error of the second kind, where $k = \alpha/f(E_2) = f(E_1)/f(E_2)$.

Finally, if we begin with prior probabilities for H_1 and H_2, and are led to the strategy S_B, with error frequencies $f_B(E_1)$ and $f_B(E_2)$, this is the same as using a minimax philosophy, having decided that type I errors are $[f_B(E_1)]/[f_B(E_2)]$ times as important as type II errors, or as selecting the most powerful test of H_2 against H_1 of size $f_B(E_1)$.

So all the philosophies are compatible! So what is all the fuss about?

But the compatibility we have just seen is obviously an illusion. I do not refer to the fact that the arguments become vastly more farfetched when we deal with more complicated problems than that of choosing between two simple alternative hypotheses by means of a test based on a sample of fixed size. I refer to the fact that a person comes to a statistical problem with certain opinions (his degree of belief, for example, that H_2 is true), *and* a certain set of values (the relative importance he in fact attributes to the two sorts of error), *and* perhaps with a certain determination not to commit an error of the first kind more than alpha of the time. To be sure, one can attempt persuasive reconciliation in the case of conflict. Thus one might argue that the distinction between prior probabilities and values is an obscure one, and that a proper behavioral assessment of either will preclude conflict; or that they should be combined into seriosities (Braithwaite's expression, I believe[14]). But this just adds a new source of conflict: initially the scientist may now have one more source of conflict—who is to say that his seriosities will not conflict with both his prior probabilities and his values? One cannot define the conflict away; one can redefine the terms of the conflict so that they are compatible, but in doing so one may only have monkeyed with language, and not with the source of the conflict. It is as if one were to say, "Since you can only pursue one strategy, it must be the case that $S_C = S_M = S_B$; therefore there is no conflict in the philosophies, since they must all indicate the same strategy."

My solution to this potential conflict of philosophies is both trivial and obvious. (In keeping with the great tradition of Western Philosophy, it consists of offering yet another point of view.) We consider first the case where both errors are regarded as equally serious. For the Bayes prior probability w, of H_2, I put a pair of probability limits w_u and w_l which in extreme cases may be the same or may be 1 and 0. On the convex set of possible strategies this pair of numbers either determines a unique pure strategy, $S_{u,l}$ or it determines a pair of pure strategies S_u and S_l such that every strategy which is optimal for a prior probability of H_2 lying between w_u and w_l lies between S_u and S_l, and S_u is the optimal strategy for w_u and S_l is the optimal strategy for w_l. The choice of the strategy is constrained to be $S_{u,l}$, or to lie between S_l and S_u.

In the example previously considered, if the upper probability of H_2 is less than .93, and the lower probability of H_2 is greater than .348, that is, if $.93 > w_u > w_l > .348$, there is only one strategy open to us, and that is S_4; if $.348 > w_u > w_l > .265$, the only strategy open to us is S_5: if $.265 > w_u > w_l > .049$ the only strategy open to us is S_6. On the other hand, if we can do no better than pin down the probability of H_2 to the interval $(0.1, 0.9)$, then all three strategies and their mixtures satisfy the Bayesian constraints. If we have no knowledge at all on the basis of which to construct a probability for H_2—a fairly rare situation, I believe—then the upper probability of H_2 is 1, the lower probability is 0, and the Bayesian constraints are empty.

I refer to S_u and S_l as constraints because on the view of probability I have offered to attribute to H_2 the probability (w_u, w_l) is to say that we know (have adequate grounds to accept) that H_2 is equivalen to $a \in B$; that relative to what we know, a is a random member of C with respect to belonging to B; and that we *know* (have adequate grounds to accept) that the proportion of C that are B (or the measure of B in C) lies in the interval $[w_u, w_l]$, i.e., we have the statistical hypothesis $H(C,B,w_u, w_l)$ in our body of knowledge. Given any frequency of B in C, we can calculate the corresponding expectation of error in applying any strategy S. Given any frequency w of B in C, in the interval $[w_u, w_l]$ we can be sure that the expectation of error under any strategy S between S_u and S_l is less than the expectation of error under any strategy outside those limits. Should we choose a strategy S (say, a minimax strategy) that falls outside those limits, we would be following a strategy that has a demonstrably greater expectation of error than some alternative strategy.

The size of the test we want to use imposes an additional—and independent—constraint. If α is larger than the frequency of error of the first kind under strategy S_u, the constraint is empty; if α is smaller than the frequency of error of the first kind under strategy S_l it rules out any strategy as satisfactory; and if α lies between these limits, it corresponds to a strategy S_α, say, and the acceptable strategies are those between S_α and S_l. For example, in the problem we have been considering, if we know only that the probability of H_2 is the interval $(0.1, 0.9)$, the Bayesian constraints allow us to use S_4, S_6, or any strategy between. If in addition, we wish to make an error of the first kind no more than 10% of the time, the strategies open to us are S_5 and S_6 and any mixture of them, and any mixture of S_4 and S_5 that contains no more than roughly half instances of S_4.

These constraints may still leave a choice of strategies (as in the last mentioned case), and the minimax procedure may serve to pick out one of these remaining strategies—e.g., the minimax mixture of S_4 and S_5.

The case in which we do not regard all errors as equally serious introduces nothing new; the axes of the diagram become expected losses rather than frequencies of error.

4. POST-EXPERIMENT CONSIDERATIONS

There are instances in which consideration of various strategies in terms of their long-term frequencies of errors (or expected losses from errors) is appropriate and relevant: in the design of an experiment, for example, or in the design of a testing procedure to be applied over and over again in industrial quality control. In general, however, in the case of informative inference, these considerations cease to be relevant after we have performed the experiment and obtained the data.

Let us suppose that a manufacturer wants to test, repeatedly, whether certain large groups of items contain ⅔ or ¼ oversize. (We need not suppose that *oversize* is a defect; we leave the utilities to one side, in view of the fact that it is clear enough, in principle, how to work them in.) A fast-talking statistician convinces him that he should use a minimax test, which in the example we have been at such pains to construct, consists of rejecting the hypothesis $p = ¼$ if a chance event of probability $^8/_{73}$ occurs and more than 4 of 12 sampled gadgets are oversize, or if a chance event of probability $^{65}/_{73}$ occurs and more than 5 out of 12 of our sampled gadgets are oversize. Put more simply: reject $p = ¼$ if more than five are oversize; reject $p = ⅔$ if less than five are oversized, and if exactly 5 are oversized, reject $p = ¼$ if and only if a chance event of probability $^8/_{73}$ occurs.

The first large lot comes out of the machine. We select a sample of 12 items (you may select them by random numbers, if you wish; we will get to randomization in a minute). Seven of them are oversized. The chance event of probability $^{55}/_{73}$ occurs. The minimax rule thus tells us to reject $p = \frac{1}{4}$. It also tells us that by following this rule, in the long run we will be in error about 6 times out of a hundred.

What Alan Birnbaum calls the *Principle of Conditionality*, however, tells us that this error figure is utterly irrelevant: the possible outcomes of experiments which might have been performed, but were not, cannot be relevant to the evidential import of those experiments that were performed.

In view of the fact that in the auxiliary experiment the most probable event occurred, the rule we were in fact following in sample was that we were going to reject $p = \frac{1}{4}$ provided more than 5 of the gadgets in our sample were oversized. *This* experiment is characterized by error frequencies of 0.050 if $p = \frac{1}{4}$ and .067 if $p = \frac{2}{3}$. We might thus say that the interval (.050, .067) characterizes the experiment better than the number .061, once we have observed the outcome of our randomizing device.

We can explain and illustrate this by reference to the conception of probability characterized earlier: before performing the complex experiment, the instance that confronts us is an application of a rule with an error frequency of .061; it is, relative to what we know before we perform the experiment, a random member of the set of aplications of that rule. The probability that it will lead us to error is therefore .061, exactly. Once we have performed the auxiliary experiment, however, it may be unreasonable to regard the instance that confronts us as a random application of the rule.

But let us pursue this line of reasoning further. In the experiment we performed, not only did the auxiliary chance event occur, but the chance result that exactly seven of the objects examined turned out to be oversized occurred. Given that we have no information about the prior probabilities of the two alternative hypotheses, the conditional probability of error in rejecting H_1, given the observations that were actually made and ignoring those that might have been made but were not, is just the prior probability of H_1—the whole interval [0,1]—"multiplied" by the ratio of the likelihood to the probability of the evidence. However we interpret this, we can only emerge with the useless interval [0,1] as the probability of error in rejecting H_1, given the observations we have made. The same argument that led us from the single number .061 to the interval (.050, .067) has now led us to the interval [0,1].

Taking the pre-experiment analysis to yield the degenerate probability interval [.061, .061], this analysis suggests that a post-experiment consideration of subclasses should lead us to a different probability *only* when the resulting frequency of error actually conflicts with the interval [.061, .061]—i.e., when [.061, .061] is not a subinterval of it. Thus Birnbaum's argument does *not* give us reason to change the probability of error after the experiment on the grounds that we know the outcome of the auxiliary experiment.

The situation changes abruptly and dramatically as soon as we have any limitations at all on the prior probability of the two hypotheses. As soon as the prior probability of H_1 is no longer the whole interval $(0,1)$ it is possible to compute non-trivial posterior measures for the two hypotheses. Given, for example, that we have found 7 oversized objects in our sample of 12, the probability of error, in the application of any rule which directs us to reject H_1 under these circumstances may be just the probability of H_1, given that evidence. The following table gives some examples:

prior probability		strategy		P(Error, given observation of n oversize objects)				
of H_1	of H_2	followed	P (Error)	n = 3	n = 5	n = 6	n = 7	n = 9
(.75,.90)	(.25,.10)	S_6 *	(.027,.052)	$P(H_2)=$ (.126,.303)	$P(H_2)=$ (.049,.133)	$P(H_2)=$ (.232,.475)	$P(H_1)=$ (.158,.278)	$P(H_1)=$ (.0043,.0127)
(.4,.7)	(.6,.3)	S_5 *	(.055,.062)	$P(H_2)=$ (.052,.162)	$P(H_2)=$ (.164,.407)	$P(H_1)=$ (.137,.355)	$P(H_1)=$ (.026,.086)	$P(H_1)=$ (.0006,.0022)
(.1,.3)	(.9,.7)	S_4 *	(.032,.059)	$P(H_2)=$ (.028,.114)	$P(H_1)=$ (.209,.481)	$P(H_1)=$ (.038,.134)	$P(H_1)=$ (.007,.026)	$P(H_1)=$ (.0002,.0006)
(.1,.9)	(.1,.9)	S_5 *	(.052,.065)	$P(H_2)=$ (0013,.1025)	$P(H_2)=$ (.049,.805)	$P(H_1)=$ (.040,.764)	$P(H_1)=$ (.007,.358)	$P(H_1)=$ (.0002,.0128)
(0,1)	(0,1)	S_6	(.010,.178)	(0,1)				
(0,1)	(0,1)	S_5	(.050,.067)	(0,1)				
(0,1)	(0,1)	S_4	(.153,.019)	(0,1)				

* When prior probability of hypotheses is given, probability of a given hypothesis, given observation, is independent of strategy.

In order to see just what has been going on in terms of randomness and our body of knowledge, let us formalize our references slightly. Let a, B, and C, as before, be the three objects such that we know that H_1 is equivalent to $a \in B$, and relative to what we know, a is a random member of C with respect to B.

Let S be the set of applications of the mixed strategy.

Let S_i now denote the set of applications of strategy S_i, regarded as a subset of S, as well as denoting the strategy itself.

Let R^{12} be the set of twelve-membered subsets of R, and let iP be the subset of R^{12}, each element of which contains exactly i members of P.

Let $E(S_i)$ be the subset of S_i in which we are led to error.

Let jS_i be the application of the strategy S_i to a sample containing j members of P.

Let s be the particular application we are making in this instance; let r be the sample we have drawn.

Let E1 be the statement that an error of the first kind is committed, and E2 the statement than an error of the second kind is committed.

Stage 1. We know only $(a, s, r) \in C \times S \times R^{12}$

$s \in E\ (S) \equiv (a, s, r) \in C \times E(s) \times R^{12}$

$H(S,E(S),\ .061,\ .061)$

$H(C \times S \times R^{12},\ C \times E(S) \times R^{12},\ .061,\ .061)$

(a,s,r) is a *random member* of $C \times S \times R^{12}$ with respect to $C \times E(S) \times R^{12}$

The probability of error before testing is

$P(H_1) = (0,\ 1)$	$P(H_1) = (.4,\ .7)$	$P(H_1) = (.1,\ .9)$
$P(\text{Error}) = (.061,\ .061)$	$(.061,\ .061)$	$(.061,\ .061)$

Stage 2. We know, in addition, that $s \in S_5$.

$s \in E(S) \equiv s \in E\ (S_5)$

$\equiv (a,s,r,) \in C \times E(S_5) \times R^{12}$

$H(S_5,\ E(S_5),\ .050,\ .067)$

$H(C \times S_5 \times R^{12},\ C \times E(S_5) \times R^{12},\ .50,\ .067)$

$H(C,B,\ .4,\ .7) \mapsto H(C \times S_5 \times R^{12},\ C \times E(S_5) \times R^{12},\ .055,\ .060)$

$H(C,B,\ .1,\ .9) \mapsto H(C \times S_5 \times R^{12},\ C \times E(S_5) \times R^{12},\ .052,\ .065)$

(a,s,r) is a *random member of* $C \times S_5 \times R^{12}$ with respect to $C \times E(S_3) \times R^{12}$, provided that the prior probability of H_1 is $[.4,\ .7]$, since $[.061, .061] \not\subset [.055,\ .060]$; (a,s,r) is still a random member of $C \times S \times R^{12}$ otherwise. The probability of error at this stage of testing is:

$P(H_1) = (0,1)$	$(.4,\ .7)$	$(.1,\ .9)$
$P\ (\text{error}) = [.061,\ .061]$	$[.055,\ .060]$	$[.061,\ .061]$

Stage 3. We know, in addition, that $r \in 7P$

$s \in E(S) \equiv H_1$

$\equiv s \in E(S_5)$

$\equiv a \in B$

$\equiv (a,s,r) \in B \times S \times R^{12}$

$\equiv (a,s,r) \in C \times E(S_5) \times R^{12}$

$H(C,B,\ .4,\ .7) \mapsto H(C \times 7P,B \times 7P,\ .026,\ .086)$

$H(C,B,\ .1,\ .9) \mapsto H(C \times 7P,\ B \times 7P,\ .007,\ .358)$

$H(C,B,\ 0,\ 1) \mapsto H(C \times 7P,B \times 7P,\ 0,\ 1)$

$H(C,B,\ .4,\ .7) \mapsto H(C \times S_5 \times 7P,B \times S_5 \times 7P,\ .026,\ .086)$

$H(C,B,\ .1,\ .9) \mapsto H(C \times S_5 \times 7P,B \times S_5 \times 7P,\ .007,\ .358)$

$H(C,B,\ 0,\ 1) \mapsto H(C \times S_5 \times 7P,B \times S_5 \times 7P,\ .0,\ 1)$

$H(C \times S_5 \times R^{12},\ C \times E(S_5) \times R^{12},\ .050,\ .067)$

The error frequencies are now all represented by intervals that include the point .061. Nevertheless, the probability of error, when the prior probability of H_1 is $(.4,\ .7)$, is still $[.055,\ .060]$, since $[.055,\ .060] \subset [.026,\ .086]$, but $[.061,\ .061] \not\subset [.055,\ .060]$.

This state of affairs may seem to have an air of paradox: where our information is least (i.e., where all we can say of the probability of the hypothesis before testing is that it is the whole interval (0, 1), our probability assessment after testing is the most precise. When we do know something about the prior probability of the hypothesis, then our posterior probability may be less precise.

But it is the appearance only of paradox, as may be illustrated by a hypothetical example. Suppose that we have a classical population of bags of balls, in each of which there are black and white balls. We might know that in the whole population exactly half of the balls are white, and at the same time have some what more limited information about the proportion of white and black balls in various bags. Thus of number seven we might know that between .5 and .7 of the balls are white. Given the knowledge merely that a ball has been chosen from the whole population, it is surely correct to take the probability that it is white to be ½. Given the further knowledge that it was drawn from bag number seven, the appropriate probability is equally clearly the whole interval (.5, .7). Our increase in knowledge has here led to a decrease in the precision of our probability. But that is no paradox and no excuse for not using what knowledge we have. The principle of total evidence which prohibits us from throwing away information to achieve more precise probabilities admits of no non-circular justification; it is simply a principle of rationality.

In general, of course, things go the other way: the more information we have about a population (e.g., as obtained by drawing samples from it) the more precise will our knowledge of its composition be, and correspondingly, the more precise will be our probability knowledge concerning future samples drawn from it.

5. RANDOM OBSERVATIONS

Ian Hacking, in a number of publications,[15] has called attention to the difference between the relevant characteristics of testing strategies before we make a test, and those that are relevant after we have observed the result of a test. He offers a number of examples to support this point; one of them is the following:

	$P(E_1)$	$P(E_2)$	$P(E_3)$	$P(E_4)$
H	0	.01	.01	.98
J	.01	.01	.97	.01

R: reject H if and only if E_3 occurs
S: reject H if and only if E_1 or E_2 occurs.

We are testing H against the alternative J. $P(E_1)$ represents a long-run frequency, or chance, or "empirical probability." Rule R and rule S are two alternative rules we are considering; they both have size .01. Rule R has power .97, however, while rule S has a power of only .02. It is clear that before a test, Rule R is to be preferred.

But after we have taken our sample, and observed it to be E_1, we *know* that rule R has led us astray. After the test, it is obvious that rule S is preferable.

In terms of the concept of probability set forth earlier, the explanation is straightforward. Before taking the sample, the probability that rule R will lead us astray is (.01, .03), provided that our application of the rule is a random member of its applications with respect to yielding the truth. The probability that rule S will lead us astray is (0.01, 0.98). The former seems preferable to the latter, since the upper bound on error is so much smaller. But after we have observed E_1, the application of either rule is no longer a random member of the set of all its applications with respect to yielding the truth. It is a member of a special subset of those applications: namely, applications in which the experimental result is E_1. And in this special subset of applications, the probability that rule R will yield the truth is (0,0) and the probability that rule S will yield the truth is (1,1).

The likelihood principle, which according to Savage (*The Foundations of Statistical Inference,*[16]) "flows directly from Bayes's Theorem and the concept of subjective probability" asserts that "the evidential meaning of any experimental outcome is fully characterized by the likelihood function determined by the observations, without further reference to the structure of the experiment." Savage offers the following example: if λ is the frequency of red-eyed flies in a population, and you have observed six out of a hundred to have red eyes, the evidential import of this observation, according to the likelihood principle, is embodied in the function $(\lambda)^6(1-\lambda)^{94}$. It is embodied in this function whether you have chosen a sample of 100 flies and counted the number that have red eyes, or counted flies until you have accumulated six that have red eyes, or counted flies until you have found 94 that do not have red eyes, or however you have chosen it, so long as the probability of the result is proportional to the function mentioned. This is in flat contradiction to the classical testing approach, according to which these are three quite different experiments.

If one adopts the likelihood principle, optional stopping is never relevant. If one adopts a classical point of view it is always relevant. According to the view adopted here, optional stopping is sometimes evidentially relevant, and sometimes not, according to what we know, and according to whether or not what we know is such as to prevent the sample from being a random one in the appropriate sense.

Thus in testing a sharp null hypothesis, it is in principle possible, given an arbitrary level of significance, to continue testing until that hypothesis is rejected at that level of significance. Such a rejection is obviously irrelevant. Why? Because if that is what a person sets out to do, his sample is clearly not a random one with respect to yielding truth under his rule of rejection. It belongs rather to a very special subclass of samples, in which the proportion of the time that the rule yields truth is known to fall into exactly the same interval as that representing the prior probability that the null hypothesis is false. On the other hand, if an investigator stops testing because he is tired, or because he has run out of money, or because he is sufficiently convinced of the falsity of the null hypothesis, or because it is five o'clock, it is perfectly possible that his arbitrarily limited sample is random with respect to yielding the truth under his rule of rejection, and therefore that his significance level does represent a genuine epistemological probability.

The attitude toward randomization that follows from the view of probability adopted here is, naturally, very similar to that of the subjectivist. A sample which is obtained with the aid of a randomizing device may or may not be random in the sense required for inference. If one is doing an agricultural experiment, and finds as a result of one's randomization that the treated plots run in orderly diagonals across the field, one will do the randomization over again. Observe that we do not *know* that such an experiment will be misleading, or even have any reason to believe it will be misleading. Thus it is still a little difficult, on purley subjectivistic grounds, to find a reason for rejecting the cogency for such an experiment. But on the view presented here, such an experiment is always imperiled by the possibility that one *might* find, for example, that fertility gradients ran diagonally across the field, and *then*, relative to this new and expanded body of knowledge, the sample would not be random in the required sense. It is to guard as best we can against such future eventualities that we randomize; and it is to guard against present defects in our experimental design that we appropriately take such randomization to be subject to check against the body of knowledge we have now.

In short, the point of view adopted here argues that neither long-run frequencies, nor the slavish adherence to mechanical rules, nor unsubstantiated opinion, should be allowed to interfere with the reasoned application of factual knowledge to the particular instances of inference with which we are concerned.

NOTES

1. Alan Birnbaum, "On the Foundations of Statistical Inference," *Annals of Mathematical Statistics*, 32, pp. 414-435, 1961.

2. Jerzy Neyman, "The Problem of Inductive Inference," *Communications on Pure and Applied Mathematics*, 8, pp. 13-45, 1955.

3. Richard Jeffrey, *The Logic of Decision*, New York, McGraw Hill, 1965.

4. Bruno de Finetti, "Foresight: Its Logical Laws, Its Subjective Sources," in Kyburg and Smokler (eds.), *Studies in Subjective Probability*, New York, John Wiley & Sons, 1964.

5. L.J. Savage, *The Foundations of Statistics*, New Jersey, Prentice Hall, 1954.

6. Harold Jeffreys, *Scientific Inference*, Cambridge, Cambridge University Press, 1957.

7. Rudolf Carnap, *The Logical Foundations of Probability*, Chicago, University of Chicago Press, 1962.

8. Jaakko Hintikka and Risto Hilpinen, "Knowledge, Acceptance, and Inductive Logic," in Hintikka and Suppes, *Aspects of Inductive Logic*, Amsterdam, North Holland Publishing Comapny, pp. 1-20, 1966.

9. *Probability and the Logic of Rational Belief*, Middletown, Wesleyan University Press, 1961.

10. This question, often formulated in terms of a lottery, was the subject of a conference last year (1970) at the University of Pennsylvania.

11. R.A. Fisher, *Statistical Methods and Scientific Inference*, New York, Hafner Publishing Co., 1956, p. 120.

12. Hans Riechenbach, *The Theory of Probability*, California, University of California at Berkeley, 1949.

13. R.A. Fisher, *Statistical Methods*, p. 32.

14. R.B. Braithwaite, "The Role of Values in Scientific Inference," in Kyburg and Nagel, *Induction*, Middletown, Wesleyan University Press, pp. 180-193, 1963.

15. Ian Hacking, "On the Foundations of Statistics," *British Journal for the Philosophy of Science* 15, (1964-65).

16. Leonard J. Savage, *The Foundations of Statistical Inference*, New York, John Wiley and Sons, 1962, p. 17.

APPENDIX

The reference classes among which we may choose are determined by the language we use, not by the nature of the world. We are thus led to specify a certain set of *expressions*—reference terms—which may appropriately occupy the second place in the metalinguistic relation Ran (a, B, C, K), just as subsets of the set of *statements* are referred to by K, and individual terms (names and definite descriptions) are referred to by a. That is: an appropriate substituend for 'a' denotes an individual term or a set-naming term, an appropriate substituend for 'B' or 'C' denotes a set naming term; and an appropriate substituend for 'K' denotes a set of statements.

No problem appears to arise in connection with a: we may let a be any term of our language.

The problem that arises in connection with K is just the problem of induction and acceptance; it is the problem of determining the criteria—perhaps relative to a number of parameters—that serve to authorize the acceptance of empirical statements. It is not my purpose to examine such criteria here. We assume that they exist, or at least that in a given situation, agreement can be reached somehow concerning what is to be regarded as background knowledge.

The set K of statements representing our body of knowledge may contain statements of the form $[H(\alpha,\beta) = p]$ *or* $[p_1 < H(\alpha,\beta) \leq p_2]$ and the like. These are the statements representing our statistical knowledge. We stipulate—as a meaning postulate, perhaps—that if α is finite, $[H(\alpha,\beta)]$ denotes the ratio of the cardinality of the set denoted by $[\alpha \cap \beta]$ to the cardinality of the set denoted by α.

B and C, however, offer problems: we can refer to all sorts of classes in an ordinary language that are totally inappropriate as possible reference classes: for example, the class consisting of tosses of this coin landing heads union the unit set of the next toss. We must therefore somehow restrict the set of possible substituends for 'B' and perhaps 'C.'

Let us first consider a language containing a finite number of one-place first-order predicate expressions, a finite or denumerable number of 0-place operation expressions (names), a two-place operation H taking pairs of sets into real numbers, and, for logical machinery, membership and identity.

Let $\Pi = \{ {}'P_0{}', {}'P_1{}', ..., {}'P_m{}' \}$ denote the set of primitive predicates.

We define $A\Pi$, the set of atomic predicates:

Definition. $A\Pi = \{\phi:\bigvee_{\psi}(\psi\epsilon\Pi\wedge\ (\phi = \Psi v\phi = [\sim\psi]))\}$.

We define the set of conjunctive propositional functions, $CA\Pi$, as follows:

Definition. $CA\Pi = \{\phi:\bigvee_{n\epsilon\omega}\ \bigvee_{\alpha_0....,\alpha_{n-1}}\ \bigvee_{\phi_0....,\phi_{n-1}\psi}\ \bigvee(\bigwedge_{i<n}(\phi,\epsilon A\Pi\wedge$
$\alpha_i\epsilon Vbl)\wedge\ \psi\epsilon LFmla\wedge\ \phi = [\psi\wedge\ \phi_0\alpha_0\wedge\ ...\wedge\ \phi_{n-1}\alpha_{n-1}])\}$.

The need for clause ψ will be apparent shortly. In powerful languages the condition that ψ contain no nonlogical terms may not be sufficient to avoid sophisticated troubles, but we suppose the intent to be clear.

Let Q be the set of strings of quantifiers of our language (existential or universal), including the empty string.

The set of reference class expressions, R, may now be defined:

Definition: $R = \{\phi:\ \bigvee_{\psi}\bigvee_{n<\omega}\bigvee_{\alpha_0...\alpha_{n-1}}\ \bigvee_{q}(\psi\epsilon CA\Pi\wedge\ q\epsilon\ Q\wedge\ \bigwedge_{i<n}\alpha_i$ is free

in $q\psi\wedge\ \bigwedge_{\beta}(\beta$ is free in $q\psi{\rightarrow}\bigvee_{i<n}\ \beta = \alpha_i)\wedge\phi = [\{\langle\alpha_0,...,\alpha_{n-1}\rangle:q\psi\}])\}$.

We observe that R satisfies the closure conditions mentioned in the text:

Theorem 1. $\alpha\epsilon R\wedge\ \beta\epsilon R{\rightarrow}\bigvee_{\gamma}(\gamma\epsilon R\wedge\ \vdash\ [\gamma = \alpha\cap\beta])$

let $\quad\alpha = [\{\langle\alpha_0,\alpha_1,...\alpha_{k-1}\rangle:q(\psi\wedge\ \phi_0\alpha_0\wedge\ ...\wedge\ \phi_{k-1}\alpha_{k-1})\}]$

let $\quad\beta = [\{\langle\alpha'_0,\alpha'_1,...\alpha'_{j-1}\rangle:q'(\psi'\wedge\ \phi'_0\alpha'_0\wedge\ ...\wedge\ \phi'_{j-1}\alpha'_{j-1})\}]$

Case I: $j \neq k$ $\qquad\vdash[\alpha\cap\beta = 0]$

$\qquad\qquad$ Since $\quad\vdash``O = \{x:P_1x\wedge\ \sim P_1x\}$'',

$\qquad\qquad\qquad\vdash[\alpha\cap\beta = \{x:P_1x\wedge\ \sim P_1x\}]$,

$\qquad\qquad\qquad$ where $``\{x:P_1x\wedge\ \sim P_1x\}''\epsilon R$

Case II: $j = k$

Rewrite the bound variables of β in such a way that the variables of q' are replaced by completely new variables foreign also to α, to obain q^* and ψ^*, and replace $\alpha'_0...\alpha'_{j-1}$ by $\alpha_0...\alpha_{k-1}$ respectively. Then

$\vdash[\alpha\cap\beta = \{\langle\alpha_0...\alpha_{k-1}\rangle:q(\psi\wedge\ \phi_0\alpha_0\wedge\ ...\wedge\ \phi_{k-1}\alpha_{k-1}\}\cap$
$\qquad\qquad\qquad\{\langle\alpha'_0...\alpha'_{j-1}\rangle:q'(\psi'\wedge\ \phi'_0\alpha'_0...\phi'_{j-1}\alpha'_{j-1})\}]$

$\vdash[\alpha\cap\beta = \{\langle\alpha_0...\alpha_{k-1}\rangle:q(\psi\wedge\ \phi_0\alpha_0\wedge\ ...\wedge\ \phi_{k-1}\alpha_{k-1})$
$\qquad\qquad\qquad\wedge\ q^*(\psi^*\wedge\ \phi'_0\alpha_0\wedge...\wedge\ \phi'_{j-1}\alpha'_{k-1})\}]$

Since none of the variables of q^* are free in the left-hand conjunct, and since conjunction is associative,

$\vdash[\alpha\cap\beta = \{\langle\alpha_0...\alpha_{k-1}\rangle$
$\qquad\qquad:qq^*((\psi\wedge\ \psi^*)\wedge\ \phi_0\alpha_0\wedge\ ...\wedge\ \phi_{k-1}\alpha_{k-1}\wedge\ \phi'_0\alpha_0\wedge\ ...)\}]$

But the right-hand side of this identity is an expression belonging to R

Theorem 2. $\alpha\epsilon R\wedge\ \beta\epsilon R{\rightarrow}\bigvee_{\gamma}(\gamma\epsilon R\wedge\ \vdash\ [\gamma = \alpha\times\beta])$

let $\quad \alpha = [\{\langle \alpha_0...\alpha_{k-1}\rangle : q(\psi \wedge \phi_0 \alpha_0 \wedge ... \wedge \phi_{k-1}\alpha_{k-1})\}]$

let $\quad \beta = [\{\langle \alpha_0'...\alpha_{j-1}'\rangle : q'(\psi' \wedge \phi_0' \alpha_0' \wedge ... \wedge \phi_{j-1}'\alpha_{j-1}')\}]$

Rewrite the variables of α and β to be all distinct.

$$\vdash [\alpha \times \beta = \{\langle \beta_1, \beta_2\rangle : \quad \bigvee_{\substack{\alpha_0...\alpha_{k-1} \\ \alpha_0'...\alpha_{j-1}'}} qq'(\beta_1 = \langle \alpha_0...\alpha_{k-1}\rangle$$

$$\wedge \beta_2 = \langle \alpha_0'... \alpha_{j-1}'\rangle \wedge \psi \wedge \psi' \wedge \phi_0 \alpha_0 \wedge ... \wedge \phi_{j-1}' \alpha'_{j-1})\}]$$

The right-hand side is clearly a member of R.

Theorem 3. $\quad \alpha \epsilon R \to \bigwedge_{n < \omega} \bigvee_{\gamma} (\gamma \epsilon R \wedge \vdash [\gamma = \alpha^n])$

let $\alpha = [\{\langle \alpha_0...\alpha_{n-1}\rangle : q(\psi \wedge \phi_0 \alpha_0 \wedge ... \wedge \phi_{k-1}\alpha_{k-1})\}]$

Choose $n \cdot (k + r)$ new variables, where r is the number of bound variables in $q\psi$. Generate n expressions of the form

$$q_i(\psi_i \wedge \phi_0 \alpha_{i,0} \wedge ... \wedge \phi_{k-1}\alpha_{i,k-1})$$

which have no variables in common.

$$\vdash [\alpha'' = \{\langle \beta_0...\beta_{n-1}\rangle : q_0...q_{n-1} \bigvee_{\alpha_{0,0}...\alpha_{n-1,k-1}} (\bigwedge_{i<n} \beta_i =$$

$$\langle \alpha_{i,0}, \alpha_{i,1},...\alpha_{i,k-1}\rangle \wedge \psi_0 \wedge ... \wedge \psi_{n-1} \wedge \phi_0 \alpha_{0,0} \wedge ... \wedge \phi_{k-1}\alpha_{n-1,k-1})\}]$$

The right hand side belongs to R.

Reference class expressions as just defined are the appropriate substituends for 'B' in 'Ran (α, B, C, K).' We can be more generous regarding substituends for 'C.' Let us call the set of appropriate substituends for 'C' the set of Predicate Class Expressions, P, to be confused neither with the set of primitive predicates, nor with the general set of propositional functions.

Definition. $P = \{\phi : \bigvee_{\psi_0...\psi_{k-1}} \bigvee_{q} \bigvee_{\alpha_0...\alpha_{n-1}} (\bigwedge_{i<k} \psi_i \epsilon CA \Pi \wedge q \epsilon Q$

$\wedge \bigwedge_{i<n} \alpha_i$ is free in $q(\psi_0 v...v\psi_{k-1}) \wedge \bigwedge(\beta$ is free in $q(\psi_0 v...v\psi_{k-1}) \to$
$\qquad\qquad\qquad\qquad\qquad\qquad\qquad\qquad\qquad\quad \beta$

$\bigvee_{i<n} \beta = \alpha_i) \wedge \phi = [\{\langle \alpha_0...\alpha_{n-1}\rangle : q(\psi_0 v\psi_1 \ v...v\psi_{k-1})\}]\}$

The set of functions referred to in the text is just the set of characteristic functions of the set of sets denoted by expressions in the set P. The domain of the functions is, as required, a set of sets. Conditions IV–IX of the text become:

T-IV $R \subseteq P$

T-V $\quad \alpha \epsilon P \wedge \beta \epsilon P \to \bigvee_{\gamma} (\gamma \epsilon P \wedge \vdash [\gamma = \alpha \cap \beta])$

T-VI $\quad \alpha \epsilon P \wedge \beta \epsilon P \to \bigvee_{\gamma} (\gamma \epsilon P \wedge \vdash [\gamma = \alpha \times \beta])$

T-VII $\alpha\epsilon P \rightarrow \bigwedge_{n<\omega} \bigvee_{\gamma} (\gamma\epsilon P \wedge \vdash [\gamma = \alpha^n])$

T-VIII $\alpha\epsilon P \wedge \beta\epsilon P \rightarrow \bigvee_{\gamma} (\gamma\epsilon P \wedge \vdash [\gamma = \alpha \cup \beta])$

T-IX $\alpha\epsilon P \wedge \beta\epsilon P \rightarrow \bigvee_{\gamma} (\gamma\epsilon P \wedge \vdash [\gamma = \alpha - \beta])$

12

Epistemological Probability

This paper is polemical, programmatic, and informal. In considering various interpretations of probability, I shall make no effort to consider all conceivable ways in which these interpretations can be applied; I shall consider only the most obvious ones. What I shall offer will be no solution to the problems examined, but merely a program which I believe will yield a solution. Finally, in view of the character of the paper, I shall allow myself to be utterly irresponsible with respect to quotes and quasi-quotes, use and mention, terms and objects, statements, sentences, propositions, and facts. In any full treatment these distinctions would be important—more directly important, I think, than in the case of deductive logic. But for programmatic purposes they are inessential.

Various interpretations of probability are available in the marketplace. None of the candidates appears to do justice to those contexts in which probability is being used to indicate the well-groundedness of an item of belief. I call these contexts epistemological, since probability so used seems to concern the worthiness (or lack of it) of a potential candidate for belief, and perhaps for acceptance. I offer here some paradigm cases of the epistemological use of probability; I shall refer to them repeatedly in what follows:

(a) It will probably be hot tomorrow.
(b) The frequency of heads on tosses of this coin is very probably very close to one-half.
(c) The probability that the next toss of this coin will yield heads is ½.
(d) The length of this table is probably in the interval 2 m plus or minus 1 cm.

Let us try out some of the traditional interpretations of probability on these examples.

Reprinted, with modifications, from *Synthese*, no. 23 (1971), pp. 309-326, by permission of the publisher. Research for the work was sponsored by the National Science Foundation under grants GS 2960 and GS 1962.

THE FREQUENCY OR PROPENSITY INTERPRETATION

I lump these two interpretations of probability together because they are both objective and general: the frequency interpretation says something objective and empirical about the class collectively; the propensity interpretation says something objective and empirical about the class distributively. A paradigm instance in which this interpretation of probability seems to make sense is, 'The probability of heads on tosses of this coin, performed in this apparatus, is ½'.

Consider statement (c). 'The next toss of this coin' has no frequency, and no propensity except simply as an instance of a general class of tosses, to which, for example, the last toss also belongs. If we wish to distinguish between the last toss, which we know landed heads, and the next toss about which we wish to adopt the correct epistemological attitude, neither a frequency nor a propensity statement is appropriate. One approach is to take statements such as (c) not to be about the *next* toss as such; but as being tacitly and implicitly about the general behavior of the coin. But statement (c) is used to indicate something about my epistemological state with respect to the *next* toss. It is true that if (c) describes my epistemological state with respect to the next toss, then it may *imply* something about my epistemological state with respect to something else, such as the general behavior of the coin; but that is another matter; that is not what it *asserts*.

This is even clearer with respect to (a). I am not attributing a frequency of being hot, or a propensity to be hot to an individual day, simply *as* an individual day. Knowing what the weather was like yesterday, I would not attribute a corresponding propensity to yesterday, nor say that yesterday it was probably hot. If the use of probability is epistemological here, it is because something is being revealed about the justified beliefs concerning *tomorrow.* To be sure, something is implied about my body of knowledge; but in this case, as opposed to the preceding one, it is much less clear what that is. In any event (a) is not the same as the statement that August days in this climate are often hot, or have a propensity to be hot.

Unpacked in accordance with the frequency-propensity interpretation, (b) says that this coin has a propensity to have a propensity to yield heads about half the time. But having a propensity to yield heads half the time is a property that the coin either has or lacks under circumstances, just as yielding heads is a property that the next toss either has or lacks. Again it could be claimed that the propensity attributed to this coin (of having such and such a propensity) is one which applies distributively to the whole class of coins under these circumstances, and hence to each coin. But the class of coins in general is not the subject of my belief, which is concerned only with *this* coin, and not with others that I may *know* to be crooked, or *know* to be fair.

Statement (d) is even more difficult to interpret in this way; we surely cannot suppose that we are talking about the propensity of the table to be one length or another, or about the frequency with which it is one length or another. We must suppose that the statement is somehow about the measuring process applied to the table, and the propensity of that process to yield errors. But again, it is not the measurement process in general or hypothetically that concerns us, but the particular result it yielded this time. We must distinguish between instances in which we know that it yielded an error, and instances in which we know that it did not yield an error, and this particular instance in which we clearly do not know either that it yielded the truth, or that it yielded an error. The distinction, by its very nature, reflects our epistemological state, what we know and don't know, and thus cannot be completely reflected in objective general statements about a measuring process.

Two remarks should be made about the frequency or propensity interpretation.

First, there is no difficulty and no circularity in speaking of propensities or frequencies of frequencies; consider the classical problem of drawing a bag from an urn full of bags and then a ball from the bag.

Second, the shortcomings cited do not depend in any way on the alleged difficulty or impossibility of coming to know propensity or frequency statements. Perhaps we can't come to know such statements. I think we can. But in any event, even if we *can* know the relevant empirical statements, this does not allow us to interpret epistemological probability statements of the sort exhibited as being statements about frequencies or propensities.

THE SUBJECTIVE INTERPRETATION

According to the subjective interpretation, what (a) says is that I'm willing to bet at better than even odds that tomorrow will be hot. If probability were simply a psychological concept, this could be so, and it may be that 'probability' is used on occasion in that sense. But when it is used this way it does not have the special force of epistemological probability. When I use the word 'probable' in (a) to indicate something epistemological, as I usually would, then I mean that my belief (as indicated by betting odds, say) is not only strong, but *justified* by what I know; I am implicitly claiming that any rational being in my epistemological circumstances would believe as I do. To be sure, this would be made more plausible by not taking beliefs to be mapped into real numbers, corresponding to betting ratios in forced-bet circumstances, but by taking beliefs to be mapped into intervals, corresponding to intervals of acceptable betting ratios.

The state of affairs is even clearer in the case of the coin, where there is a good statistical basis for picking the number one half. When I say the probability of heads on the next toss is a half, I am claiming, *among other things,* that I have *reason* to believe that the coin is normal and is being tossed under normal circumstances—that is, that in the hypothetical long run it would land heads about half the time. Note that for it to be reasonable for A to believe that the coin is normal in this sense is very different from it being *true* that the coin is normal; though of course I may justifiably claim that it is reasonable for *me* to believe that the coin is normal if and only if I may justifiably claim that the coin is normal. My 'degree of belief' is not only approximately a half, it is justified in being a half by my statistical knowledge of the behavior of the coin. Anybody who knew just what I know of the coin would be irrational to have a significantly different degree of belief.

The same thing can be said about (b) and (d) as about (a) and (c) — namely that if 'probable' is being used with epistemological force, it does not merely indicate my psychological state, but an epistemological state — i.e., a justifiable psychological state under the circumstances. As Keynes said, merely thinking something probable does not make it so.

One new difficulty arises in connection with these two statements: if the psychological state is identified with a disposition to bet, there is a problem in understanding a bet on a proposition that can't be settled. The statement about the coin is a statement about a propensity or a disposition or a frequency in a hypothetically long run of tosses; the statement about the table is a clear-cut theoretical statement. We can ask how much somebody *would* bet *if* the bet could be settled, but this puts us in a never-never land of counterfactual psychological tests that is a long way from the put up or shut up earthiness of measuring beliefs in tosses of coins. Many subjectivists or personalists tend on this ground (and perhaps others) to take general or theoretical statements to fall outside the domain of the subjectivistic probability function.

3. THE CLASSICAL LOGICAL INTERPRETATION

Although many one-time adherents of the logical interpretation of probability have moved to the subjectivistic camp, the two interpretations are radically different from an epistemological point of view. Whereas in (c) the subjectivist interpretation does not imply that there is any ultimate 'justification' for the value ½ as opposed to ¼ or 1, according to the logical interpretation there is exactly *one* real number between 0 and 1 such that the degree of confirmation of the hypothesis, 'the coin will land heads next', relative to the set of statements that constitute my total body of evidence, has that value; (c) implies, therefore, that my body of evidence is such that this value is ½. We must be careful to note what is logical and what is empirical. The proposition 'the coin will land heads' is empirical. The proposition, 'my total body of evidence is e' is empirical. But $c(h, e) = p$ is logically true, if true at all. The situation is parallel to that in deductive logic: 'All men are mortal and Socrates is a man', is empirical; 'Socrates is mortal', is empirical; but the statement, '"All men are mortal and Socrates is a man", entails "Socrates is a mortal",' is purely logical.

Thus while the subjective interpretation regards the probability value of a statement for an individual as wide open for that individual — completely undetermined except in relation to his other probability assignments—the logical interpretation regards it as absolutely and precisely fixed by his total body of knowledge, and by the purely logical character of the probability function.

In the case of (c) this precision does not seem so unreasonable. After all, we all know that the relative frequency of heads is about a half, and would tend to regard other betting ratios than even money as odd, if not crazy. But this precision seems farfetched in the case of (a). Surely, no matter how much we are willing to share our evidence, it would be hard to justify the assignment of one real number to the probability referred to in (a) rather than another arbitrarily close to it.

If the precision presupposed by the logical theory for cases like (a) seems absurd, the fact that the same precision is presupposed in the absence of *all* empirical knowledge seems monstrous. Suppose that there is a sequence of events E_0, E_1, . . . each of which may have or lack the property P. It is a property of symmetrical measure functions (nearly all logical probability functions are symmetrical) that the measure assigned to the proposition that m out of n of these events have the property P will depend only on m and n, and not on which particular events have P. (This condition corresponds to de Finetti's condition of *exchangeability*.) For a suitable property in a suitable sequence of events, it is not at all unreasonable that the prior probability, relative to tauto-logical evidence, i.e., no evidence at all, that an event in the sequence have the property P, be 0.01. The probability that one event in the sequence has the property P, relative to the evidence that consists solely of the proposition that another event in the sequence has the property P, might well be no more than 0.02, double the prior probability. In most systems of logical probability, the probability of P, relative to that evidence, would not increase so much; that fact merely strengthens our result. The result is that with no evidence whatsoever, and whatever else is true of the logical probability measure, the rational agent is committed to a degree of rational belief of at least 0.99 that no more than 11% of the events, in the *indefinitely long run*, will turn out to have the property P.

The same result would hold for the subjectivist, of course. But he needn't mind: he can shrug his shoulders and say, that's what the prior probabilities commit the subject to; perhaps, having seen that, he'll change his mind. But the logical theorist can't treat the result so lightly: in his case we are not talking about someone who happens (for some obscure reason) to have certain opinions, but about the paradigm rational being: no rational person could be less than 99% sure, given no evidence whatsoever, that this empirical hypothesis about the indefinitely long run of events E is true. Recall the very modest assumptions regarding logical probability that are required: that the probability of an event having P is *a priori* $\frac{1}{100}$; that the conditional probability that one event have that property, given that another has it is no more than $\frac{2}{100}$; and that the events be exchangeable, i.e., that the *a priori* probability that m of n of these events have P be the same regardless of the order of the events. [See appendix of this chapter for a formal proof.]

Other things can be said about the logical interpretation of probability. For example, no one has yet offered a logical interpretation suitable to a language in which the hypothesis mentioned in (d) might appear. With enormous difficulty and complication, Hintikka has managed to provide relatively plausible prior measures (that depend on a couple of arbitrary parameters) for languages in which universal generalizations can be expressed and can turn out to have finite probabilities. But whether this approach can be yet further generalized to deal with languages in which hypotheses about real-valued quantities can be expressed, seems questionable.

4. THE EPISTEMOLOGICAL INTERPRETATION

I shall now propose a conception of probability which, I claim, meets these objections, and can plausibly serve as epistemological probability. Like the logical conception, probability statements will be construed as being made relative to a rational corpus or body of knowledge; given a proposition and such a body of knowledge, the probability of that proposition, relative to that body of knowledge will be logically determinate; it will be a certain interval (rather than a real number — this, it develops, is not an inessential generalization). Given the statement S and the body of knowledge K (construed as a set of statements), the statement, 'The probability of S, relative to K, is (a, b)', if true at all, will be logically true; if false, logically false. On the other hand it is not overdeterminate, the way the Carnap-Hintikka probabilities seem to be overdeterminate. Given an empirically empty set of background statements, the probability of an empirical statement will usually be the whole interval, $(0, 1)$. It is open, and not very important in this context, whether one wants to regard this as indicated that *any* degree of belief in the statement would be admissible and rational, or to regard belief as, so to speak, spread out over the whole interval. In the latter case, one may still bet, if forced to bet, at any odds at all; no particular betting odds will be 'rational' as opposed to others. Furthermore, underlying every probability statement of the form '$P(S, K) = (a, b)$', there will be a statistical statement in K, in our body of knowledge, in which the interval (a, b) figures, and which is appropriately related to the statement S and the rest of our body of knowledge. I cannot spell out the details of 'appropriately related'; but I can give some rough indication of the idea behind the definition.

Consider first, statement (c). In uttering (c), I am implicitly referring to my own body of knowledge (as I am in the other statements exhibited). This need not always be the case: if I say, "suppose the probability were . . ." I am speaking of some hypothetical body of knowledge, the particular one supposedly made clear by the context; if I speak in this way of unknown probabilities I may be understood as speaking about a hypothetical body of knowledge that contains only true statistical statements; and so on. To return to (c). Under ordinary circumstances when I utter (c) it is in part because I know (believe with justification perfectly adequate for the occasion) that half of the tosses of this coin (or of coins in general) land heads, or that the coin has a propensity of ½, when tossed in the ordinary way, to land heads. That I know this about the coin is just as true if I consider the last toss as the first toss; but I would hardly say that the probability that the coin which I just observed to land heads should land heads was a half. So we need another condition. I take the other necessary condition (the two are jointly sufficient) to be that the next toss be a random member of the set of tosses of this coin, with respect to exhibiting heads, relative to what I know—i.e., relative to the body of knowledge K. Roughly speaking the content of this long phrase is that the next toss of this coin is a member of no subset (among those I might reasonably use as reference sets) of the tosses about which I know that the frequency of heads differs from that among the tosses of this coin in general. Thus, for example, if the next toss of the coin is performed by an amateur magician who has good control and a preference for heads, I may properly deny that it is a random member of the set of tosses of that coin in general. Observe that 'random', in the sense under discussion, is not to be regarded as something to be explicated with the help of the concept of probability, but rather the other way about: probability is being defined in terms of randomness, and randomness is defined in terms of our statistical knowledge and our knowledge of the particular instance with which we are concerned.

This reveals the truth underlying the frequentist (or propensitist) claim regarding the interpretation of probability. Of course one could not say that the probability of heads on the next toss was a half (ordinarily) if one knew that some other propensity applied to that particular coin, and indeed *unless* one knew that the coin belonged to a class that landed heads half the time under the circumstances envisaged for the next toss. But to make the probability statement is not the same as to have the knowledge of the frequency, since of course the next toss may have something which causes us to assign it to a different reference class. The frequentist problem of choosing a reference class is similar— indeed in principle the same as— the problem of defining randomness. Frequentists have grappled with it infrequently and without much success—in part because for them it was a pragmatic problem involved in the *application* of probabilities, rather than anything of fundamental philosophical interest in the nature of probability itself. Reichenbach, taking probabilities to be real numbers rather than intervals, said that one should simply choose the narrowest reference class about which one has knowledge. But often one will have knowledge of A and knowledge of B, and no knowledge of their intersection; and if one wants to take interval knowledge into account, it will always be the case that one has *some* knowledge—if only the rather uninteresting knowledge that a certain parameter lies in the interval $(0, 1)$!

Well, then, let me take it for granted (what in fact requires a vast amount of thought and analysis) that we know how to choose a reference class in a given epistemological state, or, what is the same thing, that we have a definition of randomness, relative to a body of knowledge, and with respect to a certain property or predicate. That is, give me the locution: A is a random member of B with respect to C, relative to the set of propositions K.

We can then define probability:

The probability of the statement S, relative to the set of statements K, is (a, b) if and only if there are α, β, γ, such that the S is known in K to be equivalent to $\alpha \in \gamma$; the best statistical knowledge we have concerning the frequency of γ among β is given by the interval (a, b); and, relative to the set of statements K, and with respect to membership in γ, α is a random member of β.

5. THE EXAMPLES

Consider (c) again. The next toss of this coin is α; γ is the set of tosses that land heads; β is the set of ordinary tosses. We assume that we know nothing special about the next toss; if we know something special about the next toss, then we must either suppose that the frequency of heads among such special tosses is a half, or that we do not know, at any rate, that it *differs* from the frequency among normal tosses. Under these epistemological circumstances we may say that (relative to what we know) α is a random member of β with respect to γ. We know that ordinary coins land heads with a frequency of *about* a half under these circumstances. The grounds of that knowledge are not at issue here; I am not concerned with induction, but with probability. The grounds that we might most realistically have are constituted by our general knowledge of physical laws and the limits of human skill. Under these circumstances it is reasonable for me, and for anyone who is willing to share my body of knowledge and who knows no more than I do, to have a degree of belief of close to one half in the occurrence of heads on the next toss of this coin. The probability, which is determined by the logical relationship between $\alpha \in \gamma$ and my body of knowledge K, is prescriptive for my degree of belief, and for the degree of belief of anyone whose body of knowledge is similar to mine.

Consider (b). This of course concerns the statement referred to as the foundation of the probability statement (c). Thus we have to suppose a slight change of context, for relative to the same body of knowledge K, that we spoke of before, the probability that the propensity of the coin is close to a half is exactly 1; we took this statement as part of our body of knowledge then. One such context might be the following: K might contain no information about the particular coin, but be reasonably well equipped otherwise. Then α might be this coin, γ might be the propensity of landing heads half the time, and β might be the class of coins with no obvious bends or biases and with a head on one side and a tail on the other. On general physical principles, plus a little knowledge of how coins are tossed, we might well know that all or almost all the coins in the class β exhibit a propensity of heads of a half, i.e., belong also to γ. Thus it is highly probable that this coin belongs to γ, given what we know. But this means that its frequency of heads is close to a half.

Another, imaginative and primitive, context might be the following. The rational subject has no knowledge of physics or of coins in general. He is in a stove, say, with just enough light to perform experiments on this coin. He tosses it 10,000 times, and observes 5,132 heads. Take α to be this particular set of tosses; take β to be the (hypothetical or potential) set of all sets of 10,000 tosses performed with this coin; and γ to be the set of sets of tosses in which the ratio of heads is within ε of the propensity of the coin to land heads. We choose ε so that practically all the members of β are members of γ; we can do this since it is a logical truth that most subsets of a set reflect the composition of the set. Relative to the body of knowledge of the man in the stove, α is a random member of β with respect to γ; i.e., the sample he has observed is a random member of the 10,000-member subsets of the set of all potential tosses of the coin, with respect to the property of reflecting the frequency of heads in that hypothetical population. In view of this fact, the probability is very high that the sample he has observed gives him a true indication of the frequency of heads in general, and thus that it is close to 0.5132, or roughly speaking, close to a half. In short, relative to his body of knowledge, the probability is very high that the propensity for heads is close to a half.

Now consider (d). This is a typical scientific assertion: the length of the table is 2 m plus or minus 0.01 m. But we neoclassical empiricists like to talk as if such statements could be highly probable, and thus we would like to make sense of, and in some cases establish as true, the higher-level statement: the length of this table is very probably, relative to the body of knowledge we actually have, 2 m plus or minus 1 cm. We suppose that we are employing a method of measurement M, the errors of which are normally distributed with a mean of 0 and a standard deviation of 0.5 cm, in the range in which the length of our table is known to lie. (We know perfectly well that it is more than a centimeter long, and less than a hundred meters long.) We take α to be the measurement of the table we actually performed, which yielded the value 2 m. We take β to be the set of measurements performed by method M. We take γ to be the set of measurements performed by method M which are in point of fact less than 0.01 m in error. Relative to our body of knowledge (typically) α is a random member of β with respect to γ. Therefore it is highly probable that α is in error by less than 0.01 m—indeed that probability is 0.9544. But to say that alpha is in error by less than 0.01 m, is precisely to say that the length of the table is in the interval 2 m plus or minus 0.01 m.

While in the measurement case it appears that we come up with genuine real-valued probabilities, rather than intervals, I would claim that this is an illusion. What we *know* is not that the measurement process is one which produces errors normally distributed with a mean of 0 and variance of 0.5 cm., but that it is one of which we know that it produces errors distributed *approximately* normally, with a mean of *about* 0, and a standard deviation of *close* to 0.05. Compared to other errors in the applications of our knowledge, these errors are usually trivial, and quite rightly ignored. If we are concerned with very rare events, or in some other circumstances, the degree of approximation to normality, the accuracy of the mean, the closeness of our estimate of the standard deviaiton can turn out to be exceedingly important. Thus whenever I talk as if a probability were a certain real number, I really mean that it is a small interval about that real number, for I don't believe we know any really precise empirical statistical statements.

A more usual way of reporting the length of the table, of course, would be as 2.0 m plus or minus 0.005, where '0.005' characterizes the method of measurement, being the standard deviation of the normally distribured errors generated by that method. The advantage of this technique of reporting is that it provides us with the statistical statements required for any number of probability statements: we can then talk about the probability that the table is between 1.99 and 2.01 m long, the probability that it is less than 1.95 m long (negligible), less than 2.0 m long (one half), etc. Note, however, that none of these probability statements is amenable to a propensity or frequency interpretation. The length of the table is what it is, and has no propensity to change, or to take on different values, much less to do so with determinate frequencies. What Fisher calls the pivotal quantity, the difference between the result of measurement and the true length, provides a connection between the length of the table and the measurement, *only* on the supposition (as Fisher almost saw) that α is a random member of β, with respect to the appropriate γ, relative to our body of knowledge.

It is easy enough to describe cases in which this randomness condition is not met. Cases in which a systematic error occurs in certain subsets of applications of M are the most obvious. Thus in a certain laboratory the applications of M may be characterized by an error that is normal (0.005), but there may be at the same time a lab assistant who tends systematically to get measurements that are too short; his errors, for example, may be normal $(-0.01, 0.005)$. If all we know of a measurement of the table is that it came from this laboratory, the former analysis is perfectly adequate. If we happen to know also that the measurement was made by this particular lab assistant, then the distribution that correctly yields probability statements about the length of the table is normal $(-0.01, 0.005)$.

Let us finally look again at (a). This sort of statement does not at all admit of the kind of precise analysis that the measurement example does. This does not mean, however, that the assertion is merely a matter of subjective opinion. It is one thing to say that I'll give you better than even money that it will be hot tomorrow; and something more to say that (relative to what I know) the probability that it will be hot is greater than a half. The latter suggests that there are certain things that I know, such that if any rational being knew them (and didn't know anything that in a straightforward but perhaps complicated sense superseded them), he too would be obliged, in point of logic, to agree that relative to his body of knowledge, the probability that tomorrow will be hot is greater than a half. If he were an agent, too, he should necessarily be willing to offer better than even money if he were to bet on tomorrow's being hot.

There is no problem in this case of finding an appropriate α and γ: α is tomorrow; γ is the set of hot days. But what is β, the reference set, of which, relative to what we know, α is a random member with respect to belonging to γ? And of which we know that more than half of the members do in fact belong to γ? It all depends. As an ordinary person, when I say something like (a), β may simply be the set of summer days in this region: I know that more than half of them are hot, and I don't know anything about α (tomorrow) that would lead me to put it in a different reference class. If I were a weather forecaster, I would take β to be the set of days preceded by certain characteristic weather patterns, and I would know that these weather patterns have been followed by hot days a certain proportion of the time. Thus it is that if I am an ordinary citizen, under these circumstances, I cannot claim to know more than that (say between 0.6 and 0.9 of the summer days are hot, while as a weather forecaster I may be able to know that between 0.85 and 0.95 of the days preceded by the weather patterns that tomorrow is preceded by turn out to be hot. There are a lot of possible complications in this case. They are complications that can perfectly well arise in the measurement case, though in that case, in view of the precise nature of our knowledge, and the fact that everybody who knows anything about what is going on knows roughly the same thing, they do not strike us as important or realistic. They are there; it is only that in the case of the weather they are more obvious.

6. PROGRAM NOTES

There is one difficulty about the epistemological conception of probability I have offered. Probabilities are relative to bodies of knowledge, and logically true, if true at all, relative to those bodies of knowledge. In order to know what probability statements are true for a given person or for a group of persons (there is nothing to prevent us from considering collective bodies of knowledge), we must therefore be able to tell what counts in a given context as a legitimate body of knowledge; we must be able to answer the question: in such and such a context, what may I (or you, or he, or they, or, metaphorically, chemistry or physics) legitimately and justifiably claim to know? In many—but by no means all—practical situations there is relatively little question about what belongs and what does not belong in our body of knowledge. In the practical cases in which probabilities are controversial—in which one group of people says that something is probable, and another group says that it isn't—it is far more often precisely the *logical* issue concerning whether a certain entity α is or is not a random member of β with respect to γ that is at the root of the trouble, than any question of what may legitimately be counted as part of our body of knowledge.

In a philosophical vein, however, we may and indeed must ask what the conditions of knowledge are in general. What are the criteria of knowledge, in virtue of which bodies of knowledge can be built up, relative to which probabilities can be defined? The conception of probability I have offered is epistemological in the sense that probability, in that sense, is legislative for rational belief; but for its philosophical application it requires the clarification of the concept of a body of knowledge, which itself is an epistemological problem. Thus to give philosophical flesh and bones to our conception of probability, we must at the same time develop an entire epistemology. We must consider the grounds for accepting so-called observation statements such as 'the result of this measurement was 2.00', and also such far-reaching theories as that called upon in our discussion of the coin, or that underlying our treatment of the measurement problem. Although on the view developed here probabilities are logically true, if true at all, they are so usually relative to bodies of knowledge that contain general statistical statements or complex statistical or deterministic theories. In fact the only cases in which such knowledge is not implied by the truth of a probability statement are those in which the underlying statistical assertion happens to be a logical truth, like the truth that most subsets of a set reflect the composition of the set (in a certain respect). In real life, these are rare cases.

What I have offered is therefore programmatic. It is incomplete in two respects. First, it requires that the epistemological notion of randomness be spelled out in explicit detail; this is the classical problem, essentially, of the choice of a reference class. This would suffice for practical applications of our statistical knowledge to particular instances, and also for the theory of statistical inference, since statistical inference generally consists of the application of statistical knowledge. Second, and far more grandiosely, for philosophical adequacy it requires the spelling out of a relatively complete epistemology, which will allow us to know theories and statistical generalizations as well as our toothaches. It is possible (as I have argued elsewhere) to employ the epistemological conception of probability in this construction without any circularity, vicious or otherwise. But the job has hardly been begun.

What I have tried to exhibit here is not a complete system, but merely the fact that the epistemological interpretation, rather than the frequency or propensity or subjective or classical logical interpretation, offers the best hope of solution for the plethora of problems that plague the applications of probability.

APPENDIX

Suppose that E_0, E_1, . . . is a sequence of events (or statements). Let X_I be the random quantity that has the value 1 if the ith event has the property Q (if the ith statement is true), and the value 0 otherwise. Let P be a probability measure defined over a field of events that includes all the E's. We suppose that the events are exchangeable, or that P is symmetric: i.e., that for finite set of events, say n, the probability that m specified events in the set will have the property Q is independent of *which* m events are specified. Or, to put it more precisely: given a set of m subscripts J, a set of n-m subscripts I,

$$P(\underset{i \in J}{\wedge} X_i = 1 \wedge \underset{i \in I}{\wedge} X_i = 0) = f(m, n),$$

a function of m and n only. In addition, let

$$\bar{X}_n = \frac{1}{n} \sum_{i=0}^{n-1} X_i,$$

$$P(X_0 = 1) = m_1,$$

$$P(X_1 = 1/X_0 = 1) = m_2.$$

Lemma 1:

$$P(X_i = 1) = m_1.$$

Proof:

$$P(\underset{i \in [0]}{\wedge} X_i = 1 \wedge \underset{i \in 0}{\wedge} X_i = 0) = f(1,1) = m_1.$$

$$P(\underset{i \in [j]}{\wedge} X_i = 1 \wedge \underset{i \in 0}{\wedge} X_i = 0) = m_1 = P(X_j = 1).$$

Lemma 2:

$$i \neq j \supset P(X_i = 1 \mid X_j = 1) = m_2.$$

Proof:

$$P(\underset{i \in [0,1]}{\wedge} X_i = 1 \wedge \underset{i \in 0}{\wedge} X_i = 0) = f(2,2) = m_1 \cdot m_2$$

$$P(\underset{k \in [i, j]}{\wedge} X_k = 1 \wedge \underset{k \in 0}{\wedge} X_k = 0) = m_1 \cdot m_2, \text{ provided } i \neq j.$$

$$P(X_i = 1 \mid X_j = 1) = \frac{m_1 \cdot m_2}{m_1}, \text{ provided } i \neq j.$$

Lemma 3:

$$E(\bar{X}_n) = m_1 \text{ (the mean of } \bar{X}_n)$$

Proof:

$$E(\bar{X}_n) = \frac{1}{n} \sum_{i=0}^{n-1} E(X_i)$$

$$E(X_i) = 1 \cdot m_1 + (1 - m_1) \cdot 0 = m_1$$

$$E(\bar{X}_n) = \frac{n \cdot m_1}{n} = m_1.$$

Lemma 4:

$$D^2(\bar{X}_n) = \frac{m_1}{n} + \frac{n-1}{n} m_1 \cdot m_2 - m_1^2 \text{ (the variance of } \bar{X}_n)$$

$$D^2(\bar{X}_n) = E\left[(\bar{X}_n - m_1)^2\right] \quad \text{(definition of variance)}$$

$$= \frac{1}{n^2} E\left(\sum_{i=0}^{n-1} X_i\right)^2 - 2m_1 E(\bar{X}_n) + m_1^2$$

$$\left(\sum_{i=0}^{n-1} X_i\right)^2 = \sum_{i=0}^{n-1} X_i^2 + \sum_{i=0}^{n-1}\sum_{\substack{j=0 \\ j \neq i}}^{n-1} X_i \cdot X_j.$$

Since

$$X_i = X_i^2, \ E(X_i^2) = E(X_i) = m_1$$
$$E(X_i \cdot X_j) = 1 \cdot P(X_i = 1) \cdot P(X_j = 1 \mid X_i = 1) +$$
$$0 \cdot P(X_i = 0 \vee X_j = 0)$$

$$= m_1 \cdot m_2$$

$$D^2(\bar{X}_n) = \frac{1}{n^2} n \cdot m_1 + \frac{1}{n^2}(n)(n-1)m_1 m_2 - m_1^2$$

$$= \frac{m_1}{n} + \frac{n-1}{n} m_1 m_2 - m_1^2.$$

Theorem:

$$P\left(|\bar{X}_n - m_1| \geq k \ \sqrt{\frac{m_1}{n} + \frac{n-1}{n} m_1 m_2 - m_1^2}\right) \leq \frac{1}{k^2}$$

Proof: Tchebycheff's theorem says that if Y is a random quantity, $E(Y)$ its mean, and $D^2(Y)$ its variance, then

$$P(|Y - E(Y)| \geq k \ \sqrt{D^2(Y)}) \leq \frac{1}{k^2}.$$

The theorem follows immediately by the substitution of $\bar{x}_n$ for Y, taking account of the lemmas.

Corollary: If $E_0, E_1, \ldots$ is a sequence of exchangeable events, and the probability that E_0 has Q is 0.01, and the probability that E_1 has Q, given that E_0 has Q, is between 0.01 and 0.02, then, for sufficiently large n, the probability that the frequency of Q will be no more than 0.11 among n of the events E is at least 0.99.

Proof:

$$D^2(\bar{X}_n) = \frac{1}{n}[m_1 - (m_1 m_2 - m_1^2)] + m_1 m_2 - m_1^2$$

$$= \frac{m_1}{n}[1 - (m_2 - m_1)] + m_1(m_2 - m_1).$$

By choosing n large enough, we can make the first term as close to 0 as we please.

Since

$$m_1 \geqslant m_2 - m_1, \ \sqrt{m_1(m_2 - m_1)} \leqslant m_1$$
$$km_1 \geqslant k \sqrt{m_1(m_2 - m_1)}.$$

Therefore from the theorem we have

$$P(|\bar{X}_n - m_1| \geqslant km_1) \leqslant \frac{1}{k^2}.$$

taking $k = 10$, $m_1 = 0.01$, $0.01 < m_2 \leqslant 0.02$, we have
$P(|\bar{X}_n - 0.01| \geqslant 0.10) \leqslant 0.01$, or
$P(\bar{X}_n \leqslant 0.11) \geqslant 0.99$.

Part IV. Epistemology

13

Epistemology and Induction

1. There are a lot of things we may properly claim to know: what we like and dislike, what is right and wrong in behavior, what is virtuous or sinful, mathematical truths, what is beautiful and what is ugly. But the kinds of things that have most often attracted the attention of epistemologists are things like perceptions, observations, empirical generalizations, scientific theories, and the like. It is the latter sort of knowledge with which I shall be concerned, primarily, and in a very secondary way, with mathematical and logical knowledge. We may loosely characterize these items of knowledge as matters of fact and matters of logic.

Let us begin by setting up a formal analogue of this vague general problem. We focus on a particular individual X at a particular time t. We suppose X to be a philosopher who speaks a formalized first-order language powerful enough to include whatever mathematics will turn out to be handy.

Consider first X's Ur-corpus: the set of statements to which he is most firmly committed. Some philosophers might regard the contents of X's Ur-corpus as all that he can legitimately claim to know. What goes into the Ur-corpus? Well, logical and mathematical truths in general: X may not be aware of them, may indeed be incapable of becoming aware of them (in the case of complicated mathematical truths) but is anyhow, we suppose, *committed* to them. What beyond these statements? That is a question we should not answer too quickly. The possible answers range from good old Protocol Sentences, however they might be construed, through "immediate perceptual judgments," to a categorical "*nothing* else," and a liberal "anything at all."

However we answer this question (we will return to it), there are still a lot of things we can properly claim to know that I shall suppose can't reasonably be regarded as belonging to the Ur-corpus. There are statements about the future (such as: the next time I put sugar in my coffee it will dissolve); statements about dispositional properties (sugar is soluble); general statements (all crows are black), and theoretical statements.

With regard to these statements there are two basic tacks we can take. We can say that they (some of them) are *accepted;* or we can characterize our epistemological relation to them by saying that we have a (justified) high degree of belief in them. There are philosophers (Richard Jeffrey is the most famous example) who want to claim that such statements can only be believed to a higher or lower degree—that they cannot be accepted. There is an argument for this position. To accept a statement must surely be (or at least involve) assigning it a probability of 1. It is to assume that the statement is infallible. Furthermore, if we assume that beliefs can be characterized by the probability calculus, then we must admit that if the probability of a statement is 1 then that probability cannot be changed by conditionalization according to the probability calculus: $P(h) = 1$ only if $P(h/f) = 1$, whatever f may be. Thus accepted statements are not only infallible but incorrigible on this view.

Professor Levi has introduced a happy distinction between fallibility and corrigibility, however, which allows us to talk of acceptance without being committed to incorrigibility. A statement may be accepted, on this view, and thus be regarded as infallible, without being regarded as immune to revision. In this, somewhat weakened, sense of acceptance, it surely seems appropriate to speak of the acceptance of statements other than those very special statements in the Ur-corpus. At any rate, that is the way I shall talk.

What can we say about those statements? Without introducing more distinctions than we need to, let us simply call them X's corpus of *accepted* statements, or his *rational* corpus, or his *body of knowledge,* or K. Or, as Levi puts it, X's standard of serious possiblity.

There are two ways of inquiring about this set of statements. The traditional one is to ask how the inclusion of statements in K can be justified. This is the approach of traditional epistemology. Within that approach there are a lot of alternatives: for example, we may suppose that there are incorrible statements in the Ur-corpus, and that statements get into K if and only if they are highly probable relative to the Ur-corpus. We may suppose that statements are admitted into K if and only if they cohere with other statements in K. Statements may also be supposed to enter K by observation, or by rules of the form: under such and such circumstances, enter S in K. And of course all the permutations and combinations of these methods of justifying the inclusion of S in K are also alternatives that might be considered.

Isaac Levi's approach is different. According to him what we should focus on is the problem of how to revise K; ordinarily he focuses primarily on the grounds for expanding K: When do we add S to K? This doesn't mean that we can't handle specific questions of justification: if S is in K, and we can be moved to doubt whether S ought to be in K, we can resolve the issue by deleting S from K, and then seeing if the expansion of the remainder of K to include S is a warranted expansion. Of course it isn't really this simple. There is more to contraction that deleting S, since K is a deductively closed set of statements. We must consider a set of statements K which is deductively closed and which does not include S. So we must delete from K not only S itself, but everything that implies S. In general there are a number of ways to do this—if the conjunction of A and B imply S, we have the choice of deleting either A or B from K. And this in turn may be done in a number of ways. Contraction is not a transparent notion.

The distinction to which I am drawing attention here has been called a distinction between global and local approaches to justification. It is a useful distinction; but it is one that admits of gradations. The most global sort of philosopher doesn't demand that we start with an empty set of statements and add to it only by argument. Everybody supposes that some statements, in either the Ur-corpus or the corpus K, are warranted by observations or phenomenal experiences or rules of language (incorrigible foundationalism, corrigible foundationalism), or by cohering with a whole set of statements that presents itself as a candidate for either the Ur-corpus or the corpus K (coherentist views). Anybody who is exploring a creek in imagination gives himself an imaginary paddle.

In any event, we certainly want to be able to add things to K inductively. Levi assumes that X's corpus contains theories and statistical statements. Induction involves probability one way or another, and before we return to the question of epistemology, we must take time out to say something about probability.

2. This is not the place to say a lot about my notion of probability, but it will be handy to say enough so that the contrast between Levi's approach and mine can be highlighted. According to my view, probability represents a logical relation between a set of statements regarded as "accepted" and a given statement. Since I take the relation to be logical, I am a necessitarian, in Professor Levi's scheme. But I do *not* suppose that this logical relation determines a real number representing the probability of S relative to K; I take it to determine only an interval, which may be degenerate or which may be the whole uninformative interval $(0, 1)$.

I say that the probability of S, relative to the set of statements K, is the interval (p, q) just in case:

(1) S is known in K to be equivalent to a statement of the form $\ulcorner a \in B \urcorner$
(2) The proportion of C's that are B's is known in K to be in the interval (p, q).

and (3) Relative to K, a is a random member of C with respect to B.

The statement regarding proportions mentioned in (2) I take to be a simple statistical statement, in most cases. I do not, as Levi does, require that it represent a statement concerning "objective chance," whatever that may be. It may, in certain relatively theoretical contexts—for example, in discussions of purely mathematical probabilities such as arise in connection with Bertrand's paradox, or in discussions of physically ideal dice—need to be construed modally; but certainly not in general.

The notion of randomness is more important and more difficult. It corresponds roughly to what Levi calls a Principle of Direct Inference. He and I disagree about what form the principle of direct inference should take (witness our exchange in the *Journal of Philosophy* [1], [2], [3], [4]) but we do agree that some such principle is important.

A few of the properties of my interpretation of probability will be relevant in what follows.

(1) Probability is defined for every statement of the language.

(2) If S and T are known to be equivalent (to have the same truth value), then they have the same probability.

(3) Every statement of probability is based on a known statistical statement.

(4) Given any corpus K, there is a belief function B, defined over the statements of the language, such that for every statement S, $B(S)$ is in the interval representing the probability of S relative to K, and such that B is a coherent Bayesian probability function.

(5) My system violates what Levi calls Confirmational Conditionalization.

This last point deserves comment, lest too much be made of it. First, let B be a coherent Bayesian probability function relative to K. Then clearly the two-place function, $B^*(S/T) = B(S \land T)/B(T)$, where defined, will be a coherent *conditional* Bayesian probability function. Thus conditionalization presents no problems.

This is clearly not what Levi has in mind by *confirmational* conditionalization. What he has in mind is this: Let K_T be obtained by adding T to K and forming the deductive closure. It is possible, in my system, that there is no coherent Bayesian probability function relative to K_T, say B_T, such that $B^*(S/T) = B_T(S)$.

I used to think that such violations were infrequent and unimportant. I still think they are unimportant, but their frequency depends on what you are counting. Levi is counting violations of confirmational conditionalization construed as a rule for making changes of belief. He is perfectly correct in saying that such violations are frequent—not to say endemic—on my view. What I had in mind was particular applications of conditionalization, and among those almost all conform to the Bayesian model.

For example, suppose that S is not independent of T. Suppose that S has the form $a \in M$, and T has the form $b \in N$, and that the probability of S comes from our knowledge of the frequency of M in the set X, and that our knowledge of the conjunction of S and T comes from our knowledge of the frequency of $M \times N$ in a subset of the product set $X \times Y$. (It cannot come from our knowledge of the frequency in the whole of the product set, else we would have independence; the frequency of $M \times N$ in the product set is just the product of the frequencies of M in X and N in Y.) Let this subset be R.

The frequency of $M \times Y$ in R must match the frequency of M in X (since $(a, b) \in M \times Y$ is equivalent to S, and probability is a function).

Let us now add to K the sentence T and form the deductive closure. Under ordinary circumstances the pair (a, b) will now be a random member of the intersection of R and $X \times N$: our reference class will be the subset of R consisting of pairs (a, b) in which the second term belongs to N. Certainly this will be so whenever we are dealing with the standard gambling-like situations. But of course under these circumstances no violation of confirmational conditionalization will occur.

When *will* this violation occur? Here is a plausible instance: We know that $a \in B$. To know the the proportion of B's that are C's affects the probability of $a \in C$. But to know that $a \in C$ does not affect the probability of the statement about the proportion of A's that are C's. Of course one might also want to say that knowledge of $a \in C$ *does* affect the probability of the statistical statement, but only in a trivial way. But if this is the extent of the violation of conformational conditionalization, it is clearly relatively unimportant.

What Levi shows (by example) is that violations of confirmational conditionalization, construed as a general rule, occur (potentially) whenever a probability (relative to K) is determined by a more precisely known frequency in a larger class, rather than by a less precisely known frequency in a smaller class. This is indeed a common situation, and thus violations of confirmational conditionalization occur on my view in almost every rational corpus. What should not be inferred from this, however, is that on my view it is not the case that the conditional probability that card c is a spade, given that c is black, is 1/2. All ordinary arguments and examples concerning conditional probability go through perfectly well. We should also note that violations of Bayesian conditionalization *are* allowed on Levi's way of looking at the matter.

Although Levi regards confirmational conditionalization as a basic *rule* for making changes in probability judgments, it does not determine the course of temporal credal change. There are various grounds on which one might change one's conformational commitment between one time and another, and such *temporal* changes need not conform to conditionalization. Thus at t_1, my conditional probability $P(H/E)$ may have one value, while at t_2 — even if all the new *evidence* I have acquired is E — my new probability $P^*(H)$ may have a different value. But this will only happen if I have changed my confirmational commitment between t_1 and t_2. Both Levi's view and mine conflict with conventional Bayesian wisdom. The difference is that we locate the conflict in different places: Levi in the choice of confirmational commitment, I in the principles guiding the choice of a reference class.

3. Nevertheless, in ordinary scientific situations, conditionalization will ordinarily apply over time. Let us consider an example, borrowed from Levi (oral presentation), concerning a scientist experimenting with mice, who is testing a black mouse for heterozygosity by mating it with a brown mouse. He knows that black is dominant, and therefore that if the black mouse is homozygous all of the litter will be black. If the black mouse is heterozygous, the litter may be

all black, all brown, or mixed. Let h_1 be the statement that the black mouse is homozygous, and h_2 the statement that it is heterozygous. Furthermore, let us suppose that the black mouse in question (let us call him Mickey) is the product of the union of two heterozygous black mice. We suppose that the scientist accepts as part of his background knowledge K that the chance that an off-spring of heterozygous black mouse, mated with a brown mouse, will be black is $1/2$; and that the chance of a pair of heterozygous black mice (Mickey's parents) producing a black offspring that is heterozygous is $2/3$. (This represents the prior probability that Mickey is homozygous.) Let the number of offspring of the mating be n, and let e_r be the statement that r of them are black. Given the scientist's background knowledge K, if $r < n$, h_1 will be ruled out as a serious possibility on deductive grounds. But if $r = n$, and n is large enough, it is plausible for the scientist to add h_1 to K and to rule out h_2.

The scientist performs the experiment in question and observes e_n: Mickey and his friend have n offspring, all of whom are black. What is the probability of h_2 relative to this new corpus K_{e_n}? Confirmational conditionalization gives us no answer—or rather, it gives us the uninformative conditional: If X's confirmational commitment remains fixed, then the probability of h_2 is the conditional probability of h_2 given e_n—say $Q(h_2/e_n)$. What we require is the premise that X's confirmational commitment remains unchanged between the time when he is contemplating the experiment, and the time when he has performed the experiment and added e_n to K. What is required here is *Temporal* Credal Conditionalization, which, as Levi has told us, need not be satisfied.

Note that these rules *must* be construed as applying through time: we cannot say that if the credence value of h_2 is less than q (Levi's index of caution) times M (Levi's measure of content), h_2 *is* not a serious possibility, for if h_2 is not a serious possibility its credence value is 0, not $Q(h_2/e_n)$, in direct violation of Confirmational Conditionalization. What we must say is that if at t_1 the credence value of h_2 is less than qM, then at t_2 later than t_1 h_2 may be regarded as not a serious probability. The statement h_1 cannot be added to K_{e_n} at t_1, for that would contradict our assertion that the credence value of h_2 at t_1 is $Q(h_2/e_n)$. This is a curious situation—though I hasten to add that it is a perfectly consistent way of looking at the matter. In the same way, it is perfectly consistent to believe p and to believe not-p, if you index beliefs with times and the two beliefs have different indices. (If they have the same index, you probably can't do it.)

I prefer to think of logic, both inductive and deductive, as characterizing what I am committed to in an atemporal sense. Thus suppose that the probability of h is as high as you please (less than 1) relative to K. Let h and K satisfy whatever other constraints you wish, having to do with language or information. If you construe inductive rules temporally, you can have a rule of the form: *Now* add h to K. But if you construe them atemporally, you cannot have a rule of that form at all: it follows from the fact that the probability of h relative to K is less than 1, that h is *not* a member of K.

If you are looking for an atemporal principle of acceptance, then, you really have to consider two rational corpora. You consider a corpus K of evidential statements, what I have called elsewhere a corpus of moral certainties, and also a corpus of K^* of practical certainties. Relative to a certain corpus of evidential statements, certain other statements will belong to (be accepted in) the corpus of practical certainties. Let's see how this works.

4. What counts as moral certainty and as practical certainty in a given situation depends on the situation. (Whoever supposed that what counts as adequate inductive evidence didn't depend on the context?) In the case of scientist X we are being asked to suppose that K, X's body of moral certainties, contains a certain amount of genetic theory, and the assertion that Mickey is the offspring of two heterozygous black mice.

I should mention here that it is not clear how the principle of direct inference can be applied (in Levi's form) without stipulating that this is *all* that X knows about Mickey. In fact, since Levi's form of the principle of direct inference requires that Mickey be somehow selected at *random* from the set (or maybe from the potential set) of offspring of pairs of heterozygous black mice it isn't even clear that the principle does apply here. In any event, on my view (and presumably on Levi's), we must assume that K, X's corpus of moral certainties, does not contain other information relevant to the probability that h_1 is true. For example, we assume that it contains no information regarding the composition of other litters resulting from breeding Mickey with brown females. But I shall leave to one side the question of how Levi's principle of direct inference is to be construed in a case such as this.

Scientist X now performs his breeding experiment, and observes the result e_n. At the level of moral certainty, we take this observation to warrant the inclusion of e_n in the corpus K to yield K_{e_n}.

Let us now focus on practical certainties. We suppose that a level of practical certainty (what level is suitable depends on the context) can be characterized by a real number r. What this amounts to is just the adoption of a very simple acceptance rule: S belongs to K^*, the corpus of practical certainties, just in case its probability relative to the corpus of moral certainties is greater than r. (A lower value of r presumably corresponds to a higher value of q in Levi's system.) Of course any statement in K has a probability of $(1, 1)$ relative to K, and thus comes to be included in K^*. In particular K^* contains genetic theory, Mickey's provenance, and so on.

What happens when K is expanded by the addition of e_n? Then we have a new set of moral certainties K_{e_n}. The probabilities of various statements are different relative to K_{e_n} than they are relative to K alone. A different set of statements will have probabilities higher than r relative to K_{e_n} than relative to K. Some statements will no longer belong to $K^*_{e_n}$ (the set of practical certainties corresponding to K_{e_n}. In particular, if p, the probability of h_1 is higher than r, h_1 itself will belong to $K^*_{e_n}$. The matter is just that simple. If K_{e_n} represents

X's set of moral certainties, then h_1 will belong to $K^*_{e_n}$, provided its probability is high enough to count as practical certainty in the context at hand.

Note that all of this involves only a principle of direct inference, as embodied in the epistemological notion of randomness. We do not need to invoke credal coherence. We do not need to invoke confirmational conditionalization, since what conditionalization takes place takes place on a purely statistical level. Nor do we have to demand temporal credal conditionalization, as Levi does, since his permissive rules of expansion have to be applied over time.

Despite these differences, there are important similarities. In each treatment there is a dependency on context. This dependency is reflected in different ways. For Levi it depends on the way the problem is split up—the choice of an ultimate partition U—and it depends on the choice of the index q. For me, it depends on the choice of what is to count as moral certainty and on the choice of a level of practical certainty. There is one feature of the analysis that seems to be context-dependent for Levi and is not context-dependent for me: that is the choice of a confirmational commitment. Since I am a necessitarian when it comes to probability, the choice of K—the set of moral certainties—already determines confirmational commitment.

Both Levi and I agree that members of K can be questioned; we are both committed to that view, since we are both willing to suppose that statistical statements, generalizations, and even theories can appear in K. On Levi's view, to question S is to remove it from K and then to see whether expansion of K to include S is warranted. (But recall that there are many ways to contract K so that it no longer includes S.) On my view it is to adopt a more demanding notion of moral certainty—one to which S no longer belongs—and to construe K as a set of practical certainties relative to that set of moral certainties, and then to examine the question of whether S belongs to that set of practical certainties K. An important difference is that I can consider the whole set of moral certainties K to be questionable, adopt a different stance, in which K' is my set of moral certainties, and inventory K as a set of practical certainties relative to K'. Another important difference is that I can adopt the Ur-corpus itself as my set of moral certainties, and consider a corpus of practical certainties relative to that. It may be hard to imagine motivation for being so skeptical; I myself see little point in it, except as a philosophical gambit to refute easy claims of the form: "There can be no inductive justification for S." So far as disputes concerning scientific (or ordinary) inductive inferences are concerned, it suffices for the disputants to be able to settle on the contents of a set of moral certainties and on a level of practical certainty.

5. There is still a question that needs to be addressed: the question of getting from empirical data to theories and generalizations. It is not hard to show that relative to a body of moral certainties that contains a lot of statistical data, approximate statistical generalizations can be rendered probable enough to belong to corpora of practical certainties. But "all crows are black" and the

genetic theory cannot be construed as approximate statistical generalizations. The question is: how do such statements or sets of statements come to be accepted?

To deal with this Gordian knot, I offer the following Alexandrian Sword: to accept a universal generalization or a theory is to accept—to decide to use—a language in which the generalization or the theory is characteristic of the meanings of the terms involved. Of course this immediately raises the question of *why* one should speak one language rather than another. I shall come to that in a minute, but let us begin with some observations.

First, one but rarely seems to encounter in bodies of scientific knowledge good old-fashioned generalizations of the form "all *A*'s are *B*'s." One seems rather to encounter systems of statements from which these generalizations follow. And it has always seemed very awkward to talk about the "probability" of these systems of statements. People remind us that every theory becomes obsolete, and in that sense is "probably false."

Second, when we evaluate a theory, we don't think of ourselves as computing its probability—even in a very rough and ready way—but as comparing its desirability to that of some other *given* theory or small finite set of theories.

Third, as science progresses, it is not only the theoretical structures that change, but the very notion of "observation;" what at one time is the sort of statement that can come to be regarded as morally certain on the basis of observation, at another time may simply not be regarded as that sort of statement. This characteristic of a statement—whether or not it is the *sort* of statement that can come to be accepted on the basis of observation—seems to be a reflection of its meaning, whether or not we want to go so far as to identify meaning and "use."

Fourth, probability itself is, on my view, relativized to language. The relativization is not so far-reaching as it was for Carnap, since my probabilities are based on statistical knowledge, rather than on counting state descriptions, but nevertheless, it is possible that certain sorts of change may affect certain probabilities.

These considerations suggest that we have a variety of motivations to consider principles for choosing a language in which to embody our knowledge. In this last section of my paper I shall sketch out one such principle which seems promising. I must confess that the idea has not been worked out in any detail.

Let us focus on the problem of choosing between two languages, L_1 and L_2. Each language comes complete with a set of meaning postulates, and a (recursive) set of sentences that are of the sort that admit of direct observational verification. (This need not at all be conclusive verification; it may be that such sentences can only be rendered acceptable at a certain level of moral certainty by observation.) There is a connection between the terms that occur in these sentences, and more theoretical terms that do not occur in such sentences. This is most easily seen in the case of quantitative theories. The application or testing of such a theory involves measurement, plugging values obtained from measurement into the theory, the derivation of the values of related quantities, and the measurement of these quantities. Things never work out quite right; there is always some slop. But we also have a theory of errors of measurement which allows for this looseness of fit. Now that "theory of error" is a straightforward approximate empirical statistical theory. As such, given a language, it can be rendered practically certain by the accumulation of data. Let us suppose that we have done this for each of two theories (embodied respectively in L_1 and L_2) in a given domain.

Let us now consider two bodies of knowledge, K_1^* and K_2^* written in these two languages, based on the same body of experience. It may well happen that (in this quantitative case) the practical certainties of K_1^* are stronger than the practical certainties of K_2^*: more information is embodied in K_1^* than in K_2^*. (For example, if a statement in K_1^* says that a certain observation will lie between 9 and 11, and the corresponding statement in K_2^* says that the observation will lie between 8 and 12, we would say that the former statement embodies more information than the latter.) This will occur if the theory that forms part of L_1 is better than that that forms part of L_2, for the amount of error we must assume to adjust our measurements to our theory in the first case will be less than the amount of error we must assume to adjust our measurements to our theory in the second case. Therefore when we infer from the data a statistical distribution of error, the distribution we get in the first case will be characterized by a smaller variance than the distribution we get in the second case. From this in turn it will follow that the predictions we get in the first case, at a given level of practical certainty, will involve narrower intervals than those we get in the second case.

I have worked this out, more or less, in the very simple theories of measurement that everyone takes for granted, and it seems that only very natural and pervasive principles are required. Whether it will work in detail, and whether it will work for more complicated theories, remains to be seen.

Supposing it does work, however, we have only solved the problem of determining which of two theories (that is, which of two languages) is preferable, given a certain body of experience. Two further problems then remain to be considered. First, it may turn out that theories which turn out to be indiscriminable on the amount-of-information-in-the-set-of-practical-certainties criterion, are nevertheless intuitively discriminable. Our criterion may not be fine-grained enough. Second, it might turn out that at one level of practical certainty L_1 was preferable to L_2, but that at another level of practical certainty the reverse obtained. This would call for going back to the drawing board.

This talk about choosing between languages has been very sketchy and very tentative. But let's suppose that it could all be worked out. Then we would have gone a long way toward understanding the epistemology of empirical statements. Given a corpus of moral certainties in language L, we can tell whether or not a given statement S belongs to the corresponding set of practical certainties of level r. Given two languages L_1 and L_2, and a set of morally certain observation statements of each corresponding to the same body of experience, we can decide whether the theory-laden language L_1 is preferable to the theory-laden language L_2, or vice versa, or whether neither is preferable to the other. We would thus have achieved very powerful machinery not only for the criticism and revision of bodies of knowledge, but for choosing among theories and languages on the basis of empirical knowledge. The latter part is, to be sure, merely programmatic. But an interesting program is worth pursuing.

BIBLIOGRAPHY

[1] Levi, Isaac, "Direct Inference," *Journal of Philosophy* 74, 1977, pp. 5-29.

[2] Kyburg, Henry E., Jr., "Randomness and the Right Reference Class," *Journal of Philosophy* 74, 1977, pp. 501-520.

[3] Levi, Isaac, "Confirmational Conditionalization," *Journal of Philosophy* 75, 1978, pp. 730-737.

[4] Kyburg, Henry E., Jr., "Conditionalization," *Journal of Philosophy* 77, 1980, pp. 98-114.

14

Conjunctivitis

I

Consider a set S of statements that may be taken to represent an idealized body of scientific knowledge. Let s_1 and s_2 be members of S. Should we regard the conjunction of s_1 and s_2, also as a member of S? It is tempting to answer in the affirmative, and a number of writers, whose systems we shall consider below, have indeed answered this way. An affirmative answer is conjunctivitis, which may be expressed by the following principle:

The Conjunction Principle: If S is a body of reasonably accepted statements, and s_1 belongs to S and s_2 belongs to S, then the conjunction of s_1 and s_2 belongs to S.

This principle is clearly equivalent to the following principle.

The Conjunctive Closure Principle: If S is a body of reasonably accepted statements, then the conjunction of any finite number of members of S also belongs to S.

Already the intuitive plausibility of the conjunction principle begins to fade; while it seems reasonable enough to want to accept the conjunction of two relatively elementary statements that are individually acceptable, it seems quite unreasonable to accept all the enormously long conjunctions of elements in S. But the reasonableness or unreasonableness of the principle will depend, of course, on what other principles one also accepts.

One principle which is, so far as I know, universally accepted[1], is the principle that anything entailed by a member of S should also be a member of S. If it is reasonable to accept s_1, and s_1 entails s_2, then it is reasonable to accept s_2. I shall call this the weak deduction principle.

The Weak Deduction Principle: If S is a body of reasonably accepted statements, and s_1 belongs to S, and $s_1 \supset s_2$ is a theorem of our underlying logic, then s_2 belongs to S.

Reprinted from Marshall Swain, ed., *Induction, Acceptance, and Rational Belief* (Dordrecht, Reidel, 1970), pp. 55-82, by permission of the publisher. Research for the work was supported by the National Science Foundation under grants GS 708, GS 1179, and GS 1962.

Another principle which I am sure is universally accepted is that the set of reasonably accepted statements S should contain no contradictions. Whether or not it is psychologically possible to believe a contradiction (with practice perhaps it is), we do not want to regard it as rational. This I shall call the weak consistency principle.

The Weak Consistency Principle: If S is a body of reasonably accepted statements, then there is no member of S that entails every statement of the language.

In 1961 I offered an argument from the weak consistency principle and the weak deduction principle to the denial of the conjunction principle. This argument has come to be called the lottery paradox, and has engendered a number of principles designed to restrict the contents of S in such a way that all three of the principles mentioned so far hold.

The argument is this: Consider a fair lottery with a million tickets. Consider the hypothesis, 'ticket number 7 will not win'. Since this is, by hypothesis, a fair lottery, there is only one chance in a million that this hypothesis is false. Surely, I argued, this is reason enough to accept the hypothesis. But a similar argument would provide reason to accept the hypothesis that ticket i will not win, no matter what ticket number i may be. By the conjunction principle, we obtain from 'ticket 1 will not win' and 'ticket 2 will not win', the statement 'neither ticket 1 nor ticket 2 will win'; from the last statement, together with the statement 'ticket 3 will not win', by the conjunction principle, 'neither ticket 1, nor ticket 2, nor ticket 3 will win'; and so on, until we arrive at the reasonable acceptance of a long conjunction which can be briefly expressed as: 'For all i, if i is a number between one and a million inclusive, ticket i will not win'. But we may also suppose that S contains the statement that the lottery is fair; and this statement entails the statement: 'For some i, i is a number between one and a million inclusive, and ticket i will win'. By the weak deduction principle we must therefore include this latter statement in S. By the conjunction principle we must therefore include the conjunction of the universally quantified statement and the existentially quantified statement in S. But this conjunction is an explicit contradiction from which any statement will follow in violation of the weak consistency principle. I concluded that it was worthwhile to hang onto the weak deduction principle and the weak consistency principle, and therefore that the conjunction principle should be abandoned.

Quite a number of people, finding the conjunction principle more plausible than I do, have attempted to spike this argument here or there. One of the earliest attempts was made by Salmon [14], who suggested that one ought not to accept particular statements (such as 'Ticket 7 will not win the lottery'), but restrict one's acceptances to general statistical or universal generalizations. Since a number of writers have followed Salmon in this ploy, it is worth stating a statistical version of the same argument.[2]

Consider a finite population P of entities, each of which either has or lacks a certain quality Q. We draw a random sample (in any sense of 'random' you choose) of n of the P's. A certain proportion of the members of the sample, f, have the property Q; we know that in the parent population P some unknown proportion p have the property Q. Now consider hypotheses of the form 'p lies in the interval i'; for example: 'p lies in the interval $(f - .1, f + .1)$', 'p lies in the interval $(f - .0001, f + .675)$', etc. There are a number of principles of inference that one might adopt for arriving at acceptable statistical statements of this form. I shall consider two, though what I say will apply to other principles as well. Let us call them the Bayesian Acceptance Principle and the Classical Acceptance Principle.[3] In accordance with the Bayesian Principle, we shall accept a statistical hypothesis if its posterior probability is greater than $1 - \epsilon$, i.e., if the probability of its negation is less than ϵ. According to the Classical Principle, we will accept a hypothesis provided the probability of rejecting it by mistake is less than ϵ. Since the argument is slightly different in the two cases, I shall treat them separately.

Bayesian case: There are any number of intervals i such that the hypothesis '$p \in i$' is acceptable, under the assumption that the prior distribution of p is continuous between 0 and 1. Let i_c be the intersection of all these intervals. By the conjunction principle, '$p \in i_c$' is acceptable. Again under the assumption of continuity, it is possible to divide any interval i and in particular i_c into a finite number of subintervals i_1, i_2, . . . , i_m, such that the posterior probability of '$p \in i_k$' is less than ϵ, for all k, $1 \leqslant k \leqslant m$. But this is just to say that the posterior probability of '$\sim p \in i_k$' is greater than $1 - \epsilon$ for all k, $1 \leqslant k \leqslant m$, and thus that the hypothesis '$\sim p \in i_k$' is acceptable for all k, $1 \leqslant k \leqslant m$. The conjunction principle then entails that '$\sim p \in i_c$' is acceptable, in virtue of the fact that $i_c = \cup\, i_k$. Thus by the conjunction principle we have '$p \in i_c$ & $\sim p \in i_c$' in our body of acceptable statements in violation of the weak consistency principle.

Classical case: Again there are any number of intervals i such that the probability that we will falsely reject the hypothesis '$p \in i$' when we observe f is less than ϵ. To be more precise (and more classical), to each of these intervals i_j there will correspond an interval E_j, such that if we reject the hypothesis '$p \in i_j$' if and only if the observed frequency f falls outside the interval E_j, then we will falsely reject the hypothesis no more than ϵ of the time. Of those hypotheses '$p \in i_j$' such that in point of fact f falls in the corresponding interval E_j, we say that they 'are not rejected at the ϵ level of significance'. In particular, to each hypothesis of the form '$p \in (a, b)$' there will correspond a test interval $(a - d, b + e)$ (it will always include the *closed* interval $[a, b]$), such that if we reject the hypothesis if and only if we observe a value of f not falling in the test interval, we shall falsely reject it less than ϵ of the time. Consider two hypotheses '$p \in (a, f)$' and '$p \in (f, b)$'. At any level of significance, the value f of the observed frequency will fall within the test interval corresponding to each of these hypotheses.[4] Thus at any level of significance we will accept both the hypothesis '$p \in (a, f)$' and the hypothesis '$p \in (f, b)$'. By the conjunction principle, we must then accept their conjunction. But there is no number that belongs both to (f, b) and (a, f); again we find a violation of the weak consistency principle.

II

Among those who have adopted principles of acceptance satisfying the principle of conjunction, the weak principle of consistency, and the weak principle of deduction, are included Hempel [3], Hintikka [7], Lehrer [12], and Levi [13]. In the ensuing sections I shall consider the principles proposed by each of these writers in turn, both from the viewpoint of strength and from the viewpoint of plausibility. We begin with Hempel. In his well-known paper, 'Deductive-Nomological vs. Statistical Explanation', Hempel lays down certain "necessary conditions of rationality in the formation of beliefs," I shall discuss them one by one.

(CR1) Any logical consequence of a set of accepted statements is likewise an accepted statement; or, K contains all logical consequences of any of its subclasses.

An obviously equivalent formulation is the following:

The Principle of Deductive Closure: The set S is closed under deduction.

It should be observed that this principle is not equivalent to the weak deduction principle. Hempel's criterion entails the weak deduction principle, but the converse does not hold. For example, the set: 'S', '$S \supset P$', '$S \vee \phi$', '$\sim P \supset \sim S$', '$S \& T$', 'T', . . . of which 'P' is not a member satisfies the weak principle, but not Hempel's strong lprinciple. However, the conjunction principle, together with the weak deduction principle, are equivalent to the principle of deductive closure:

Theorem 1: Principle of deductive closure $\equiv$ (principle of conjunction and weak deduction principle).

Proof: If S satisfies the principle of deductive closure, then if s_1 and s_2 belong to S, so do all their consequences; among their consequences is the conjunction of s_1 and s_2. Thus the principle of conjunction. And if S satisfies the principle of deductive closure, then if s_1 belongs to S, so does any consequence of s_1. Thus the weak principle of deduction. Now suppose S satisfies both the principle of conjunction and the weak deduction principle; then suppose that $s_1, \ldots, s_n$ each belong to S, and that s follows from $s_1, \ldots, s_n$ as premises. By the principle of conjunction, the conjunction of $s_1, \ldots, s_n$ belongs to S; by the standard deduction theorem, plus the weak deduction principle it then follows that s belongs to S.

What is questionable about the strong principle of deductive closure is, I think, precisely the principle of conjunction. This may involve a matter of intuition: I simply don't believe that everything I believe on good grounds is true, and I think it would be irrational for me to believe that. Other people seem to think the opposite. I suspect that at root there is a confusion of quantifiers: of everything that I believe, it is correct to say that I believe it to be true; but it is not correct to say that I believe everything I believe to be true. In symbols:

(1) (x) (I believe $x \supset$ I believe x to be true).
(2)   I believe (x) (I believe $x \supset x$ is true).

Statement (1) seems true, statement (2) false.

Hempel's second condition of rationality is a consistency condition

(CR2) The set K of accepted statements is logically consistent.

Although it might be possible to construe this as the weak principle of consistency above, it is more likely that Hempel has in mind a strong principle of consistency:

Strong Principle of Consistency: If S is a body of reasonably accepted statements, then there is no finite subset of S, $s_1, \ldots, s_n$, such that every statement of the language follows from $s_1, \ldots, s_n$ as premises.

Again conjunction plays an important role. In the presence of the conjunction principle, the strong principle of consistency and the weak principle of consistency are equivalent.

Theorem 2: Conjunction principle $\supset$ [strong principle of consistency $\equiv$ weak principle of consistency].

Again one can question the plausibility of the strong principle. I probably cannot believe a contradiction, or act on one. But I can certainly believe, and even act on, each of a set of statements which, taken conjointly, is inconsistent. Indeed, when I lend my moral support to a lottery, without buying a ticket, this is one way to describe what is going on; though a more adequate and complete description would involve expectation.

Hempel's third criterion is, he claims, "simply a restatement of the requirement of total evidence" (p. 151).

(CR3) The inferential acceptance of any statement h into K is decided on by reference to the total system K.

This criterion, though it is not strictly relevant to the problem of conjunctivitis, is worth a comment or two. It is clearly in conflict with the principles of fallibilism and empiricism which underly much of what Hempel writes. Surely it is a consequence of these principles that even if a statement s becomes a part of our body of reasonable beliefs, we will, if the evidence begins to go the other way, be ready to reject it. But if we incorporate the statement h into the body of beliefs K, then, whatever else we add to that body of beliefs, its probability, relative to that body of beliefs, is going to be unity. Once accepted, no added evidence can ever render h improbable. The suggestion—which requires a great deal of development—is that we shall have to keep our evidential base separate from the body of reasonable beliefs erected on that base. There is also a new path to inconsistency opened by this principle. Let us suppose that there is a set

P, 99% of which are Q_1; that 99% of the Q_1 are Q_2; . . . that 99% of the Q_n are R. There is nothing inconsistent in supposing this, and that at the same time 99% of the P are not-R. But there is obviously something inconsistent about accepting the statement that an arbitrary P is not-R (since it is a P and that's all we know about it), and accepting the statement that an arbitrary P is R (since it is a P and that's all we know about it).

Hempel finally proposes a measure of epistemic utility (related to the content of a statement in terms of a logical measure function) according to which the principle of maximizing utility leads to the rule:

Tentative rule for inductive acceptance: Accept or reject h, given K, according as $c(h, K) > 1/2$ or $c(h, K) < 1/2$; when $c(h, K) = 1/2$, h may be accepted, rejected, or left in suspense (p. 155).

It is clear that this rule is not only, as Hempel puts it, "too liberal," but leads directly, through the strong principle of deduction, to inconsistency, provided only that there are three hypotheses, jointly exhaustive, whose probabilities, relative to k are all less than a half.

III

A recent paper by Hilpinen and Hintikka develops an inductive acceptance rule that is demonstrably consistent, and satisfies a number of criteria similar to those discussed above. Their system uses Hintikka's 1965 system of inductive logic [4], in which nonzero degrees of confirmation come to be assigned to general sentences. This system of inductive logic is applicable in principle to all first-order languages (without identity), but is developed in detail only for monadic languages. In point of fact, the system developed by Hilpinen and Hintikka satisfies the strong consistency principle, and the strong principle of deductive closure. Put in terms of the most finely articulated statements above: their system satisfies the weak deduction principle, the weak consistency principle, and the conjunction principle. (Since these three principles are independent, it seems best to refer to them separately.)

Since Hintikka's system is not as well known as it should be, a brief review of its features may be helpful here. Consider a language L, containing k primitive monadic predicates 'P_i'. By means of these predicates, one can characterize $K = 2^k$ kinds of individuals, corresponding to Carnap's 2^k Q-predicates. For the sake of simplicity we suppose that instantiation of each of the Q-predicates is logically possible, or in Carnap's terms, that the primitive predicates are logically independent. These Q-predicates are called by Hintikka 'attributive constituents'. A *constituent* consists of a specification, for each of the K Q-predicates or attributive constituents, of whether or not it is instantiated in the world. There are $2^K - 1$ possible different constituents (because it is logically false that *no* constituent be instantiated in a non-empty universe).

238 / Conjunctivitis

There are various ways of assigning *a priori* probabilities to the constituents. One might take the probability of a constituent to be proportional to $(w/K)^\alpha$, where α is an arbitrary constant, and w is the number of Q-predicates that are alleged to be instantiated by the constituent. For our purposes the simpler assignment of equal probabilities to each constituent (also worked out by Hintikka and Hilpinen) will suffice.

Let e be a sentence that asserts, for each member of a sample of n individuals, and for each of our primitive predicates 'P_i', either that that individual has the property P_i or that it has the property $\sim P_i$. Since we may order the Q-predicates in an arbitrary way there is no loss of generality in supposing that our sample of n individuals provides instantiation of the first c Q-predicates. The constituents that are consistent with our evidence all have the form:

$$(\exists x)\, Q_1(x)\, \& \,(\exists x)\, Q_2(x)\, \& \,\ldots\, \& \,(\exists x)\, Q_c(x)\, \& \,(\exists x)\, Q_{i_1}(x)$$
$$\& \,(\exists x)\, Q_{i_2}(x)\, \& \,\ldots\, \& \,(\exists x)\, Q_{i_m}(x)\, \& \,(x)\, (Q_1(x) \vee Q_2(x)$$
$$\vee\, \ldots\, Q_c(x) \vee Q_{i_1}(x) \vee \ldots \vee Q_{i_m}(x)),$$

where $i_j < i_k$ whenever $j < k$, and $i_1 > c$.

Let C_c be the constituent that asserts that just those Q-predicates instantiated by our evidence are exemplified in the universe (i.e., $C_c = $ '$(\exists x)\, Q_1(x)$ $\& \,\ldots\, \& \,(\exists x)\, Q_c(x)\, \& \,(x)\, (Q_1(x) \vee \ldots \vee Q_c(x))$', and let C_w be any other constituent consistent with our evidence. Then it is possible to show:

(1) $P(C_c, e) > P(C_w, e)$
(2) $\lim_{n \to \infty} P(C_c, e) = 1$
(3) $\lim_{n \to \infty} P(C_w, e) = 0$.

One further fact is important:

(4) Every consistent general sentence h of L_k can be transformed into a disjunction of constituents; thus $P(h, e) = \sum_i P(C_i, e)$, where the summation is extended over all those constituents in the disjunction equivalent to h.

It is possible to show ((2) and (3) give an intuitive justification) that for given $\epsilon < 1/2$, we can calculate an integer n_0 such that if $n > n_0$, one and only one constituent will have a probability, relative to e, greater than $1 - \epsilon$. This constituent will of course be C_c.

We now adopt the following for our rule of acceptance: Accept a *general* statement h, given evidence e, if and only if: the probability of h is greater than $1 - \epsilon$, and more than n_0 objects have been examined. Formally (p. 11):

(D.Ac) $Ac(h,e) =_{Df}$ (i) $P(h, e) > 1 - \epsilon$, where $0 < \epsilon \leqslant 0.5$
                              (ii) $n > n_0$.

In virtue of (4) a hypothesis h can have a probability greater than $1 - \epsilon$ only if the constituent C_c appears in its distributive normal form; thus every hypothesis that is acceptable must be consistent with C_c; and thus they must be jointly consistent. The strong consistency condition, and thus the weak consistency condition also are satisfied.

The principle of conjunction is also satisfied. If h_i and h_j are acceptable, then C_c must occur in the distributive normal form of each of them, and thus C_c will occur in the distributive normal form of their conjunction. The probability of their conjunction will therefore be greater than $1 - \epsilon$, and their conjunction will therefore be acceptable.

The principle of deductive closure so far fails, however, even in its weak form. Let '$(x)A(x)$' be an acceptable generalization; one of its deductive consequences is '$A(a)$'. But there is no clause in (D.Ac) that will allow us to accept '$A(a)$'.

Deductive closure does hold, however, for *general* statements. Suppose that the general statements $h_1, \ldots, h_n$ are all acceptable, and that they entail a factual general statement h. Since C_c occurs in the distributive normal form of each h_i, C_c must also occur in the distributive normal form of h itself. Thus h must be acceptable, and, so far as general statements h (containing no individual constants) are concerned, the strong principle of deductive closure is satisfied.

Theorem 3: If K is the set of all those statements h such that $Ac(h, e)$, then K satisfies the conjunction principle and the strong consistency principle, but neither the strong nor the weak deduction principle. The strong and weak deduction principles are satisfied if we restrict their range of application to completely general sentences.

The system so far provides us with no way of accepting singular statements of the form $M(a_i)$, where M is a molecular predicate equivalent to a disjunction of Q-predicates, and a_i an individual constant. Hintikka and Hilpinen show that in order to preserve consistency, our rule for the acceptance of singular predictions must be:

(D.Ac sing) A singular hypothesis $A(a_i)$ is acceptable if and only if the generalization $(x)A(x)$ is acceptable (p. 18).

Let A_c be the disjunction of the c Q-predicates in C_c. '$(x)A_c(x)$' is acceptable, and the probability of the conjunction of any arbitrary number of statements of the form $A_c(a_i)$ is at least $1 - \epsilon$. Indeed:

$$\lim_{r \to \infty} P[A_c(a_1) \& \ldots \& A_c(a_r)] = P(C_c, e)$$

Let us look at consistency and deductive closure. Suppose the singular statements '$A_1(a_1)$', '$A_2(a_2)$', $\ldots$ '$A_n(a_n)$' are acceptable as being instances of acceptable universal generalizations, and that the compound statement S is deducible from them. Since '$(x)A_c(x)$' is the strongest universal generalization, '$A_1(a_1)$' is deducible from '$A_c(a_1)$', '$A_2(a_2)$' is deducible from '$A_c(a_2)$' etc., and the statement S is deducible from the conjunction '$A_c(a_1) \& A_c(a_2) \& \ldots \& A_c(a_n)$', therefore S is deducible from '$(x)A_c(x)$'. This ensures that the probability of S will be at least $1 - \epsilon$. But we have no grounds for either asserting or denying that S is acceptable; acceptability has been defined only for completely general statements, and for singular statements of the form $A(a)$. Deductive closure thus far fails. Acceptability in general, however, would presumably be defined in this way:

(Acc)   A statement S is acceptable if and only if it belongs to every class K of statements, closed under deduction, containing e, such that each member of K that is completely general is acceptable by (D.Ac), and such that each statement acceptable by (D.Ac) is a member of K.

The separate principle (D.Ac sing) is deducible from this principle.

Theorem 4: If K is the set of all statements h, such that h is acceptable by the principle (Acc), then K satisfies the conjunction principle, the strong consistency principle, and the strong deduction principle.

Proof:

(a) Conjunction Principle: The conjunction of s_1 and s_2 belongs to every class K closed under deduction to which both s_1 and s_2 belong, and therefore to every class K closed under deduction and meeting further requirements as well to which both s_1 and s_2 belong.

(b) The Strong Consistency Principle: By hypothesis e is consistent, and consistent with the strongest acceptable generalization, '$(x)A_c(x)$'. Other statements are obtained only by deduction, but deduction cannot introduce inconsistency.

(c) The Strong Deduction Principle: Since the classes K are closed under deduction the deduction principle is satisfied automatically.

The set of statements characterized as acceptable by this principle consists essentially of C_c and e, together with all of their deductive consequences. This set is essentially the set of deductive consequences of a single statement. We shall find this to be characteristic of those acceptance rules for which deductive closure holds, and which are demonstrably consistent.

There are certain shortcomings to the system of Hintikka and Hilpinen. In the first place, as it stands, it does not allow us to take account of the relative frequencies with which the Q-predicates are exemplified. In a similar system proposed by Hintikka [6] the probability that an individual a will have a certain molecular property M will depend on the relative frequencies with which Q-predicates have been observed to be exemplified; but in the system under discussion we can never accept $A(a)$ unless the universal generalization $(x)M(x)$ is acceptable. This is a general feature of these systems, and necessarily so. All of these systems accept the principle of conjunction, and it follows directly from the principle of conjunction that if an arbitrary predictive inference of the form '$A(a)$' is acceptable, then its universal generalization '$(x)A(x)$' is acceptable, at least when restricted in scope to the unobserved part of the universe of discourse. This should be stated formally.

Theorem 5: If the principle of conjunction is accepted, and if for any arbitrary individual a among the unobserved individuals, the singular predictive in-

Conjunctivitis / 241

ference '$A(a)$' is acceptable, then the universal generalization '$(x)A(x)$' is acceptable, when restricted in scope to unobserved individuals.

Proof: Let the evidence e mention only k individuals, as failing to satisfy the predicate 'A'; let these individuals be $a_1 \ldots a_k$ (k may be 0). Then if the principle of conjunction is accepted, then if in general any singular predictive inference of the form '$A(a_i)$' ($i > k$) is acceptable, then every finite conjunction of statements of this form is acceptable, and the universal generalization '(x) $(\sim x \in \{a_1, a_2, \ldots, a_k\} \supset (A(x)))$' is acceptable in a finite language. For an infinite language, we need only note that '$A(a_{k+1})$' is acceptable, and that if the restricted universal generalization is acceptable for all individuals up to the nth, then by the principle of conjunction it is acceptable also for all individuals up to the $(n + 1)$st. A plausible induction principle yields the conclusion. In systems such as Hintikka's without identity we cannot express a generalization that takes account of exceptions; but the same result follows in those systems for cases when $k = 0$.

The problem of extending the system of Hintikka and Hilpinen to a full first-order logic is very knotty. Some steps have been taken in this direction by Hintikka, who has defined constituents quite generally. Hintikka's approach to inductive logic is applicable in principle to all first-order logics, though the definition of (Acc) would obviously have to be enormously complicated even to deal with a language containing two-place predicates. Tuomela [15] has begun the attempt to construct an inductive logic for monadic languages with identity. But in virtue of the fact that the essence of the acceptance rule is that we are directed to accept a single statement $(C_c \& e)$, together with all of its deductive consequences, any such system will be open to objections of the sort that will be applied below to proposals of Levi and Lehrer.

Finally, it should be observed that in order to do statistical inference, we need a general higher-order logic. In particular, we need to be able to speak of the set of n-membered subsets of a set S, if not in general, at least for sets of fairly high order. We also need a language rich enough for measure theory. Such a language, of course, is enormously more powerful than anything hitherto considered by Hintikka, Hilpinen, or Tuomela. To be sure one must start somewhere. But it is difficult to see what principles, analogous to those adopted for the monadic predicate calculus, could be used to avoid the statistical versions of the lottery paradox described above.

IV

The sytem of inductive acceptance described by Levi [13] has the overwhelming advantage of being applicable to very rich languages. It is thus the sort of system we can apply in the kinds of circumstances that we can actually find ourselves in. It can be applied, for example, to the problem of accepting statistical hypotheses on given evidence. Two new concepts must be explained before the rule can be stated. The most important and most novel concept is that of an *ultimate partition*. Levi argues that the inductive inference maker does not conduct his inquiries in a vacuum; he does so in a context determined in part by a felt need, a problem which he is seeking to solve. Thus before the inquiry starts, an investigator has an idea, which may be quite clear, or, unanalyzed, may be rather confused, as to what would constitute a relevant answer to his problem. These answers can be related to relatively atomic relevant answers, which constitute an ultimate partition, U, in the following way. Following Levi, we suppose that there is a certain statement b which represents background information, not up for test in the inquiry, and a certain statement e, which represents the body of evidence of the inquiry. The ultimate partition U_e is a (usually finite) set of sentences in L (the language of the inquiry, which may be as rich as you please), such that each element of U_e is consistent with b and e, and such that the conjunction of b and e entails (i) that some member of U_e is true, and (ii) that at most one member of U_e is true, and (iii) every relevant answer is logically equivalent to the disjunction of zero or more members of U_e, where we understand the disjunction of zero members of U_e to be the conjunction (inconsistent with b and e) of all the members of U_e. The set of sentences M_e represents the canonical standardized list of relevant answers. For an ultimate partition containing n members, M_e is the set of 2^n statements, constructed by forming the disjunction (in alphabetical order) of m $(1 \leqslant m < n)$ elements of U_e, and adding to that list S_e, the disjunction of all the members of U_e and C_e, the conjunction of all the members of U_e. The subscript 'e' reflects the evidence e. An initially ultimate partition would be designated by 'U', and its set of ultimate answers in canonical form by 'M'. Given some evidence e, the initially ultimate partition would be reduced by the deletion of any elements of U that were inconsistent with e. This produces a truncated ultimate partition U_e, and leads to a new (and correspondingly truncated) set of relevant answers M_e.

The other crucial concept is content. Content is defined relative to ultimate partitions. Each element of the initial ultimate partition is taken to have the same content, on the grounds that any difference in content would lead to a finer ultimate partition. To arrive at the conditional content of a hypothesis H, given certain evidence e, one merely applies the same principle to the truncated ultimate partition: one takes each element of U_e to have the same content. This leads to the conclusion that in general,

cont$(H, e) = m/n$, where n is the number of elements in U_e, and m is the number of elements in U_e that are inconsistent with H (p. 70).

With these two concepts at hand, we can state Levi's Inductive Acceptance Rule (p. 86).

Rule A: (a) Accept b & e and all its deductive consequences.
(b) Reject all elements a_i of U_e, such that $p(a_i, e) < q$ cont $(\sim a_i, e)$

i.e., accept the disjunction of all unrejected elements of U_e as the strongest element in M_e accepted via induction from b & e.

(c) Conjoin the sentence accepted as strongest via induction according to (b) with the total evidence b & e and accept all deductive consequences.

(d) Do not accept (relative to b, e, U_e, the probability distribution, and q) any sentences other than these in your language.

The number q referred to in the acceptance rule may be construed as an index of boldness; it ranges from 0 to 1, and the larger it is, the less cautious will one be in accepting statements not entailed by the background knowledge and evidence b & e. The number q reflects the "relative importance of the two disiderata: truth and relief from agnosticism."

As it stands, Rule A obviously leads to the acceptance of a set of statements satisfying the strong principle of deductive closure (indeed Levi takes the condition of deductive cogency, as he calls it, as a condition of adequacy), and thus also the conjunction principle; the strong consistency principle is satisfied because q must be less than or equal to 1, and the probability level at which elements of U_e are rejected must therefore be less than $1/n$, where n is the number of elements of U_e. Even if q is taken to be 1, and the number of elements n of U_e is taken to be 2, the inequality in (b) preserves us from inconsistency. The general principle is the same as that embodied in Hintikka's system already discussed: what is accepted is essentially a single (strongest) hypothesis H, together with its deductive consequences.

Unlike Hintikka's system, in Levi's system a high probability is not necessary for acceptance. Levi's system has a rule of rejection which is not purely probabilistic, but is dependent on content (as determined by the number of elements in the ultimate partition) and on the index of caution q. One may perfectly well end up accepting a proposition on the evidence whose probability relative to that evidence is less than 1/2, so long as it is more probable than any competing alternative. The canonical example is that in which there are three elements in U_e, each (therefore) having content $1/3$, q is 1, and the probabilities of a_1, a_2 and a_3 are respectively 0.4, 0.3, and 0.3. We are directed to accept a_1 and all the deductive consequences of a_1 & b & e. Strong consistency is nevertheless preserved.

While Hintikka's system appears to be the prototype of a global approach to problems of belief and acceptance, and thus to be limited by the choice of a language, and open to the difficulties of attempting to develop a similar system for richer languages, Levi's system is frankly local and problem dependent. Another way of construing the relation is to say that for Hintikka, the language we use determines the ultimate partition, while for Levi the ultimate partition is determined both by a language and by a particular problem; or perhaps it could be put this way: the partition is determined by a particular problem together with the language in which we represent that problem to ourselves.

The fact that Levi's rule of acceptance is relativized to a given language L, background knowledge b, evidence e, and a probability distribution P, raises no eyebrows; we surely expect that what a plausible acceptance rule will dictate will depend on these factors. That what we accept should depend in some way on how cautious or bold we are being, as expressed by the number q, also seems reasonable enough. The important question concerns the relativization to an ultimate partition. Given the language, b, e, the probability distribution, and q, it is clear that different ultimate partitions may lead to the acceptance of different sets of statements. It would be blatantly contrary to the whole pragmatic spirit of Levi's approach to suppose that there is some special, preferred, universal, ultimately ultimate partition. All ultimate partitions must be treated on a par, though at a given time, under given circumstances, we may not *consider* or *think about* more than one. But we could consider several. Levi asks rhetorically, " . . . why is it impossible for conditions K and K' to prevail at the same time, such that a man believes a deductively consistent and closed system of sentences Γ based on K and simultaneously a deductively consistent and closed system of sentences Γ' based on K'? To be sure he will believe, and believe rationally, all sentences in the set $\Gamma \cup \Gamma'$, and this set may very well be neither consistent nor [deductively] closed. But . . . why should this be objectionable?" (p. 94).

One answer to this rhetorical question might consist in quoting the arguments Levi adduces elsewhere in his book in favor of the Principle of Deductive Cogency. Whatever reason there is for demanding that the set Γ based on K should be deductively consistent and closed, are these not also reasons for demanding that $\Gamma \cup \Gamma'$ be deductively consistent and closed? But I rather agree with Levi that there is nothing at all objectionable about a man believing rationally all the sentences in the set $\Gamma \cup \Gamma'$, where this set is neither consistent nor deductively closed. Indeed, since for any hypothesis that has a high probability, we can construct an ultimate partition which will lead to the acceptance of that hypothesis, we are in essentially the same state, so far as statements with high probability are concerned, as we are in one of my rational corpora. Levi points out (p. 95) that his Rule A " . . . requires that this set [of rationally accepted sentences] must be divisible into subsets which are consistent and closed relative to the total evidence and the ultimate partitions detached at that time." But since we can detach any partition we want, this latter requirement is empty; and it is trivial to divide any set of sentences satisfying my conditions for a rational corpus into subsets that are deductively cogent. Indeed, it is trivial to do this for any purely probabilistic rule of acceptance.

Theorem 6: If $S \in K$ if and only if Prob(S, e) $> r$, then K may be divided into subsets which are consistent and closed—i.e., for which the strong consistency principle and the strong deduction principle are satisfied.

Proof: For each sentence S of K, let K_S consist of S, together with all of its deductive consequences. The K_S are the required division. If $T \in K_S$, then T

is entailed by S. But if S entails T, the probability of T cannot be less than that of S (on *any* interpretation of probability) and so T belongs to K. Conversely if $S \in K$, then $S \in K_S$. So $K = \cup K_S$. The sets K_S are deductively closed; they satisfy the Conjunction Principle. It remains to show that they are consistent. An inconsistency can appear only if it is entailed by some sentence S of K. But the probability of an inconsistency (on any interpretation of probability) is 0, and if S entails it, the probability of S cannot be greater than 0; and so S cannot be a member of K on purely probabilistic grounds.

Let us examine the set of statements that might come to be accepted (by means of some ultimate partition or other) in Levi's system. Levi points out that this set of statements will not in general satisfy either the strong deduction principle or the strong consistency principle. It is interesting to observe that these sets of statements do satisfy the weak deduction principle and the weak consistency principle.

Theorem 7: If Γ_ω is the set of all those statements S such that there is an ultimate partition U_e, relative to which, and b, e, and q, S comes to be accepted by Rule (A), then Γ_ω satisfies the weak deduction principle and the weak consistency principle.

Proof: Every statement that comes to be accepted in this set of statements is accepted originally in relation to some ultimate partition. But Rule A demands that when S is accepted relative to some ultimate partition, all of the deductive consequences of S & b & e should also be accepted; thus the weak deduction principle. As for consistency, if S is inconsistent in itself, it can never come to be accepted by Rule A, and thus cannot be a member of the set of accepted statements relative to any ultimate partition.

There is one further kind of consistency we might ask about. The pair of statements $(S, \sim S)$ is perfectly consistent in the weak sense—i.e., it contains no inconsistent statement among its elements—and yet seems rather flatly wrong, somehow. What I shall call the Principle of Pairwise Consistency stipulates that a body of accepted statements should not contain any such pairs of statements.

Principle of Pairwise Consistency: If K is a body of reasonably accepted statements, then for no statement S of the language is it the case that both S and the denial of S belong to K.

In a similar manner we may define for every n a principle of n-wise consistency:

Principle of n-wise Consistency: If K is a body of reasonably accepted statements, then for no set of statements s_1, s_2, . . . , s_{n-1} is it the case that each of $s_1, s_2, \ldots , s_{n-1}$, and $\sim(s_1$ & $s_2, \ldots , s_{n-1})$ is a member of K.

We should first observe that any purely probabilistic acceptance rule (with acceptance level greater than $1/2$) satisfies the Principle of Pairwise Consistency, and any purely probabilistic acceptance rule with acceptance level greater than $n/(n+1)$ satisfies the Principle of n-wise Consistency.

Theorem 8: If $S \in K$ if and only if $\text{Prob}(S, e) > r$ (where $r > 1/2$), then K satisfies the Principle of Pairwise Consistency. If $S \in K$ if and only if $\text{Prob}(S, e) > n/(n+1)$ then K satisfies the Principle of n-wise Consistency.

Proof: For ordinary point probabilities, the probability of S is one minus the probability of $\sim S$, so both probabilities cannot be greater than 1/2. For my interval probabilities, it is possible to show that $\text{Prob}(S) = (p, q)$ if and only if $\text{Prob}(\sim S) = (1-q, 1-p)$; so the same argument goes through.

$$\text{Prob}\sim[S_1 \& S_2 \& \ldots \& S_{n-1}] =$$
$$\text{Prob}[\sim S_1 \vee \sim S_2 \vee \ldots \vee \sim S_{n-1}]$$
$$\text{Prob}[\sim S_1 \vee \sim S_2 \vee \ldots \vee \sim S_{n-1}] \leqslant$$
$$\text{Prob}(\sim S_1) + \text{Prob}[\sim S_2 \vee \sim S_2 \vee \ldots \sim S_{n-1}]$$
$$\leqslant \text{Prob}(\sim S_1) + \text{Prob}(\sim S_2) + \ldots + \text{Prob}(\sim S_{n-1})$$
$$\text{Prob}(S_i) \geqslant n/(n+1); \text{Prob}(\sim S_i) \leqslant 1-n/(n+1) = 1/(n+1)$$
$$\text{Prob}\sim[S_1 \& S_2 \& \ldots \& S_{n-1}] \leqslant (n-1)\, 1/(n+1) = (n-1)/(n+1)$$
$$< n/(n+1).$$

Therefore $\sim[S_1 \& S_2 \& \ldots \& S_{n-1}]$ is not probabilistically acceptable.

Now let us observe that Levi's general sets of rationally accepted statements, although they do in fact satisfy the weak consistency principle, do not satisfy the Pairwise Consistency Principle. Consider a three-ticket biased lottery, in which ticket 1 has the probability 0.4 of winning, and the tickets 2 and 3 have the probablity 0.3 of winning. Relative to the ultimate partition: [ticket 1 wins, ticket 2 wins, ticket 3 wins], we will be able to accept the statement 'ticket 1 wins' together with all its deductive consequences. Relative to the ultimate partition [ticket 1 wins, ticket 1 does not win], we will be able to accept the statement 'ticket one does not win' together with all of its deductive consequences. Thus in the union of the statements accepted relative to each of these ultimate partitions, we will find both a certain statement and its denial. (We assume $q = 1$.)

It is interesting to observe that while Levi takes me to task for abandoning the rule of conjunction in my system (and with it the strong deduction principle and the strong consistency principle), the set of rationally accepted beliefs that he comes up with not only abandons all three of these principles (conjunction, strong deduction, strong consistency) but also fails to satisfy the pairwise consistency principle, which my own system, like that of any other purely probabilistic system, does satisfy. It is also interesting to note that the requirements of Rule A, construed locally and not globally, are satisfied by *any* probabilistic rule of acceptance (including mine).

V

Keith Lehrer discusses a purely probabilistic rule of inductive inference, and what amounts to the strong consistency condition. He shudders with horror at what he regards as an abandonment of consistency, and attempts to provide a rule of inductive inference which will satisfy the three strongest principles: the conjunction principle, the strong principle of consistency, and the strong principle of deduction. The principle he comes up with contains as parameters P, an appropriate probability function, e, a body of evidence, and L, a formal language. There is no parameter corresponding to degree of caution, or level of practical certainty. There is no relativization to a given set of hypotheses. The rule is:

RDI: $D(k, e)$ [k is directly inducible from e] if, for any h, if it is not the case that $e \& k \vdash h$, then $P(k, e) > P(h, e)$.

IR: $I(h, e)$ [h is inducible from e] if and only if h is a member of a set I_e such that $I_e = I_1 \cup I_2 \cup \ldots \cup I_m$, [where]
I_1 = the set of hypotheses h_j such that $D(h_j, e)$,
and letting C_n be a conjunction of the members of I_n that is logically equivalent to I_n,
I_2 = the set of hypotheses h_j such that $D(h_j, C_1 \& e)$
I_3 = the set of hypotheses h_j such that $D(h_j, C_2 \& e)$
. . .
I_m = the set of hypotheses h_j such that $D(h_j, C_{m-1} \& e)$.

We may elucidate the 'logical equivalence' of a statement (C_n) and a set of statements (I_n) in the obvious way: C_n is derivable from the set of statements I_n, and every member of I_n is derivable from C_n. It might be wondered if, for every I_n, there is a finite conjunction of members of I_n from which every member may be derived. In a finite language this is the case; in an infinite language C_n may turn out to be an infinite conjunction. It is possible to prove that the set of statements induced by IR from consistent evidence satisfies the conjunction principle (if h and k are inducible from e by IR, so is their conjunction); that this set of statements is deductively closed (if $h_1, \ldots, h_n$ are inducible from e by IR, and $h_1, \ldots, h_n \vdash k$, then k is inducible from e); and that it is strongly consistent (it contains no set of statements $h_1, \ldots, h_n$ such that $h_1, \ldots, h_n \vdash k \& \sim k$).

But we have achieved our goal of an inductive rule that satisfies these strong principles at essentially the same cost as that paid for Hintikka and Hilpinen's rule, namely: there is essentially only *one* hypothesis that we may induce from given evidence. Anything else we are allowed to induce will turn out to be merely an implicate of the evidence and that one strongest hypothesis. Indeed the situation for Lehrer's system is even stranger; at a given level we cannot induce all the deductive consequences of the strongest hypothesis we can induce, but only a string of implicates, of which each implies *all* the statements lower in the string.

Lemma: If h belongs to I_m, then h belongs to I_{m+1}.

Proof: I_{m+1} is the set of hypotheses h_j such that $D(h_j, C_m \& e)$, i.e., such that for any h, if it is not the case that $C_m \& e \& h_j$ entails h, then $P(h_j, C_m \& e)$

$> P(h, C_m\&e)$. But $C_m\&e$ does entail h, so h is directly inducible from $C_m\&e$.

Theorem 9: If h and k are directly inducible from e, then either $k\&e$ entails h or $h\&e$ entails k.

Proof: Suppose that $k\&e$ does not entail h. Then $P(k, e) > P(h, e)$. Suppose that $h\&e$ does not entail k. Then $P(h, e) > P(k, e)$. Therefore either $k\&e$ entails h or $h\&e$ entails k.

Observe that this means that if h and k are any two members of C_n, then either $C_{n-1}\&e\&k \vdash h$ or $C_{n-1}\&e\&h \vdash k$.

(Now, incidentally, we see why the conjunction principle holds. If h and k are directly inducible from e, then so is their conjunction, simply because their conjunction is equivalent, given e, to one of them alone: i.e., either e entails $k \equiv h\&k$, or e entails $h \equiv h\&k$.)

We now come to the main theorem regarding Lehrer's system, which is that there is essentially only *one* statement inducible from e. In order to show this rigorously for infinite languages we must allow ourselves infinite conjunctions; two observations on this move are in order. It seems to be only in pathological cases that the move to infinite conjunctions is required. This move must be allowable in Lehrer's system, since he says to let "C_n be a conjunction of members of I_n that is logically equivalent to I_n", and in the pathological cases no finite conjunction will do. I suspect, however, that worry about the infinite case is academic.

Theorem 10:

(a) For every n, there is a statement, k_n, which is either inducible from C_{n-1} and e, or which is an infinite conjunction, each member of which is inducible from C_{n-1}, such that every member of I_n is entailed by k_n and e.

(b) There is a statement, k_s, such that every statement inducible from e is entailed by e and k_s, and such that k_s is inducible from e, or is an infinite conjunction, each member of which is inducible from e.

Proof: For every two statements in I_n, either the first, in conjunction with e and C_{n-1}, entails the second, or the second, in conjunction with e and C_{n-1}, entails the first. This relation gives a partial ordering of the hypotheses inducible from C_{n-1} and e. Either (as would in general be true) there is a hypothesis k such that every element of I_n is derivable from $k\&e\&C_{n-1}$, and then k is the k_n whose existence is asserted in (a), or else there will be an infinite sequence of hypotheses inducible from $C_{n-1}\&e$, $k_1 \ldots, k_m \ldots$, such that $k_i\&C_{n-1}\&$ e entail k_{i-1}, but $k_{i-1}\&C_{n-1}\&e$ do not entail k_i. In this case we let k_n be the infinite conjunction of the hypotheses k_i. (Observe that in this case, C_n will have to be an infinite conjunction, too. We may, of course take k_n as C_n itself in this case.) Therefore $k_n\&e\&C_{n-1}$ does entail h.

In a similar way, either there is an n^* such that for n and m greater than n^*, C_n and e entail C_m and e and conversely, or else, for every n, C_{n+1} and e entail C_n, but C_n and e do not entail C_{n+1}. In the former case k_n is the k_s of (b). In the latter case, there is an infinite conjunction, C^*, such that every member of

C^* is inducible from e, and every finite conjunction of members of C^* is inducible from e, which is such that for any statement h whatever, if h is inducible from e, h is deducible from C^*; namely the conjunction of all k_n.

It is perhaps worth observing that the conjunction principle does not hold for infinite conjunctions. Consider a sequence of hypotheses, $k_1, \ldots, k_n$ each of which, with e, entails the preceding hypotheses, but is not entailed by them (with e). The probability of the conjunction $k_1 \& k_2 \& \ldots \& k_n$ given e, is just the probability of k_n given e. The probability of the infinite conjunction $K_1 = k_1 \& k_2 \& \ldots, k_n \ldots$ is thus just the $\lim_{n \to \infty} P(k_n, e)$. Each of the k_i will be inducible provided that for any h not entailed by $k_i \& e$, $P(k_i, e) > P(h, e)$. But $P(h, e)$ could be $\lim_{n \to \infty} P(k_n, e)$ (since $P(k_i, e) > \lim_{n \to \infty} P(k_n, e)$), and h might not be entailed even by e and the infinite conjunction of the k_i. Thus the infinite conjunction would not be inducible, even though each of its members was. Thus k_n and k_s may not themselves be acceptable.

VI

The system of Hintikka and Hilpinen and the system of Lehrer are unsatisfactory for essentially the same reason. They boil down to the claim that given a language and a body of evidence, there is essentially just one strongest statement that can be accepted. This approach to induction is global with a vengeance. It suggests that as scientists or even as people we do not induce hypothesis by hypothesis, but that induction consists in principle of inducing at each stage of inquiry—i.e., for each body of evidence e—a single monumentally complex conjunctive statement. Observe that we cannot even consider parts of the complex hypothesis in isolation from other parts. Although the evidence may have the form $e_i \& e_j$, and e_i may be utterly irrelevant to h_j, the fact that h_j is inducible from e_j will have no bearing at all on whether h_j is inducible from $e_i \& e_j$. A hypothesis h_i, not entailed by h_j and e_i and e_j may always turn out to be more probable on $e_i \& e_j$ than h_j is. Indeed, one may wonder if the exceedingly high confirmation of the hypothesis that the speed of light is finite will not preclude the acceptance of *any* hypothesis concerning the cause of cancer, the existence of life on Mars, or the amount of inflation to be anticipated in the coming year.

It may be argued that any global system in which the conjunction principle is satisfied will suffer from these shortcomings. In any such system there will be a statement from which every acceptable statement follows, and which is either acceptable itself, or is an infinite conjunction each finite conjunct of which is acceptable.

Theorem 11: If the conjunction principle is satisfied for an inductive acceptance rule in the language L, then there is a statement C^* in L, or an infinite conjunction C^* every component of which is in L, such that if h is a finite statement, h is inductively acceptable if and only if h is entailed by C^* and the basic evidence e.

Proof: Entailment given e provides a partial ordering of the statements in L. Suppose first that there are two statements in L, h_1 and h_2, each of which is inductively acceptable, and neither of which is ranked above the other in the partial ordering. By the conjunction principle their conjunction must also be acceptable, and by the partial ordering, their conjunction must be ranked higher than either one alone. Either there is an acceptable hypothesis of maximum rank (from which all the other hypotheses then follow, given e) or else for every hypothesis h, there is a stronger one h' which, conjoined with e, entails h, but which is not entailed by h conjoined with e. If this is the case, an argument like that of a preceding theorem will give a C^* satisfying the conditions of the theorem.

Given the conjunction principle, as I showed earlier, it also follows that the strong and weak consistency conditions are equivalent, and that the strong and weak deduction principles are equivalent. Thus I think it is appropriate to focus on the conjunction principle as a source of the pecularities to which such systems as those we have looked at give rise.

It is difficult to give an argument against the conjunction principle, partly because it is so obvious to me that it is false, and partly because it is so obvious to certain other people that it is true. The most persuasive arguments perhaps are those which stem from the last theorem presented; it seems preposterous to suppose that all of our inductive knowledge has to be embodiable in a single fat statement. It seems too limiting to say that I have to believe the conjunction of everything I have a right to believe (there cannot be very much, then, that I have a right to believe), and it seems even more unreasonable to claim to have a right to believe the conjunction of everything I have a right to believe. Although I claim to have good reasons for believing every statement I believe, I claim also to have good reasons for believing that some of those statements are false. I think both of those claims are perfectly sound; and if they are, the conjunction principle is false.

VII

The system of rational beliefs I have developed elsewhere accepts the failure of the principle of conjunction. It is an attempt at a global theory, and for a global theory the conjunction principle seems flatly false. Having abandoned the principle of conjunction, it becomes possible to distinguish strong and weak deductive closure, strong, weak, pairwise and n-wise consistency. In what follows I will briefly characterize a simplified version of the original system, freed, of course, from the original inconsistency.

We begin (as always) with a language L; we suppose it to contain a set theory, terms denoting operations, properties, relations, etc., which may be of a theoretical as well as of an observational character. We let B denote a set of statements that are accepted as evidence or background information. In a given context B represents the basic rational corpus, or body of knowledge. We suppose, by hypothesis, that B is pairwise consistent, and satisfies weak deductive closure. B thus contains all the theorems of our language. To be sure, if we pick the wrong axioms for set theory—inconsistent ones—in our language, the set B will be empty. But we must always suppose, so long as we know no better, that the language we speak is consistent. We do not suppose that we believe in any active or behavioristic sense every statement in B; rather we say that the contents of B are what we are *committed* to believing.

Axiom I: $S \in B \supset {\sim}nS \in B$ ('nS' denotes the denial, in L, of S).

Axiom II: ThmS cd T & $S \in B \supset T \in B$ ('S cd T' denotes the conditional whose antecedent is S, and whose consequent is T; 'Thm S cd T' says that the statement S cd T is a theorem of L).

There is no need here for defining the probability relation; there are certain properties of that relation I shall refer to, which I shall state as axioms. It should be observed that on the basis of a definition of probability like that I have provided elsewhere, these axioms turn out to be theorems. Probability I take to be relative to a body of knowledge or rational corpus B; it is a relation that holds between a statement S, the rational corpus B, and a pair of fractions p and q. We say, relative to B, the probability of S is the pair of fractions (p, q), and we symbolize this assertion: '$\text{Prob}_B (S, p, q)$'. It should be observed, not as part of the formal development here, but simply as background information, that on the definition I have offered, every probability statement is based on a *known* statement concerning relative frequencies, i.e., that if the relation $\text{Prob}_B (S, p, q)$ holds, there is as a member of B some corresponding statistical statement asserting that a certain relative frequency or measure lies between the ratios denoted by p and q. The properties of probability that we shall need are the following:

Axiom III: $\text{Prob}_B (S, p, q) \supset \text{Prob}_B (nS, 1{-}q, 1{-}p)$.

Axiom IV: [Thm S cd T & $\text{Prob}_B (S, p, q)$ & $\text{Prob}_B (T, p', q')$] $\supset$ Thm p' gr p ('p' gr p' denotes the statement in abbreviated notation consisting of the fraction p', followed by '$>$', followed by the fraction p).

Axiom V: $S \in B \supset \text{Prob}_B (S, 1/1, 1/1)$.

Our final axiom requires an auxiliary notion, that of a biconditional chain in B. Since we have not assumed deductive closure in B, it is perfectly possible that S b T (the biconditional whose antecedent is S and whose consequent is T) is a member of B and that T b R is a member of B, when S b R is not a member of B. But we want to say that S and R are related by a biconditional chain in B anyway. In general we shall say that S and R are related by a biconditional chain in B, in symbols, S bc_B T, when S b T belongs to every set of statements containing P b Q whenever P b Q belongs to B, and containing P b R whenever it contains both P b Q and Q b R. Formally:

Definition 1: S bc_B T = df$(K)((P) (Q) (R) ((P$ b $Q \in B \supset P$ b $Q \in K)$ & $(P$ b $Q \in K$ & Q b $R \in K \supset P$ b $R \in K)) \supset S$ b $T \in K)$.

The final axiom simply says tht any two statements related by a biconditional chain have essentially the same probability.

Axiom VI: $(S$ bc_B T & $\text{Prob}_B (S, p, q)$ & $\text{Prob}_B (T, p', q')) \supset (\text{Thm } p$ id p' &

Thm q id q') ('x id y' denotes the statement in abbreviated notation consisting of x followed by '=' followed by y).

We are now in a position to characterize the set of statements B_r which may be induced from B, at the level r. Note that we cannot simply include a statement in B itself on the grounds that its probability is at least r, unless we take r to be 1, for the probability of S, relative to B, can be less than one only if S is not a member of B.

Theorem 12: $(\text{Prob}_B\ (S, p, q)\ \&\ \text{Thm '}1 > p') \supset {\sim}S \in B$ (Axioms V and VI).

Let us define B_r to be the set of statements whose probability, relative to B, is at least r, where r denotes a ratio greater than a half.

Definition 2: $B_r = \text{df}\big\{S: \text{Prob}_B\ (S, p, q)\ \&\ \text{Thm } p \text{ gr } r\big\}$.

B_r is thus a set of statements accepted on purely probabilistic grounds. We can show that B_r satisfies the weak consistency principle, the weak deduction principle, and the pairwise consistency principle, which, recall, failed for Levi's general system.

Theorem 13: $(S \in B_r\ \&\ \text{Thm } S \text{ cd } T) \supset T \in B_r$ (Axiom IV, D-2).

Theorem 14: ${\sim}(\exists S)\ (S \in B_r\ \&(T)\ (\text{Thm } S \text{ cd } T))$.

Proof: If (T) (Thm S cd T), then Thm nS. Thus $nS \in B$. $\text{Prob}_B(nS, 1, 1)$. By Axiom III, then $\text{Prob}_B(S, 0, 0)$. By the (hypothetical) consistency of B, we have ${\sim}\text{Thm '}0'$ gr r, and thus ${\sim}S \in B_r$.

Theorem 15: (Pairwise Consistency and n-wise consistency for n such that $n/(n+1) < r$)

$(S)\ (S \in B_r \supset {\sim}nS \in B_r)$ (Axiom III).

$(S_1)(S_2)\ \ldots\ (S_{n-1})\ [(S_1 \in B_r\ \&\ S_2 \in B_r\ \&\ \ldots\ \&\ S_{n-1} \in B_r) \supset {\sim}n(S_1 \text{ cj } S_2 \ldots \text{ cj } S_{n-1}) \in B_r]$

(where S cj T represents the conjunction of S and T).

Lehrer makes a point of the consistency of what is induced with the evidence on the basis of which it is induced. This condition is satisfied here for single statements given that B is deductively closed, which may not be an unreasonable supposition for 'observation statements'.

Theorem 16: $(S)\ (B \vdash S \supset S \in B) \supset (S)\ (S \in B_r \supset {\sim}(B, S \vdash \text{contradiction}))$.

Proof: If $B, S \vdash \text{contradiction}$, then $B \vdash nS$. By the hypothesis of the theorem, then, $nS \in B$, and $\text{Prob}_B\ (S, 0, 0)$, and ${\sim}S \in B_r$.

As I pointed out earlier, there are parts of any system like this which are strongly consistent and deductively closed. The relation between statements S and T, Thm S cd T. provides a partial ordering of the elements of B_r. Let us define a strongest acceptable statement, in symbols STR, to be a statement such that no other statement in B_r bears the relation in question to it, unless it also bears that relation to the statement. Thus:

Definition 3: $STR_{B_r}\ S = df\ S \in B_r\ \&\ (T)\ ((T \in B_r\ \&\ \text{Thm } T \text{ cd } S) \supset \text{Thm } S \text{ cd } T)$.

The set of consequences of any strongest statement in B_r satisfies the strong deduction principle, the strong consistency principle, and (!) even the conjunction principle.

Theorem 17: $STR_{B_r}S \supset [(\exists A)\,(T)\,(\text{Thm } S \text{ cd } T \equiv T \in A) \supset (\sim\!A \vdash \text{contradiction} \,\&\, (R)\,(A \vdash R \supset R \in A) \,\&\, (R)\,(T)\,((R \in A \& T \in A) \supset R \text{ cj } T \in A))]$.

Perhaps, in these terms, it is the fact that most of our beliefs are not strongest beliefs that has led people to feel that our beliefs belong to systems of beliefs which satisfy the conjunction principle.

There are a number of other theorems we can prove. For example, we can prove that if a complex statement S is like a complex statement T, except for containing occurrences of the statement P where T contains occurrences of the statement Q, and if P and Q are connected by a biconditional chain in B, then S will be a member of B_r if and only if T is a member of B_r. In a similar fashion it is possible to define the concept of an identity chain in B. Then it is possible to prove that if S is like T except for containing occurrences of the term p where T contains occurrences of the term q, and p and q are connected by an identity chain in B, then S will be a member of B_r if and only if T is a member of B_r. Even without complete deductive closure, there is a lot that can be shown to hold in B_r.

The issue is only whether or not there is a single strongest statement in B_r — i.e., whether there is a statement S^* such that $(T)\,(T \in B_r \supset \text{Thm } S^* \text{ cd } T)$. When stated thus baldly, the answer is obvious; it is gratuitous to suppose that there is any such statement. Indeed the supposition that there is is one of the secondary symptoms of the disease I have called conjunctivitis.

NOTES

1. Except in one of Keith Lehrer's systems, described in this volume.

2. A muddier version of this argument was presented in [11]; a cleaned-up version is mentioned by Harman in [2].

3. These principles are not essential parts of the Bayesian or classical statistical theory. One can develop the theory of statistical inference without considering the question of acceptance one way or the other. The classical theory requires us to *reject* certain hypotheses, but it is hardly necessary to point out (as statisticians of this persuasion inevitably do) that to reject a statement is not (necessarily) to accept it. Bayesian theory is sometimes coupled with a philosophy according to which one *never* accepts any *hypothesis*.

4. The test interval for '$p \in (a, f)$' will include the closed interval $[a, f]$ and the test interval for '$p \in (f, b)$' will include the closed interval $[f, b]$.

BIBLIOGRAPHY

[1] R. B. Braithwaite, *Scientific Explanation*, Cambridge 1953.

[2] Gilbert Harman, 'Detachment, Probability and Maximum Likelihood', *Nous* 1 (1967) 401-11.

[3] Carl Hempel, 'Deductive-Nomological vs. Statistical Explanation', in *Minnesota Studies in the Philosophy of Science*, III (ed. by H. Feigl and G. Maxwell), Minneapolis 1962.

[4] Jaakko Hintikka, 'Towards a Theory of Inductive Generalization', in *Proc. 1964 Inter-*

national Congress of Logic, Methodology, and Philosophy of Science (ed. by J. Bar-Hillel), Amsterdam 1965.

[5] Jaakko Hintikka, 'Distributive Normal Forms in First-Order Logic', in *Formal Systems and Recursive Functions* (ed. by Crossley and Dummett), Amsterdam 1965.

[6] Jaakko Hintikka, 'A Two-Dimensional Continuum of Inductive Methods', in *Aspects of Inductive Logic* (ed. by J. Hintikka and P. Suppes), Amsterdam 1966.

[7] Jaakko Hintikka and Risto Hilpinen, 'Knowledge, Acceptance, and Inductive Logic', in *Aspects of Inductive Logic* (ed. by J. Hintikka and P. Suppes), Amsterdam 1966.

[8] Richard Jeffrey, *The Logic of Decision,* New York 1965.

[9] Henry E. Kyburg, Jr., *Probability and the Logic of Rational Belief,* Middletown 1961.

[10] Henry E. Kyburg Jr., 'Probability and Randomness', *Theoria,* 29 (1963).

[11] Henry E. Kyburg Jr., 'Probability, Rationality, and Rule of Detachment', in *Proc. 1964 Congress for Logic, Methodology and Philosophy of Science* (ed. by J. Bar-Hillel), Amsterdam 1965.

[12] Keith Lehrer, 'Induction, Rational Acceptance, and Minimally Inconsistent Sets, in *Induction, Probability, and Confirmation* (ed. by Grover Maxwell and Robert M. Anderson, Jr.), Minnesota Studies in the Philosophy of Science, Minneapolis, 1975.

[13] Isaac Levi, *Gambling With Truth,* New York 1967.

[14] Wesley Salmon, private correspondence.

[15] Raimo Tuomela, 'Inductive Generalization in an Ordered Universe', in *Aspects of Inductive Logic* (ed. by J. Hintikka and P. Suppes), Amsterdam 1966.

15

Probability, Rationality, and a Rule of Detachment

Carnap and many other writers on induction and probability deny that there is a rule of detachment in inductive logic. According to their view the relation among evidence, hypothesis, belief, and action is the following: A scientific hypothesis *H* is rendered probable to such and such a degree by evidence *E*. *E* is understood to include all of the relevant information we have concerning *H*. We *ought* to have a degree of belief in *H* corresponding to its probability. We should never *accept* *H*—not even provisionally. We may *act* in accordance with *H*, but the basis for our action is a straightforward calculation of the mathematical expectation of our various alternatives.

Another behavioristic school of thought that has been rapidly growing in influence is that of the subjectivistic statisticians. For these writers, probability is no longer even a logical relation between hypothesis and evidence, but a measure of subjective confidence that satisfies certain rules (the axioms of the probability calculus). It would be possible for the subjectivists to talk about the *acceptance* of a hypothesis, but not in any interesting way. To accept a hypothesis *H* would be to assign to it a personal or subjectivistic probability of unity. But the only way that we can assign a conditional probability of unity to *H* on evidence *E* is to assign an *a priori* probability of unity to *H*. (The probability of *E* must be the same as the probability of the conjunction of *H* and *E*.) This is clearly of no interest to us.

The majority of writers on statistical inference fall into an even more explicitly behavioristic camp. Let us call Carnap and the subjectivists *Bayesians,* and these other writers *non-Bayesians.* Many non-Bayesians formulate the problem of statistical inference, from the outset, as a problem of choosing between alternative courses of action. Neyman, for example, talks only of inductive *behavior,* not of inductive inference. We have here also the work that stems from Wald's fundamental research in decision theory and the theory of testing hypotheses.

Reprinted from Yehoshua Bar-Hillel, ed., *Proceedings of the 1964 International Congress for Logic, Methodology and Philosophy of Science* (North Holland, Amsterdam, 1965), pp. 301-310, by permission of the publisher.

Sometimes the behavioristic character of these approaches is thinly veiled by confusing terminology—there are writers who use the phrase "Accept hypothesis H_i," to mean "Follow the course of action A_i which would be most appropriate were H_i true." "Most appropriate," of course, means most appropriate *under the conditions of the problem*. But I don't think this terminological confusion need bother us; *we* know that when a decision theorist or a hypothesis tester tells us to *accept* hypothesis H_i, he means for us only to adopt a certain course of action in the present circumstances, and nothing more.

One objection to this behavioristic view of science is that it doesn't seem to be true: scientists (and other people) simply do *accept* hypotheses, when the evidence in their favor becomes overwhelming. When there is a good deal of evidence in favor of a hypothesis, so that we surely ought to believe it to some extent, there may still be circumstances in which it would be imprudent to act on it. But on any behavioristic analysis it is absolute nonsense to say "believe H, but don't act on it." I am sure that an overpowering ordinary language argument could be constructed in favor of the thesis that scientists accept hypotheses; but in these technical regions I find ordinary language arguments rather less than persuasive and rather more than a little dull, and so I shall spare you one.

There is one argument against the behavioristic approach to scientific inference that does strike me as interesting enough to mention. According to this approach, there are exactly three things we are concerned with in the practice of science: (1) we have a certain body of evidence, consisting of statements asserting the occurrence of particular events; (2) we have a certain number of courses of action open to us; and (3) we have a certain utility function which assigns values to the possible outcomes of the actions that are open to us. There is much that might be said concerning the nature of evidence-statements. (I would claim, for example, that many of the statements that we *accept* as evidence statements are acceptable, or indeed, intelligible, only in virtue of an *accepted* body of theoretical scientific knowledge.) It may also be questioned whether values can be plausibly assigned to the outcomes of actions except within the framework of some general, accepted, theory. But leaving these two points aside, the strikingly paradoxical consequences of the behavioristic approach is that scientific hypotheses—those grand, elegant creations of the human intellect, that have been ranked by some above the works of Bach and Michelangelo—turn out to be altogether redundant and useless. They are, to invert a metaphor of Bergson, the pretty but useless colored sparks that fall away from the tail of the soaring rocket. *Having* hypotheses may be useful—they may help to simplify the computations of the utilities to be associated with various actions—but they add nothing whatever to our view of the world, or to the factual basis of our actions.

In Carnap's *Logical Foundations of Probability*, theories not only turned out to be redundant, but also to have zero probability. They were not only useless, but incredible. Carnap was not satisfied with that, and has since worked on metrics for degree of confirmation which will allow theories and universal hypotheses to have degrees of confirmation greater than zero. But observe that *even then* a universal statement or a theory is redundant. It is a useless intermediary (no matter what its degree of confirmation) between the evidence statements and the statements of outcomes of particular courses of action in a particular concrete situation. We need only be concerned with *evidence, utility,* and *action.*

There are those for whom the creation and testing of hypotheses is the very soul of science. In America for many years the prevalent view of scientific practice had it this way: formulate hypotheses; test them; accept them provisionally so long as they continue to pass tests. To accept a hypothesis provisionally is of course to accept a hypothesis. In England Karl Popper and his followers have argued for a view of science in which one of the key elements is the provisional *acceptance* of hypotheses. As a guide to the acceptance of hypotheses, Popper has proposed a concept of 'degree of corroboration'. This is not a probability concept; it is based on a notion of logical measure, but it does not satisfy the axioms of a probability calculus. (Other writers, e.g., Kemeny and Oppenheim, Rescher, Finch, have proposed other measures of factual support; these proposals are systematically compared in my "Recent Work in Inductive Logic," *American Philosophical Quarterly*, I (1964), pp. 1-39.)

The question naturally arises as to the possibility of finding some bridge between the two approaches. Carl Hempel began the attempt to construct such a bridge with the help of the concept of *epistemic utility.* That is, given a body of statements K, including evidence statements, we can consider three courses of epistemic action with respect to a hypothesis H: We may accept H, adding it to the set K; we may reject it, adding its negation to K; or we may suspend judgment and add neither it nor its negation to K.

Isaac Levi has applied this notion of epistemic utility to the analysis of Popper's proposed 'degree of corroboration', and argued that "All utility functions that can be generated from possible analyses of $C(h, e)$ into a measure of expected gain [i.e., into a sum of the utilities of alternatives, each multiplied by its logical probability] require that the utilities assigned to the outcome of accepting h when it is true and to the outcome of accepting h when it is false vary with $P(h, e)$—the probability of h given e. This amounts to saying that scientists change their preferences with changes in evidence."[1] This violates our intuitions, as well as the conventions of every decision-theoretic approach, Bayesian or otherwise. Indeed Levi's conclusion is quite general: Any Bayesian decision rule which attempts to take such factors as simplicity and explanatory power into account in the calculation of utilities is committed to saying that scientists change their preferences with changes in evidence.

Non-Bayesian strategies may offer some way out of the problem: e.g., perhaps one can plausibly apply a minimax strategy to $C(h, e)$. But this is another problem, and one that I cannot go into here.

At this point it will be helpful to introduce Hempel's criteria of adequacy for an inductive rule of detachment.[2] These criteria, he says, state *"certain necessary conditions of rationality in the formation of beliefs."* The first three of these conditions seem innocuous enough. They are:

"CR 1. Any logical consequence of a set of accepted statements is likewise an accepted statement; or K contains all logical consequences of any of its subclasses."

"CR 2. The set K of accepted statements is logically consistent."

"CR 3. The inferential acceptance of any statement h into K is decided on by reference to the total system K."

The third condition is merely a requirement of total evidence. The first two conditions are ambiguous as they stand, as I shall show shortly, and except on the weakest interpretation, one of them must be rejected.

The specific rule that Hempel suggests makes use of a content measure function m defined over statements in an appropriate formalized language for science, and a confirmation function c satisfying the usual probability calculus. When h is the hypothesis and k the conjunction of statements in K, he takes the epistemic utility of accepting h when it is true to be $m(h \vee {\sim}k)$ and of accepting h when it is false to be $-m(h \vee {\sim}k)$. The utility of leaving h in suspense is 0. It is shown, after some computation, that this leads to the following rule:

"(12.4) *Tentative rule for inductive acceptance:* Accept or reject h, given K, according as $c(h, k) > 1/2$ or $c(h, k) < 1/2$; when $c(h, k) = 1/2$, h may be accepted, rejected, or left in suspense."[3]

It is interesting that the measure of information drops out of the picture, and that we are led to this rule (as Hempel observes) regardless of what confirmation function we start with.

Hempel realizes that rule 12.4 is far too liberal. In another context he presents a version of the lottery paradox, but he does not explore the implications of this paradox for his acceptance rules. We can do so easily. Consider this example:

"There are three balls in this urn, a blue one, a red one, and a green one."
"A ball is about to be drawn from the urn by a blindfolded man."

This is surely a plausible basis for a body of knowledge K_1, isn't it? Yet by 12.4 (taking any ordinary confirmation function) we find we must add the following statements to K_1:

"The ball will not be blue."
"The ball will not be red."
"The ball will not be green."

By CR 1, then, we have: "A ball is about to be drawn from an urn containing only a red ball, a blue ball, and a green ball and this ball will be neither red nor blue nor green." But this is in clear violation of CR 2.

Can we fix matters by making the criterion 12.4 mention a higher degree of confirmation? For example, 0.999 instead of 1/2, so that we accept h only if $c(h, k) > 0.999$ and $\sim h$ only if $c(h, k) < .001$, and otherwise suspend judgment? Clearly this won't work. Take any ϵ you wish; put a number N of counters greater than $1/\epsilon$ in an urn; the counters to be numbered successively from 1 to N. Take K_2 to include the two sentences:

"There are N consecutively numbered counters in this urn."
"One counter is to be drawn by a blindfolded choirboy."

Again it is easy to show that this K_2 does not satisfy Hempel's conditions.

This already seems to me to be a serious problem; why on earth shouldn't a set of statements such as K_2 be a perfectly plausible set of statements to be believed or accepted?

Wesley Salmon has made one proposal (in correspondence) which would take care of the difficulty in which we find ourselves now; his idea is to limit inductive rules of acceptance to rules for accepting *general* statements; particularly, statistical hypotheses. Hempel suggests (as a cure for the overliberality of his 12.4) that we search for a more plausible measure of epistemic utility. I am sure that many of you are thinking that such sets of statements as K_1 and K_2 are so outrageously silly and arbitrary that it is a waste of time to worry about the fact that they fail to satisfy Hempel's very natural conditions. CR 1 and CR 2 are not only natural, but have been explicitly defended as epistemic principles by Chisholm and by Martin. They hold for some of the concepts defined by Hintikka.

But I shall now show that Salmon's proposal will not correct the situation; that Hempel's hope that a better definition of epistemic utility would help is unwarranted; that the problem is a real and serious one even in the *practice* of statistics; and that the difficulty stems from CR 1, CR 2, and *any* probabilistic rule of detachment like Hempel's 12.4.

All this is revealed by the following example. Let there be a population of 100,000 balls in a very large urn. Those who are of a very practical turn of mind may think of this as representing the products of an automatic screw machine; telephone receivers; eggs; live births at a hospital; micro-organisms in a bottle, etc. Some of the balls are black. (Some of the parts are defective; some of the births are births of males, etc.) No statistician will deny, I think, that there *are* occasions when Bayesian inference is appropriate. Let this be one of those occasions. For frequency theorists this amounts to stipulating that we have a prior distribution for the parameter p that represents the proportion of black balls in the urn. For subjectivistic and logical theorists this amounts to no stipulation at all. We now draw a sample of 10,000 balls; we stipulate that the sample is *random* in whatever sense is regarded as appropriate. Again this is a condition that can be met in some cases, one way or another, whatever your views on probability. In this sample, 4,867 balls are black. With the help of Bayes's theorem, we calculate a posterior distribution for the parameter p.

260 / Probability, Rationality, Detachment

Now statements of the form "p lies between p_1 and p_2" are certainly general statistical statements— they meet Salmon's criterion for detachment. They *might* be said to vary in content of information, but surely two such statements in which the difference between the upper and lower bounds was the same would have to be granted the same information content. (I.e., when $|p_1 - p_2| = |p_1' - p_2'|$.) Thus if one of these statements meets a modified Hempelian criterion for detachment, so will the other if its probability is the same. Suppose now that the level of probability chosen as the criterion for detachment of general statistical statements is $1 - \epsilon$. Then there is no trouble at all, obviously, in finding numbers p_1, p_2, and p_3, where $p_2 < p_3 < p_1$, such that the statements,

".4867 $- p_1 < p < .4867 + p_2$"
".4867 $- p_2 < p < .4867 + p_1$"

have the same probability and are *acceptable*, and also such that the statement,

"It is not the case that $.4867 - p_3 < p < .4867 + p_3$"

is also overwhelmingly probable and must be accepted. For example, take $p_1 = 0.10$, $p_2 = .005$, and $p_3 = .006$. (The information content of this statement may not be the same as the information content of the first two; but the fact that we may adjust the parameter p_3 to make this statement as probable as we please allows us to compensate for the effects of any difference in information content. Remember that we are merely constructing a possibility that could occur in a practical situation; we do not have to suppose that this sort of thing occurs frequently, or at all.)

The triple of sentences that I have just described clearly leads to a violation of Hempel's first two conditions. Changing the level of acceptability, changing the definition of information content, restricting ourselves to realistic situations— none of these things have allowed us to avoid this form of the lottery paradox.

If we are to hold on to a probabilistic rule of detachment like Hempel's, there is clearly only one thing to do in this situation, and that is to reject one or both of CR 1 and CR 2. I mentioned before that these conditions are ambiguous. So far I have been interpreting them as Hempel intended; but there is another interpretation in which they hold for my own system of *Probability and the Logic of Rational Belief.* Let us take CR 1 to mean *not* that every logical consequence of the *conjunction* of the statements of K belongs to K, but only that every logical consequence of each *single* element of K belongs to K. Thus if P and Q belong to K, their conjunction may not belong to K, unless it is included in K on independent grounds. In conjunction with a probabilistic rule of detachment this interpretation of CR 1 is very natural— it is clear that P can be overwhelmingly probable, and Q can be overwhelmingly probable, without their conjunction being overwhelmingly probable.

The same interpretation may be given to CR 2. Rather than demand that K

be consistent in the sense that no contradiction be deducible from the *conjunction* of all the elements of K, we may rest content with the stipulation that there be no statement S such that K contains both S and the negation of S. (An even weaker stipulation would be that K contain no *self*-contradictory statement.)

The rule of detachment in *Probability and the Logic of Rational Belief*[4] is a purely probabilistic one. I take probability to be a logical relation defined for classes of equivalent sentences of a formalized language. I take the probability of a sentence S, relative to a rational corpus K, to be the *interval* (p, q), when there are terms a, b, and c such that in K, S is known to be equivalent to "$a \in c$"; relative to K, a is a random member of b with respect to membership in c; and it is known in K that the proportion of b's that are c's lies in the interval $(p; q)$. I take rational corpora to be based on a certain fund F of 'observation statements', but like Hempel I leave to one side the question of what sort of statements these might be. I define a sequence of rational corpora, based on the set of statements F; the sequence of levels corresponds to levels of 'practical certainty' suitable to different practical situations. The highest level of rational corpus consists of F and the logical consequences of $F-$ including the truths of logic and mathematics. The contents of lower-level rational corpora is determined entirely by a general rule of detachment:

D S belongs to the rational corpus of level i and basis F, if and only if the probability of S, relative to the rational corpus of level $i+1$ and basis F, is $(p; q)$, where $p > r_i$ (r_i being the critical probability level of acceptance for the rational corpus of level i).

It is possible to show that the rational corpora of my system satisfy the modified Hempel conditions CR 1 and CR 2. The lottery paradox fails to arise initially because, even if S_1 and S_2 and . . . and S_n are so probable that they are to be included in the rational corpus of level i, it will *not* generally be the case that their conjunction is that probable. We detach any statements that are probable enough—but we do not necessarily accept the conjunctions of the statements we accept.

This sounds quite plausible, but Fred Schick has shown[5] that the lottery paradox still arises, though in a slightly different way. I showed in my book that if S_1 is a statement in the rational corpus of level i, and a conditional whose antecedent is S_1 and whose consequent is S_2 is in the rational corpus of level $i+1$, then S_2 will also belong to the rational corpus of level i. Since $S_1 \supset (S_2 \supset (S_1 \cdot S_2))$ is a logical truth that appears in every rational corpus, this means that the conjunction of S_1 and S_2 will appear in the rational corpus of next lower level to that in which S_1 and S_2 appear separately. In other words, if S_1 belongs to the rational corpus of level i and S_2 belongs to the rational corpus of level i, then their conjunction belongs to the rational corpus of level $i-1$.

So far, so good. This sounds reasonable. But what Fred Schick pointed out was that the process could be continued. Let $S_1, S_2, \ldots, S_n$ belong to the rational corpus of level i. Since $S_1 \supset (S_2 \supset (S_1 \cdot S_2))$ is logically true, $S_2 \supset (S_1 \cdot S_2)$ also belongs to the rational corpus of level i. The same argument supports $(S_1 \cdot S_2) \supset (S_1 \cdot S_2 \cdot S_3)$ in virtue of the logical truth of $S_3 \supset ((S_1 \cdot S_2) \supset (S_1 \cdot S_2 \cdot S_3))$; $(S_1 \cdot S_2 \cdot S_3) \supset (S_1 \cdot S_2 \cdot S_3 \cdot S_4)$ in virtue of the logical truth of $S_4 \supset ((S_1 \cdot S_2 \cdot S_3) \supset (S_1 \cdot S_2 \cdot S_3 \cdot S_4))$; etc. By the principle mentioned above, this leads to the conclusion that the conjunction of all of the statements in the rational corpus of level i will appear in the rational corpus of level $i - 1$.

The lottery paradox now arises in the following way. Let F contain the statement of K_2 above concerning chips in an urn. Let S_i be the statement "Chip number i will not be drawn." Clearly these statements may be so probable as to be detached in a certain rational corpus. But then the rational corpus of the next lower level will contain the explicit contradiction: "One chip will be drawn and it will not be chip number 1, and it will not be chip number 2, and . . . and these are all the chips there are."

I have a solution for this paradox, but it is not one that I am particularly happy with. I should like to think of something better. Nevertheless, I offer it to you for what it is worth.

We can avoid the lottery paradox in my system by dealing with only two levels of rational corpora at a time. The highest one we regard as containing only genuine, unquestioned 'certainties'—it might be regarded as a body of philosophical knowledge. It would, in any given context, correspond to the highest level rational corpus of my original system. The other rational corpus would be of a level corresponding to *practical* (as opposed to philosophical) certainty in the given situation. This level would vary from situation to situation—it might be characterized by a detachment parameter of 0.7 in one situation, by one of 0.95 in another, and by a detachment parameter of 0.99995 in yet another. But we would consider only *one* level of practical rational corpus at a time. The practical rational corpus would contain statements that were appropriately probable relative to the highest level rational corpus. The practical rational corpus would not be logically closed, of course. It, like the rational corpus of level i above, might contain S_1 and S_2, but not their conjunction. Now the only place where we allow an inductive rule of detachment is in getting statements into the practical rational corpus on the basis of their probability relative to the highest level rational corpus. We keep the definition of probability unchanged; we can make probability statements relative to the lower-level rational corpus; but we do not allow a statement to be detached from its evidence in virtue of its probability relative to the lower-level, practical, rational corpus.

The lottery paradox is now avoided simply by virtue of the fact that the rule of detachment is allowed to operate at only one level in a given context. While the philosophical or highest-level rational corpus may contain such statements that for $1 \leqslant i \leqslant N,$ the statement "Chip number i will not be drawn" is an ingredient of the practical rational corpus, there *is* no *next* lower rational corpus in which the conjunction of these statements will appear.

One may argue about whether or not it is reasonable to look for an inductive rule of detachment; I have presented some arguments in favor of looking for one. (But I have not refuted Bar-Hillel's argument, presented at the Wesleyan Conference on Induction. His argument was: "Who *needs* a rule of detachment?") But given that one *is* going to look for a rule of detachment, there is a great deal to be said about the characteristics of the bodies of knowledge to which it leads. Nearly all writers on epistemology, and nearly all proposers of inductive rules of detachment, have accepted conditions of complete logical closure and consistency. Levi has shown that the non-probabilistic proposals involving degrees of corroboration or factual support break down if they are made the basis of a Bayesian approach to inference. I have attempted to show that probabilistic rules—as generally outlined by Hempel—lead to the lottery paradox so long as we hang onto the ideal of consistency and the ideal of logical closure. If this is so, Hempel's conditions *cannot* be satisfied by a probabilistic rule of detachment. In my own system these ideals are abandoned in favor of much weaker conditions of consistency and logical closure. And in this system— as modified above—we have a rule of detachment which can lead to the acceptance of scientific theories and generalizations, as well as of individual predictions, and which yet does not generate the lottery paradox. Defective as the modified system may turn out to be, I still hope that *some* of my beliefs are rational. Hope springs eternal.

NOTES

1. Levi, Isaac, "Decision Theory and Confirmation," *Journal of Philosophy* 60, 1963. p. 623.

2. Hempel, Carl, "Deductive Nomological vs. Statistical Explanation" in Feigl, H. and Maxwell, G., *Scientific Explanation, Space and Time,* Minnesota Studies in the Philosophy of Science, Vol. III, University of Minnesota Press, Minneapolis, 1962, pp. 150-151.

3. Hempel, "Statistical Explanation," p. 155.

4. Kyburg, Henry E., Jr., *Probability and the Logic of Rational Belief,* Wesleyan University Press, Middletown, 1961.

5. Schick, Frederick, "Rationality and Consistency," *Journal of Philosophy* 60 (1963) 5-19.

16

Local and Global Induction

I

In 1967 Isaac Levi introduced a distinction which has had a serious impact on the direction of research into inductive problems. The distinction itself was not new in principle; people for years had been aware that the problem of justifying a particular inductive conclusion in a practical scientific context was quite different from the general problem of justifying inductive conclusions whole-sale. But Levi made the distinction sharper, and, more important, turned what had been taken to be the philosophical point of the distinction on its head. Traditionally, the point of the distinction was this: as philosophers we are not concerned with the particular problems of how a sociologist, for example, should justify his argument from an observed sample to a population; the sociologist, after all, can rely on a whole body of knowledge whose justification is not (for him) at issue. As philosophers (so the traditional view went) we are interested in the general and abstract problem of justification; to justify an inductive conclusion I by reference to principles which themselves are just as much in need of ultimate justification as I itself, is to accomplish nothing of philosophical interest. Levi argues, on the contrary, that there are profound and interesting philosophical problems in local induction: it is not at all a simple matter to say what it is that justifies the sociologist in accepting his inductive conclusion, even *given* his background knowledge. Although Levi neither claims nor argues that the concern with global induction is philosophically uninterest-ing, his language suggests that that concern is less than vital: "No attempt will be made to justify the criteria offered by deriving them in some globalistically impeccable manner from the incontrovertibly evident."[1]

The local problem of induction is the problem of providing an analysis of justification appropriate to a particular scientific problematic situation. Here the *evidence* "will consist of those of the investigator's findings and beliefs that are relevant to the problem at hand and are not likely to be questioned by any

Reprinted from R. J. Bogdan, ed., *Local Induction* (Reidel, Dordrecht, 1976), pp. 191-215, by permission of the publisher.

participant in the inquiry . . . ."[2] As contrasted with this, the global problem is to show that a whole body of beliefs are justified; in dealing with this problem we wish to admit as evidence only those statements that are not subject to doubt: the direct evidence of our senses, for example, or intuitively apparent necessary truths. It is well known that there are problems associated with the global approach: while people tend to agree that necessary truth is limited to logical truth, the extent of logical truth is not altogether clear; the effort to find data that are suitably incorrigible and will serve as a basis for global justification of what we know has been perpetually frustrated.

Under these circumstances, it is not surprising that Levi's suggestion that inductive logicians concentrate on the problems of local induction has been followed enthusiastically. Lehrer has written extensively from this point of view;[3] Hintikka and his students may also be construed as having adopted the same point of view. Most recently, Niiniluoto and Tuomela have both taken it for granted that theories may be counted among the evidential statements relative to which we assess probabilities, and for them, even the choice of a probability function is an empirical matter, guided by considerations outside of and prior to the problem of local justification. It is even a 'condition of adequacy' for the explication of hypothetico-inductive inference that the required probability function *not* be determined by logical considerations alone.[4]

The local-global distinction is an important one, and it is increasingly clear that there are interesting and important local problems. This is clear particularly in statistical inference, where foundational questions are a lively source of debate and disagreement even among practicing statisticians. Often what is at issue in questions concerning the acceptance of statistical hypotheses is precisely the question of what, in a given context, with a given common store of background knowledge, constitutes good inductive evidence. Since in every form of scientific inference we must take account of error—even in the most 'deductive' parts of celestial mechanics—these statistical considerations are not special or peripheral, but central to the whole inductive enterprise. I shall argue, in Sections two and three, that most of the work that has been done on the problems of local induction has suffered from just the disease that the local-global distinction was supposed to cure us of: the disease of excessive generality. It thus provides relatively little help in cases in which there is genuine disagreement or puzzlement on a local level. If we are going to adopt a Deweyan stance, and claim that it is not in the abstract that inductive problems should be resolved, but in down-to-earth practical situations in which there is a felt problem, then the theory of local induction should make it possible (often, if not always) for two people who are holding conflicting views concerning the bearing of a specific body of evidence on a specific set of hypotheses, to resolve that conflict. This is not to say that the context may not have to be broadened in order to achieve a resolution, but that the theory should indicate the direction in which a resolution should be sought.

On the other hand, in Sections four and five, I shall argue that if 'broadening the context' is an acceptable move, then we must take the global problems seriously. The traditional problems of induction—some of them, at any rate—are just the problems at which you arrive when you 'broaden the context' as much as you can. In order to be *sure* that a local conflict will be resolvable, you must be confident that no matter how the context must be broadened, it will be possible to apply the general inductive theory. But this in turn means that we must, even if only hypothetically and artificially, be capable in principle of justifying a whole body of beliefs.

There is another class of problems that pushes us toward global justification: the problems of epistemology. Here we have traditional philosophical problems, which, in view of their traditional philosophical generality, require an understanding of more than local induction for their resolution. It may be that they are false problems, in the sense that no resolution is possible. But as yet there has been no persuasive argument to that effect, and indeed the work that has been done on global approaches to induction has shed some light on these philosophical problems.

II. LOCAL NON-PROBABILISTIC INDUCTION

There are two reasons why local non-probabilistic induction has received relatively little attention.[5] The first is that, being demonstrative, it employs no novel or interesting logical relationships. It just employs the same old logic we know all about. Furthermore, even when a local inductive conclusion is entailed by the evidence for it combined with background knowledge, that reconstruction seems simplistic because it ignores the pervasive presence of error. I shall present and comment on the same old problem by way of illustration.

An organic chemist creates a new organic compound. It is crystalline at ordinary temperature and pressure. He performs an experiment to test the melting point. After one experiment, he concludes, with perfect generality, that all samples of this compound, past, present and future, tested and untested, will melt under standard pressure at T degrees centigrade. No one will come up to him and say, "Aha! you have no evidence for that; your sample of one surely can't lead to such a strong conclusion; and even if you had done the experiment thousands of times, that wouldn't indicate that in the *future* the compound would continue to melt at that temperature; and of course you have no evidence at all that untested samples of the compound *would have* melted at that temperature, had they been tested." In that context, the argument (idealized though it may be) is deductive in character. We can reconstruct it as follows. (I use second-order logic as being more intuitive here; but of course a first-order reconstruction in set theory is just as easy.)

Before the experiment the chemist (and you and I, insofar as we believe chemical doctrine—and that's not what is at issue here) accepts the general statement:

(1) (F) (F is a crystalline chemical compound $\supset (t)[(\exists x)$ (x is a specimen of F x melts at $t) \supset (x)$ (x is a specimen of $F \supset x$ melts at $t))]$.

Loosely translated: If something is a crystalline chemical compound and any sample of it melts at a certain temperature under standard conditions, then every sample of it melts at that temperature.

Before the experiment the chemist (and you and I, insofar as we are not taking issue with his laboratory techniques) accept that his new compound, c, is indeed a crystalline chemical compound.

(2) c is a crystalline chemical compound.

Finally, when the chemist performs his test, he concludes that a sample of c melts at standard conditions at T degrees. Again, assuming we are not taking issue with his techniques or his state of mind, we also accept that conclusion.

(3) a is a sample of c and a melts at T degrees.

From (1) and (2) and (3) it follows deductively that all samples of c melt at T degrees.

(4) (x) (x is a sample of $c \supset x$ melts at standard pressure at T degrees).

There is nothing particularly exciting about the logic of this inductive inference, or about the fact that it entails its conclusion. One might well nevertheless be able to find, in journals devoted to chemistry or physics or even biology, arguments complex enough to have an interesting structure which could still be construed in this deductive fashion.

There is still something that seems to be left out: it isn't all this easy to establish a new physical constant. Surely the chemist would not be satisfied to conduct one melting point experiment, but would perform the experiment several times. The reason for this is not far to seek: it lies in the insecurity of statement (3). If we could be quite certain that one sample of c melted at T degrees, we would be quite certain of the general conclusion. But any process of physical measurement has associated with it a pattern of error, and thus all we can be sure of when we conduct the melting point experiment is that the reading for that run is T. We replicate the experiment in order to ensure that the melting point is (close to) T. We do not, in fact, accept statements of the form (3), but only statements of the form:

(3′) a is a sample of c, and a melts at T plus or minus ϵ degrees,

where ϵ is characteristic of experimental procedure. Statement (3′) in fact is a result of another inference, which is statistical and problematic, and which therefore calls for another analysis. Nevertheless, the deductive pattern does represent something that is going on in the scientific inference, which we may explicate by reference to a notion of practical certainty.

Statements (1), (2), and (3′) may all be challenged. The first statement may be defended as (partially) analytic of what we mean by a crystalline chemical compound, or it may be defended as part of a physical theory. In either event, it can (in some way or other, I am supposing) be defended as at least practically certain. It is not up for question in the same way that the melting point of this brand-new chemical substance is open to question. The second statement is somewhat more open to question: it isn't hard to be mistaken in thinking that you have a chemical compound when in fact you have a mixture of chemical compounds. But there are various laboratory tests (one of which is sharpness and consistency of melting point — but for the purposes of this example we leave that to one side) for determining whether c is a crystalline chemical compound. In the local context of determining the melting point of c, we are accepting (2) as practically certain. It is tempting to construe 'practical certainty' in terms of probability, and in fact I think that approach, though complicated and requiring a good deal of clarification, is the right one. If we do that, and if the evidence (consisting of one or several tests of melting point) is such as to render (3') just as probable, or just as 'practically certain' as (2), then (4') will follow deductively from (1), (2), and (3'), and will do so in a relatively realistic way.

(4') (x) $(x$ is a sample of $c \supset x$ melts under standard pressure at T plus or minus ϵ degrees C.).

What has now become problematic is the statistical inference that renders (3') so probable as to be practically certain. We therefore turn to probabilistic inference in general.

III. LOCAL PROBABILISTIC INDUCTION

This is the area in which most of the work on local induction of recent years has been done. This is the area that Levi singled out, that has been taken as paradigmatic by Lehrer, that has been discussed by Niiniluoto and others of Hintikka's school. Our treatment of local probabilistic induction will reflect, of course, our views regarding probability itself. We shall therefore look at the local problems as they appear under each of three views regarding probability: the logical and subjectivistic, the objective, and the epistemological. Furthermore, there are two degrees of inference that we may have in mind: the degree of inference according to which one comes to *accept* a statistical hypothesis (or to choose one against an alternative, or to choose one set of hypotheses as against another set); and the degree of inference according to which one merely *assigns a probability* to a statement (general or particular), or, more generally, according to which one assigns a probability distribution to some quantity, which may be a parameter in a statistical hypothesis. In the first case, we might come to accept that the measure of tosses yielding heads is a half, or is in some interval around a half, or that a certain quantity is distributed normally (m, s) or is distributed approximately normally with mean between m_1 and m_2, and variance between s^2 and s^2. In the second case we might assign a distribution to the parameter p characterizing the coin and tossing apparatus.

The subjectivistic interpretation of probability seems tailor-made for local probabilistic induction in the second degree. The situation is typically described as follows: We begin with a set of statements b representing our background knowledge. The prior probability of the hypothesis in question, h, is p. We accumulate evidence e. The conditional probability of h on e (and the background knowledge) is q. The conditional probability q may be very much greater than the prior probability p. More generally, we begin with a prior distribution D for a random quantity; we accumulate evidence e, and, by Bayes's theorem, obtain a posterior distribution D_e for that random quantity.

Two familiar problems must be dealt with. First, since probabilities on this view represent personal degrees of belief, there is no "standard" prior probability or prior distribution. Two people may with equal right have widely differing prior probabilities. Their posterior probabilities will then also differ. Second, this approach throws no light on the question of acceptance. To *accept* a statement on this view, is to assign it probability one, and conditionalization cannot lead to unit probabilities except in trivial and uninteresting cases.

There are two sets of answers to these questions, one provided by the practicing statisticians who have adopted a Bayesian approach in their professional work, and the other provided by philosophers concerned with the problem of learning from experience.

(1) The statisticians' answers: There is no 'standard' prior distribution, but there is nevertheless rough agreement in many practical instances. There is a certain amount of conventional wisdom on which the statistician may draw. Furthermore, it is generally the case (subject to some very weak conditions), that as the amount of evidence increases, two people will come to agree more and more closely regarding their posterior distributions, even if they begin with quite divergent prior distributions. You may have a probability of one-tenth for a coin to land heads; my probability may be nine-tenths; but after we have tossed it a thousand times your conditional probability and my conditional probability for heads on the thousand and first toss will be very close together, unless one of us is adamantly pig-headed. Finally, there are many circumstances under which the prior distributions may vary extremely widely, without having more than a very tiny effect on the posterior distribution. As for the other problem—the problem of acceptance—that is no problem at all: whatever the parties to an investigation agree to accept is acceptable as background knowledge, evidence, or whatever. Since they are concerned with statistical inference, the question of coming to accept hypotheses simply does not arise; they are concerned only with obtaining a posterior distribution on which to base a practical decision.

(2) The philosophers' answers: Philosophers also refer to the convergence of posterior distributions, but they also sometimes suggest constraints that prior distributions should satisfy. These constraints have been formulated only for first-order (and, usually, monadic) languages. (Carnap is the classical figure in this approach, but it has also been followed by Hintikka and his students.) These

constraints may be construed as purely logical (Carnap) or as reflecting empirical commitments (Niiniluoto and Tuomela). There are, in the construction of probability measures for these languages, one or two free parameters (λ of Carnap's λ-system; λ and η in his New System; α and λ in Hintikka's system). Although the parametrization of degrees of belief imposes certain restrictions on the prior distribution of belief, posterior probabilities will depend on the choice of the parameters. People choosing different values for the parameters cannot be expected to agree on their posterior distributions.

There are two philosophical approaches to the problem of acceptance. Richard Jeffrey shuns acceptance: there are certain experiences that may *cause* us to assign probability one to certain statements, but in general not even evidence statements can be assigned probability one. An evidence statement, on his view, is a statement in which a shift in probabilities *originates;* its probability may leap from 0.1 to 0.9 as a result of an observation. Jeffrey then gives us an algorithm for computing the effect of this shift on our other probabilities. William Harper has broadened this approach so that, given a certain shift in a set of basic probabilities, we move to a new probability function for all the statements of our language which is, in a sense yet to be made precise, the *closest possible* probability function to our original one. The other approach is that derived from Hintikka's work. As Hilpinen and Hintikka show,[6] it is possible to define a rule of acceptance, in terms of both probability and a minimum sample size, which is demonstrably consistent. Levi formulates a rule of acceptance (rule A) which is also demonstrably consistent;[7] Lehrer has developed rules similar to Levi's.[8]

What is to be said about the bearing of all this on the problems of local probabilistic induction? The philosophical approach that devises an acceptance rule based on logical or constrained subjectivistic probability is (so far) applicable only to very simple languages. It cannot be applied directly to practical instances of scientific inference. In any such situation, we have a large body of information, relevant in varying ways, which cannot even be formulated in a first-order monadic language. This holds of all the philosophical approaches to local probabilistic induction based on constrained subjectivistic or logical probability, whether they involve a rule of acceptance or not. Furthermore, these approaches do not provide the one thing that we might reasonably demand: a framework within which it is possible to discuss and come to agreement concerning whether a given posterior distribution (or given acceptance) is justified by the evidence, unless we begin with not only the same body of knowledge, but the same belief structure. To be sure, we should perhaps not demand a simple algorithm which will crank out a result automatically, but we should at least be able to focus on the kinds of items we have in our real bodies of knowledge that are relevant to the argument.

The out-and-out subjective Bayesians are in a slightly better position. They can take the prior probability measure to be defined over our native language. There may not be a natural way to do this, but in principle we can determine the degree of belief a person has in any arbitrary statement of his own language. (How large a set of statements one can test this way before running into incoherence is open to question. And how one handles the incoherencies that one does run into is also open to dispute—dispute, note, that the theory is powerless to adjudicate. Savage, the most thoroughgoing subjectivist, says that it is a matter of the person distinguishing between degrees of belief of which he feels 'more sure' and degrees of belief of which he feels 'less sure'.) Furthermore, subjectivistic Bayesian statisticians have in fact made important contributions to the solution of the very problem we are concerned with: much of what they have done is directly relevant to the problem of local probabilistic induction. There is just one constraint on the applicability of their techniques: it is required that the prior distributions of parties to an inductive episode be similar, in the sense that the differences among the prior distributions do not give rise to significant differences in the posterior distributions. (We have learned that the differences in prior distributions can be rather large in many cases without being dissimilar in the sense at hand.) But this doesn't amount to much: the thesis appears to be that if our probability distributions aren't too different to start with, they won't be too different afterwards. What we are looking for, as philosophers at least, is some way of resolving disagreements about what is how much evidence for what, in this local situation. This is just what the subjectivistic approach fails to give us. Talk about how *further* evidence will lead non-extreme opinions ever closer together is irrelevant here. We each have a prior distribution, we observe a given amount of evidence, and we each obtain a posterior distribution. If our posterior distributions are still divergent, the subjectivistic approach gives us no way of approaching agreement, or even discussing the disagreement fruitfully with an eye to reducing it.

In short, subjective approaches to probability are failures at the one thing we might expect of a theory that is to make sense of local probabilistic induction. They work where there is nothing at issue (i.e., where the prior distributions of participants to an inference are not 'too' dissimilar), and they are impotent in the face of disagreement.

Objectivistic (frequency, propensity) approaches to probability do not fare better. In fact, the one thing that can be obtained on the basis of such approach is a characterization of statistical tests. As was true of the Bayesian approach to statistics, there are local situations to which these considerations apply. If we can agree that a given local problematic situation is one to which the objectivistic techniques apply, then we are in good shape. But if we cannot agree, we are out of luck. The objectivistic considerations are not even potentially relevant to the question of accepting singular statements characterizing an experimental situation, and thus there is no way this approach can be called upon to adjudicate disputes of this nature. Again, the objectivistic techniques of local induction work productively when there is nothing at issue; and again, they are impotent in the face of disagreement.

The epistemological interpretation of probability, though it has yet to be put to extensive test, does seem to promise to do better. To begin with, it does supply criteria for picking out those situations in which Bayesian techniques are appropriate and for picking out those situations in which objective techniques are appropriate.[9] Epistemological probability is defined for first-order languages only, but we may suppose that these languages include set theory, so that almost anything is sayable in them. Most important, epistemological probability supplies a framework within which it is possible to make a constructive effort to resolve disagreements about the import of evidence in the case of local probabilistic induction. It is important to see how this takes place, at least in outline, in order to see that the 'nothing at issue or impotent to resolve disagreement' charge does not apply here.

The definition of epistemological probability is a long and complicated story, which has been given in detail elsewhere.[10] Here a few remarks will suffice to bring out the aspects that are relevant to our special problem.

(1) Probability is defined relative to a body of knowledge, construed as a set of statements of a first-order language that is strong enough to include set theory, and, in particular, the mathematics required for statistical inference. At this juncture we are not concerned about how items get into a body of knowledge, but we may suppose that they can get in by 'observation' in some sense, and perhaps by inductive inferences as well. So long as we are concerned merely with the local induction, the source of our (common) body of knowledge is irrelevant. We agree that there is a certain set of things that we take for granted. Of course we couldn't list them; but, as items become relevant to our discussion, they can be listed.

(2) Every probability is based on a known statement of relative frequency or propensity. Since we are concerned here with local induction, we may suppose that all parties to any controversy accept the same statistical background knowledge.

(3) The third required ingredient of a probability statement is an assertion of randomness. Like probability, randomness is metalinguistic and epistemological. It is construed as a four-termed relation, holding between a term (denoting an object), a term (denoting a reference class), a term (denoting another class), and a set of statements, representing a body of knowledge. The probability of '$a \in b$' is the interval (p, q) just in case there is a term 'c' denoting a reference class, such that the randomness relation holds between 'a', 'c', 'b', and our body of knowledge. Probability is defined for equivalence classes of statements, where two statements belong to the same equivalence class if they are connected by a biconditional in our body of knowledge—i.e., s and t belong to the same equivalence class if the biconditional '$s \leftrightarrow t$' is in our body of knowledge.

Given a body of knowledge, there exists a probability for every statement in the language. Finding that probability, however, may be a non-trivial exercise in logic in virtue of the complexity of the randomness relation. It is here, I think, that the material controversies that arise in local induction originate, and it is through the analysis of this relation that we can provide a framework in which they can be constructively resolved.

Consider a statement s; it gives rise to an equivalence class $[s]$. Now consider the set of all triples of terms $\langle a, b, c \rangle$ such that '$a \in b$' is a member of $[s]$, '$a \in c$' is a member of our body of knowledge, and 'c' is a reference term—a term denoting a (potential) reference class. The problem of randomness is essentially the problem of choosing a reference class.[11] There are two ways in which our knowledge of potential reference classes may conflict: (1) the interval (p', q') that represents our knowledge of the proportion of c' that is b' may *differ* from the interval (p, q) that represents our knowledge of the proportion of c that is b, in the sense that neither interval is included in the other; (2) one interval may be properly included in the other, in which cases we say that the statistical statement mentioning the shorter interval is *stronger than* the statement mentioning the including interval. Suppose that $\langle a, b, c \rangle$ conflicts with $\langle a', b', c' \rangle$ in the first sense. There are two circumstances under which we might still want to maintain that the randomness relation held among the terms a, b, c, and our body of knowledge: (a) If we knew that c was included in c'; this reflects the maxim 'choose the narrowest reference class'. (b) If we knew that c was included in a potential reference class c'' that was a cross product, and such that either a subset of c' is the first term of the cross product, or that c includes the cross product of a term and a subset of c' as a special case.[12] This reflects the maxim 'use Bayes's theorem when you can'.

A certain number of our triples of terms $\langle a, b, c \rangle$ are now ruled out; in fact there are no conflicts in sense (1) remaining.. For if our knowledge of b and c differs from our knowledge of b' and c', at most one of the two triples $\langle a, b, c \rangle$, $\langle a', b', c' \rangle$ can remain a candidate for determining a probability. The remaining group of candidates can then be ordered by 'strength': we want as reference class that class about which we have the most precise knowledge. Of course there will be more than one—in fact there will be an infinite number—of the same maximal strength. But since the corresponding statistical statements all mention the same intervals, we may suppose that all the randomness assertions mentioning triples of this last set are valid.

It is no doubt worth examining a couple of instances in which considerations like those just alluded to abstractly can be relevant to the validity of a local induction.

Suppose we are interested in the proportion of A's that are B's, and we take a large sample of A's and count the number of B's. Suppose that in our sample of n, a proportion r are B's. We may argue as follows (taking the mathematics for granted). Let a sample be ϵ-representative, if the proportion of B's in it differs by less than ϵ from the proportion of B's among A's in general. The proportion of ϵ-representative n-fold subsets of A—the proportion of ϵ-representative members of A^n—varies according to the proportion of B's among A's. It is 1, of course, if either all or none of the A's are B's; it decreases as the proportion in question differs from 0 or 1, and it achieves a minimum if the proportion of A's that are B's is 0.5. Let the proportion of ϵ -representative subsets of A in the last mentioned case be p. Then, whatever the proportion of A's that are B's, the proportion of ϵ -representative subsets of A (containing n items) will lie between p and 1. Suppose the sample we have drawn is denoted by s, and the set of ϵ -representative samples by e. Then if the randomness relation holds of the triple $\langle s, e, A^n \rangle$ we may conclude that the probability is $(p, 1)$ that $s \in e$. Since probabilities are defined to be equal for statements known to be equivalent, this will also be the probability of the statement: the proportion of A's that are B's lies between $r - \epsilon$ and $r + \epsilon$.

It is obvious to everybody that such local inductive arguments do not always go through. It should be a task of a theory of local induction to provide an explanation of precisely when and why they fail, or at least to provide a framework within which two people who share the same background knowledge can come to agreement—or at least work constructively *toward* agreement—about which inductive argument goes through in a particular case. Let us see how the framework I have provided serves this function.

(1) Let p' be greater than p, and suppose it is claimed that the probability of our hypothesis (that the proportion of A's that are B's lies between $r - \epsilon$ and $r + \epsilon$, henceforth abbreviated as H) is $(p', 1)$. If this claim is to be justified, there must be a triple of terms $\langle a, b, c \rangle$ such that '$a \in b \leftrightarrow H$' is a member of our background knowledge, such that the proportion of c's that are b's is known to lie between p' and 1, such that we know '$a \in c$', and such that the randomness relation holds among a, b, c, and the set of statements constituting our agreed-upon knowledge. Three examples: (a) Our sample s_n was obtained by a certain method of which we know that it yields representative samples more often than 'random' sampling. Let the set of applications of this method be m. It would be being claimed then that the randomness relation holds among $s, m, e,$ and our body of knowledge. (b) We know in advance of sampling that at least three quarters of the A's are B's. Then the minimum proportion of ϵ-representative samples among the members of A^n is that corresponding to a proportion of ¾, and that is represented by p'. (c) A belongs to a certain class of classes, $\mathscr{A}$, among which a proportion between p' and 1 are characterized by having a proportion of B's lying between $r + \epsilon$ and $r - \epsilon$—let us denote the set of such classes by $\mathfrak{R}$. It would be being claimed that the randomness relation holds between $A, \mathscr{A}, \mathfrak{R}$, and our body of knowledge.

Rebuttal of the claim that the probability of H is the interval $(p', 1)$ would take the same form in the two cases in which it is possible. Under (b), no rebuttal is possible, since no question of randomness is at issue. If we truly share the same background knowledge, I simply made a mistake when I said that the proportion of ϵ-representative samples in A^n lay between p and 1: I know more than that. Under (a) and (c) the rebuttal of the claim consists in exhibiting a triple of terms $\langle a, b, c \rangle$ concerning which our statistical knowledge *differs* (in the sense described earlier) from the interval $(p', 1)$, and that the conflict cannot be avoided by either of the two gambits mentioned on page 273. Thus, for example, in the case of claim (a) we might argue that the sample was obtained under circumstances C—let the set of samples so obtained be denoted by c—and that the proportion of such samples that are ϵ-representative lies between q and q', where q is less than p' and q' less than 1; and (we would also have to argue) there is no subset of c to which we know that our sample belongs in which the relevant proportion is $(p', 1)$, and there is no cross product set m', such that a subset of c is the first term in the cross product, or such that the second term of m' includes the cross product of a term and a subset of c. An example of this circumstance will be given shortly.

The rebuttal of the rebuttal would consist of showing that in fact the conflict can be avoided by one of the gambits mentioned on page 273. At every stage there is a constructive procedure to follow: the *onus probandi* is on a determinate one of the claimants, and can be satisfied—so far as that stage is concerned— by a finite amount of argument.

(2) Let q be less than p, and q' be less than 1, and suppose it is claimed that the probability of H is (q, q'). There must exist, then a triple of terms $\langle a, b, c \rangle$ such that '$a \in b \leftrightarrow H$' is a member of our background knowledge, such that the proportion of c's that are b's is known to lie in the interval (q, q'), such that we know '$a \in c$', and such that the randomness relation holds between a, b, c, and our background knowledge. Two examples: (d) we already know the proportion of A's that are B's; suppose that proportion is r^*. Then, according as r^* lies in the interval $(r - \epsilon, r + \epsilon)$ or not, we *know* whether the sample is representative or not, and the probability is $(0, 0)$ if it is not. We have, in this case, that s is a random member of $\{s\}$ with respect to being ϵ-representative, and if the difference between r^* and r is greater than ϵ, we know that the proportion of ϵ-representative members of $\{s\}$ is exactly 0. Since $\{s\}$ is a subset—and known to be a subset—of A^n, the conflict is resolved in favor of $\{s\}$. (Note that while we always know that s is a member of $\{s\}$, and that $\{s\}$ is a subset of A^n, this knowledge has a bearing on the probability in question only when we know whether s is ϵ-representative or not; when we lack this knowledge we know only that the proportion of members of $\{s\}$ that belong to e lies between 0 and 1, and this knowledge doesn't *differ* in our sense from any other statistical knowledge.) (e) we know that A is a member of a set of sets $\mathscr{A}$, among which various proportions of B's are distributed according to one of a set D of distributions. Our sample s is ϵ-representative just in case the pair $\langle A, s \rangle$, which belongs to the set of pairs consisting of populations and samples from them, say s, has the property that s is ϵ-representative of A, or belongs, say, to $\mathscr{E}$. Given a member of D, we may compute the frequency with which the pair belongs to those pairs in which the second member is ϵ-representative of the first by straight-forward Bayesian techniques. Given the set D, we may therefore compute a maximum and a minimum frequency for this to occur. It is claimed that $\langle\!\langle A, s \rangle, \mathscr{A}\mathit{s}, \mathscr{E} \rangle$, and our body

of knowledge satisfy the randomness relation. In particular although s, A_n, and e conflict with $\langle A, s \rangle$, $\mathscr{A}s$, and $\mathscr{E}$, the conflict is resolved in favor of the latter by the following argument: There is a subset of A^n — namely those exhibiting the frequency r — which is a special case of a subset of a cross product — namely $\mathscr{A}s$ itself — in which the relevant frequency is just the same as it is in $\mathscr{A}s$.

A concrete example may help to illuminate the last abstract example. Suppose we are interested in the mean weight θ of a strain of laboratory animals — say, white rats. We might suppose it well known that the variance in any of a related group of strains is 4, and thus that it is in this one. The difference between the mean and the sample average in a sample of one will therefore be distributed normally with mean 0 and variance 4. Let a be the sample of one, B the set of samples of size one, and C be the set of samples in which the sample mean does not differ by more than 1.96 standard deviations from the population mean θ; 95% of the members of B are also members of C. Thus *if* a is a random member of B with respect to belonging to C, relative to what we know, *then* the probability for us, having observed a weight of 75, that θ lies between 71.08 and 78.95, is exactly 0.95.

Now we probably, from previous experience, have some idea of the distribution of the means among the strains in the subspecies to which the strain in question belongs. The extent of that knowledge determines whether or not the randomness condition is met. Suppose we know merely that the means are distributed roughly normally among the strains, with an overall mean of between 20 and 100, and a variance somewhere between 9 and 16. The conditional distribution of θ, after our observation, will then be one in the set of normal distributions:[13]

$$\left\{ N\left(\frac{75/4 + m/\sigma^2}{1/4 + 1/\sigma^2}, \frac{1}{1/4 + 1/\sigma^2} \right) : 20 \leqslant m \leqslant 100 \wedge 9 \leqslant \sigma^2 \leqslant 16 \right\}.$$

The range of the measures for the interval (71.08, 78.92) will thus have a maximum at $m = 75$, $\sigma = 9$, and a minimum when $m = 20$ and $\sigma = 9$. The lower measure is 0, and the upper is 0.982. Let P be the population, A be the set of strains. Then if the pair, $\langle a, P \rangle$ is a random member of the set [$\langle x, y \rangle$: $x \in y$ $y \in A$ $wt(x) = 75$] $= S$ with respect to membership in the set of pairs $\langle x, y \rangle$ such that y has a mean (θ) in the interval (71.08, 78.92) — let the set of such sets be R — relative to what we know, then the probability that θ lies in that interval is (0, 0.982). Under the circumstances we have described, the former assertion of randomness is true, the latter false. The frequency of R among members of $P \times A$ does not *differ* from the frequency of C among members of B.

Now suppose our knowledge of the subspecies is a little more precise. We might know that the distribution of means among the members of A is roughly normal with a mean between 50 and 60, and a variance of between 9 and 16. The set of conditional distributions will then be:

$$\left\{ N\left(\frac{75/4 + m/\sigma^2}{1/4 + 1/\sigma^2}, \frac{1}{1/4 + 1/\sigma^2}\right) : 50 \leqslant m \leqslant 60 \wedge 9 \leqslant \sigma^2 \leqslant 16 \right\}$$

The range of the measures for the interval (71.08, 78.92) is now from 0.012 to 0.68. This range does *not* overlap (include) the previous measure of 0.95, and so indeed the two frequencies are known to differ. Now we shall show that nevertheless $\langle a, P \rangle$ is a random member of S, but a is not a random member of B with respect to C.

Of the gambits mentioned on page 273, the first—choose the narrowest reference class—is no help. Neither of the sets at issue is known to be a subset of the other, nor is there any way of transforming the problem so that this will be the case. The complicated gambit, (b), is the relevant one. There is indeed a potential reference class—namely S itself—which is a cross product, and which is such that the competing class—namely B—is known to have a subset—namely, the set of one-membered samples having a mean weight of 75—such that the cross product of P and this set is known to be included in S as a special case. We are thus directed to use Bayes's theorem.

The probability, therefore, that θ lies between 71.08 and 78.92 is (0.012, 0.68). The shortest interval whose minimum probability is 0.95 turns out to be roughly (63.7, 75.6).

Finally, if we suppose that we know that the distribution of mean weights among the subspecies A is normal with mean 55 and variance 10, the unique posterior distribution for θ is normal with mean 69.29 and variance 2.86. The object $\langle a, P \rangle$ is a random member of S, and the probability is exactly 0.95 that θ lies between 63.68 and 74.90.

Note that in this last example we have an illustration of the manner in which the epistemological interpretation of probability provides a precise criterion for when our background knowledge is extensive enough that Bayesian procedures properly take over from confidence techniques.

IV

Techniques of local induction can guide collective inquiry, just in case the participants share the same body of knowledge, or the same opinions, at least in relevant respects. To be sure, this condition is vacuous for Robinson Crusoe, at least before the appearance of Friday. But even Robinson Crusoe, to the extent that he wishes his inquiries to be controlled and objective, should on occasion step outside himself and play the part of a critic of Robinson Crusoe. Barring such exceptional cases, however, we want the theory of local induction to provide a framework within which to criticize particular inductive inferences; we want the theory to be capable of leading a group of scientists to agreement about what the evidence warrants in a particular case. (This is not to say that it will force them to agreement about their beliefs: it is perfectly possible that for someone to say' "Yes, the evidence does indicate H, but I still feel that there is another and deeper explanation.") Theories of local induction, as we have seen, can do this only if the scientists in question share the relevant parts of a body of knowledge, or (in the subjectivistic case) the relevant degrees of belief. What is the scope of the word 'relevant' here? It is well known that inductive logic is peculiar in the sense that if a set of premises inductively yields a conclusion, an enlarged set of premises may not yield that conclusion. Thus it is difficult to limit the scope of relevant knowledge. We thus seem pushed, even in the application of local induction to well-circumscribed problems, to consider relatively global matters.

Furthermore, we should be able to achieve some sort of agreement about what the evidence warrants, even if we don't start with the same body of knowledge or the same opinions. We can only be assured of being able to do this if we can apply the techniques of local induction to an ever wider set of circumstances: if, given my background knowledge, you agree that the evidence supports H, but you lack a certain item in my background knowledge, I should be able, using the *same techniques* of local induction, to convince you that the evidence warrants the inclusion of that item in your background knowledge, too. What we require, in short, is that the context of local induction be arbitrarily expandable. But if a theory of local induction has this property, it is already almost a global theory. If my fellow scientist protests ignorance of (almost) everything, and my theory of local induction is arbitrarily expandable, I should be able to fill in his background knowledge to the point where he will agree that the evidence supports H. (Note that this does not mean that I have to teach him *everything* I know; but it means that I have to be able to teach him any *particular* thing I know, and that without presupposing a common body of background knowledge.) The conclusion we draw is that the application of local induction is either dependent on the solution of those very problems that constitute the problem of global induction, or else its scope is so limited as to be uninteresting.

Of course it may be that the scope of local inductive logic is severly limited — perhaps even limited to those whose epistemological states are extremely similar. I know of no general arguments to this effect. There are arguments stated within a point of view regarding local induction: thus the subjectivist Bayesian will give limits within which the opinions of participants in an inference must fall in order that they end up in close agreement after observing the evidence. There are general arguments concerning the formation of theories: if you don't accept the same paradigms as I, you will formulate a different hypothesis to account for a given phenomenon. But we are here concerned with the most elementary and straightforward statistical kinds of inductive inference; we leave to one side the question of the case made for the paradigm-dependence of scientific hypothesizing.

To provide a formulation of this problem neutral with respect to the approach to local induction, let us refer to the background *state* of the investigator, rather than to his background knowledge or his prior distribution of belief. In this framework the problem is this: Given a certain background state S, given certain evidence E, a theory of local induction yields an inductive result R (which may be the acceptance of a statement, or the adoption of a new degree of belief in a statement or set of statements). Suppose two scientific workers have different background states S and S'. Given the same evidence E, they will not necessarily obtain the same inductive result. Let the difference between S and S' be represented by D. We suppose that the difference D does not represent merely a difference in data or evidence, for under ordinary circumstances I will not question your data, unless I have some theoretical or general grounds for doubting it. D thus represents inductive results that one worker has obtained and the other not. If local induction is going to resolve the issue between the two workers as to whether or not the inductive result R is yielded by the evidence E, it must first resolve the issue of the difference D between S and S', by leading to the inclusion of the inductive results of D in both S and S', on the basis of a common background state S^0 that both workers can put themselves in. But if we can do this in general, we may simply suppose that the background state S^0 contains no inductive results at all, and we will have at hand a solution to the global problem of induction. A successful local theory would seem to imply a global theory.

V

To what extent can the theories of local induction discussed previously be expanded to take account of differences in background state?

Let us consider first the subjectivistic approach. If our prior probabilities are the same, before we obtain the evidence E, then our probabilities conditional on E will be the same. This is the situation in which local induction applies without any problems. Now suppose our prior probabilities are not the same. They may differ within certain limits without leading our conditional probabilities to be widely different; but suppose they differ more than that? We are stymied. If we could put our finger on a difference in evidence which would account for the difference in prior probabilities, we could get started. But (a) even if we could cite such evidence, its efficacy would depend on our beliefs prior to that evidence being in close enough conformity so that the evidence will constrain us to have similar beliefs, and (b) it need not be the case that we *can* cite evidence: the prior beliefs relevant to the inductive conclusion may just be prior beliefs—not formed by induction and relative to evidence, but just bare facedly prior. A logical view would resolve the latter difficulty—but only for those who accept the same purely *a priori* logical distribution of probability over sentences of the language. As is well known, there are no compelling reasons for accepting one logical measure function rather than another.

Now it may be that as we bracket more and more empirical evidence, we will come more and more to share the same degrees of belief. If so, then the subjectivistic approach will yield a solution to the global problem. It would be an unsatisfactory solution, however, since it depends on what, from a logical point of view, must be regarded as sheer coincidence. Is it possible that we could find an evolutionary justification for the primordial predilections to believe? Perhaps; but we are now far off in a speculative realm that has so far been relatively unexplored.

How about objectivistic approaches? Whether or not a certain objectivistic statistical technique can be applied in a certain situation is a matter of what we know or don't know. Can we assume that X is distributed normally with known variance and unknown mean? Should we suppose that X is normally distributed with both mean and variance unknown? Should we suppose only that it has a distribution of a certain type? Answers to these questions depend on accepting the results of prior inductions. If we know the variance of X, for example, and that X is normally distributed, student's test, appropriate for the case of an unknown variance, is just plain wrong. It is true that we can 'back' up' to a certain extent. If A claims that the variance is known, and B claims that it is not, it is possible to review the evidence which supports A's claim; we can test for the variance. And if what is at issue is whether or not the distribution of X is normal at all, we can test for normality, or review the evidence on which a claim of normality is made. How far can we go in this way? It seems unlikely that we can go very far. There is no provision, in ordinary objectivistic theories, for the acceptance of singular statements—for that matter, there is no way in which probabilities can be assigned to such statements. There is no mechanism for the acceptance of extreme statistical hypotheses assigning parameters of 1 or 0 to probability measures. There is no mechanism for accepting universal generalizations. These are required for the characterization of the testing situation. Such statements must be accepted if we are to be able to know that a certain kind of test is appropriate to a certain situation. We need background knowledge which is not itself of the form of testable statistical hypotheses. Furthermore most objectivistic writers make a sharp distinction between accepting a hypothesis (which is never regarded as legitimate) and failing to reject a hypotheses (which is the appropriate outcome of a statistical test). If this distinction is maintained, then there is obviously no way in which the background knowledge required for the application of statistical tests can itself be obtained by means of statistical tests.

The epistemological approach can take account of differences in background state only with the help of a rule of acceptance. But in this case a rule of acceptance does not seem unattainable. Suggestions have been made in *The Logical Foundations of Statistical Inference*. We suppose that in a given context there is a degree of probability that constitutes practical certainty. The body of knowledge relative to which we judge probabilities in that context is a set of statements, each of which is acceptable (with that degree of practical certainty), relative to a body of knowledge of some higher degree of practical certainty, and to every degree of practical certainty between it and the given degree of practical certainty. If two people share the same body of knowledge, then as outlined earlier, they will be able to come to agreement, eventually concerning probabilities, and this includes the probabilities of inductively founded statements.

Suppose they do not share the same body of knowledge of a given degree of practical certainty. There are two possibilities: first, that they fail to share the same data; second, that the bodies of statements they regard as acceptable on the basis on that data differ. With respect to the first possibility, the epistemological interpretation of probability offers no help; but this is not surprising: if two investigators do not share each other's data, there can be no way for them to come to agreement. If I insist that your data are cooked or falsified, I will not accept the inductive conclusions you draw from that data. The second possibility cannot occur, for the following reasons: Let A and B share the same data (we suppose that data may be accepted directly into bodies of knowledge of degrees of practical certainty less than one; if we count as data only things of which we are "absolutely" sure, the argument is simplified). Let us assume that the bodies of practical certainties for A and B differ significantly — by which I mean that they differ with respect to those statements that come up in the attempt to adjudicate the probability statement at issue. That is, assume there is a degree of practical certainty such that the body of statements acceptable at that degree of practical certainty for A differs from the body of statements acceptable at that degree of practical certainty for B. Then there is a highest such degree of practical certainty, say p. The bodies of knowledge of A and B of any degree of practical certainty higher than p will then agree in their contents. But then probabilities for A and B, relative to these higher-level bodies of knowledge will agree; and since a statement will be acceptable in a lower body of knowledge depending on its content (independent of anybody's body of knowledge), and its probability (which will be the same for both A and B), the contents of the body of knowledge of level p for both A and B will agree, contrary to our hypothesis.

Now of course two scientists A and B do not have identical bodies of knowledge: scientist A knows he had scrambled eggs for breakfast, and scientist B is ignorant of this fact. There are a vast number of bits of data — and induced propositions — that are part of A's body of knowledge that are not part of B's body of knowledge. What is required of a global approach to induction is not that A and B should be forced into epistemological conformity in *all* respects, but (a) that, assuming they have agreed to share data, without which science is impossible, they should be forced into agreement in all *relevant* respects — i.e., in all respects that have a bearing on the arguments concerning the probability of the inductive conclusion at issue, and (b) that there should be no *a priori* constraints as to what is potentially relevant. It may turn out that what scientist

A had for breakfast *is* a bit of relevant data; but if it is relevant, its relevance will come out in the dialectic regarding randomness, and, as a piece of data, it will come out shared. Nor does this approach eliminate the role of intuitions and good guesses. Choice of a local research program—how we shall go about finding out about *X*—is often a matter of lucky guesses. Within a general paradigm, it may be possible to find patterns of discovery, to provide arguments supporting one program of research as against another. But within a shared language and shared data, it should not be an open question whether or not a given inductive conclusion is probable, or whether it is acceptable at a given level of practical certainty.

VI. CONCLUSIONS

Philosophical work that has oriented itself toward problems of local induction has shed little light on inductive inference. The premises required for demonstrative induction have been phrased wiht excessive generality by philosophers (e.g., 'The set *S* includes a necessary and sufficient condition for *E*'), with the result that there are no real-life instances of demonstrative induction in which very much more specific and limited (and powerful) premises are not acceptable. The search for generality here has led away from realism and from relevance. With respect to probabilistic induction, philosophical treatments have suffered from even more serious defects. To the extent that local probabilistic inductions can be put into the frameworks provided by various philosophical approaches, they presuppose the very fundamental agreement that they should be capable of engendering: they require that opinions not differ too much (subjectivism) or that background knowledge not be at issue (objectivism). To the extent that these conditions are not satisfied—as they will not be in controversial instances of inductive argument—the local philosophical theories must be capable of being broadened. A theory which was capable of being broadened in all respects and without limit would be a global theory. Thus a local theory will be either redundant and unnecessary (when everybody is agreed that the inductive conclusion follows from the evidence for it, 'conclusion', 'follows', and 'evidence' being construed broadly enough to include the case that the 'conclusion' is a certain degree of belief in the hypotheses, the 'evidence' is a set of degrees of belief in other statements, and the 'following' consists in adherence to coherence and a principle of belief change) or it will be impotent to resolve disagreements (when our prior degrees of belief differ too much, or when our background knowledge differs to the extent that the objectivistic test appropriate to your circumstances differs from the objectivistic test appropriate to mine).

Different local theories are capable in different degrees and different ways of being broadened in the face of controversy or disagreement. To the extent that they are capable of that broadening, they approach global theories. Levi, though the earliest proponent of local approaches to induction, himself provides an approach that is relatively capable of arbitrary broadening. (His set of 'answers' to the 'problem' can be indefinitely expanded.) This suggests that the ultimate desideratum is, after all, a global theory of induction. Furthermore the global theories that have been proposed have contributed as much or more to the solution of local problems as those theories that are avowedly local. Thus the approach of Reichenbach, developed further by Salmon, has helped to focus attention on the problem of the choice of a reference class, which is fundamental and controversial in a wide range of local problems. The approach of Carnap, originally global in intent, helped to focus attention on the role of languages — again something highly relevant to the discussion of local problems of induction.

A theory of global induction seems to be required in order to avoid the dilemma that faces theories of local induction: irrelevance or impotence. But a plausible theory of global induction must be tied up intimately with an epistemology. There are a host of problems here, of course; but the artificial and technical ones contemplated by theorists of local induction are not among them.

NOTES

1. Isaac Levi, *Gambling with Truth*, Knopf, New York, 1967, p. 6.

2. *Ibid.*, p. 4.

3. K. Lehrer, 'Induction: A Consistent Gamble', *Nous* 3 (1969), pp. 285-297; 'Induction, Reason, and Consistency', *British Journal for the Philosophy of Science* 21 (1970), pp. 103-114; and elsewhere.

4. I. Niiniluoto and R. Tuomela, *Theoretical Concepts and Hypothetico-Inductive Inference*, Reidel, Dordrecht, 1973, p. 18.

5. It was discussed in my old paper 'Demonstrative Induction', *Philosophy and Phenomenological Research* 21 (1960), pp 80-92; a similar example is used by Niiniluoto and Tuomela, *Theoretical Concepts*, p. 240.

6. R. Hilpinen and J. Hintikka, 'Knowledge, Acceptance and Inductive Logic', in Hintikka and Suppes (eds.), *Aspects of Inductive Logic*, North Holland, Amsterdam, 1966, pp. 1-20.

7. Levi, *Gambling with Truth*.

8. Lehrer, "Induction."

9. H. Kyburg, *The Logical Foundations of Statistical Inference*, Reidel, Dordrecht, 1974, Chapter 15.

10. *Ibid.*

11. This is perhaps not intuitively clear. For more detail see pp. 224 and 366 of *Logical Foundations*.

12. This possibly cryptic characterization will perhaps be elucidated by an example to be considered shortly; the circumstances in question are characterized explicitly and in detail in *Logical Foundations*.

13. See, e.g., D. V. Lindley, *Introduction to Probability and Statistics*, Vol. 2, Cambridge University Press, Cambridge, 1965. p. 2.

Part V. Theory and Generalization

17

How to Make Up a Theory

It is now a commonplace that if you begin with a theory meeting certain requirements of explicitness, you can replace it by another theory which has precisely the same observational consequences as the original theory, but which avoids reference to any 'theoretical' terms. Like all commonplaces, this one deserves to be challenged once in a while. How do you go about getting this "other" theory, it may be asked? It is perfectly true, one may admit, that Craig's interpolation theorem shows how to replace a *theory*, with a set of theoretical terms, with internal structure, with mixed sentences containing both observational terms and theoretical terms, by a recursively axiomatizable "theory" that involves only observation terms, and that is observationally equivalent to the original theory, in the sense that all and only those statements expressed in observational terms alone that are consequences of the original theory are consequences of the truncated theory. But this is not to say that you could have a different *theory*, with a different structure and different primitive terms, which would have the same observational consequences. And one might even issue the challenge: it has never been done; what reason have we to believe that it can be done if it hasn't ever been done? In what follows I shall give a recipe for constructing a theory for a given observational domain, observationally equivalent to a given theory, which exhibits your favorite theoretical structure and employs as theoretical terms your favorite theoretical terms.

Let T be the first theory, represented as a sextuple $\langle L_O, L_T, L_{TO}, A_O, A_T, A_{TO} \rangle$, where L_O is the observation language—that is, the set of sentences employing the observational vocabulary only; L_T is the theoretical language; L_{TO} is the mixed language containing both L_O and L_T, as well as sentences employing terms of both vocabularies. A_O is the set of axioms (if any) involving only observational terms; A_T is the set of theoretical axioms; and A_{TO} is the set of bridge axioms or coordinating definitions or reduction sentences—what you will—that provide the connection between theoretical predicates and observation predi-

Reprinted from *The Philosophical Review*, no. 87 (1978), pp. 84-87, by permission of the publisher.

cates. Clearly $A_O \in L_O$ $A_T \in L_T$, and $A_{TO} \in L_{TO} - L_O - L_T$. Since the logic of the theory is rarely at issue, we shall suppose that the logic of the theory is standard first-order logic. The observational content of the theory is the set of sentences Cn_{L_O} (T)— the set of consequences of the axioms of T that are in the observational language L_O. We suppose, of course, that A_T, the set of theoretical axioms, A_O, the set of observational axioms, A_{TO}, the set of mixed axioms that provide connections between the observational vocabulary and the theoretical vocabulary, the theoretical vocabulary itself, L_T, and the observational vocabulary L_O are recursive, we must be able to tell one part of the vocabulary from the other, and we must be able to tell an axiom from other sorts of sentences. We suppose the theory to be consistent.

Let L_{T*} be your favorite theoretical language, and let A_{T*} be the set of axioms that attributes your favorite (consistent) theoretical structure to the entities referred to by this vocabulary. We shall construct a theory $T^* = \langle L_O,$ $L_{T*}, L_{T*O}, A_O, A_{T*}, A_{T*O} \rangle$ having the same observational vocabulary and the same observational axioms as our original theory, and whose observational consequences are the same as those of the original theory. Furthermore, it will be a theory in which the theoretical language L_{T*} and axioms A_{T*} play an *essential role* in the derivation of observational consequences, so long as the same is true of the original theory.

Step I: Construct the Craigian axiomatization of the observational consequences of T. (The Gödel numbers of proof of statements in the vocabulary L_O are recursive enumerable; we take as axioms all theorems of the form $S \wedge S \wedge$ . . . $\wedge S$, where S is a sentence of L_O, and the number n of conjuncts in the conjunction is the Gödel number of a proof in T of S.) We order these axioms by the number of conjuncts. We may thus represent these axioms as an infinite recursive enumerable sequence $[0_i]_{i<\omega}$.

Step II: Construct the Craigian axiomatization of the theoretical consequences of A_{T*}; order them in the same way, and represent them as the infinite recursive enumerable sequence $[T^*_i]_i [I_i^*]_{i<\omega}$.

Step III: Adopt as bridge principles, coordinating definitions, or what-have-you, the infinite recursive enumerable set of statements:

$$[\ulcorner T_i \to 0_i \urcorner]_{i<\omega}.$$

We now assert that T^* has the desired properties.

(a) $Cn_{L_{T*}}(A_{T*})$ has just the vocabulary and structure we wanted. Obvious.

(b) $Cn_{L_O}(T^*) = C_{L_O}(T)$. Suppose that S is an observational consequence of T. Let N be the Gödel number of a proof of S. Then for some i, there will be a Craig axiom 0^*_i of the form $S \wedge S \wedge$ . . . $\wedge S$, where the conjunction contains N conjuncts. The i'th bridge axiom of T^* is $\ulcorner T^*_i \to 0^*_i \urcorner$ where T^*_i is an M-termed conjunction, M being the Gödel number of a proof of a theorem t from the axioms A_{T*}. Thus we can obtain a proof of t in T^*, and thus a proof of an M-fold conjunction each of whose conjuncts is t, and thus (via the ith bridge axiom) a proof of $O_i{}^*$, and thus, by simplificlation, a proof of S.

We now show that if S is an observational consequence of T^* it is also an observational consequence of T. Suppose that $L_T \cap L_{T^*} = \phi$ (if not, we may achieve this end by judicious rewriting). Let E be the expanded language containing the theoretical terms of both T and T^*. A proof in T^* of S is a proof of S in the expanded language E from premises $A_O \cup A_{T^*} \cup A_{T^*O}$. The members of A_{T^*O} are provable from premises $A_O \cup A_T \cup A_{TO}$ in the expanded language, since they have the form of conditionals whose consequents are theorems of theory T. Thus in E

$$A_O \cup A_T \cup A_{TO} \cup A_{T^*} \vdash S$$

Since we assume an ordinary underlying logic, we have therefore, for some finite $K \in A_{T^*}$

$$A_O \cup A_T \cup A_{TO} \vdash \ulcorner K \to S \urcorner$$

Since $K \in L_{T^*}$ and $L_{T^*} \cap (L_T \cup L_O \cup L_{TO}) = \phi$ this can only happen (by the soundness of our logic) if $\vdash \ulcorner \sim K \urcorner$ or $A_O \cup A_T \cup A_{TO} \vdash S$. Since we have assumed that T^* is consistent, the latter must be the case. The observational consequences of T^* are, therefore, just the observational consequences of T.

(c) The theoretical structure of T^* is essential to the derivation of observational consequences of T^*. Of course we can replace T^* by a Craigian form of theory with new axioms that will yield exactly the observational theorems of T^*, but we could do that with T, too. In T^* as it stands, however, we need the axioms A_{T^*} in order to derive any observational theorems that are not consequences of A_O alone. The theoretical structure of T^* is just as essential to the derivation of observational results as the theoretical structure of T.

There are several lessons to be learned from this trivial exercise. First, it is possible to construct a *theory* (not mrely a list of observation sentences) which will have the same observational consequences as an old theory, and which will embody an interesting and relevant theoretical structure.[1]

Second, it has been argued by many authors that one of the factors on the basis of which we choose between theories is the simplicity of their respective theoretical structures. Since, however, we can design a theory that has given observational consequences, and an arbitrary and thus arbitrarily "simple" theoretical structure, this approach seems wrong. In particular, there seems to be little point in looking for measures of theoretical simplicity. If simplicity is to be a factor in our choice among theories, it must take account not only of the theoretical structure itself, but also of the "bridge principles" that tie the theoretical vocabulary to the observational vocabulary.

Third, other authors have argued that the intelligibility and coherence of the theoretical structure should guide our choice between theories. Again, such considerations cannot be focused merely on the purely theoretical structure of the theory, but must take account of the "bridge principles" as well.

Fourth, we cannot judge the explanatory excellence of a theory by attending to the theoretical structure only; we must consider not only A_T, but also A_{TO} — the sentences that connect theoretical and observational terms.

Fifth, since in point of fact we can and do choose between theories, and do so on rational grounds according to all scientists and most commentators on science, principles of choice should be sought that involve the bridge principles as well as the purely theoretical principles of the theory. Indeed, it may be that it is the bridge principles that should be the focus of our attention. It is these principles that we need in order to pass from the world of ordinary experience to the theoretical realm, and in order to pass from the theoretical realm back to the world of ordinary experience. As any scientist or engineer will readily admit, both transitions are fraught with potentials for error. Perhaps a crucial guide to the choice between theoretical structures is to be found in the simplicity and accuracy of the largely statistical connections between observations and theoretical assertions.

NOTE

1. We have considered the theory by itself; if we consider consequences whose derivation involves "auxiliary hypotheses" that provide connections between the theory under consideration and theories from related domains, the equivalence, of course, will not hold. It seems likely, though, that by making some assumptions about these "auxiliary hypotheses" and at the cost of some added complications, we could handle this situation as well.

18

An Interpolation Theorem
for Inductive Relations

Theorem: Let L be a language with a theoretical vocabulary V_T and an observational vocabulary V_B; let P be a conditional logical probability function defined on pairs of sentences of L. Let T be a conjunction of theoretical axioms and correspondence statements (or an interpretive system), and let O_1, O_2, and E be statements employing only the observational vocabulary. Then, if the probability of O_2 is high relative to O_1, E, and T, and if O_1 does not undermine the acceptance or high probability of T, the probability of O_2 relative to accepted evidential statements *in the observational vocabulary alone* will be at least as high. The theory T, whether accepted or merely highly probable, will not enable us to stretch the import of our observational evidence insofar as it bears on other observation statements.

This is not a very surprising result, when you stop to think about it, but it conflicts with the opinions of a number of writers with regard to the role of theoretical terms in inductive systematization.[1] Most of these writers have supposed that inductive relations can be captured with the help of a measure function defined (à la Carnap or Hintikka) over a formal language. The question of the treatment of theories is more complicated. According to some writers, theories are rendered probable by the evidence in their favor, but are never "accepted." According to others, theories do come to be accepted, either on the basis of high probability, on the basis of high probability combined with other factors, or on the basis of other factors alone, without high probability being required. We assume here that, whatever the mechanism of its acceptance, once a theory has been accepted it has a probability of unity, relative to the corpus of data on the basis of which it was accepted. Thus if E represents the background data that, by whatever means, authorizes the acceptance of the theory T, we suppose that $P(T/E) = 1$. We leave open the question of whehter T is "added" to E. I am unclear as to what it would mean to "accept" T, while at the same time assigning a low probability to it. I assume that this case can be handled in the

With apologies to Professor William Craig; reprinted from the *Journal of Philosophy*, no. 75 (1978), pp. 93-98, by permission of the publisher.

same way as the "high-probability case. (See Lemma 4 and the comment appended thereto, recalling that nobody said that ϵ and δ *have* to be small.) We also suppose that the observation statement O_1 does not undermine this relation. When we assume that theories may be rendered probable, but need not be accepted, we suppose that the addition of O_1 to the evidence does not decrease the conditional probability of T. This is the background, then: we assume a logical probability function; we assume that theories either are rendered highly probable or are accepted under certain circumstances, and that when they are accepted they are assigned probability 1.

It has been claimed (by the writers mentioned in note 1, among other) that, although Craig's theorem shows that a theory cannot provide *deductive* systematization, it is possible that a theory can provide *inductive* systematization that cannot be provided by sentences of the observation language alone.

There are several interpretations of this claim. The claim may be:

(1) The theory T is accepted in the light of observational evidence E. O_1 is added to our evidence E. T and O_1 entail O_2. Therefore O_2 may be rendered more probable (and thus also more acceptable) by the evidence E and O_1 through the deductive agency of the accepted theory T than it would be otherwise.

(2) The theory T is taken as probable relative to our evidence E, and at least as probable relative to the combined evidence E and O_1. O_1 is added to our evidence E. T and O_1 entail O_2. Therefore O_2 may be rendered more probable by the evidence E and O_1 through the deductive agency of the probable theory T than it would be otherwise.

(3) The theory T is accepted in the light of the observational evidence E. O_1 is added to our evidence E. O_2 is probable (perhaps even acceptable) relative to T and E and O_1. Therefore O_2 may be rendered more probable (or acceptable) by the evidence E and O_1 through the inductive agency of the accepted theory T than it would be otherwise.

(4) The theory T is taken as probable relative to our evidence E, and at least as probable relative to the combined evidence E and O_1. O_1 is added to our evidence E. O_2 is probable relative to T and E and O_1. Therefore O_2 may be rendered more probable by the evidence E and O_1 through the inductive agency of the probable theory T than it would be otherwise.

What we require in the way of machinery from the probability calculus are the following principles:

(A) If $e \vdash \ulcorner w \rightarrow s \urcorner$, then $P(w/e) \leqslant P(s/e)$

(B) $P(\ulcorner w \wedge s \urcorner /e) = P(w/e) \times P(s/\ulcorner w \wedge e \urcorner)$

(C) If $e \vdash w$, then $P(w/e) = 1$

Lemma 1: Claim 1 is false.

Formal statement of claim (1): It is possible that

$$P(T/E) = P(T/\ulcorner E \wedge O_1 \urcorner) = 1 \qquad (T \text{ is accepted and continues to be accepted.})$$

$T, O_1 \vdash O_2$ (T and O_1 entail O_2.)

$P(O_2/\ulcorner T \wedge E \wedge O_1 \urcorner) = 1$ (Therefore, the probability of O_2 given T, E, and O_1 is high.)

$P(O_2/\ulcorner E \wedge O_1 \urcorner) < 1$ (But the probability of O_2 on E and O_1 is not high.)

Refutation of claim (1):

   (i)   Assume first three clauses.

   (ii) $P(O_2/\ulcorner E \wedge O_1 \urcorner) \geqslant P(\ulcorner O_2 \wedge T \urcorner / \ulcorner E \wedge O_1 \urcorner)$ by (A)

   (iii) $P(\ulcorner O_2 \wedge T \urcorner / \ulcorner E \wedge O_1 \urcorner) = P(T/\ulcorner O_1 \wedge E \urcorner) \times P(O_2/\ulcorner E \wedge O_1 \wedge T \urcorner)$ by (B)

   (iv) $P(O_2/\ulcorner E \wedge O_1 \wedge T \urcorner) = 1$ by (C) and (i)

   (v) $P(O_2/\ulcorner E \wedge O_1 \urcorner) = 1$ by (i), (iii), and (iv)

Lemma 2: Claim (2) is false.

Formal statement of claim (2): It is possible that

$P(T/\ulcorner E \wedge O_1 \urcorner) = 1 - \epsilon$ (The probability of T on E and O_1 is high.)

$T, O_1 \vdash O_2$ (T and O_1 entail O_2.)

$P(O_2/\ulcorner T \wedge E \wedge O_1 \urcorner) = 1$ (Therefore, the probability of O_2 on T, E, and O_1 is high.)

$P(O_2/\ulcorner E \wedge O_1 \urcorner) < 1 - \epsilon$ (But the probability of O_2 on E and O_1 is not high.)

Refutation of claim (2):

   (i)   Assume first three clauses.

   (ii) $O_1 \vdash \ulcorner T \wedge O_2 \leftrightarrow T \urcorner$ by (i)

   (iii) $P(T/\ulcorner E \wedge O_1 \urcorner) = P(\ulcorner T \wedge O_2 \urcorner / \ulcorner E \wedge O_1 \urcorner)$ by (A) and (ii)

   (iv) $P(O_2/\ulcorner E \wedge O_1 \urcorner) \geqslant P(\ulcorner T \wedge O_2 \urcorner / \ulcorner E \wedge O_1 \urcorner)$ by (A)

   (v) $P(O_2/\ulcorner E \wedge O_1 \urcorner) \geqslant 1 - \epsilon$ by (i), (iii), and (iv)

Comment: Of course the probability of O_2 relative to E and O_1 may be less than the probability of O_2 relative to the theory and the observational evidence; but remember that T itself has only probability $1 - \epsilon$, so we haven't got anywhere using T if the probability of O_2 is *already* more than $1 - \epsilon$. For a more detailed consideration of these matters, see the comment following the proof of Lemma 4.

Lemma 3: Claim (3) is false.

Formal statement of claim (3): It is possible that

$P(T/\ulcorner E \wedge O_1 \urcorner) = 1$ (T is accepted.)

$P(O_2/\ulcorner T \wedge E \wedge O_1 \urcorner) = 1 - \epsilon$ (O_2 is probable, given T and the evidence.)

$P(O_2/\ulcorner E \wedge O_1 \urcorner) < 1 - \epsilon$ (But O_2 is not so probable without T.)

Refutation of claim (3):

   (i)   Assume first two clauses.

(ii) $P(\ulcorner O_2 \wedge \bar{T}\urcorner / \ulcorner E \wedge O_1\urcorner) = P(T/\ulcorner E \wedge O_1\urcorner) \times P(O_2/\ulcorner E \wedge O_1 \wedge \bar{T}\urcorner)$ by (B)

(iii) $P(\ulcorner O_2 \wedge \bar{T}\urcorner / \ulcorner E \wedge O_1\urcorner) = 1 - \epsilon$ by (ii) and (i)

(iv) $P(O_2/\ulcorner E \wedge O_1\urcorner) \geqslant 1 - \epsilon$ by (iii) and (A)

Lemma 4: Claim (4) is false.

Formal statement of claim (4): It is possible that

$P(T/\ulcorner E \wedge O_1\urcorner) = 1 - \delta$ (T is probable, relative to the evidence.)

$P(O_2/\ulcorner E \wedge O_1 \wedge \bar{T}\urcorner) = 1 - \epsilon$ (O_2 is probable, relative to the theory and the evidence.)

$P(O_2/\ulcorner E \wedge O_1\urcorner) < (1 - \epsilon)(1 - \delta)$ (But O_2 is not probable relative to the evidence alone.)

Refutation of claim (4):

(i)   Assume first two clauses.

(ii) $P(\ulcorner O_2 \wedge \bar{T}\urcorner / \ulcorner E \wedge O_1\urcorner) = P(T/\ulcorner E \wedge O_1\urcorner) \times P(O_2/\ulcorner T \wedge E \wedge O_1\urcorner)$ by (B)

(iii) $P(\ulcorner O_2 \wedge \bar{T}\urcorner / \ulcorner E \wedge O_1\urcorner) = (1 - \epsilon)(1 - \delta)$ by (i) and (ii)

(iv) $P(O_2/\ulcorner E \wedge O_1\urcorner) \geqslant (1 - \epsilon)(1 - \delta)$ by (iii) and (A)

Comment: As in the case of claim (2), the probability of O_2 relative to the observational evidence alone may be less than the probability of O_2 relative to the evidence and theory conjoined. But since T itself has only probability $(1 - \delta)$, the latter probability $-(1 - \epsilon)-$ could clearly not be taken as legislative for our belief in O_2. The most natural thing to do is to take our belief in O_2, given the observational evidence and the high probability of the theory, to be the probability of O_2 relative to the assumption of the theory and the evidence, multiplied by the high probability of the theory relative to the evidence. This is the way I have interpreted claim (4) above. An alternative way of looking at the matter is the following: Our belief in O_2 may be higher than the product just mentioned: it will be the sum of the proability of O_2 relative to the assumption of T, multiplied by the probability of T, *plus* the probability of O_2 relative to the assumption of the denial of T, multiplied by the probability of the denial of T. That is, it will be:

$$P(O_2/\ulcorner T \wedge E \wedge O_1\urcorner) \times P(T/\ulcorner E \wedge O_1\urcorner) + P(O_2/\ulcorner \sim T \wedge E \wedge O_1\urcorner) \times P(\ulcorner \sim \bar{T}\urcorner / \ulcorner E \wedge O_1\urcorner)$$

But since, of course, this is just the same as

$$P(\ulcorner O_2 \wedge \bar{T}\urcorner / \ulcorner E \wedge O_1\urcorner) + P(\ulcorner O_2 \wedge \sim \bar{T}\urcorner / \ulcorner E \wedge O_1\urcorner) = P(O_2/\ulcorner E \wedge O_1\urcorner)$$

the theory T is not much help here, either.

We are now ready to prove the main theorem. Let L be the theoretical language, with vocabulary V_T and V_B of theoretical and observational terms, respectively. Let E, O_1, and O_2 employ only the vocabulary of V_B. Let T_1 be a conjunction of statements not entirely in the vocabulary of V_B which have probability 1 relative to E and O_1. (Note that we are perfectly free to let T_1

employ, and even include as fragments if we want, some statements in the vocabulary V_B. Let T_δ be a finite statement, not entirely in the vocabulary of V_B, whose probability relative to E and O_1 is $1 - \delta$. Again, we need not worry about having bits of the language V_B mixed in. Then

$$P(O_2 / \ulcorner E \wedge O_1 \urcorner) \geqslant P(O_2 / \ulcorner E \wedge T_1 \wedge O_1 \urcorner) \quad \text{(Lemmas 1 and 3)}$$

$$P(O_2 / \ulcorner E \wedge O_1 \urcorner) \geqslant P(O_2 / \ulcorner E \wedge T_1 \wedge T_\delta \urcorner) \times P(T_\delta / \ulcorner E \wedge O_1 \urcorner) \quad \text{(Lemmas 2 and 4)}$$

The probabilities we compute in the observational language alone are at least as high as those we get when we compute our probabilities in the whole language L and attempt to take advantage of a helpful theory T.

So much, one might think, for the helpfulness of theoretical terms.

Alternatively, this theorem might be construed as an argument, not against the thesis that theoretical terms provide inductive systematization, but against the notion that inductive systematization can be explicated by reference to probabilities related to logical measures. And of course we might conclude *both* that theoretical terms are unnecessary, *and* that logical measures are no help in explicating inductive notions.[2]

NOTES

1. For example, C. G. Hempel, "The Theoretician's Dilemma," in Feigl and Scriven, eds., *Minnesota Studies in the Philosophy of Science*, II (Minneapolis: Minnesota Press, 1956), pp. 37-98; I. Scheffler, *The Anatomy of Inquiry* (New York: Knopf, 1969), part II; K. Lehrer, "Theoretical Terms and Inductive Inference," *American Philosophical Quarterly*, Monograph Series 3, pp. 30-41. Carnap himself, in "Replies," P. S. Schilpp, ed., *The Philosophy of Rudolf Carnap* (LaSalle, Ill.: Open Court, 1963), p. 962, expresses explicit agreement with Hempel's treatment of inductive systematization. Most of those who have followed Hempel's lead have supposed that inductive relations can be captured with the help of a Carnapian measure function. Even if acceptance is taken to require more than high probability (in the logical sense), no one has proposed that evidence which increases the logical probability of a statement can decrease its acceptability, other things being equal; and that is all that need concern us here.

2. Largely as a matter of faith, so far, I think a case can be made for the significance of theoretical terms, on the basis of probabilistic considerations. It is a case that rejects the Carnapian notion of probability, in favor of a quite different logical notion, and takes theories to be characterized in crucial respects by their accompanying theories of error. But the story is much too long for a footnote.

19

All Acceptable Generalizations Are Analytic

1. INTRODUCTION

According to my data, the probability is the interval (0.99, 1.0) that between 95% and 98% of introductory philosophy courses mention the statement "All generalizations are false." So far as I know, relatively few people have observed that all general truths are analytic, including that one. (That is, non-observational generalizations: "There are no elephants in this room," need not be taken as analytic.) But it is a thesis that has interesting consequences; among other things it entails that all our fancy theories in physics, biology, chemistry, sociology, psychology, if they are construed as universal generalizations, are completely without content: without observational content, without theoretical content, without any content at all. Furthermore, it enormously simplifies the problem of induction: if generalizations are analytic, their probability is unity, and any evidence whatever will serve to confirm them to the maximum degree. The constraint on explanation, that the theoretical premises be true, becomes satisfied automatically, since all generalizations and theories will turn out to be true. I am sure one could go on indefinitely citing the interesting and valuable consequences of the thesis that all acceptable generalizations are analytic.

The only cloud that looms on the horizon is the doubt that the thesis is true. (Note that it is not self-certifying in the sense that "All generalizations are false" is self-refuting.) It requires a certain amount of argument to see that it is true; analytic though it be, it is not one of your self-evident analyticities.

Let us make the thesis a bit more precise. Consider any first-order language appropriate to a certain body of scientific knowledge. Let a body of knowledge be construed simply as a set of statements in this language. (1) Certain statements come to be accepted into this body of knowledge on the basis of what happens to us. In a certain sense we can *observe* that these statements are true. (2) Certain other statements will become acceptable on the basis of statistical inference. We have in our body of knowledge a set of data representing observa-

Reprinted from *American Philosophical Quarterly*, no. 14 (1977), pp. 201-210, by permission of the publisher.

tions. These statements support a statistical hypothesis so strongly that it becomes (in a slightly weaker sense) also acceptable. It is statements of these two sorts that I shall take to represent the empirical content of our knowledge. (3) And then there are the scientific statements most people mostly consider: simple universal generalizations. "All samples of table salt are soluble," "Yellow phosphorus melts at 42 degrees centigrade," "All whales are mammals," "All creatures with hearts have kidneys," and of course, "All ravens are black." These statements, I shall maintain, are analytic. (4) Finally, we have the crowning glories of the sciences, theoretical systems: relativity theory, quantum mechanics, genetic theory, and so on. These, especially, I shall maintain are barefacedly analytic.

To defend this thesis, and to show that even if true it does not constitute a massive reduction to triviality of our most cherished beliefs, requires that we attend to each of these kinds of statements in turn, as well as to two other matters. One of these matters is, of course, the notion of analyticity I have in mind. The other is the notion of error. We shall then look briefly at some of the ways in which the thesis might provide a new focus for certain problems in the philosophy of science.

2. OBSERVATION STATEMENTS

It is traditional to divide the vocabulary of the first-order language I mentioned into an observational part and a theoretical part, and (usually) to suppose that we can come to know, without inference and with absolute certainty, certain of the statements expressed in the observation language. I shall make an assumption that is somewhat weaker, but roughly within this tradition. I shall assume that within our formal language, we can provide a recursive characterization of a set O of statements that are *potentially* capable of being accepted on the basis of observation. I recognize that scientific languages change, and one of the ways in which they can change is by an alteration in the membership of O. Whereas in one language one might simply observe the motion of the sun, in another one might only be able to observe the *apparent* motion of the sun (thereby opening the possibility of the question as to whether or not it *really* moves). It is obvious that we come to accept a lot of the statements of O, not on the basis of what happens to us, but on the basis of inference from other statements we accept, on the basis of reliable authority, and so on. Note that O itself is the set of all *potentially* acceptable observation statements: thus it contains contraries such as "the next rose I see is red" and "the next rose I see is yellow." The point of singling out this set of statements is to contrast them with statements that we cannot properly be said to know directly on the basis of our experience, such as "Half the draws from this urn yield a black ball," "Three quarters of the peas produced by such and such a cross have red flowers," "All creatures with hearts are creatures with kidneys," "All ravens are black," and "$f = ma$."

In one way I depart from tradition, though perhaps only slightly, and perhaps not from the intent of the founders of the tradition. That is, I shall not assume that when we come to know these statements in *0*, we come to know them with absolute certainty. This relieves us of *some* of the burdens of trying to justify the selection of a particular set of statements to be put in *0*, and also relieves us of some of the traditional problems of epistemology. This is not the place for me to develop or defend a foundationalist epistemology which eschews certainty, but I will mention one typical problem that leads me in this direction. When a person looks at a penny, unless he is a philosopher he will see that it is round. This is certainly true of a naive subject who has no theory of vision, no notion of the rectilinear path of light rays, no projective geometry, to tell him that the pattern on his retina is elliptical. Indeed, were such a subject to claim to see an ellipse, he would be making a mistaken claim; what he *ought* to say he sees, and what (almost) every such person sees, is a round penny. Now of course he may also be mistaken in the traditional way: that is, he may think it is a round penny he is seeing, when in fact it is a trick elliptical penny. In the real world he won't make that mistake very often, but the possibility is there. So philosophers enamoured of certainty, and, more important, who are in possession of a whole presumably empirical theory of vision, will attempt to save the certainty of observation by saying that he does not *observe* the roundness of the penny, but rather *observes* the elliptical character of its projection, and makes an unconscious (and possibly erroneous) inference to its circularity. We are thus led to replace a simple observation (that the penny is round) with an unconscious observation (that the projection of the penny is elliptical) that is not even accessible to the naive subject until he learns a whole theory of light and vision, and then combine this unconscious observation with an unconscious inference which may not even be truth-preserving! There may be good reasons for doing this (though I don't know them), but it certainly seems worthwhile to start from the outset by accepting the principle that even observation statements may be in error, that we can accept observation statements on the basis of what happens to us, but that we need not suppose that they are incorrigible.

This approach imposes on us an obligation to have a theory of acceptability and a theory of error. We shall consider theories of error in a little while. As for acceptability, we need not go into very great detail, but we should say a few things. I shall take acceptability to be related to *moral certainty* and *practical certainty*, in the following rather technical senses. A statement is morally certain for me, if there is no more than a tiny chance that it will turn out to be in error. What is a tiny chance? That could be taken as a matter of context; I shall suppose that moral certainty can be indexed by a number close to 1, whose exact value can depend on the context. Thus for ordinary purposes I can be morally certain that I am now before my desk; but if the fate of the world were at issue, I might limit my moral certainties to "seeming" statements, and see how strong an argument I can construct on that basis in favor of the proposition that I am before my desk. Practical certainty is a weaker notion: a statement may be practically certain just in case it has a small (as opposed to tiny) chance of being wrong. I suppose that some observation statements are so well supported by what happens to me that they are moral certainties for me. I suppose that other observation statements are well supported, so that I may accept them as practically certain, without their being so well supported as to be morally certain.[1] In addition, there are statements so probable, relative to my body of moral certainties, as to be practically certain, even though they are not "observation" statements.

I have already said that the population of O depends on the state of our scientific art, and thus changes through time. But just to give some idea of what, in ordinary contexts at least, we take to be observation statements, they might include such statements as: "There is a table before me," "The penny is round," "The dial reads 10.3," "The current is turned on," "This object is longer than that object," "The scale reads 5.8 grams," "Tom is angry," "There is a cat on the roof," etc. They are to be contrasted with: "The table is a complex structure of cellulose molecules," "The penny is composed mainly of a metal of atomic number 29," "There is a current of 10.3 amperes flowing in the apparatus," "Electrons are flowing through the apparatus," "This object is 3.20 meters long," "This object weighs 5.8 grams," "Tom is suffering from an Oedipus complex," "The cat on the roof is suffering from enteritis."

These statements—the observation statements—all have empirical content in an obvious sense. If I come to accept one of them, I thereby cut down the worlds which are possible relative to what I accept. If I accept it on the basis of what has happened to me, it is the world that has done it: my interaction with the world has caused me to accept it. There are a number of problems here, to be sure, and this whole thesis needs to be provided with some epistemological, and maybe some metaphysical underpinnings. But I assume the general idea is relatively clear for present purposes.

3. STATISTICAL STATEMENTS

Suppose that I am morally certain that I have examined a sample of 10,000 draws from an urn, and that 5,891 of them have produced black balls. (I could have miscounted, been the victim of hallucination, and so on—but remember we are talking of moral certainty only, not absolute philosophical certainty.) Under certain circumstances the probability that between 0.54 and 0.64 of the balls drawn from the urn will be black is at least 0.99—more properly, the interval (0.99, 1.0). If we take 0.99 as our level of practical certainty, this means that we could simply accept, in our corpus of practical certainties, the statistical statement: the proportion of black draws from this urn lies between 0.54 and 0.64. This is an example of what I mean by a statistical statement; it is the sort of statement we can accept as a practical certainty; it is a statement having empirical content. Our bodies of knowledge are full of statements like this: "Roughly half the tosses of coins yield heads;" "Close to 51% of human births are births of males;" and so on.

There are other kinds of statistical statements as well; it is necessary to say something about one other sort, because it will play a large role in our later discussion. Furthermore, although acceptance of statistical statements of this second sort involves no new principles, one principle which we cleverly glossed over in the previous case will come out with clarity and simplicity in this case, and this is a principle which will turn out to have a lot to do with universal generalizations and theories.

In real-life statistics the normal distribution is pervasive. This is due to the fact that there are a lot of quantities that are distributed normally; and that in turn is due to a pair of facts: that a lot of things can be construed as additive mixtures of other things; and as a matter of mathematics, almost all additive mixtures of things are roughly normally distributed. In particular, any sum or average of a large number of identically and independently distributed random quantities will be normally distributed, *regardless* of how the random quantities themselves are distributed.

Let us consider the problem of weighing an object on a beam balance of known sensitivity. We assume that we know the sensitivity and that the balance has no systematic error. The readings we obtain will be normally distributed with a mean equal to the true weight of the object, and a standard deviation which is represented by the known sensitivity. As you know, if we looked at the potential infinite set of readings, and plotted them on a graph, knowing the true value of the weight, t, they would look like this:

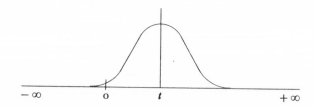

(This familiar bell-shaped curve is referred to as a curve of error, as well as the normal curve.)

Our problem is that we don't know the true weight of our object, and must obtain that from a sample of readings. To keep things very simple, we shall suppose our sample consists of a single reading, r. The set of readings, we noted, was distributed with a mean of t, the true value of the weight, and a standard deviation of d, representing the sensitivity of the balance. It follows (purely analytically) that the distribution of the quantity $(t - r)/d$, or error divided by standard deviation, is distributed normally with a mean of 0 and a standard deviation of 1. This is what is tabulated in all those tables at the backs of textbooks in various sciences. The area under the curve is unity (as was the area under the other curve); and the area between two points a and b is the frequency (loosely speaking) with which we will encounter an error less than b and greater than a.

Let us fix on a probability level, say 0.99. There are a number (a very large number: the number of the continuum) of events that have a probability of 0.99 given that appropriate conditions of randomness are met:

The probability is 0.99 that the reading will not be more than 2.5 standard deviations greater than the true value.

The probability is 0.99 that the reading will not be more than 2.5 standard deviations less than the true value.

The probability is 0.99 that the reading will differ by at least 0.01 standard deviations from the true value.

The probability is 0.99 that the reading will differ from the true value by no more than 2.64 standard deviations.

The probability is 0.99 that the reading will either be greater than the true value, or will be at least 2.4 standard deviations less than the true value.

And so on. There are as many such events as there are ways of finding Borel sets on the real line such that the integral of the normal frequency function (corresponding to area under the curve) over the Borel set is 0.99.

Now we weigh our object, and we get a value V. What do we want to say, what *can* we say, about the true value? With probability 0.99 we can say that the true value is less than $V + 2.5d$; with the same probability we can say that the true value falls *outside* the region $V + 0.01d$; with the same probability we can say that the true value falls inside the interval $V \pm 2.64d$.

We all know which statement of probability 0.99 we are interested in: the last one. Why? It represents what statisticians call a "shortest" confidence interval. Intuitively, it is because it seems to provide more information than the other statements.[2] In this case, the most informative statement is the one that assigns the shortest interval to the possible range of weights of the object. In general, we might accept that statistical statement (remember, assigning the weight to an interval is just another way of characterizing a parameter in the distribution of the results of weighings) which has given probability and which assigns the parameter (which may be multidimensional) to the Borel set in parameter space of smallest Lebesgue measure. In any event (jargon aside) we shall suppose we have some way of picking the most informative (complex) statistical hypothesis from among those equally probable, and that this warrants our accepting such statistical hypotheses in our corpus of practical certainties.

All of these things, in my view, are language dependent. Probability is defined relative to a specified formal language; among the specifications of the language is a recursive characterization of certain terms we take to denote potential reference classes, and a recursive characterization of certain functors we take to denote random quantities, i.e., functions from objects to real numbers or vectors. If we are going to have a general theory of scientific inference, we must therefore either have a way of generating an ideal language (not very likely) or a way of choosing between alternative languages in the case in which we have alternatives to choose between (rather more realistic).

4. UNIVERSAL GENERALIZATIONS

So far we have in our rational corpus of practical certainties some statistical hypotheses, e.g., that between 0.49 and 0.51 of coin tosses result in heads; that the distribution of readings of the weight of this object is normal with a mean between $V - 2.6d$ and $V + 2.6d$ (i.e, the weight of the object lies between these limits); that the mature weight of species X of frogs is normally distributed with a mean between m_1 and m_2 and a standard deviation between d_1 and d_2.

Now let us consider how these statements are used. According to my notion of probability, such statements are ingredients in probability assertions. If we know that between 40% and 60% of A's are B's—that is, if the corresponding statement is a member of our set of practical certainties—and if x is a random member of A with respect to B, relative to what we know, then the probability that x will be a B is the interval (0.4, 0.6). Suppose, as is not unreasonable, that what we know is that between 0.99 and 1.0 of the A's are B's, and that we know this at a level of practical certainty of 0.99. Then if x is a random member of A with respect to B, the probability that it will be a B is (0.99, 1.0). This is perfectly adequate grounds simply to *accept* that x is B in any lower level rational corpus.

Now suppose that for any term x in the whole language, if "$x \in A$" is added to our rational corpus, then either: (1) x is a random member of A with respect to B, relative to that possibly enlarged rational corpus, or (2) it is known already in that rational corpus that x is a member of B. If this is so, then for any term x, if "x is a member of A" is in our rational corpus, "x is a member of B" will be in the rational corpus of any lower level. This is tantamount to either: (1) accepting in the rational corpus of practical certainties, the generalization, "All A's are B's," or (2) adopting as a material rule of inference (a Sellarsian P-rule) for getting from statements in the set of practical certainties to statements in any body of beliefs of lower level: From "x is A," infer "x is B."

It looks as though we are well on our way to a classical reconstruction of scientific inference: we have shown how, in effect at least, a universal generalization can come to be accepted on the basis of enumerative evidence. I used to be more or less persuaded of this, but now I have my doubts. I shall express those doubts in a strong form: the situation described in the preceding paragraphs never happens.

We might say it never happens because all synthetic universal generalizations are false; but this would be a misleading way of putting the matter. A more explicit argument depends on looking more closely at what the observation terms of a language are, and how they are used. Let us suppose first that they are used incorrigibly: then if S is an observation statement (belongs to the set O mentioned earlier), and things happen to our bearer of a rational corpus that lead him to include S in his body of moral certainties, there's an end of the matter, and S is eternally a moral certainty for him. Now if observation statements are used in this way, it is very hard to think of any universal generalizations that don't have exceptions: Bear appearances, for example, are usually, but not always, palpable; they rarely, but sometimes, become person appearances, or disappear altogether. The phenomenal world, if taken seriously, would be a rather spooky place; and the reason it would be spooky is that it is undependable: there are no universal generalizations we can depend on to hold. This is not to say that we could not found our knowledge on statements expressed in such a phenomenological language (nor is it to say that we could: that issue may remain open for the purposes of this argument), but simply that all of our knowledge expressed in those terms would be statistical in character, and would not contain universal generalizations even of the sort described above.

Alternatively, suppose that the observation statements are more ordinary ones: "The cat is black," "The scale reads 10.5," "A is longer than B," and so on. Then it is quite plausible indeed to suppose that we have in our bodies of knowledge universal generalizations relating the terms that appear in these statements: "All samples of table salt are soluble," "All samples of yellow phosphorus under standard conditions melt at 42 degrees C.," "All ravens are black," and so on. But now we can no longer suppose that these terms are used in an error free way. If the right (or wrong) things happen to the bearer of a rational corpus so that he comes to take S to be morally certain, it is always possible that other things may happen to him so that he will withdraw S, or correct it. Thus if our generalizations concern raven appearances and apparent blackness we have at best a rough statistical generalization connecting the terms: a few raven appearances have apparent blueness, a few turn out to be colorless, and so on. If our generalization concerns ravens and blackness, then we cannot (to use the immortal words of John Pollock) *know* a raven when we see one. The claim that something is a raven is corrigible. Here is the crux of the element of novelty in my treatment of observation statements: I suppose that they may be corrigible, and at the same time that we do not need *arguments* to support them. They are directly probable.

Now let us suppose that a person has a lot of statements about A's and B's in his stock of moral certainties, and indeed that he has (rationally) accepted in his body of practical certainties the statement that "practically all A's are B's." He cannot accept the universal generalization, since there are also statements in his body of moral certainties to the effect that *this* A is not a B, and *that* A is not a B, and perhaps a few more. These statements are not incorrigible; we assume that circumstances may arise when they must be rejected. What circumstances? We have a possible candidate right to hand: we are on the verge of a nice universal generalization, which we could accept, were it not for these troublesome counter-examples. To accept the generalization *requires* interpreting the counter-examples as erroneous, and expunging them from our stock of moral certainties. And is this not precisely the hallmark of analytic truths? — that in the face of counter-examples we are committed to regarding the counter-examples as erroneous? So what we can do is make a language shift: regard the terms *A* and *B* to be connected analytically, by virtue of their meanings, come what may (as long as we continue using that language), and to take the judgments we make about *A*'s and *B*'s to be subject to error.

In point of fact, this approach is not so very novel. I have spared you footnotes so far, but it will be worthwhile mentioning here two other writers. Wilfrid Sellars,[3] says that one of the things that may happen when we find a lot of Φ that are Ψ, and no exceptions, is to decide to adopt the material move from "*x* is Φ" to "*x* is Ψ" and to reflect this decision by using the modal, "Φ's are necessarily Ψ's." "This constitutes, of course, an enrichment of the conceptual meanings of 'Φ' and 'Ψ'." Robert Binkley,[4] considers the possible charge of equivocation, if it is argued that when we accept a generalization we change the meanings of the terms involved: the evidence is expressed in old meanings, and the generalization in new meanings. But no equivocation occurs. "When Jones seeks to justify his lawlike statement to Smith . . . he does so by trying to convince Smith that they both have reason to want to change the use of language . . . [to] do as good a job as possible of explaining and predicting what goes on in the world." [p. 73] When one considers that in point of fact when one does accept a generalization, it is often the case that there *are* (in the old terms) exceptions, the change-of-meaning gambit seems very realistic.

What is lacking in these accounts — and in any accounts that I know of — is a treatment of the arguments that Jones might *rationally* employ to convince Smith that he has a *good reason* to change his language. In the case of theories (as opposed to simple generalizations) Kuhn and Feyerabend seem to deny that there can be rational arguments. We shall return to this issue — and to Kuhn and Feyerabend — in due course.

Meanwhile, when we accept it as analytic that all *A*'s are *B*'s, what has happened to all that evidence we collected? What has happened to the empirical content of our body of knowledge? Should we throw our notebooks away? Surely we cannot regard that evidence as supporting a generalization that is already analytic. No, the evidence is still an important part of our body of knowledge. But rather than supporting the generalization that all *A*'s are *B*'s — which is now without empirical content — it supports a theory of error regarding the terms *A* and *B*. The theory of error tells us that our *A* and *B* judgments are almost always veridical, but sometimes erroneous; and tells us how often. "All *A*'s are *B*'s" has become analytic and incorrigible, but our judgments concerning *A*'s and *B*'s are now corrigible (before they were merely uncertain) and the mass of data we have accumulated tells us how often they are in error. Our body of knowledge as a whole still has the same empirical content; but the empirical content has shifted from the statement "practically all A's are B's" to the statement, "A and B attributions are practically never in error."

Now this doesn't seem to have gotten us very far: there seems little to choose between a body of knowledge that contains the analytic truth that all ravens are black, and the contingent error statement that practically all things that look like ravens in fact are ravens, and the body of knowledge that contains the statistical hypothesis that practically all ravens are black, and embodies the convention that we can tell a raven when we see one. But if we consider a number of statistical generalizations: almost all ravens have such and such feeding habits; such and such mating habits; such and such nesting habits; and so on, then it may well turn out that the errors associated with these various attributions are not independent. This allows us to attain a more finely articulated theory of error; and a more informative set of statistical error hypotheses. Thus in principle we can base our choice of language on precisely the same criterion we employed in choosing among alternative statistical hypotheses: choose the one that gives the most information.

A simple numerical example would be very helpful here, but it will have to be extremely artificial. Suppose we have examined a thousand A's, and found that 990 of them are B's, that 992 of them are C's, that 995 of them are D's, that all of them are E's, and so on. By straightforward statistical inference we could infer that almost all A's are B's, that almost all A's are C's, etc. On the other hand, if we took our recognition of A's to be subject to a 1% error (1% of the time when we think we are examining an A, in fact it turns out that it is not a "true" A), if it happened that in each case it was the same A's that turned out to be recalcitrant, we could accept as analytic that all A's are B's, that all A's are C's, that all A's are D's, that all A's are E's, etc. Of course I am being a little provocative by using the term "analytic," but what I mean is, "necessarily," "irrefutably," . . . you may choose a less provocative word, such as *a priori.* The content that originally lay in the collection of statistical statements, now lies in the statistical statement that we are in error about A's only about 1% of the time. And of course future experience could refute or modify this statement. We could never find an A that wasn't a B, and a C, and a D, and an E, etc.; but we could easily *suppose* that something was an A, and discover, in virtue of the fact that it was not a B, that it was not an A after all. If this sort of thing happened a lot, we would have to suppose that the frequency of error in making A attributions was much higher than the 1% that was originally justified. And if that should happen, we might well be led to suppose that our linguistic "reform" was misguided, and that we would be well-advised to return to our former language.

One question remains: the claim that we choose between languages on the same basis as we choose between statistical hypotheses, i.e., on the basis of information content. Roughly speaking, we would say something like the following: before the language reform, we had (say) four statistical statements in our body of practical certainties which assigned parameters to the four intervals i_1, i_2, i_3, and i_4, each including the number 1 as an endpoint. The deficiency of information might be measured by the sum of the lengths of these intervals. After we accept the universal generalizations, these intervals all become degenerate: the sum of their lengths is 0. But after the language reform we must also take account of the statistical hypothesis regarding errors in making A-attributions, and this will give rise to another interval i_5, in this instance also including 1 as an endpoint. It seems *prima facie* reasonable to compare the length of i_5 to the sum of lengths of the other intervals. Things ae not quite this simple, and this is a complicated matter that would take us too far astray to pursue wholeheartedly; again, you will have to be satisfied with a promissory note. But that is the nature of the subject: epistemology is written on the backs of IOU's.

The obvious objection to all this is that sometimes universal generalizations do get refuted. A classical case in point: the black swans of Australia. Suppose that at a certain point we had accepted it as analytic that all swans are white. How could we then be led to reject that generalization on the basis of the observed black swans of Australia? I ask you to put yourself seriously in the situation of an 18th century Englishman, who *knows* that all swans are white.

A disheveled sailor, somewhat the worse for drink, whom you meet in a pub, tells you that in Australia he saw some black swans. Do you regard this as refuting the generalization? Hardly. You suppose that he made a mistake, or is lying, or is just telling sea stories, or was tricked by a can of black paint. "All swans are white" remains analytic for you, but your theory of ornithological error has been given a little nudge: it's just possible that the man saw some black birds that he mistook for swans. The theory of error is given a rather larger nudge when the Australian Ambassador tells you, at a formal reception, that there are whole flocks of black swans in Australia. But even this does not (need not, should not) lead you to abandon your universal generalization; you still hold it "come what may," though now your notion of how easy it is to tell a swan when you see one undergoes a radical change; the Ambassador is no ornithologist, but he is probably as good at telling swans as you are. In fact, we may find ourselves in the following situation: we don't know whether to change our language, so that "all swans are white" no longer appears among its analytic truths, or whether to suppose that there is a new species of birds, quite like swans, which makes it difficult to tell when you see a swan. Note that there is no question of "analyzing" the "concept" of a swan to find an answer: the concept is what we make it, not some entity in a glorious academic mental realm that we can go and look at.

If we are going to maintain that these birds in Australia are swans, then we shall have to change our language so that it is not a mistake to speak of black swans. If we are going to maintain that those birds in Australia are not swans, then we shall have to change our empirical theory of swan-error. The point is that both options are open to us; and another and even more important point is that *we* are not competent to choose between them: that is a task for an ornithologist. What the ornithologist can do, and we cannot, is to assess the effect on the whole set of ornithological error functions: swan error, gizzard error, feather error, wing-shape error, color error, mating-habit error, nesting error, feeding-habit error, and so on. Depending on what the observations do to his error functions, he will recommend (and we will adopt) a change of language so that *Swanhood* no longer entails *Whiteness*, or he will give the swan-like birds in Australia a name they lacked before.

5. THEORIES

When it comes to theories, the thesis I am proposing is not so novel. Sellars, for example, writes that a number of predicates are implicitly defined if they appear in a set of synthetic sentences "specified as axioms . . . by the *rules of the language* to which they belong." It is true that Sellars calls these sentences "synthetic," but he also says that they are "unconditionally assertable,"[5] and "assertable by the rules of the language." It is primarily these latter properties that I have in mind when I call generalizations and theories analytic. (There may be a deeper sense of "analytic," but I am unclear as to what it is.) Feyerabend speaks of "different languages and different idealogies."[6] Kuhn insists that Newtonian "mass" and Einsteinian "mass" "must not be conceived to be the same."[7] Hockney, whose language is closer to my own, says that S_1 may be analytic in the language L_1 of the theory θ_1, but false in the language L_2 of theory θ_2, and "hence, my reasons for rejecting or accepting analytic sentences are just my reasons for accepting or rejecting theories."[8]

Of course this raises a serious problem: what are the reasons, if any, for rejecting or accepting theories? According to Feyerabend " . . . the freedom of action and thought" of rational people has been considerably restricted by the supposition that there are "certain and infallible rules"[9] according to which one should decide whether or not to accept a theory. It is a matter, not of argument, but of propaganda, not of logic, but of rhetoric.[10] Kuhn too, seems to regard the fundamental choice between two linguistic frameworks for science as a matter of persuasion. "As in political revolutions, so in paradigm choice—there is no standard higher than the assent of the relevant community."[11] Sellars, as might be expected, is not so pessimistic: " . . . the problem concerns the grounds on which a decision to use—that is, to teach ourselves—*this* language rather than *that* can be justified. And to play the language game in which we can be confronted by the need for such a decision, is to know what would constitute a good reason for making it one way rather than another."[12] Thus according to one view, there simply are no "good reasons" for employing one language rather than another, and that is why Science pursues such a jumpy, halting, and irregular course; and according to the other view, all competent scientists (i.e., those who know the rules of the language game) know perfectly well what constitutes such a "good reason," and that is why Science progresses, even if a bit jumpily. The truth, I think, lies somewhere in between. Specifically, I suppose that scientists (and everybody else) have an implicit, inarticulate, and vague intuition of what the "good reasons" in question amount to; but being implicit, inarticulate, and vague, the intuition is not reflected in formal rules of sound argument, but rather becomes a matter of persuasion. (And in persuasion, anything goes!) If we can render these reasons articulate, we might be able to perform a useful function.

It is quite true that the classical approaches: verification, confirmation, and falsification, have not turned out well. As Putnam remarks, regarding such statements as "$f = ma$" and "$e = 1/2mv^2$," "These statements, then, have a kind of preferred status. They can be overthrown, but not by an isolated experiment. They can be overthrown only if someone incorporates principles incompatible with these statements in a successful conceptual system."[13] As Kuhn puts it, when scientists are confronted by anomalies, they do not "treat [them] as counterinstances . . . once it has achieved the status or paradigm, a scientific theory is declared invalid [from the present point of view, an excellent choice of word: not "falsified," not "refuted," but "invalid," a word appropriate to argument forms, to theorems] only if an alternative candidate is available to take its place." And he goes on to remark: "No process yet disclosed by the historical study of scientific development at all resembles the methodological stereotype of falsification by direct comparison with nature."[14] It has been pointed out, particularly by Kuhn and Feyerabend, that the data on which two alternative theories with the same subject matter are based may be roughly the same: the data that might be said to verify them; the data that might be used to compute degrees of confirmation or corroboration for them; the data which might be alleged to refute one or the other. We are confronted with a problem posed by Quine: " . . . when two theories agree in point of all possible sensory determinants they are in an important sense not two but one. Certainly such theories are, as wholes, empirically equivalent."[15] And indeed this is the typical case for scientific theories: to be sure, not all "observations" are "explained" by each theory; but each theory recognizes that it must come to terms with the observations that exist and no particular observation can be taken as flat-out refuting a whole theory.

One response to this situation has been to suppose that scientific terms are simply *vague*. Thus Scriven: " . . . no exact definition [s] could be adopted which would exhibit significant advantages over the present 'vague' definitions . . . for the crucial terms of theoretical and observational science."[16] Thus Ziff: Our generalizations are hedged about with implicit conditions concerning "ordinary" and "normal" circumstances and objects, whose precise content cannot be unpacked.[17] And Putnam goes so far as to say that even in ichthyology there are no necessary and sufficient conditions for a technical term such as "fish."[18] But this is obviously all wrong; in pursuing science we *do* have necessary and sufficient conditions for the terms we use. (Not, of course, "observationally" necessary and sufficient conditions; that distinction was a clumsy one anyway.) For example, an entomologist on a trip to the Congo can tell when he has discovered a new strain of mosquito (every entomologist must dream of such an occurrence) precisely because a mosquito he finds fails to satisfy the necessary and sufficient conditions for membership in any *known* strain. It is true that *one* specimen won't suffice to convince the scientific community that his is a new strain; one individual may be a sport; from one individual alone it may be hard to infer what the necessary and sufficient conditions for membership in the new strain should be; and thus the successful mosquito catcher must find three or four examples of his new mosquito. But this surely suggests that in the use of scientific terms, at a given time we *do* employ necessary and sufficient conditions. I say at a given time, for we must recognize that scientific language changes, and I am supposing that it changes almost constantly. Thus it is not surprising that if you look at the behavior of a scientific word over a period of time, you will find that there are no necessary and sufficient conditions for it that have remained constant. But the proper interpretation is not that there are no such conditions, but rather that they have changed with the accumulation of data and the consequent development of theory and acceptance of generalizations.

But if this is so, if scientific language is constantly changing, how can one theory be compared with another? We come up against the problem of sheer incommensurability that has been so lengthily discussed by Feyerabend. If Newtonian mass has one meaning, and Einsteinian mass has another, how can statements about them be said to contradict each other? And if it is to be maintained that this is the case even for terms (such as *raven* and *black*) that are closely tied to observation language, how can we even compare the "all swans are white" theory with the alternative, "not all swans are white?"

Kuhn hints at what I think is the true answer: " . . . it is precision of articulated paradigm that leads to the recognition of anomaly."[19] This ties in with what I said earlier about error. Every theory—even a common sense theory, implicitly—has associated with it a theory of error that carries the burden of empirical content associated with the theory. The axioms of the theory are analytic; they "implicitly define" (if we want to use that phrase) the terms that appear in the theory. They thus have no content, so far as the theory is concerned. But there are certain terms that are taken to be directly connected with our experience, not in an incorrigible way, but with a certain implicit chance of error. In advanced sciences, these are measurement terms. We have a theory of "experimental error" which connects the observed magnitudes with true magnitudes. (Note that in exact sciences errors are taken to be distributed normally, which means that *no* observation, however far from the theoretical prediction, could even conceivably *contradict* the theory.) In more primitive and taxonomic sciences, even in common-sense knowledge about the world (which I take merely to be a science without a fancy vocabulary), there is a rough and ready theory to the effect that errors don't occur often; but that there are errors is entailed by the existence of generalizations that we take to hold universally. It is to save these generalizations that we introduce misperception, hallucination, inaccurate perceptions, and the like.

All of this may be descriptively accurate, but it doesn't solve the problem we set ourselves: that of articulating the good reasons that lead us to prefer one scientific linguistic framework to another. It does suggest that the place to look is in the theory of error associated with the frameworks. And our earlier suggestion regarding universal generalizations provides a hint as to how to measure the content of the theory of error. Roughly, it is this: that the more closely the theory of error packs the frequency of error to the extremes 0 and 1, the more information carried by our body of knowledge. The language which takes the perception of an elephant to be a necessary and sufficient condition for its existence will have to deal with the fact that there are no useful generalizations about elephants: they come in all colors, they sometimes disappear, they sometimes turn into rocks, and so on. (One might hesitate even to call this a theory — precisely on the ground that it does not seem to have associated with it a theory of error!) A theory which takes elephant perceptions to be sometimes erroneous (and which therefore allows any number of fascinating analytic generalizations about elephants) will have associated with it a theory of error, according to which we are almost never mistaken about elephants under ordinary daylight circumstances, but rather more often mistaken at night, or when we have been drinking heavily. More generally, we might be able to evaluate two theories by looking at the number of statistical generalizations that assign the lower bounds of parameters to a small interval close to one. We might, that is, if we could devise an algorithm for counting numbers of statistical generalizations. I don't know how to do that yet, and if I did this would be neither the time nor the place to do it; but I think there is in this direction some hope of being able to measure the useful empirical content of a theory: i.e., of a set of analyticities plus a body of data, plus statistical generalizations.[20]

NOTES

1. I wonder if the phrase "morally certain" means: it is moral, proper, justifiable, to act as if it were certain?

2. Of course we cannot *accept* as practically certain all of these statements: in fact they cannot all be true—they are, considered jointly, self-countradictory. So if we are going to accept one of the statements (under *ordinary* circumstances: there may be circumstances that call for special treatment, as when we don't care, for some special purpose, whether the object weighs more than so and so much; we just want to be sure that it doesn't weigh less than so and so much), then we should accept the most informative statement.

3. Wilfrid Sellars, *Science, Perception and Reality* (London, 1963), p. 357.

4. Robert Binkley, "Conceptual Change" in Glenn Pearce and Patrick Maynard (eds.) *Conceptual Change* (Dordrecht 1973).

5. Sellars, *Science, Perception and Reality*, p. 303.

6. Paul Feyerabend, "Against Method" in Michael Radner and Stephen Winokur (eds.) *Minnesota Studies in the Philosophy of Science* IV (Minneapolis, 1970), p. 47ff.

7. Thomas Kuhn, *The Structure of Scientific Revolutions* (Chicago, 1962), pp. 100-101.

8. Donald Hockney, "Conceptual Structures," in Pearce and Maynard, *Conceptual Change*, p. 162.

9. Feyerabend, "Against Method," p. 101.

10. *Ibid.*

11. Kuhn, *Revolutions*, p. 93.

12. Sellars, *Science, Perception and Realtiy*, p. 356.

13. Hilary Putnam, "The Analytic and the Synthetic," Herbert Feigl and Gover Maxwell (eds.) *Minnesota Studies in the Philosophy of Science* III (Minneapolis, 1962) p. 372.

14. Kuhn, *Revolutions*, p. 77.

15. W. V. O. Quine, *Word and Object* (Cambridge, Mass., 1960). p. 78.

16. Michael Scriven, "Definitions, Explanations, and Theories" in Herbert Feigl, Michael Scriven, and Grover Maxwell (eds.) *Minnesota Studies in the Philosophy of Science* II (Minneapolis, 1958), p. 106.

17. Paul Ziff, "Something about Conceptual Schemes" in Pearce and Maynard, *Conceptual Change*.

18. Hilary Putnam, "Explanation and Reference" in Pearce and Maynard, *Conceptual Change*.

19. Kuhn, *op. cit.* p. 69.

20. Research leading to this paper has been supported by the National Science Foundation.

פה

Index

Index

A priori probability. *See* Probability, prior
Acceptability, 298-99
Acceptance rules: mentioned, 75-76, 154, 257-58; atemporal, 226*ff.*; Hempel on, 235-37; Hintikka and Hilpinen on, 237-41; Levi on, 241-46, 270; Lehrer on, 246-49, 270; different positions on, 269-70
Aggregation, 9, 10

Ballie, Patrician, viii
Bar-Hillel, Yehoshua, 263
Bayes's Theorem, 53, 58, 95, 136, 147-48, 188, 198, 259-60
Bayesian Decision Theory, 90
Bayesian inference, 133-34, 137-38, 148-49, 255, 257, 263
Behrens-Fisher problem, 137
Belief, 21
Belief, degrees of. *See* Degrees of belief
Bergson, Henri, 256
Bernoulli's theorem, 112, 121, 122
Bertrand's paradox, 155, 223
Biconditional chain, 161, 251
Birnbaum, Alan: mentioned, 136, 137-38; on intrinsic confidence limits, 147; on informative inference, 180, 183; Principle of Conditionality, 194-95
Body of knowledge. *See* Rational corpora
Boole, George, 135
Boolean algebra, 24, 25
Borel sets, 154, 173
Braithwaite, R. B., 60, 133, 192

Carnap, Rudolf: view of probability, 54, 181, 209; mentioned, 63, 64, 67, 71, 77, 80, 82, 133, 135, 138, 153, 237, 291; on probabilities and evidence, 70; on prior probabilities, 96; on rule of detachment, 255; on degrees of confirmation, 256-57; on rules of acceptance, 269-70; and global and local induction, 283
Causality, 45
Chance interpretation of probability. *See* Probability, chance interpretation
Chihaha, Charles, viii
Club of Rome, 3
Club of Rome report, vii, 5, 11-13
Commoner, Barry, 13
Computer simulation, 16
Conditionalization, ix, 95-96, 157, 224-28
Confidence intervals, 137, 138, 146
Conjunction, ix
Conjunction Principle, 232, 239, 240, 249-50, 252-53
Conjunctive Closure Principle, 232
Consistency, ix, 29, 37
Content, 242
Corrigibility, 39-40, 42
Craig, William T., x
Craig's Lemma, 24
Craig's theorem, 287, 292
Cramér, Harald, 20
Crucial experiments, 41

Darwin, Sir Charles Galton, 8, 11
de Finetti, Bruno, 24, 55, 63, 66, 67, 71, 75, 76, 79, 133, 181, 208
Decision theory, 43, 133-34
Deductive closure, ix, 29, 36-37, 154, 159-61, 186, 239-40

Degrees of belief, 20-22, 31-32, 54-55, 64, 65, 68-69, 77, 82-97
Detachment rule, 255, 261
Direct inference, 102, 223-28
Dispositions, 22
Dutch Book Argument, viiii, 81, 82-85
Dutch Book Theorem, 27, 65, 67

Economic growth, 4, 15-16
Edwards, Ward, 86, 135
Empirical probability. *See* Probability, frequency interpretation
Energy conservation, 13-14, 15
Enterprise of Knowledge, The, 26
Epistemological probability. *See* Probability, epistemological interpretation
Equivalence condition, 186-87
Equivalence relation, 161
Evidence, 69-71, 184
Exchangeability, 66, 208
Expected utilities, 86

Feyerabend, P. K., 307, 308
Fiducial probability. *See* Probability, fiducial
Finch, Henry A., 257
Finetti, Bruno de. *See* de Finetti, Bruno
Fisher, Ronald A., viii, 133, 136, 137, 140-44, 149, 185, 187
Forrester, Jay, 3
Fraassen, Bas van. *See* van Fraassen, Bas
Frequency interpretation of probability. *See* Probability, frequency interpretation

Gambling with Truth, 26
General Addition Law, 165
Generalizations, 228-31, 296-311. *See also* Universal generalizations
Global induction, 264-83
Goodman, Nelson, 178

Hacking, Ian, 197-98
Harper, William, 96, 270
Hempel, Carl, 235-37, 257-61, 263
Hilpinen, Risto, 237, 247, 249, 270
Hintikka, Jaakko: mentioned, 81, 96, 182, 235, 243, 247, 249, 291; interpretation of probability, 209; on acceptance rules, 237, 269-70; and local induction, 265
Hockney, Donald, 307

Hume, David, 10, 44

Identity, 105
Independence, 172
Inductive systematization, x
Informative inference, 136, 180-81, 188
Instrumentalism, viii, 27
Irrationality, 21

Jeffrey, Richard, 89, 90, 97, 181, 222, 270
Jeffreys, Harold, 54, 132-33, 135, 181

Kahn, Herman, 9
Kemeny, John G., 63, 257
Kennedy, Ralph, viii
Keynes, John Maynard: mentioned, 54, 138, 153, 207; on partial beliefs, 64; on probabilities and evidence, 70; logical interpretation of probability, 135; and randomness, 163
Koopman, B. O., 54, 64, 79
Kuhn, Thomas, 307, 308, 309

LaPlace, Pierre Simon, 134-35
Law of negation, 165
Lehman, E. L., 63
Lehrer, Keith: mentioned, 235, 241, 252; on acceptance rules, 246-49, 270; and local induction, 265
Leibniz, Gottfried Wilhelm, 169
Levi, Isaac: propensity interpretation of probability, viii; mentioned, ix, 26, 106, 107, 108, 112-15, 121, 122, 127-28, 235, 263, 282-83; on Dutch Book Theorem, 65; on fallibility and corrigibility, 222; on rational corpora, 222-23; on Confirmational Conditionalization, 224-28; on direct inference, 224-28; on acceptance rules, 241-46; 270; on epistemic utility, 257; on local and global induction, 264-65, 268
Likelihood principle, 198
Limits to Growth, The, 3-16
Lindeman, Harold, 135
Lindley, D. V., 133
Local induction, 264-83
Logical closure. *See* Deductive closure.
Logical probability (Carnap and Keynes). *See* Probability, logical interpretation

Logical probability (Kyburg). *See* Probability, epistemological interpretation
Logical Foundations of Statistical Inference, The, 26
Lottery paradox, ix, 36-37, 233-34, 261-63

Mathematical expectation, 51-52, 88-89
Mathematical Logic, 158
Meadows, Dennis, 3
Minimax strategy, 189-91, 193, 194
Mises, Richard von. *See* von Mises, Richard
Models of Doom, 5

Nagel, Ernest, 67
Next Million Years, The, 8
Neyman, Jerzy, 133, 136, 137-38, 180, 255
Niiniluoto, Ilkka, 81, 265, 270
Non-Bayesian inference, 257

Observation statements, 297-99
Oppenheim, Paul, 257

Pearson, Igan, 136
Personalistic probability. *See* Probability, subjectivistic interpretation
Pollock, John, 303
Popper, Karl, 257
Prediction, 5-9
Preference ranking, 88-91
Prince Hogarth, tale of, viii, 57-62
Principle of Conditionality, 194-95
Principle of Conjunction, 235ff.
Principle of Deductive Closure, 235, 239
Principle of n-wise Consistency, 245-46
Principle of Pairwise Consistency, 245-46
Prior probabilities. *See* Probability, prior
Probability: constraints on functions, 25, 26, 27; values as intervals, 26, 28, 33; and randomness, 30; single case, 30-31; objective, 32; relation to statistical inference, 20, 33-36; and ethics, 44; calculus of, 52-53, 156-57; interpretations of, summarized, 53-62; intensionality of, 99, 104-29; prior, 133-34, 135, 181, 194-97, 238, 270-71; statements as metalanguage, 184-85; conditional, 187-88
— Chance interpretation, 99, 101, 102-29
— Epistemological interpretation: mentioned, viii, ix; described, 28, 32, 42-46, 101-2, 138-40, 153-57, 182-83,

209-18, 271-73; relation to fiducial probability, 140-45; relation to frequency interpretation, 145-46; relation to subjectivistic interpretation, 146; application to local induction, 273-77
— Fiducial, viii, 140-45
— Frequency interpretation, viii, 20, 45, 53-54, 55-62, 133-34, 145-46, 181-82, 205-6
— Logical interpretation, viii, 54, 55-62, 67-68, 71-77, 133-34, 181, 182, 207-9
— Propensity interpretation, viii, 32-33, 44, 45, 99, 101, 205-6
— Subjectivistic interpretation: mentioned, viii, 28, 32; described, 20-25, 54-62, 81, 135-36, 206-7; defended, 63-68; critiqued, 68-77; reasons for popularity of, 79; as empirical decision theory, 85-87; as normative decision theory, 87-91; as empirical theory of degrees of belief, 91-93; as normative theory of degrees of belief, 93-96; relation to epistemological interpretation, 146; and informative inference, 181, 182; and local induction, 269
Propensity interpretation of probability. *See* Probability, propensity interpretation
Putnam, Hilary, 308

Quine, W. V. O., 158

Ramsey, Farnk P.: interpretation of probability, 55, 64; mentioned, 63, 66, 67, 79, 93; on laws of probable belief, 65; and the Dutch Book Argument, 81-82
Ramsey's Theorem, 24
Randomness, 33-36, 102, 139-40, 144-45, 156, 158-79, 187, 195-97, 199, 210-11, 213, 223-24, 225
Randomness condition, 186-87
Rational corpora, 29-30, 154, 184, 195-97, 221-23
Rationality, 66
Redistribution of wealth, 14-15
Reference terms, 155-156
Reichenbach, Hans: mentioned, 33, 77; view of relative frequencies, 63-64; on randomness, 187; interpretation of probability, 210; and local induction, 283

318 / Index

Rejection rules, 188, 243
Rescher, Nicholas, 257
Robbins, Herbert, 138

Salmon, Wesley, 77, 233, 259, 283
Sampling, 167
Savage, L. J.: mentioned, 55, 63, 66, 68, 79, 135, 136, 137; on probabilities and evidence, 70; view of probability axioms as normative, 87-89; on degrees of belief, 92, 271; and subjectivistic interpretation of probability, 181; on likelihood principle, 198
Schick, Fred, 261-62
Scriven, Michael, 308
Sellars, Wilfrid, 304, 307
Shimony, Abner, 63
Special multiplication law, 165
Spielman, Stephen, ix
Statements, 23-26
Statistical condition, 186-87
Statistical hypotheses, 184-85
Statistical hypothesis, strongest, 185-86
Statistical inference, 20, 33-36
Statistical statements, 107-16, 162-63, 299-302
Statistics: foundations of, ix; history of, 19-20; personalistic, 22; hypothesis-testing approach to, 180-81; Bayesian approach to, 181, 189-91; minimax strategy in, 189-91
Stochastic relations, 99, 100

Strong Consistency Principle, 239, 240, 244-45, 252-53
Strong Deduction Principle, 239, 240, 244-45, 252-53
Strong Principle of Consistency, 236
Strong Principle of Deductive Closure, 243
Subjectivistic probability. *See* Probability, subjectivistic interpretation
Sussex, report from University of, 4-11
System Dynamics, 3

Tuomela, Raimo, 81, 241, 265, 270

Ultimate partition, 242, 243, 245
Uncertainty, 50-51
Universal generalizations, 37-39, 302-7. *See also* Generalizations
Utility, epistemic, 237, 257

van Fraassen, Bas, 106, 122, 125-26
von Mises, Richard, 20

Wald, Abraham, 255
Weak Consistency Principle, 233, 234-35, 246
Weak Deduction Principle, 232, 235, 239
Weiner, Anthony, 9
Wesleyan Conference on Induction, 263

Year 2,000, The, 8

Zero population growth, 13, 15
Ziff, Paul, 308

Henry E. Kyburg, Jr., earned his bachelors degree in chemical engineering at Yale University and his Ph.D. in philosophy at Columbia. He has taught mathematics and philosophy at Wesleyan, Rockefeller, and Wayne State universities and at the University of Denver, and he is now Burbank Professor of Moral and Intellectual Philosophy at the University of Rochester. His major works include *Probability Theory, Probability and the Logic of Rational Belief,* and *The Logical Foundations of Statistical Inference.* Kyburg is a Fellow of the American Association for the Advancement of Science and a recipient of the Nicholas Murray Butler Medal from Columbia University.